Hermeneutics of Form

for Heinrich + Eve
in friendship +
with best wishes for
the year ahead

Cyrus
New Year 1998

Cyrus Hamlin

Hermeneutics of Form

*Romantic Poetics
in Theory and Practice*

New Haven
Henry R. Schwab Publishers
1998

Cataloging data:
Library of Congress Catalogue Card Number: 98-69299
ISBN (clothbound) 0-939681-04-8
ISBN (paperbound) 0-939681-05-6
PN1261 H35 1998
Hamlin, Cyrus.
Hermeneutics of form: Romantic poetics in theory and practice /
Cyrus Hamlin.
New Haven: Henry R. Schwab Publishers, 1998.
442 p.; 22 cm.
Includes bibliographical references and index.
1. Poetry, Modern 19th century History and criticism Theory, etc.
2. Poetics.
3. Romanticism.
4. Hermeneutics.
5. English poetry 19th century History and criticism Theory, etc.

Printed in the U S A on acid-free paper.

Illustration: "Chalk Cliffs of Rügen"
by Caspar David Friedrich
c. 1818; oil on canvas; 90.5 x 71 cm.
Reproduced by courtesy of
Museum Oskar Reinhart, Winterthur

Hermeneutics of Form may be ordered
by calling toll free 888 999 7177.
Prices of copies of the first printing are:
Paperbound: $19.95 plus $3 for shipping in the USA
Clothbound: $39.95 plus $5 for shipping in the USA

Contents

Acknowledgments

Earlier versions of the essays collected here appeared in the following journals and books:

Chapter 1: "The Limits of Understanding: Hermeneutics and the Study of Literature," *Arion. A Journal of Humanities and Classics*, N. S. III, 4 (1978), 385-419.

Chapter 2: "The Negativity of Reading," written for a conference on *Theories of Literary History* at the University of Toronto in 1979, has not previously been published.

Chapter 3: "The Conscience of Narrative: Toward a Hermeneutics of Transcendence," *New Literary History*, XIII (1981-82), 205-30.

Chapter 4: The Poetics of Self-Consciousness in European Romanticism: Hölderlin's *Hyperion* and Wordsworth's *Prelude*," *Genre*, VI (1973), 142-77.

Chapter 5: "The Hermeneutics of Form: Reading the Romantic Ode," *boundary 2. A Journal of Postmodern Literature*, VII, 3 (1979), 1-30.

Chapter 6: "The Temporality of Selfhood: Metaphor and Romantic Poetry," *New Literary History*, VI (1974), 169-93.

Chapter 7: "Platonic Dialogue and Romantic Irony: Prolegomena to a Theory of Literary Narrative," *Canadian Review of Comparative Literature*, II (1976), 5-26.

Chapter 8: "Strategies of Reversal in Literary Narrative," in: *The Interpretation of Narrative*, ed. M. J. Valdés and O. J. Miller (University of Toronto Press, 1978), 61-77.

Chapter 9: "The Faults of Vision: Identity and Poetry (A Dialogue of Voices, with an essay on Coleridge's "Kubla Khan")," in: *Identity of the Literary Text*, ed. M. J. Valdés and O. J. Miller (University of Toronto Press, 1985), 119-145.

All the essays have been revised and expanded, in some cases extensively. Permission to reprint published material is gratefully acknowledged.

Permission was also received to reproduce the painting by Caspar David Friedrich, "Kreidefelsen auf Rügen," from the Oskar Reinhart Museum in Winterthur, Switzerland, and to reprint the poem by Richard Howard, "Chalk Cliffs of Rügen," *Findings* (New York, 1971), 14-17, from the poet.

Preface: *Caspar David Friedrich*

"Chalk Cliffs of Rügen," one of the best known oil paintings by the German artist Caspar David Friedrich (1774–1840), is located in the collection of Oskar Reinhart in Winterthur, Switzerland. During the early 1990s, while the building which houses this collection was being restored, the painting was exhibited both in the Altes Museum in Berlin and in the Metropolitan Museum in New York. This provided an opportunity for many, including myself, to view the painting with care and at close hand. In conjunction with the early stages of preparing this collection of essays for publication, Friedrich's painting provided a visual focus for the guiding concern of my own work on hermeneutics. The choice of this image as a symbol for the hermeneutics of form thus seems in retrospect to have been inevitable.

The date of origin for the painting is uncertain, though it is generally thought to serve as a document for the journey made by Friedrich in the summer of 1818 with his wife Caroline and his brother Christian to the island of Rügen, located in the Baltic Sea not far from the painter's native city of Greifswald. Friedrich had by that time been living for many years in Dresden, where earlier in the same year at the age of forty-four he and his wife had been married. The visit to Rügen could thus be regarded as a wedding trip. A biographical interpretation of the painting is very tempting, where the three figures in the foreground may be identified with the three travellers. Which of the two men should be identified as Friedrich himself seems uncertain, but the figure standing at the right with the floppy 'old German' style hat, gazing out to sea, would correspond to similar figures in other paintings by Friedrich, which are traditionally identified with the painter. The scene represented in the painting is the Stubbenkammer, a well-known point of attraction for visitors at the edge of a sharp descent with an open vista toward the sea through the distinct V-shaped formation of the chalk cliffs.

The painting conveys, however, much more than a sense of documentation either for a wedding trip or for the representation of a vantage point for tourists. As with so many of the landscapes painted by Friedrich, the viewer senses that a symbolic significance is intended by the image, though the painter himself provides no accompanying narrative, not even a title, to suggest what the symbolic message might be. The titles assigned traditionally to Friedrich's paintings, including this one, derive from the scholars and critics of his work. Nor have the commentators on Friedrich hesitated to impose their own interpretive readings, often constructing a fairly specific system of figurative attributions. The most familiar and the most extreme of such allegorical readings derives from the leading scholar of Friedrich, Helmut Börsch-Supan, Director of Museums in the administration of the Staatlichen Schlößer und Gärten in Berlin and Professor of Art History at the Free University. I would like briefly to consider his discussion of this painting, contained in his monumental catalogue and commentary on Friedrich.[1]

With reference to the central figure in the painting, whom he takes to represent Friedrich himself, Börsch-Supan comments that "he is gazing over the precipice into the abyss of death, while holding fast to the grass which symbolizes the transience of life." He also argues that Friedrich "developed a system of colour symbolism," associating the blue coat of the central figure with faith, the red dress of the woman with love, and the green outfit of the third figure with hope. The Christian implications of such color symbolism are apparent. The third figure stands, he adds, "with great daring" at the very edge of the cliff, "leaning against a tree-stump, which signifies death," and he "gazes out over the abyss to the distant sea, where two boats can just be seen, symbolizing the soul seeking eternal life." In conclusion, Börsch-Supan insists that this realistic image of the view from Rügen deriving from Friedrich's wedding journey nonetheless conveys an allegorical meaning: "In this picture he depicts the threat to life posed by death with an unprecedented explicitness, though at the same time in an unusually cheerful mood."

How should a viewer of this painting respond to such allegorization? According to Börsch-Supan nothing contained in Friedrich's image signifies itself. Everything is symbol, conveying a meaning which stands in relation to the visual medium only as an abstract doctrine. To an untutored eye such doctrine appears to be an arbitrary imposition, a narrative supplement to the visual image as such. The painting represents a scene at the edge of the chalk cliffs of Rügen, where three travellers, each portrayed with a separate and distinctive stance, gaze outward and downward toward the open vista of the sea. Yet we also sense that the image conveys more than itself, even if we resist the kind of reductive allegorization imposed by Börsch-Supan.

Quite a different and more imaginative response to this painting is conveyed in a poem entitled "The Chalk Cliffs of Rügen" by the contemporary American poet Richard Howard.[2] Howard dramatizes the scene depicted as an implied exchange of views among the three figures, each of whom is characterized and named in quite distinctive and ironic manner. The woman is called Ottilie (a name perhaps derived by Howard from Goethe's novel *Die Wahlverwandtschaften*), the central male figure with top hat and cane is called Walther, and the third, perched precariously on the protruding bush to the far right gazing out to sea, is Franz.

Ottilie, last to be described in the poem, is presented with reference both to her gesture and to her dress: "Ottilie clings to an alderstump, pointing / down to where the orifice widens / in thunders of white silence / against the singing sea. Franz had begged her / to accept the cloth—a red casheen—/ for her new riding habit..., but now the brute / will not so much as deign to glance across / the gully to where she sits."

Walther is called "a true lawyer," presented initially with reference to his patron, the "Grand Duke"– sponsor of a visit in the preceding year to this Prussian island "for the first Goethe-Jubilaeum" (it is not clear what Howard has in mind; could it be a celebration of Goethe's birthday? On August 28, 1819, the poet, still very much alive, turned seventy). "Ever illustrating the obvious, / explaining the evident," Walther's stance is elucidated at some length toward the end of the poem. "Walther is kneeling / now, at the brink, parting the grass-stems: / who can tell if he follows / Ottilie's finger down where the cliffs fall, / weightless, to the surf, or merely hunts /

for more relics in the turf? / Why has he cast away his hat and stick?"

Franz is viewed as the Romantic misfit among the three, a moody loner or outsider – "three days out of the week /...Absurd, three days mediocre, / and one day sublime." Further evidence about him is also offered, apparently derived from physiognomy: "his Organ of Destructiveness is large, / the Combative Lobe pronounced." Franz's petulance is further developed by Howard in an imagined exchange with Walther about the paintings of David in response to what Ottilie calls her "Récamier attitude...(one lovelock carefully loosened)" – thus associating her pose in Friedrich's painting with that of David's portrait of Mme. Récamier.

This invective would seem to imply, if we may attribute such a motive to Howard's poem, that Friedrich's painting offers a corrective to the leading painter of the French Revolution and the Napoleonic era. "He [David] seems to have formed his mind from three sources: / the scaffold, the sick-room, the brothel – / it is all so laborious," so argues Franz, "...so tasteless." Walther then responds in defense of the French master: " – but plausible, / ...His foliage being / of the Single Leaf, and that / chiefly laurel, grape and bell-vine." But Franz has the last word, and it is presumably the word which Howard himself would offer in defense of Friedrich: "Let us hear / earth's voices as they are, and the water's / lovely dishabille – I would see *that!*"

In its response to Friedrich's "Chalk Cliffs," Howard's poem, however playfully, offers a striking contrast to the reductive allegorizing of Börsch-Supan. Yet such a free-ranging narrative, perfectly suited to an imaginative exercise in ekphrasis, also poses a challenge for the viewer of the painting. What should our interpretive response be? How should we attempt to formulate an adequate sense of what this image conveys? Before offering an answer to this question in terms which anticipate the argument of this book regarding the hermeneutics of form, let me cite the concluding effusion of Howard's poem, where a purposefully generic response is expressed, free of association with any one of the three figures at the edge of the cliff. The poem acknowledges this openness in its concluding line: "And you will never know / which of us has told you this." Howard's description here slips by design into an interpretive mode.

> There are two boats
>   on the Hiddensee. The sun,
>   hewing the cliffs, is mighty now. Perhaps
>   we have discovered what their shape, sharp
>   against the water beyond,
>   reminds us of: it is a womb, a birth,
>   a spanning of the earth no longer
>   just a grave, delivering
>   Ottilie splayed against her alder-stump,
>   and Walther sprawled at the verge, and Franz
>   under his birch. So we are
>   born, each alone, in chaos while that waiting
>   silence glows.

Such a general statement also approaches allegory, though Howard's poem, in contrast to the sequence of categorical identifications offered by Börsch-Supan, earns the right to its surmise on the basis of its imaginary narrative and its playful dialogue among the characterized figures who also observe the scene. Every narrative about the painting, however, must remain unavoidably a supplement to the image itself, even though the image clearly demands from every observer some form of interpretive response. Like the figures in the painting themselves, we cannot view the image in a merely passive way. The configuration of the three, perched along the edge of the cliff, looking downwards and outwards toward the open space of the distant sea, imposes on the viewer of Friedrich's work a corresponding obligation to interpret what is seen. I would define this obligation as a hermeneutical imperative.

The crucial insight of Richard Howard's poem concerning the meaning of Friedrich's painting occurs in the lines quoted above about the shape of the cliffs as "a womb, a birth, / a spanning of the earth no longer / just a grave...." The implication would seem to be that at a symbolic level the figures in the foreground may be regarded as the offspring of that peculiar configuration of the earth, which establishes a kind of visionary conduit toward the openness of the sea as source. Significantly, such a view implies a dynamic movement of vision that proceeds inward from that source as much as outward through the gaze of the observer toward the indeterminate openness of sea and sky. The key to such a reading of Friedrich's image resides within the design or structure of its representation. The central hermeneutical challenge of the painting derives from an awareness of its inner form, or *Gestalt* (to use a term from Goethe's aesthetic and scientific sense of form.)[3]

Not only the chalk cliffs, which arch upward vertically along both the right and left sides of the canvas, but also the curvature of the two trees, which arch across the top of the painting to form a kind of cover or ceiling to the foreground of the image: these define a sense of frame. Equally, with a gentle parabolic curve, such as Friedrich often employs to delineate a sense of threshold for his paintings, the edge of the cliff extends along the bottom of the canvas to define a precarious ground or surface, upon which the three figures are perched in their respective poses. This completes the sense of a foreground which encircles the entire image and delineates the central space that opens toward an indeterminate and seemingly endless vista. Also striking in the representation of this vista toward the sea is the placement of the horizon line so near the top of the painting, essentially at the level where the cover of foliage is joined together. It is as if the vision of the open sea were filling the central space like a vessel or container. What stretches inward at the center of the canvas is thus entirely ocean, and, despite the presence of the two distant and quite insignificant sailing vessels, this expanse of water remains essentially undifferentiated. Only the muted modulation of colors in the vertical design of the sea defines a sense of spatial and perhaps qualitative difference: from the splotches of light green upon the neutral light blue of the water near the bottom to the emergence of an increasing intensity of rosy hue near the top. Such shifting color suggests perhaps that the surface of the sea as it stretches away from the opening in the cliffs catches the light of the sun and reflects it back toward us.

In thus describing the image perceived by the viewer of the

painting as the erasure of all particularity in the object of the gaze (excepting only the two diminutive sailing vessels), it becomes apparent that a programmatic contrast is established between the frame of the foreground, where the three figures are located, who share in this act of looking downward and outward, and the undifferentiated openness of the vision. We also share with these figures as viewers of this openness an identical sense of contrast between the particular and the universal, for we also stand at the threshold of this foreground looking inward. The three figures thus thematize the act of vision *for us,* as they stand with their backs turned upon the viewer, subtle variants of the *Rückenfigur* which Friedrich so frequently employs in his paintings.

What specifically do they see? There is no way to answer this question with any certainty. Clearly the woman points downward, gesturing perhaps—if we may construct an approximate sightline – toward the lowest point of the sea on the canvas, where the curves of the cliffs with their several vertical thrustings come together at the bottom. The central male figure leans over the edge on his hands and knees, looking at who knows what? Howard's poem, as quoted above, also acknowledges the indeterminacy of his gaze, whether focussed on the edge of the verge or upon something far below. Only the third figure, somewhat meditative or self-absorbed, perched vertically and precariously upon the branches of the bush to the right, stares straight before him out to sea.

And does not such an act of staring, combined with a suitable gesture of meditation and self-reflection, serve as a paradigm for the stance of vision in many of the most famous paintings by Friedrich? One thinks immediately of the diminutive Capuchin monk in "Monk at the Edge of the Sea," the large canvas exhibited in Berlin in 1810 and purchased by the Crown Prince of Prussia, currently located in the Gallery of the Romantics at Schloß Charlottenburg;[4] or the lonely figure standing with his back to us at the summit of a high mountain in "Wanderer over a Sea of Mist," which was painted at approximately the same time as "Chalk Cliffs of Rügen" and is now in the Kunsthalle in Hamburg.[5] In both instances a sense of solitude in the face of an infinite vista prevails.

Such solitary and meditative vision into the infinite is emblematic of the sublime and constitutes a paradigm for European Romanticism. Caspar David Friedrich has belatedly been recognized as the supreme master of such imagery, and "Chalk Cliffs of Rügen" would seem to affirm such a thematic concern. Yet this painting may also symbolize more than the mere act of gazing into the boundless openness of the sea. Through the contrasting poses of the three figures in the foreground a sense of diversity or difference in the act of gazing is achieved. The depiction of a natural frame for the foreground of the painting, including (as indicated) the vertical rise of the cliffs at both sides and the arching branches of the trees at the top, as well as the parabolic curve of the cliff's edge at the bottom on which the three figures stand, establishes a significant sense of place in its unique particularity over against the undifferentiated openness of the sea.

The painting is thus focussed, in the way a photograph would be, upon the foreground, and what it thematizes is the very act of looking or gazing itself, through the differentiated stances of the three figures and through the sense of natural frame within which this activity of observation is located. The viewer of Friedrich's painting, furthermore, is engaged in precisely the same kind of activity: we look at the canvas the way they look at the sea. And the central moment of communication between viewer and painting consists in the form of a recognition.[6] We become aware that our act of viewing the painting is essentially identical with the act of gazing and observing in which all three figures standing at the foreground are engaged. More than this, however, we also recognize in this figure of analogy or shared activity that the figures in the painting come to symbolize *for us* postures of thought or a stance of self-reflection, whereby the outward gaze is turned back upon itself as an act of meditation or interpretation, which includes the consciousness of self within the structure of such experience. This process of self-reflection may be called the drama of a hermeneutical consciousness.[7]

How this event happens may well remain a mystery for the mind that experiences it. It depends upon the capacity of the viewer to recognize the intentional analogy between the represented act of gazing and the act of gazing at what is represented. The moment of affirmation which signals this hermeneutical consciousness necessarily includes the reflective turn of the mind upon itself. We project a corresponding reflectivity upon the figures in the painting in such a way that the painting comes to symbolize our own reflective turn of thought. We surmise that these three figures, like ourselves, are also engaged in more than the mere act of looking. We imagine that they also, like ourselves, are thinking about themselves as looking in the very act of doing so.[8] Such at least is the implied intention of Friedrich's painting. A tacit recognition takes place of a reciprocal reflectivity.

The shape of Friedrich's painting may thus resemble – as Richard Howard's poem about it suggests – a kind of womb, or an act of giving birth, where the earth (as he says) is "no longer just a grave." Yet, equally, the vision of ocean here revealed, with its varied but undifferentiated spectrum of modulating color, may symbolize *for us* a kind of cosmic eyeball (to borrow the famous image from Emerson's *Nature*),[9] which reflects back upon the viewer whatever thought may be projected upon it through the labor of our meditation. We thus seem to catch the universe in our gaze as a figure of sublime reciprocity. To adapt a phrase from Coleridge's late poem "Limbo," which is discussed at the end of chapter 4 below: "We seem to gaze at that which seems to gaze on us."[10] The entire image of Friedrich's painting thus stands as a figure of capable imagination, where the work of art comes to signify an act of recognition for the self, an act which the German poet Hölderlin, in an essay fragment concerned with the poetic process (discussed in chapters 6 and 8 below), called the "metaphor of an intellectual intuition."[11] My own phrase for describing this kind of poetic experience, used as the collective title for the essays contained in this book, is the *hermeneutics of form*. Precisely what is implied by such a phrase will be clarified step by step, though always through the occasion of an interpretive reading, in the argument of the nine chapters that follow.

The Chalk Cliffs of Rügen

For Robert Rosenblum

Every authentic work is conceived in a sacred moment, created in a blessed one....The painter must present not only what he sees before him, but what he sees within. Otherwise his pictures will resemble screens behind which may be found only invalids or even corpses.
–Caspar David Friedrich

This is the largest Prussian island,
on which we have spent the day:
Ottilie and Walther, and of course Franz.
There are ferry connections at Bug,
should we desire to return,
and at Binz across the Baltic, were it
opportune to extend an outing
into a real excursion.
Rügen, a stronghold of Germanic tribes
(the Rugii), fell to the Slavs or Scyths
of old, and as recently
as last summer, when our Grand Duke came here
for the first Goethe-Jubilaeum
Picknick and Recitation,
bits of bronze would wash up the tidestrewn shore,
where the dishevelled seaweed dyes the sea.
"Bits indeed," Walther explained,
"vestiges of a horse culture which carved
its bridles with combat signs." To which
the Duke replied that the place
was rather like Paestum without the temples,
the beach as passive as any stone
inured to wine-libations,
and that such beauties imparted to it
an amenity and an elegance

hardly to be found elsewhere.
Franz, forever jealous of his spiritual
            attachments, as of his spiritual
                        liberties, muttered he found
no inhabitants here but time, ever
            demolishing in silence. The phrase,
                        one recalls, is Marmontel's.
No matter. Walther, a true lawyer, resumed,
            ever illustrating the obvious,
                        explaining the evident.
And the Grand Duke generally uttered
            no more than "Ha," his convenient
                        suspensive expression, or
laughed as if laughter could kill and he knew it,
            thinking of an enemy. Whereas
                        Franz—three days out of the week
Franz is absurd, three days mediocre,
            and one day sublime. So much for that.
                        We are not at Bug now, but above
the pale cliffs at Putbus; before us lie
            the sacred spaces of the sea, fields
                        of light without a focus,
and to conceive our enchantment, you must
            imagine to yourself how a pearl
                        might appear in a burning-glass . . .
That is the Hiddensee, as it is called,
            wrinkling beyond the turreted V
                        of chalk cliffs plunging from high
above us to far below. Already, Franz
            rejoices at having this time reached
                        our perch without the Grand Duke,
whose liaison with Frau Korn, he grumbles,
            is no more than a macabre copy
                        of Lord Byron's career but
conducted with one woman, on a less grand
            level, and in slower motion. One

thing about Franz, evident
as he stands, bare-headed, staring out to sea:
his Organ of Destructiveness is large,
the Combative Lobe pronounced.
Ottilie clings to an alder-stump, pointing
down to where the orifice widens
in thunders of white silence
against the singing sea. Franz had begged her
to accept the cloth–a red casheen–
for her new riding-habit
(Scarpelain swore it was the true Parisian
gorge de pigeon so fashionable
this season), but now the brute
will not so much as deign to glance across
the gully to where she sits, merely
folding his arms and squinting
against the sun. "Little islands are all
large prisons," he announces, and when
Ottilie pouts and assumes
(one lovelock carefully loosened) what she calls
a Récamier attitude, Franz inveighs
against David: "Loathsome work –
he seems to have formed his mind from three sources:
the scaffold, the sickroom, the brothel –
it is all so laborious,"
he declares, "so tasteless–" "–but plausible,"
Walther puts in, "his foliage being
of the Single Leaf, and that
chiefly laurel, grape and bell-vine." "Devil
take ten-thousand of them!" Franz will have
nothing neo-classic: "Let us hear
earth's voices as they are, and the water's
lovely dishabille–I would see *that*!"
Ottilie shifts her pose, and
staring past the white ramparts to the sea,
calmly remarks, "I shall live always

        –that is for me; I am living
here, at Rügen, eighteen-hundred twenty
        –that is for you. All is given us,
            Herr Fuessli says, and we have
nothing to ask for." Walther is kneeling
        now, at the brink, parting the grass-stems:
          who can tell if he follows
Ottilie's finger down where the cliffs fall,
        weightless, to the surf, or merely hunts
          for more relics in the turf?
Why has he cast away his hat and stick?
        For answer he merely murmurs on
          in that absent drone of his,
"It is no naive illusion which makes men,
        and you too, my dear, seek eternal
          life. A limited future
makes our past unbearable. Nothing consoles,
        for nothing replaces . . ."–
               There are two boats
        on the Hiddensee. The sun,
hewing the cliffs, is mighty now. Perhaps
        we have discovered what their shape, sharp
          against the water beyond,
reminds us of: it is a womb, a birth,
        a spanning of the earth no longer
          just a grave, delivering
Ottilie splayed against her alder-stump,
        and Walther sprawled at the verge, and Franz
          under his birch. So we are
born, each alone, in chaos while that waiting
        silence glows.
             And you will never know
        which of us has told you this.

           –Richard Howard
           Findings (New York, 1971), 14-17

Foreword

This book consists in a series of essays, all of which were written independently of one another, each for a particular occasion, over a twelve-year period from 1971 to 1983, when I was teaching at the University of Toronto. Only in retrospect has it become fully clear to me that they trace a coherent line of inquiry into the poetics of Romanticism with specific regard to what is designated in the title as the hermeneutics of form. At the encouragement of a number of friends and sympathetic readers, I began several years ago to revise and (in a number of instances) to expand the argument, simplifying and strengthening (I hope) the writing, while also attempting to delineate more fully the underlying coherence of concern. What has emerged has been for me an affirmation of many assumptions about critical and interpretive reading which were often only implicit and half understood at the time of writing the original versions.

As indicated in the lead footnote for each essay, the sequence of the essays is neither chronological nor exactly linear, though chapter 9 on "The Faults of Vision" was indeed the last to be written. The first three chapters include a common programmatic concern with the nature of hermeneutics, which should help to clarify for any reader what I take to be the central implications of this often puzzling and poorly defined technical term for current theoretical views of literary criticism and interpretation. The two central essays, which are also the longest, entitled "The Poetics of Self-Consciousness" and "Reading the Romantic Ode," document my attempt to clarify the two most complex focal points for my own approach to the hermeneutics of reading, both derived from sources crucial to Romantic theory, especially in Idealist philosophy: self-consciousness (*Selbstbewußtsein*, in Fichte's sense) and poetic form (as *morphé* or *Gestalt*, in Goethe's sense). Both essays document moments of breakthrough in my own thinking about hermeneutics. Chapters 6, 7 and 8 address specific issues in poetic practice, as indicated by the titles: metaphor, irony and narrative reversal. Each of these concepts developed in my own thinking from the experience of teaching, especially in graduate seminars on the history of literary theory, and each of the three essays was written for a conference sponsored by the Graduate Program in Comparative Literature at the University of Toronto, which I chaired for six years during the mid-1970s. The final essay was also intended for a series of lectures sponsored by the same program, addressing the identity of the literary text, but the argument took on a direction of its own, developing into a dialogue for three distinct voices. Without my intending it by conscious design, the essay became a summation of my inquiry into poetics and hermeneutics, which had been the central concern of my work for more than a decade of continuous effort. Finally, the brief discussion of Caspar David Friedrich's painting "The Chalk Cliffs of Rügen," which is contained in the Preface, was written as a preliminary demonstration of the hermeneutics of form in the visual arts and may also serve – within the chronology of composition – as a kind of coda for the collection as a whole, even though it is located at the very beginning.

At several points in this book I emphasize one of Hans-Georg Gadamer's central convictions about hermeneutics, namely that in Aristotle's sense it pertains to the domain of praxis (it is a *Praxiswissenschaft*).[1] For me this has included a commitment as priority to the interpretive engagement with specific texts. A theory of hermeneutics as such, insofar as that is at all possible, can only emerge from the experience of hermeneutical reading. This may seem in retrospect a defensive stance for a practitioner of criticism to have assumed during an era when "literary theory" threatened to displace all concern with the study of actual works of literature. The challenge of such reading for the study of literature remains a priority, but that which used to be called "practical criticism" presumably no longer needs to be defended in a book on the hermeneutics of form.

The choice of authors and texts for discussion in these chapters should be beyond challenge, even though many decisions about the examples for inclusion were dictated by contingency or convenience or mere personal preference. The focus on Sterne's *Tristram Shandy* and the *Confessions* of St. Augustine in chapter 3, for instance, could equally well have been replaced at that time by Dante's *Divine Comedy* and Joyce's *Ulysses,* both of which are briefly considered at the beginning and end of the essay. Dante at least provided subsequently a central focus for the argument of chapter 2, which ranges from the Bible to late Hölderlin, though in its original draft version the essay also concluded with a reading of a sonnet by Mallarmé. More essential to the agenda of the argument for the book as a whole is the inclusion of Plato's dialogues in the essay on irony (chapter 7), as well as *The Republic* in the dialogue of chapter 9, as likewise is the discussion of Schiller's aesthetic theory in both chapter 1 and chapter 6. To a large extent the theories of Plato and Schiller may resonate against each other as the proper parameters for defining the hermeneutics of form.

Two continuing preoccupations for my own reading and teaching during those years in Toronto will also be apparent throughout.

On the one hand, representative texts from English Romantic poetry are crucial for my argument, in particular in the treatment of Wordsworth's *Prelude* in chapter 4 and the close reading of Coleridge's ode "Dejection" in chapter 5 and "Kubla Khan" in chapter 9. The later poems of Coleridge, which have largely been ignored by critics of Romanticism, are also considered briefly at the end of chapter 4 under the heading of a poetics of despair. The addendum to chapter 5 concerning Keats and Shelley as practitioners of the Romantic ode may perhaps seem too brief and tentative to serve as more than a supplement to my main argument about Coleridge; just as the brief glance at Shakespeare's *Troilus and Cressida* in chapter 8 can only hint at the enormous challenge of a hermeneutical reading of that work.

On the other hand, at the very center of my continuing concern stands the unique achievement of German Idealist thought for any discussion of hermeneutics. My long-term preoccupation with Hölderlin pervades the book, even though relatively little is said about his poetry. The novel *Hyperion* assumes a position alongside *The Prelude* in chapter 4 with regard to a poetics of self-consciousness, and Hölderlin's theory of poetic composition, in particular the "modulation of tones" (*Wechsel der Töne*) and the notion of a caesura of thought in discourse, are discussed in chapters 1, 6, and 8. It is my hope to gather my essays on Hölderlin's poetry for subsequent publication as a separate, though related, book. Hegel's dialectical method offers a singular challenge for any theoretical discussion of hermeneutics, and my own longstanding struggle with the complexities of his writing will be apparent throughout, notably in chapter 1, where the concept of "reciprocal recognition" from *The Phenomenology of Spirit* is considered; in chapter 5, where Hegel's theory of Romantic art is discussed with reference to the ode as genre; and in chapter 8, where the "speculative sentence" as defined in the Preface to the *Phenomenology* serves as a central example for the hermeneutics of reversal in narrative. Throughout the book, furthermore, Hegel's concept of negativity, which enters explicitly in chapters 2 and 5, guides my thinking about Romanticism and the hermeneutics of form.

It remains only to acknowledge my personal debt to a range of eloquent and learned mentors, with whom I have had the good fortune to come into personal contact during my academic career. Each chapter in the book, more or less accurately, indicates a sense of indebtedness to the particular person to whom it is dedicated, though in many instances that indebtedness extends to everything I have written, often beyond my conscious awareness. I offer here a brief tribute to those named in these dedications.

First and foremost, my esteemed teacher from undergraduate years at Harvard in the mid-fifties should be mentioned: I. A. Richards, whose readings of poetry and theories of reading first inspired me to take the task of interpretation and teaching seriously. Richards was truly a powerful, but intuitive, hermeneuticist – though he never used the term, so far as I am aware – as I have argued in a commemorative essay published shortly after his death in 1979.[2]

Second, let me mention a sincere debt to my teacher in Comparative Literature at Yale, René Wellek, who directed my doctoral dissertation in the early sixties and who became subsequently a continuing source of encouragement and reassurance during the years prior to his final infirmities and death in 1995. It was Wellek above all who urged me to gather these essays into a book, even if he remained somewhat skeptical about hermeneutics.

Third, as an added source of spice to the stimulus of my intellectual development, I mention Paul de Man, with whom I studied at Harvard in the late fifties, when he first began to teach, who introduced me to the serious challenge of Hölderlin and Romanticism, and who remained a good friend despite developing differences between us about critical method during the years of deconstruction at Yale, when I was located safely in Toronto working on these essays. Chapter 6 was written in large part as a response to de Man's seminal essay "The Rhetoric of Temporality,"[3] and it benefited from his perceptive and often quite pointed criticism during several rewritings.

Three powerful and resourceful mentors in hermeneutics directly influenced the development of my thinking and writing during the years in Toronto, when the ideas pursued in these essays first began to come clear to me.

First and foremost among these was Hans-Georg Gadamer, whose semester as Visiting Professor of Comparative Literature coincided with my arrival in the fall of 1970. I had at that time begun serious study of *Wahrheit und Methode,* which first became fully accessible to me through direct tutelage from the author. I remain extraordinarily grateful for the opportunity, extending now over more than a quarter century, to meet frequently, in Toronto and more recently in Heidelberg, with the leading philosopher of hermeneutics in this century. Chapter 1 was originally written as a review essay in response to the first English translation of Gadamer's book.

Second among these senior mentors in hermeneutics in Toronto was Paul Ricoeur, who also came twice for a semester as Visiting Professor in Comparative Literature: first to teach a seminar on metaphor, which subsequently became his book *La métaphore vive;*[4] and second to teach a seminar on narrative and history, which later produced his three volume work on *Temps et recit.*[5] Chapter 6 on metaphor in Romantic poetry and chapter 8 on reversal in narrative could not have been written without the immediate impact of Ricoeur's teaching in hermeneutics.

Finally, I wish to acknowledge with particular gratitude the close collegial relation which developed for me during those years in Toronto with Northrop Frye. He served as the initial Chairman of Comparative Literature in Toronto and assisted me in countless ways during my years as his successor. I also recall with pleasure the experience of team teaching with Frye the lecture course on Shakespeare in Victoria College, as also the opportunity to discuss with him various hermeneutical problems pertaining to the Bible as he was completing *The Great Code*. Frye never indicated an explicit commitment to hermeneutics in his writing, but to those who knew him and worked with him there were few readers of literature who could measure up to his interpretive skills.

Two influential scholars and friends in Germany should also be mentioned, to whom I owe a singular debt for insights into hermeneutical issues at crucial stages in my own thinking on the subject. Wolfgang Iser from the University of Constance also visited Toronto to teach a seminar on his book *The Act of Reading* prior to its initial publication in German.[6] From him I learned to appreciate the importance of negativity, a concept derived from Hegel, as a necessary component in the hermeneutics of reading. Dieter Henrich, the leading historian of German Idealism, whom I first met in Heidelberg in the mid-sixties, and subsequently visited in Harvard and in Munich in the eighties, engaged me in a productive and ongoing dialogue on Hölderlin. He also challenged me in various ways as a reader of Idealist philosophy, Hegel in particular, with regard to hermeneutical questions. It was in immediate response to Henrich's seminal essay on "Fichte's original insight" that the issue of self-consciousness in Romantic poetics first became apparent to me.[7] I doubt that either Iser or Henrich would agree with everything I have written in this book, but no doubt they could recognize their influence in virtually every essay.

My last acknowledgement of indebtedness must be directed to my students, many of whom became friends, especially those graduate students in Comparative Literature at Toronto who reminded me in seminar sessions again and again that the only lasting value for hermeneutical insights is established through a dialogical exchange in response to the careful reading of texts that are shared. I cannot remember all their names, but I do appreciate how much I learned from those many lively discussions throughout such privileged years. It is my hope that the publication of these essays as revised and collected here may win other readers to the challenge of the hermeneutics of form.

It remains only to express my thanks to the team of coworkers who helped to prepare this book for publication. I offer my sincere thanks to Henry Schwab for his idea of a monograph series by Yale authors, for which this is a kind of pilot project; to Alvin Eisenman, grand master of design and a true philosopher of the book, whose expertise and vision about the technology of book production and its future have made this work such a pleasure to plan and produce; to Jennifer Kaufman for conscientious copy editing beyond the limits of what was reasonable and for help in preparing the index; to Vincent Oneppo at Yale's Reprographic Imaging Service for his patience and expertise in making innumerable corrections and changes in the book; to Richard Benson, Dean of the Yale School of Art, for scanning the transparency of Friedrich's "Chalk Cliffs of Rügen" and fine-tuning the digitized image for reproduction; and last but not least, to my son Hannibal for his dedicated and exacting scrutiny in proofreading. In certain ways the intimacy and the commitment of producing this book probably has resembled the early heroic days of print, but in its use of the new electronic and computer technology the book points forward toward developments in the next millennium.

To my wife Rosamond, who has sustained my hermeneutical readings with patience and understanding for the past forty years, I owe more than words can say.

Chapter 1 : The Limits of Interpretation

For Hans-Georg Gadamer, with gratitude.

But where danger is, grows
what rescues also.
–Hölderlin, "Patmos"

The place of interpretation in criticism used to be taken for granted;
lately it has been called into question. The heritage of New Criticism from T. S. Eliot and I. A. Richards to Cleanth Brooks and
Robert Penn Warren, René Wellek and W. K. Wimsatt, seemed to
reflect an easy confidence in the texts of literature.[1] We learned
from them how to read closely, and our preoccupation with patterns, structures and forms of language in literature seemed fully
adequate to the task of understanding. Yet radical doubts have
arisen in recent years about the value of such skills through efforts,
admirably motivated by social conscience or by philosophical commitment, to go beyond the text, beyond New Criticism and beyond
its apparent formalism. The most outspoken of these innovators, in
particular a group of colleagues at Yale, described as deconstruc-
tionists,[2] tell us that the task of criticism is to deformalize literature
and that the only reading of texts which is of interest or value must
be a misreading. It has even been asserted by Jonathan Culler that
an era of interpretation is now past, having been replaced by an era
of theory, in which the texts of literature will serve at most as
instances or examples.[3]

    Within such a climate of radical change, which brings with it
reactions at equal extremes of enthusiasm and dismay, the publica-

tion in English translation of works by the leading philosopher of hermeneutics, Hans-Georg Gadamer, is timely indeed.[4] Gadamer's monumental outline of a philosophical hermeneutics, to paraphrase the subtitle of *Wahrheit und Methode,* appeared in Germany in 1960.[5] To a large extent this book constituted (and must have been conceived as) the recovery of a humanistic tradition in German thought that had been interrupted and largely destroyed during the Nazi era. Gadamer writes as a follower of Husserl in phenomenology and, even more purposefully, as a spokesman for the Marburg school of hermeneutics, where Gadamer was a colleague of Rudolf Bultmann and Martin Heidegger during the 1920s.[6] Behind the argument of the book stands the tradition of historical studies in Germany, from Wilhelm Dilthey back through the work of nineteenth-century universal historians, e.g., Droysen and Ranke, to the fathers of modern hermeneutics during the Romantic era, the theologian Schleiermacher and the philosopher Hegel. Much of this tradition is familiar in North America within the historical and theological disciplines, where the assimilation and application of European ideas are further advanced. In literary criticism, however, the situation is quite different. Apart from isolated academic centers, usually under the aegis of Comparative Literature and almost always through the direct influence of European critical theory, hermeneutics remains an unfamiliar concern and consequently a suspect term.

Gadamer himself anticipated the difficult reception of his ideas in North America. Preliminary studies in hermeneutics were published by E. D. Hirsch and Richard Palmer.[7] Important books by Paul Ricoeur, available in English for some time, have also established a valid perspective for hermeneutical theory closely related to Gadamer's position.[8] Nor have Gadamer's frequent visits to universities in Canada and the United States since 1970 been without impact. The English text of his book, entitled *Truth and Method,* finally appeared in 1976 after years of effort and negotiation. The cumbersome style of the translation, yielding the author's insights only after painstaking study, bears witness to the difficulty of making Gadamer over into English. Fortunately, the much revised second edition by Joel Weinsheimer and Donald G. Marshall is both more accurate and more readable. Versions of Gadamer's shorter pieces, contained in *Philosophical Hermeneutics* and *Hegel's Dialectic*, are more forceful and lucid, hence more accessible. The complex process of responding to Gadamer's work and applying his ideas to literary criticism, however, has only begun.

I contend that hermeneutics offers a direction for criticism that is more viable than theories of deconstruction. Indeed, the greatest impact of Gadamer's work may occur in a domain where the practice of criticism still remains an urgent concern. The crucial challenge for interpretation is education itself, especially within the curriculum of literary studies in departments of English, classics and modern languages at the university level. The implications of hermeneutic theory for the traditional historical approach to literature are revolutionary indeed. Hermeneutics calls into question the basic assumptions of traditional literary history as a fixed body of texts arranged in a chronological order of epochs or periods, rather than a hypothetical body of knowledge immediately accessible to understanding. Even more important, the historical implications of hermeneutics as mediation between text and reader, as indicated by Gadamer's crucial concept of effective-history (*Wirkungsgeschichte*, translated in the revised English version of *Truth and Method* as "history of effect"), clash with traditional views of the historical basis of meaning in literary texts. Hermeneutics is preeminently a branch of practical philosophy in the Aristotelian sense, as Gadamer emphasizes,[9] which addresses issues of reading and understanding in ways that reaffirm the central place of literature in education.

Gadamer's *Truth and Method*

Gadamer's *Truth and Method* has been the subject of many reviews and discussions, debates and polemical exchanges, particularly for the theory of science or the problem of ideology.[10] It is not my intention here to survey the argument or to review the reviews, especially since so much of Gadamer's impact has been felt primarily within Germany. What makes his book so difficult for readers unfamiliar with the German tradition of *Geisteswissenschaft,* or humanistic science, is that Gadamer develops his position at several stages in his argument through a detailed survey of that tradition. This also introduces a complex vocabulary of philosophical terms, many of them highly specialized, abstract and difficult to render in English. If this tradition is unfamiliar, the basic premises of the argument are likely to remain obscure and seemingly arbitrary. Even worse, the entire book is likely to be regarded as special pleading for an alien, very narrow and peculiarly Germanic mode of thought. To have the text of *Truth and Method* available in English does not relieve that discomfort. For many students of literature, furthermore, especially those trained in New Criticism, this sense of strangeness will be compounded by the sheer effort of thinking theoretically about so practical an exercise as interpretation. How often I have heard the claim, in characteristic Anglo-Saxon candor, that if you can do criticism, you should not have to theorize about it.

My own remarks will move in a direction opposite from Gadamer's argument. I shall consider only two of the central concepts in hermeneutic theory: effective-history and the hermeneutic circle – specifically as applied to the interaction of text and reader – in order to impose upon this theory an argument derived from the historical context of German Romantic aesthetic and ethical theory. I shall outline a point of implicit disagreement between Friedrich Schiller and G. W. F. Hegel concerning the ethics of aesthetic response, followed by a brief outline of the implied hermeneutics in Hölderlin's poem "Patmos." These distinctions will indicate the appropriate place of hermeneutics in the study of literature, both for the experience of reading and for methods of criticism, in a way that will clarify Gadamer's position from a separate vantage point. Except for an initial distinction between two kinds of historical understanding, which Gadamer derives respectively from Schleiermacher and Hegel, I shall limit my use of material from *Truth and Method* to the second section of Part Two, entitled "Foundations of a Theory of Hermeneutical Experience."

HISTORICAL UNDERSTANDING

Gadamer's survey of the development of hermeneutics in Germany during the nineteenth century is guided by one single conviction. From Schleiermacher to Dilthey, he argues, the interpretation of texts was primarily, if not exclusively, committed to the reconstruction of meaning as historical truth.[11] Hermeneutics served the science of history as a supportive discipline (*Hilfsdisziplin*). Such a view of meaning reflects the presuppositions of historicism, which was established in the later eighteenth century, notably in secular theories of universal history beginning with Herder. According to this view, all works of literature, art and culture embody and address particular aspects of the historical era in which they originated. Implicit in such a concept of historical origin is a psychological attitude toward the poet or artist as the spokesman of his age, or a more comprehensive notion about the relation of art and literature to the life of nations and the development of human culture. The basis of meaning in any particular work is thus the Spirit of the Age, the *Zeitgeist*.

This historical approach to humanistic studies, though new and exciting in the early nineteenth century, is now so familiar to our university curricula that the presuppositions of historicism sound like truisms or clichés, which may be regarded, according to opposing predilections, as either self-evident and true or old-fashioned and out-of-date. Gadamer's point, which seems correct to me, is that the function of hermeneutics for historicism consisted entirely in the authoritative, legitimate and objective recovery of that original historical context which was thought to constitute the meaning of any work of literature or art. More recent discussions of hermeneutic theory in the works of Schleiermacher and Dilthey have demonstrated complexities that Gadamer overlooked or oversimplified; yet the validity of his argument about hermeneutics and historicism still holds. His summary of this reconstructionist theory of interpretation, attributed to Schleiermacher, is as follows:

If we acknowledge that the work of art is not a timeless object of aesthetic experience but belongs to a "world" that alone determines its full signifi-

cance, it would seem to follow that the true significance of the work of art
art can be understood only in terms of its origin and genesis within that
"world." Hence all the various means of historical reconstruction – re-
establishing the "world" to which it belongs, re-establishing the original
situation which the creative artist "had in mind," performing in the original style, and so on – can claim to reveal the true meaning of a work of art
and guard against misunderstanding and anachronistic interpretation.
(*WM* 159, *TM* 166)

Gadamer totally rejects such a subordinate role for interpretation in the service of historical reconstruction. He does this, surprisingly, by substituting the authority of Hegel for that of Schleiermacher in hermeneutic theory. The development of a phenomenological hermeneutics in this century, argues Gadamer, from Husserl
to Heidegger and on to his own work, restored a view of meaning
already established in Hegel's *Phenomenology of Spirit*, which
opposes the basic suppositions of historicism. Hegel recognized the
essential futility of all historical reconstruction. The ruins of time
remain ruins for Hegel, and the distance of the past from the present remains a gap which separates us from what is irretrievably
lost. The exercise of historical understanding thus becomes an act
of remembrance, where the object from the past is not recovered as
if it were no longer lost to us, but interpreted *for us* within the horizon of our understanding (a crucial concept for Gadamer), despite
the fact that the object itself remains lost. Hermeneutics in Hegelian terms becomes an essential part of philosophy, as part of the
reflective or conceptual capacity of the mind to comprehend the
past as its memory. Such a positive, recollective role for interpretation diametrically opposes the hypothetical elimination of self-
awareness in the exercise of objective reconstruction, as if we were
after the thing itself, in traditional historical studies. As Gadamer
asserts of Hegel, in explicit opposition to Schleiermacher:

Hegel raises [understanding] to the level on which he has established philosophy as the highest form of absolute Mind. The self-consciousness of
spirit that, as the text has it, comprehends the truth of art within itself "in
a higher way," culminates in philosophy as absolute knowledge. For Hegel,

then, it is philosophy, the historical self-penetration of spirit (*die geschicht-liche Selbstdurchdringung des Geistes*), that carries out the hermeneutical task. This is the most extreme counterposition to the self-forgetfulness of historical consciousness. (*WM* 161, *TM* 168)

For Gadamer the exercise of understanding is less conceptual, less philosophical than for Hegel, but it nonetheless requires a conscious act of mediation, whereby history is no longer the *origin* of meaning, but rather the *medium* through which the mind must move in comprehending that meaning for itself. The concept of effective-history is developed from this view of history as mediation. The true place of hermeneutics, argues Gadamer (*WM* 279, *TM* 262–63), is found in the tension between an alien distance and an achieved familiarity, a sense of separation across historical time and the participation in an appropriated tradition. The true historicity of understanding, as Gadamer defines it, does not pertain to the historical object as such, but to the relation between the knower and what is known, involving simultaneously the reality of history and the reality of historical understanding in general. The goal of hermeneutics, then, is a fusion of these separate realities, as a blending of two horizons into one. This fusion of horizons (*Horizontverschmelzung*) is what constitutes understanding. Gadamer describes such a process of fusion under the rubric of effective-history, as follows:

Real historical thinking must take account of its own historicity. Only then will it cease to chase the phantom of a historical object that is the object of progressive research, and learn to view the object as the counterpart of itself and hence understand both. The true historical object is not an object at all, but the unity of the one and the other, a relationship that constitutes both the reality (*Wirklichkeit*) of history and the reality of historical understanding. A hermeneutics adequate to the subject matter would have to demonstrate the reality and efficacy (*Wirklichkeit*) of history within understanding itself. I shall refer to this as "history of effect" (*Wirkungsgeschichte*). *Understanding is, essentially, a historically effected event.* (*WM* 283, *TM* 299–300)

Gadamer acknowledges that his position is essentially Hegelian. Understanding is the mediation between a sense of history and a sense of truth. This experience is conscious of itself as mediation, and is termed "historically effected consciousness" (*Wirkungs-geschichtliches Bewußtsein*, WM 323, TM 340–41). Gadamer's entire theory of hermeneutics proceeds from this position.

THE HERMENEUTIC CIRCLE

The second aspect of Gadamer's argument that I wish to consider concerns the so-called hermeneutic circle. This concept has been central to theories of interpretation since the Romantic period, but Gadamer revises the traditional view of circularity, applying it to the basic dialogical relation between text and reader in the act of reading. In doing so, Gadamer also acknowledges his debt to Heidegger's ontological definition of the hermeneutic circle (*WM* 250–56, *TM* 265–71).

The classical formulation of the hermeneutic circle was made in an obscure work by Friedrich Ast, a contemporary of Schleiermacher who published a handbook of philology under the aegis of *Alter-tumswissenschaft*, the discipline of classical studies developed by Friedrich August Wolf. Whether Ast himself deserves credit for the crucial insight into the nature of interpretation which underlies his formulation is open to question. He may have been indebted to unpublished work by Schleiermacher and Friedrich Schlegel. Nor would Ast's argument still be known at all, I surmise, had not Schleiermacher later made it the subject of his important address to the Academy of Sciences in Berlin, one of the few texts published by Schleiermacher on hermeneutics.[12] Ast's definition of the hermeneutic circle is as follows:

The basic law of all understanding and of all cognition is to find out the spirit of the whole from the particular and to comprehend the particular through the whole. The former is the analytical, the latter the synthetic method of cognition. Both, however, depend upon each other and are closely interrelated, so that the whole may not be conceived without the part, as its unit, nor the part without the whole, as the sphere within which it lives. Neither is therefore prior to the other, since each determines the other reciprocally and both together are one single harmonious life.[13]

The circle of understanding, asserts Ast, where *a, b, c,* etc. (as a series of particulars) may only be known through *A* (as their totality) and *A* may only be known through *a, b, c,* etc., is irresolvable (*unauflöslich*). Gadamer summarizes this position with explicit reference to Ast in essentially the same terms:

Fundamentally, understanding is always a movement in this kind of circle, which is why the repeated return from the whole to the parts, and vice versa, is essential. Moreover, this circle is constantly expanding, since the concept of the whole is relative, and being integrated in ever larger contexts always affects the understanding of the individual part. (*wm* 178, *tm* 190)

In our century this circular structure was reaffirmed by Martin Heidegger, as Gadamer acknowledges, in the argument of *Being and Time,* as necessary and appropriate to the ontological status of interpretation. To be caught up in a circle appears vicious to common sense, as it is also contrary to all the assumptions of deductive reason. Such a view, argues Heidegger, is based on a fundamental misunderstanding. Gadamer quotes from paragraph 32 ("Understanding and Interpretation") of *Being and Time,* where Heidegger states:

The circle of understanding is not to be reduced to the level of a vicious circle which is merely tolerated. In the circle is hidden a positive possibility of the most primordial kind of knowing. To be sure, we genuinely take hold of this possibility only when, in our interpretation, we have understood that our first, last, and constant task is never to allow our fore-having, fore-sight, and fore-conception to be presented to us by fancies and popular conceptions, but rather to make the scientific theme secure by working out these fore-structures in terms of the things themselves.[14]

These peculiar Heideggerian terms, fore-having (*Vorhabe*), fore-sight (*Vorsicht*) and fore-conception (*Vorgriff*), which are introduced and explained in the pages preceding the passage quoted, have to do with what Heidegger calls "the existential *fore-structure* of *Dasein* itself." The circle of understanding reflects the manner in which the mind comprehends its own existential situation. Heidegger thus extended the theory of the hermeneutic circle, as Gadamer emphasizes, to more essential philosophical concerns than the part-whole relations within a text, as had been the case in the tradition of Ast and Schleiermacher.

Gadamer accepts Heidegger's argument concerning the ontological basis of the hermeneutic circle. He even goes a step further to suggest that our sense of the unity or totality of meaning in a text (Gadamer's term is *Vollkommenheit*) derives from this fore-structure of understanding.[15] It might be argued that the universality of art itself may be grounded in such hermeneutical circularity. Even more important for critical theory is the application of such fore-structuring to the act of reading as an unavoidably purposive endeavor, where readers construct the meaning of the text for themselves through the act of reading. The fore-structure of understanding thus provides the basis for a phenomenological theory of reading as the construction of a sense of totality for the text being read.[16] The circular interrelation between part and whole is thus extended to the complex interaction between text and reader in the act of reading. More precisely, this involves bringing together the horizon of awareness or expectation in the mind of the reader and the entire fabric of historical and literary associations called into play by the text. The result is that conscious coordination or fusion of horizons which, as Gadamer argues, is essential for understanding. He summarizes his views on the hermeneutic circle in this way:

The circle, then, is not formal in nature. It is neither subjective nor objective, but describes understanding as the interplay of the movement of tradition and the movement of the interpreter. The anticipation of meaning that governs our understanding of a text is not an act of subjectivity, but proceeds from the commonality that binds us to the tradition. But this commonality is constantly being formed in our relation to tradition. Tradition is not simply a permanent precondition; rather, we produce it ourselves inasmuch as we understand, participate in the evolution of tradition, and hence further determine it ourselves. Thus the circle of understanding is not a "methodological" circle, but describes an element of the ontological structure of understanding. (*WM* 277, *TM* 293)

Gadamer achieves his deepest insight into the act of interpretation by applying this position to the relationship between text and reader. This relationship is described as an exchange, following the model of question and answer in dialogue. The text speaks to its reader *as if* it were a partner in dialogue, raising questions, either explicit or implicit, which the reader must answer through interpretive response. Through this dialogical, or intersubjective, relation between text and reader the essential dynamic status of tradition is defined. A sense of tradition is established through the experience of reading, and participation in such a tradition is what constitutes the role of interpretation, specifically the study of literature, in education. Again, to quote Gadamer:

Hermeneutical experience is concerned with *tradition*. This is what is to be experienced. But tradition is not simply a process that experience teaches us to know and govern; it is *language* – i.e., it expresses itself like a Thou. A Thou is not an object; it relates itself to us. It would be wrong to think that this means that what is experienced in tradition is to be taken as the opinion of another person, a Thou. Rather, I maintain that the understanding of tradition does not take the traditionary text as an expression of another person's life, but as meaning that is detached from the person who means it, from an I or a Thou. Still, the relationship to the Thou and the meaning of experience implicit in that relation must be capable of teaching us something about hermeneutical experience. For tradition is a genuine partner in dialogue, and we belong to it, as does the I with a Thou. (*WM* 340, *TM* 358)

Making use of the dialectical method in the philosophy of Plato and Hegel, Gadamer argues that the basic model of hermeneutics is the dialogical structure of discourse. On the authority of these philosophers he also insists that the meaning thus communicated and shared by the participants in dialogue, even where one of the participants is a text, goes beyond the limits of the particular, individual, subjective existence of the participants. Meaning is thus general, in the sense of a community or a tradition which is shared. The basis for such a tradition, as established through dialogue, is language itself, the medium or field of discourse which is shared by the participants as the basis of understanding. Language, thus achieved through dialogue, is both a presence and a resource, involving a mutual transformation of the partners into a community. Gadamer believes that such a mutual transformation may also occur in the act of reading, in a manner which corresponds directly to the genuine dialectic of education. The eloquence and the conviction of his comments on this point, which constitutes the climax of his entire argument, reveal Gadamer's commitment as a teacher and a philosopher to the tradition of humanistic studies that extends back beyond his immediate sources in German thought through the entire Christian-Platonic heritage of the West:

Every conversation presupposes a common language, or better, creates a common language. Something is placed in the center, as the Greeks say, which the partners in dialogue both share, and concerning which they can exchange ideas with one another. Hence reaching an understanding on the subject matter of a conversation necessarily means that a common language must first be worked out in the conversation. This is not an external matter of simply adjusting our tools; nor is it even right to say that the partners adapt themselves to one another but, rather, in a successful conversation they both come under the influence of the truth of the object and are thus bound to one another in a new community. To reach an understanding in a dialogue is not merely a matter of putting oneself forward and successfully asserting one's own point of view, but being transformed into a communion in which we do not remain what we were. (*WM* 360, *TM* 378–79)

Romantic Hermeneutics

Gadamer's concept of dialogical form for the hermeneutic relation between reader and text derives in large measure from Hegel's *Phenomenology of Spirit*. He openly acknowledges this debt near the end of his argument, where a philosophical theory of experience is outlined in Hegelian terms (*wm* 329–44, esp. 336ff.; *tm* 346–62, esp. 353ff.). He does not elaborate on the specific implications of a Hegelian theory of experience for hermeneutics. This is not a failing on Gadamer's part, especially since he has subsequently developed his views on Hegel and hermeneutics in his book of essays *Hegel's Dialectic* (see note 4); yet I doubt that even a careful reader of the *Phenomenology of Spirit* would see from the argument of *Truth and Method* how Hegel serves as the source for the concept of dialogical form.

The crucial issue is raised when Gadamer asserts that Hegel's theory of absolute knowledge is incompatible with hermeneutic experience. For Hegel the dialogical relation between individuals established through language is part of the ethical structure of objective spirit. Absolute knowledge lies beyond, in the domain of philosophy and science, achieved through a transcendence, or sublation (*Aufhebung*),[17] of individual concern, when the spirit affirms its self-certainty as conscience ("der seiner selbst gewisse Geist," as *Gewissen*)[18] in a form acknowledged by others to be universal. This form is achieved, as Hegel emphasizes, in language, presumably the language of his own *Logic*, where the medium of dialogue collapses into the truth of absolute knowledge. Gadamer alludes in passing to this crucial and extremely difficult section of the *Phenomenology*. He emphasizes that such an attitude toward experience, from the vantage point of an absolute that must lie beyond the limits of the experiential process, is antithetical to hermeneutic consciousness. "The dialectic of experience," Gadamer concludes, "has its proper fulfillment not in definitive knowledge, but in that openness to experience that is made possible by experience itself" (*wm* 338, *tm* 355).

An issue emerges from Gadamer's discussion of the dialogical form of hermeneutic experience which I take to be crucial to the status of literary criticism. In order to clarify this I shall comment briefly on Hegel's theory of absolute knowledge in contrast to Schiller's concept of aesthetic experience, as formulated in his *Letters on Aesthetic Education*. Hegel has Schiller's views in mind, along with other post-Kantian positions in moral philosophy, throughout his discussion of conscience as the affirmation of spirit in its self-certainty.[19] Self-certainty, or self-fulfillment, as a comprehensive reintegration of consciousness and the objects of its knowledge, was envisioned by Schiller as the goal of what he called aesthetic education. Hegel responds by rejecting all aesthetic criteria for such a state of mind, offering instead his theory of absolute knowledge. My own conviction, based on a reading of *Truth and Method,* is that hermeneutics resides between these radical alternatives in the domain of dialogue, distinct from either aesthetic experience or absolute knowledge. On the basis of such distinctions one might argue that, contrary to various claims by contemporary theorists who would regard the critic as either a poet or a scientist, criticism as a discipline is neither an art nor a science, but a dialogue with tradition through the hermeneutic encounter with texts.

The juxtaposition of Schiller and Hegel in terms of an implicit hermeneutic theory, which neither consciously espoused, will provide a broader historical basis for the claim put forward by Gadamer that the interpretation of texts belongs to the domain of practical philosophy. This is essentially part of what both Schiller and Hegel would have regarded as the ethical dimension of education, involving the dialogical interaction between texts and readers. Such an argument also demonstrates both the value and the limit of literary studies for education.

SCHILLER'S *LETTERS ON AESTHETIC EDUCATION*

One can demonstrate the crucial contribution that Schiller's aesthetic theory makes to hermeneutics by examining the end of his fifteenth letter. There he describes ideal beauty as "living form," which he earlier defined as the manifestation of freedom (*Freiheit in der Erscheinung*).[20] Schiller does not distinguish between beauty as a formal principle in art and beauty as a quality or condition of the self. The argument that he develops in the middle sequence of letters (eleven to fifteen) adapts principles of ethical theory derived from Kant and epistemological concepts concerning the dialectical structure of experience from Fichte to an aesthetics of individual development. The goal of this development is conceived as an ideal of harmonious self-fulfillment, where freedom and beauty are achieved as identical attributes of the self. The highest principle of integration, called the "play-impulse" (*Spieltrieb*), involves the reconciliation of opposing forces or impulses in the mind. Schiller's concept of play is virtually synonymous with what elsewhere in Romantic aesthetics is termed the poetic imagination. Schiller does not address himself to the ethical implications of such a concept for human society, i.e., as a principle of harmonious interaction between individuals. Instead he discusses the work of art as an ideal manifestation of this quality. In response to the work of art, he argues, individuals may become aware of beauty and freedom as latent in themselves and thus orient their thoughts and actions toward the achievement of such a state. Beauty thus becomes the goal of human development and education. The work of art in its ideal form provides an instance of man's essential humanity – "die Idee seiner Menschheit," as Schiller puts it in the fourteenth letter – and serves simultaneously as "a symbol of man's accomplished destiny" and as "a manifestation of the Infinite."[21]

Aesthetic experience results from the interaction between a work of art and its beholder. Insofar as the beholder may comprehend and consciously understand this experience as it occurs, his or her aesthetic response must also include an implicit hermeneutic dimension. Schiller does not concern himself in any way with the verbal or cognitive structures involved in understanding such experience. The norm of art which he selects as an instance of ideal beauty is, not surprisingly, Classical sculpture, where the form perceived is spatial or plastic and the mode of perception is purely visual. At the end of the fifteenth letter he describes the colossal bust of Juno Ludovisi in the collection of antiquities at the Vatican in Rome. Goethe greatly admired this statue and had it copied in a plaster cast during his Italian journey. Schiller presumably knew of it only through Goethe, since the cast was not sent to Weimar until 1823, where it found a prominent place in Goethe's house. Such indirect access to the work strengthens the hermeneutic implications of Schiller's description. He writes at the distance of hearsay, as if he and his reader together could behold the statue only through his verbal description. Schiller thus describes an aesthetic response to this work of art in terms which translate visual perception into verbal form. What he offers is the language of a hermeneutic consciousness:

It is not Grace, nor is it yet Dignity, which speaks to us from the superb countenance of a Juno Ludovisi; it is neither the one nor the other because it is both at once. While the woman-god demands our veneration, the god-like woman kindles our love; but even as we abandon ourselves in ecstasy to her heavenly grace, her celestial self-sufficiency makes us recoil in terror. The whole figure reposes and dwells in itself, a creation completely self-contained, and, as if existing beyond space, neither yielding nor resisting; here is no force to contend with force, no frailty where temporality might break in. Irresistibly moved and drawn by those former qualities, kept at a distance by these latter, we find ourselves at one and the same time in a state of utter repose and supreme agitation, and there results that wondrous stirring of the heart for which mind has no concept nor speech any name.[22]

Schiller here pays eloquent tribute to the ideal of beauty in Classical sculpture, as it had been defined in German aesthetics during the eighteenth century from Winckelmann to Goethe. He also indicates, at least implicitly, how the experience of art may indeed blend a sense of harmony and repose as a symbol of humanity with an intuition of the infinite or divine. Schiller asserts that the statue reveals the presence of the goddess in a unity of affect where the beautiful and the sublime become identical. But Schiller also asserts that the beholder – and this includes the reader of his letters along with himself as hypothetical respondent to the statue – achieves a conscious understanding that this aesthetic experience constitutes the ideal of humanity. Indeed, the eloquence of his rhetoric, both as description of the statue and as description of an aesthetic response to it, suggests that for both Schiller and his reader the conscious understanding of this experience and the verbal description of it will be commensurate with, if not identical to, the experience itself.

Aesthetic experience and hermeneutic consciousness, Schiller implies, are thus fully correlative and mutually compatible. At the same time, however, he asserts that the aesthetic response to those qualities of beauty and nobility embodied by the statue includes a sense of wonder and communion which goes beyond language and even beyond thought. The experience of art thus includes a sense of identity between consciousness and its object. At this point a limit of hermeneutics is defined, which also reflects the limit of language itself, at least for the purpose of cognition and communication. It is also at precisely this point that Hegel's rejection of Schiller would occur, replacing aesthetic experience as the norm for art with an alternative model of language based on the demands of philosophy.

HEGEL'S *PHENOMENOLOGY OF SPIRIT*

Not by accident did Schiller select a Classical statue as his example, specifically the head of a statue thought to represent a goddess. Implicit in his model of aesthetic fusion between the mind of the beholder and the beautiful object beheld is a theme familiar from traditions of love poetry, where the pleasure inspired by beauty is akin to erotic desire. Juno Ludovisi, as described by Schiller, could serve as an ideal woman, such as Beatrice or Laura, as Schiller, no doubt, was aware. The kind of communion thus attributed to aesthetic experience, however complex, resembles the satisfaction of desire in either a religious or a secular context.

Hegel opposes such a model of fusion or communion for experience and insists that self-consciousness, which is the necessary prerequisite to understanding, results from a reciprocal opposition or tension between the mind and its object. In place of the erotic response to Classical beauty, Hegel introduces the model of a mutual acknowledgment between opponents in conflict, the lord and the servant, or master and slave, whose relation to each other results from a life-or-death struggle. That Hegel intentionally reversed the model of aesthetic fusion from Romantic theories of art, whether or not he had Schiller specifically in mind, need not be questioned. My present argument is concerned to show what this familiar passage in the *Phenomenology* has to do with hermeneutics.

Spirit for Hegel is the intersubjective dimension through which individuals interact with one another. Self-consciousness, his central concept for defining the manifestation and comprehension of spirit, is achieved through a reciprocal response among separate individuals. By acknowledging each other they establish for themselves that interrelationship which constitutes, for Hegel, the ethical substance of spirit and which he calls mutual recognition (*gegenseitiges Anerkennen*).[23] Hegel summarizes the dialectical process through which such a reciprocal relationship is achieved in a difficult paragraph just preceding his example of master and slave.[24] It will be instructive to paraphrase this summary, keeping Schiller's description of aesthetic experience in mind for contrast.

Each individual achieves self-consciousness, in and through the Other, in three stages. First, the Other becomes, as undifferentiated self or "I," an immediate object of knowledge *for me*. Second, this immediacy is perceived *by me* to be an absolute mediation, whereby the self-sufficiency of the Other is transformed *for me* by Desire. The satisfaction of this Desire is achieved through what Hegel terms the reflection of self-consciousness in itself – i.e., as mediated between the two selves – so that *my* self-certainty becomes truth (mutual and reciprocal to both). Self-consciousness understands its truth to be a double reflection. The "living form" – Schiller's term for ideal beauty – of *my* self-consciousness loses its self-sufficiency through the dynamics of my interaction with the Other – i.e., I affirm myself for myself through the Other. Exactly the same process also occurs for the other self, which served as *my* object, in its relation to *me*. It is affirmed for itself in and through its own negativity – i.e., as it is known *by me*. In this way, Hegel concludes, the self is universalized as a type (*Gattung*): both I and the Other mutually recognize ourselves through our reciprocal knowledge of each other. This state of achieved Spirit Hegel calls "living self-consciousness."

Despite the cumbersome terminology so characteristic of Hegel (which I have attempted to modify into more workable English), it is apparent that he avoids the sense of communion that Schiller attributed to aesthetic experience. He does so by emphasizing a sense of opposition, or negativity, to the relationship between the participants in this dialectic. By substituting this principle of opposition or negativity, Hegel makes an awareness of difference the basis for mutual self-understanding. The best example of this that Hegel can offer, in conscious contrast to the model of love in Romantic aesthetics, is the bond of opposition that unites master and slave. Both acknowledge their interdependence in terms of this opposition. In the struggle between these two opponents one overpowers the other and thus asserts himself to be master. He is acknowledged as such by the defeated other, who thereby assumes the role of servant or slave and is so acknowledged by the master. Each is mutually dependent on the other for recognition of what he is. In itself, of course, this example of mutual recognition has no importance for hermeneutics, although it could easily be applied to a theory of understanding.

Much later in his argument in the *Phenomenology* – at the end of the long chapter "Spirit," under the heading of "Conscience" – Hegel reintroduces the same dialectic of mutual opposition, but this time at a higher level of consciousness, namely as a form of language.[25] The self-certainty of spirit is affirmed through a dialectic of self-assertion and denial in language, which also achieves a mutual recognition through a sustained sense of difference. For my argument concerning the dialogical structure of hermeneutic experience what matters is the role of language in the extremely complex process of self-fulfillment described by Hegel. At the risk of oversimplification I shall attempt to outline this role from the context of Hegel's discussion.

Conscience as the final stage of self-certainty in the spirit makes an absolute claim to truth. The validity of this claim depends upon the acknowledgment of the community in which this claim is made. As in the case of a prophet or an evangelist – and Hegel presumably has in mind the supposedly privileged truth claims of radical religious sects in the eighteenth century – the question is how an individual may make such an absolute assertion for others. If we assume, for instance, that such a claim is made in a text – as in a Romantic ode on the intimations of immortality or the constancy to an ideal object – then we must ask what substantiates that claim other than the subjective certainty of the speaker. The *content* of the claim, so Hegel argues, cannot indeed be more than subjective. Such a verbal act by the individual self attests to no more than its own conviction. Yet the *form* of its declaration, specifically as verbal structure, establishes its validity for those who hear and respond. The statement of a subjective individual becomes universal through the mediation of form, which requires an authentic hermeneutic consciousness shared between speaker and audience, or between a text and its readers. The highest kind of mutual recognition, which Hegel earlier argued to constitute Spirit, is the mediation of truth in the forms of language that are shared between speaker and audience. Hegel summarizes this point in terms that may be directly applied to hermeneutic theory:

> . . . whoever says he acts in such and such a way from conscience, speaks the truth, for his conscience is the self that knows and wills. But it is essential that he should *say* so, for this self must be at the same time the *universal* self. It is not universal in the *content* of the act, for this, on account of its specificity, is intrinsically an indifferent affair: it is in the form of the act that the universality lies. It is this form which is to be established as actual: it is the *self* which as such is actual in language, which declares itself to be the truth, and just by so doing acknowledges all other selves and is acknowledged by them.[26]

This mutual acknowledgment is achieved through a radical crisis of opposition and denial. Hegel traces an extremely complex dialectical development, which cannot be presented in detail here,[27] whereby the individual self makes the claim of truth as a beautiful soul (*schöne Seele*, a phrase that was adapted from the vocabulary of pietism to aesthetic theory by Goethe and Schiller).[28] This claim is rejected by those to whom it is made through a categorical negative judgment, which Hegel calls evil (*das Böse*) and even hypocrisy. The self in its extremity as a hardened heart (*das harte Herz*) is reduced to a spiritless unity of being, as an insubstantial mist or a kind of madness (described in terms which suggest an allusion to extremes of Romantic subjectivism).[29] At this point of denial a catastrophic reversal occurs, so that the moment of tragic collapse is followed by a mutual act of forgiveness (*Verzeihung*). Opposition and denial are thus replaced by a genuine reconciliation, where each self acknowledges the other as equal in their respective differences. This sense of shared community, concludes Hegel, constitutes the Absolute Spirit:

> The word of reconciliation is the *objectively* existent Spirit, which beholds the pure knowledge of itself *qua universal* essence, in its opposite, in the pure knowledge of itself *qua* absolutely self-contained and exclusive *individuality* – a reciprocal recognition which is *absolute Spirit*.[30]

Hölderlin's "Patmos"

We may now return to Gadamer's theory of hermeneutic experience as a dialogue between an I and a Thou, in order to assess the critique he makes of Hegel's concept of absolute knowledge. The claim for philosophy as scientific system is apparent in the original title intended by Hegel for the *Phenomenology – The Science of the Experience of Consciousness (Wissenschaft von der Erfahrung des Bewußtseins)*.[31] Gadamer develops his own theory of experience, as indicated earlier, from Hegel. Insofar as the historical and temporal nature of human experience may be subsumed within a dialectical form as a development of consciousness, there is no quarrel with Hegel. Nor does Hegel's concept fail to address the essential dialogical or intersubjective form which experience must assume in language. This form, especially where it is defined by the interaction of text and reader in the act of reading, is essentially hermeneutic. The difficulty arises when Science (*Wissenschaft*) is proclaimed as the goal for the experience of consciousness in the domain of the absolute spirit, where the self achieves a certainty of itself in knowledge ("die Gewissheit seiner Selbst im Wissen," as Gadamer formulates it [*WM* 337; *TM* 355]).

Gadamer rejects such a goal for hermeneutics and substitutes a familiar idea from Greek tragedy, as formulated in the opening chorus of Aeschylus's *Agamemnon*: πάθει μάθος ("wisdom is only

achieved through suffering"). Translated into the terms of hermeneutic theory, this may be restated: *understanding is only achieved
through experience.* And such understanding must also include, as
Gadamer emphasizes, a sense of the limits of experience, due to the
unavoidable limitation of human existence. "Thus experience," he
concludes, "is experience of human finitude" (*WM* 339, *TM* 357). The
place of hermeneutics remains within the limits of understanding,
located on a middle ground between opposing ideal norms of coalescence: aesthetic experience, on one hand, as evoked by Schiller,
and absolute knowledge in Hegel's sense, on the other.
Hermeneutics is limited to the medium of dialogue, where one
mind speaks to another, even if the one is fixed in the form of a
text; and the experience thus communicated and understood is
shared according to a reciprocal sense of historical and existential
difference. In itself such dialogue remains open, of course, and as
limitless as language and the history of human culture. The limits
on understanding within that scene of dialogue apply to all who
participate in it, since each of us – as we are mortal, born at a
moment of time beyond our control and destined to die at some
time equally beyond our control – enter the dialogue of tradition
and break off from it somewhere else quite arbitrarily.

In support of this argument we may consider an alternative to
the opposing positions of Schiller and Hegel, established by Hölderlin in his Pindaric hymn "Patmos," written, conveniently for my
argument, in the middle of the decade which separates the *Letters
on Aesthetic Education* from the *Phenomenology of Spirit.*[32] The poet
of "Patmos" develops a complex imaginative identification of perspectives between his own vision and that of Saint John the
Apostle. Since John is regarded as the author of both the Fourth
Gospel and the Book of Revelations, "Patmos" includes an implicit
hermeneutic response to these texts. The poet asserts near the climax of the poem that he has gathered the materials that he needs
with which to construct an image of Christ as he truly was:

So hätt' ich Reichtum,
Ein Bild zu bilden, und ähnlich

Zu schaun, wie er gewesen, den Christ.
(164–66)

[Thus would I have riches sufficient
to build an image and to behold
the Christ, similar to what he was.]

Needless to say, these "riches" are verbal, and they derive from
the poet's reading of Scripture. But he resists the temptation to
form an image of Christ by poetic imitation, thus denying to his
poem that quality of ideal beauty which Schiller attributed to the
statue of Juno. He describes instead a danger which would result
from such an attempt. The language of this conditional statement is
radically ambivalent, collapsing finally in a breakdown of syntax at
the dash:

Wenn aber einer spornte sich selbst,
Und traurig redend, unterweges, da ich wehrlos wäre
Mich überfiele, daß ich staunt' und von dem Gotte
Das Bild nachahmen möcht' ein Knecht –
(167–70)

[But if someone spurred himself on
and, speaking sadly, underway, since I would be defenseless,
fell upon me, so that I was astonished, and wished
to imitate the image of the god, a servant –]

The question of who is doing what to whom is left unclear.
Superimposed upon the metaphor of a sculptor imitating the god is
another metaphor of an encounter on a journey, involving an
ambush of the poet, who declares himself to be defenseless. These
metaphors are crucial for the implied hermeneutics of the poem.
Who is the servant or slave referred to at the end of the passage?
The poem offers no further elaboration, nor does the grammar
allow any certainty of reference, whether the servant is the author
of the imagined image or another who seeks to imitate the image.
Is it the poet or his reader? The context of Hölderlin's biblical

source suggests however that such ambivalence of reference is appropriate to such an act of imitation, especially when the object imitated is Christ as Lord. This relationship between the Lord and his servant may be juxtaposed with Hegel's example of self-consciousness as the relation between master and slave. The terms are the same for both and derive from the idiom of Luther's German Bible: *Herr* and *Knecht.* This connection might seem arbitrary indeed, were it not likely that both Hölderlin and Hegel had the biblical tradition in mind. The paradoxical relation of Christ to his followers is prefigured in the primal displacement of bondage in Exodus, when Israel went out of Egypt. The slaves who had been subject to Pharaoh freely establish a covenant with the God of Moses as their Lord, thus transforming their state through a kind of Hegelian sublation into a nation that is free, even though the people acknowledge that they are the Lord's servants.

For Hölderlin the heresy of a hermeneutics which seeks to identify the reality of the divine with the object of poetic imitation may indeed be regarded as a perversion of just such a free covenant, reinterpreted (as "Patmos" shows) through the example of the love and death of Christ. My point for a theory of hermeneutics is that the poetic object relates to understanding in precisely the manner of Hölderlin's hymn to the reality of Christ as divine. The danger mentioned in the opening lines of the poem – "Wo aber Gefahr ist" – which the poem seeks to avoid, is the desire to "grasp" (*fassen*) the God, to achieve an imaginative identity or fusion with the divine, "to build an image of Christ as he was." "Patmos" rejects the model of aesthetic fusion between the beautiful object and its beholder, as described by Schiller. The reason for this rejection is a sense of the appropriate limit to understanding. Such an act of imitation would endanger the poet, as if through a kind of ambush against one who deserves no more than to be a servant of the Lord. Hölderlin's point applies also to the reader of his poem, expressed in the statement just following the lines quoted: "nicht, daß ich seyn sollt etwas, sondern / Zu lernen" [Not that I should be something, but to learn].

The passages from "Patmos" that I have cited here indicate a thematic concern by the poet for issues of hermeneutics, in particular regard to the limits of understanding. By denying the possibility of imitating the divine in the language of his poem, Hölderlin displaces all claims for the sublime and grounds his poetic vision within a hermeneutical consciousness. Such a sense of limit for poetry is affirmed by the form of dialogue established between the poem and its reader. In the final line of the hymn, Hölderlin asserts this hermeneutical care (*Pflege*) to be the task of German song. The breakdown described as an ambush and embodied in the language as a syntactical collapse must also be perceived by us as part of the experience of reading. And what, finally, is the stance that the poet assumes in the poem? Vigil and service, like a monk in his cell, studying Holy Scripture. Nor is the text of his German song committed to more than exegesis and translation. The role of the poet in the poem, responding to the biblical texts by Saint John, is essentially the same as our own role in reading and interpreting the poem. "Patmos" as a text reproduces a hermeneutic response to the New Testament, and our interpretation of it is constructed accordingly upon a conscious sense of difference between reader and "Patmos" or between "Patmos" and New Testament within the dialogical form of the poem. Interpretation is thus, so Hölderlin concludes, the highest service which may be offered to God:

> . . . der Vater aber liebt,
> Der über allen waltet,
> Am meisten, daß gepfleget werde
> Der veste Buchstab, und bestehendes gut
> Gedeutet. Dem folgt deutscher Gesang.
> (222–26)

> [But the father who rules over all
> loves most of all that care
> be given to the fixed letter
> and what is established be well
> interpreted. This is the task of German song.]

Hölderlin demonstrates such service through his own poem. An imagined fusion of horizons (Gadamer's term) is established between the poet as mental traveller and John the Apostle on the island of Patmos. This relationship is in fact a metaphor for the poet's interpretive response to the text of Scripture. A dialogical form is established which extends to the hermeneutic consciousness of Hölderlin's reader, in a manner that resembles what Hegel calls mutual recognition. "Patmos" affirms that quality of *wirkungs- geschichtliches Bewußtsein* (historically effected consciousness), which mediates between the past and the present, here represented as a visionary journey from Germany to Asia Minor and back.

At the outset of the poem the poet prays for the means, indeed the medium, whereby he may go across the abyss of time, as in the journey of a mountaineer from one summit to another, and subse- quently return to his own historical, cultural perspective. At the end of the poem, despite his denial of the possibility that his language might construct a viable image of Christ, the poet nonetheless affirms the continuity of historical time between the era in which Christ lived and died and the situation in which he lives and speaks. In a cosmic oxymoron Hölderlin affirms the continuing presence of divinity despite its apparent absence. The sign of God is silent in the thundering sky, even though the lightning serves pre- cisely as such a sign. This is the storm of historical time, and the one alone who stands beneath it his whole life long is Christ. For he still lives:

> Still ist sein [des ewigen Vaters] Zeichen
> Am donnernden Himmel. Und Einer stehet darunter
> Sein Leben lang. Denn noch lebt Christus.
> (203–5)

> [Silent is the sign of the eternal father
> in the thundering sky. And one alone stands beneath it
> his whole life long. For Christ still lives.]

Such affirmation through the medium of the poem, both as experi- ence and as interpretation, demonstrates at the highest level of hermeneutic form the completion of the circle of dialogue, where difference itself bears witness to Absolute Spirit. A continuity in the consciousness of effective-history is also affirmed, where the experiential structure of the poem recapitulates the theological paradox of presence across the abysses of historical time.

As motto for this chapter I cited two lines from the famous opening of "Patmos":

> Nah ist
> Und schwer zu fassen der Gott.
> Wo aber Gefahr ist, wächst
> Das Rettende auch.
>
> [Near is,
> and hard to grasp, the god.
> But where danger is, grows
> what rescues also.]

On first reading of the poem these opening lines would appear to address a fundamental theological and existential dilemma: the danger for the self of the proximity of the divine. Yet the lines also offer a somewhat cryptic reassurance that from such danger a form of rescue will grow. Only in retrospect after a careful reading of the poem do the hermeneutical implications of these lines become apparent. The nearness of the god, and the difficulty of grasping (i.e., comprehending) him, refers to the experience of reading Scripture. The text conveys a sense of presence—as when the mind is seized by the power of a "Genius," which is said in stanza two of the poem to have carried the poet away from his German homeland into the dazzling light of revelation over the mountain ranges of Asia, leading finally to the retreat of the poet to the island of Patmos, where St. John once found refuge. Such transport defines the effects of danger upon the mind in response to the revelatory power of Scripture. Rescue is received, however, from the capacity of a hermeneutical response, which follows the example of the visionary disciple in his retreat to the safety of the sacred grotto on the island, where the Book of Revelation was written in response to the vision of God. The poet's poem thus constitutes an imitative form, where the danger of divine presence is mediated through the interpretive labor of language. Hölderlin's "Patmos" defines an exercise in hermeneutics, through which the danger of the proximity of God is relieved through the growth of a poetic rescue that offers service (*Pflege*) to the overwhelming power of such revelation by retreating into the milder light of exegesis.

The fundamental difference between Hölderlin's hermeneutical stance in "Patmos" and the respective opposition between Schiller and Hegel outlined earlier is crucial for the argument of this essay concerning the limits of interpretation. To reiterate: 1) Schiller celebrates an ideal of coalescence or fusion between the beautiful work of art and the perceiving subject as a norm for aesthetic experience; 2) Hegel insists upon the irresolvable conflict of individual perspectives, even within the essential form of the language that constitutes self-consciousness, which may only be resolved through a mutual act of forgiveness (*Verzeihung*), a dialectical sublation into a reciprocal recognition (*gegenseitiges Anerkennen*) which is Absolute Spirit; and 3) Hölderlin evokes the recreative power of poetic recollection through the encounter with Scripture, whereby an image of the absent Christ could be constructed within the medium of his poem, but he proposes as alternative to such a dangerous, hybristic endeavor that faithful care (*Pflege*) be devoted to the text as that which abides (*das Bestehende*) and which must be well interpreted (*gut gedeutet*). Such care and such good interpretation are the fundamental tasks of hermeneutics.

The Task of Interpretation

Let me conclude, returning briefly to the remarks made at the outset concerning the place of interpretation in criticism and the place of literary studies in education, with three points which emerge from this discussion about the limits of understanding. This will suggest tentatively the direction in which a defense of reading might proceed against whatever heresies of deconstruction or misreading may be conjured against such study.

The first point has to do with the historicity of texts and the role of historical understanding in literary criticism. The attempt to recover a sense of the truth through the interpretation of texts resembles the effort to commune with spirits of the dead, even though the texts of literature provide us with a supremely privileged form of documentation. What we achieve through our study is at best a reconstruction of the tradition shared between us, which enables the text to mediate between the past and the present through the dialogue of hermeneutic consciousness. The meaning that is constructed by interpretation stands in a problematic relation to any criterion of truth or reality from the past, simply because this construction is the product of dialogue and necessarily reflects our own limits and the limits of our understanding. On this point Hegel's concept of recollection or memory (*Er-Innerung*), as the essential quality of what we understand, indicates also the appropriate limit to the validity our interpretations may claim. It has been the fundamental error of historicism in humanistic studies to ignore the status of understanding as a reconstruction or recollection, as if scholarship could ever gain access to absolute truth. The truth of hermeneutic understanding must never be confused with some objective or systematic model of scientific knowledge.

My second point concerns the ethical dimension of criticism and education. The limit of interpretation constitutes the basis for a system of values shared as a sense of community by those who engage in dialogue with the text and who come to share in the tradition and continuity thus communicated. The most crucial aspect of hermeneutic experience, in agreement with the Hegelian model of ethical interaction, is a mutual recognition of difference as the basis of understanding in the dialogical structure shared by the participants. The dream of a fixed and authoritative meaning to texts has always invited the hope of an identity shared by all readers, analogous to the model of a mystical communion among the faithful in the church. Certain texts may invite such a hope, including the texts of Scripture upon which such faith is based. It is the task of hermeneutics, however, including the domain of biblical interpretation, to offset such expectations with an awareness of difference in the varied responses of readers which constitute what Gadamer calls effective-history. It is therefore beneficial for criticism to emphasize that the experience of reading can achieve at best a sense of participation in an ongoing dialogue which remains open and without end.

My final point, which follows directly from the first two, concerns the centrality of hermeneutics for education. We need to recognize that a sense of difference and of limit, not only in the study of literature, is an essential aspect of that dialogical form of experience which, since Plato and even since Homer, has constituted education and has been the prerequisite to self-knowledge. Insofar as all education involves communication through language, all systems of thought and value must be subject to the unavoidable human limits of experience and understanding. This applies equally to the ideals of philosophy and to the theories of science. Science and philosophy may continue to draft models of systematic knowledge, which also provide norms for education, in Plato's sense of the love of wisdom and in Hegel's sense of the absolute spirit. Yet the community of scholarship and learning, to which our institutions of education are committed, not only in humanistic studies, can only be established through the practice of interpretation as a form of open dialogue.

Plato still provides the most eloquent demonstration of the essential form of education in his Socratic dialogues, even while expressing through these dialogues a commitment to the ideals of philosophy. Alongside Hegel, furthermore, whose claims for Absolute Spirit assume an authority equal to Plato's Ideas, Hölderlin writes as a kind of poetic conscience for systematic thought, demonstrating a powerful, even tragic sense of limitation to the possibility of affirming human experience in poetic language. Hölderlin's poem thus affirms the truth of Aeschylus's tragic vision that "wisdom is only achieved through suffering." Hans-Georg Gadamer would welcome, I expect, the association of his work in hermeneutics with the dialogues of Plato and the poetry of Hölderlin. This company is deserved. Gadamer, more than any other theorist of our time, has demonstrated with authority the place of hermeneutics in criticism and education, in terms of both the need to understand and the limits of understanding.

Afterthought (1997)

The initial draft of this essay was written as a review of the first, badly flawed translation of *Truth and Method* during the mid-seventies. At that time, as indicated in the essay, the term and concept of hermeneutics was still very new and often alien to the habits of literary criticism in North America. Since then the work of Gadamer has become much more accessible in English, not only through the excellent revised translation of his major book but also through the publication in translation of many of his lesser writings, collected under a variety of headings. Gadamer himself, who will shortly celebrate his own centennial to coincide with the new millennium, has also completed editing his collected works in ten magisterial volumes.

In the face of such a triumphant career, unequalled perhaps in the history of philosophy for its longevity, a student of his hermeneutics may well ask whether the skills of interpretation in literary study have benefitted in significant ways from his teaching. The answer to such a question within the American academic scene would have to be largely negative. Theories of interpretation have had relatively little impact on the practice of reading. Not that the poets are any more neglected in the curricula of university courses; nor is there any lack of sympathetic respondents among the generations of students, each seemingly less sophisticated than the last. But the temper of the times goes contrary to the needs of interpretation, as ever more alien and hostile motives govern what is taught and written about literature.

Gadamer himself in the serenity of his advancing years – he is repeatedly referred to as the *Nestor* of philosophy – does not seem troubled by the vicissitudes of taste and time. The word of the poets stands as fixed and secure as always, and the challenge of critical service and care – "daß gepfleget werde/Der veste Buchstab," to quote again from Hölderlin's "Patmos" – remains as ever for those readers who choose to respond. The task of hermeneutics thus abides through all the shifting heresies of taste, and the place of interpretation for reading remains as central for us today as it was for Gadamer, also for Hölderlin, and even for Plato himself. In that conviction these essays were undertaken and are presented here.

Chapter 2: The Negativity of Reading

In memory of Northrop Frye

But conversation
Is good and to speak
The heart's opinion
–Hölderlin, "Andenken"

"In exitu Israel de Aegypto." Readers of Dante will recall this line of Latin from canto 2 of the *Purgatory*, which indicates a quotation from the 114th Psalm in the Vulgate Bible.[1] The poet-pilgrim of *The Divine Comedy*, newly emerged from his journey through the *Inferno* into the early dawn of Easter Sunday at the shore of Mount Purgatory, hears this psalm sung in unison by a group of souls newly dead, arriving in a boat from the River Tiber to begin their penitential climb toward salvation. Why did Dante choose this particular psalm for these souls to sing? Several reasons for this deserve consideration in some detail.

An important comment on the meaning of this same psalm is provided by Dante in his famous epistle to Can Grande de la Scala, where he refers to the traditional fourfold reading of Scripture, in order to suggest that his own poem be read in the same way.[2] Scholars have long regarded this document as crucial for defining the allegory of *The Divine Comedy*, even if they often disagree on how to apply the doctrine of the four levels to the text of the poem. I would like to add my name to those who have taken Dante's emphasis on this fourfold structure seriously by looking closely at the context of the psalm and its use by the poet. The medieval theory of the four levels of meaning will emerge in the course of my argument as important for a theory of literary history and hermeneutics, with regard to both the intertextual status of tradition and the reappropriation of that tradition through the act of interpretation. Close attention to Dante and his use of the biblical psalm will lead to more general questions of meaning in modern poetry and the interrelation of criticism, theory and history.

In the letter to Can Grande Dante surveys the fourfold reading of Psalm 114, addressing in turn the *literal,* the *allegorical,* the *moral* and the *anagogical* as follows: "If we consider the letter alone, the thing signified to us is the going out of the children of Israel from Egypt in the time of Moses; if the allegory, our redemption through Christ is signified; if the moral sense, the conversion of the soul from the sorrow and misery of sin to a state of grace is signified; if the anagogical, the passing of the sanctified soul from the bondage of the corruption of this world to the liberty of everlasting glory is signified."[3] Earlier in the same paragraph Dante introduces his reading by distinguishing categorically between the meaning conveyed "by the letter" [per literam] and the meaning conveyed "by what the letter signifies" [per significata per literam]. There is for Dante, in other words, a basic distinction between the literal meaning and the figurative, or "allegorical" and "mystical," reading of the *polysemous* (Dante's term) poetic text. The last three levels of the fourfold reading constitute such figurative meaning. What Dante has in mind as the literal meaning is the apparent referential or occasional sense of a text in both historical and literary terms; the figurative levels introduce, as his letter makes clear, the whole range of typology from the tradition of Christian exegesis. What interests me here is how the act of reading moves from the literal level of meaning to an awareness of the figurative levels. I shall argue in the course of this essay that such a move is only possible through a cognitive process which may best be termed *negation.*

Psalm 114

The historical event to which the opening line of Psalm 114 refers is clear and unambiguous: it is the exodus of the people of Israel from their bondage in Egypt, as narrated in the biblical book of Exodus. The first level of meaning for the psalm is thus seen to be *not* a reference to the actual historical event so much as an allusion to the narrative of that event in Exodus, which constitutes the official, sacred, textual account. The psalm assumes an awareness of this history as an intertextual referent, which constitutes its *literal* meaning. Dante also intended the reader of *The Divine Comedy* to have the entire psalm in mind, as indicated by the fact that the souls in the boat are said to sing "the rest of that psalm as it is written."[4]

As we read through the psalm, however, the question of literal reference quickly becomes complicated and more ambiguous.[5]

1 When Israel went forth from Egypt,
    the house of Jacob from a people of strange language,
2 Judah became his sanctuary,
    Israel his dominion.

The opening verse contains a twofold repetition. "The house of Jacob" and "Israel" are synonymous, each referring to the people of the Exodus; and the place of bondage, "Egypt," is, in effect, synonymous with the people of that alien nation: "de populo barbaro." In the second verse the twofold reference to the promised land, which became the home of the people of Israel, is more ambiguous. Judah is called *sanctuary,* which suggests (to some scholars)[6] an allusion to the Temple, later built on the hill of Zion in Jerusalem under King Solomon, which then became a part of the southern kingdom of Judah. Israel is called *dominion,* which would be a puzzling attribute indeed, were an allusion intended only to the northern kingdom during the divided monarchy. Here, as in the opening phrase of the psalm, Israel must therefore refer to the whole nation, itself regarded as both the sanctuary and the dominion of the Lord.

The biblical context removes all ambiguity of historical and geo-

graphical reference; yet such reference also must include an awareness of the historical narrative of the Exodus and also the entry of
the Jews into the promised land, as well as the founding of the
monarchy and the building of the temple. The text of the psalm
thus imposes upon its reader a retrospective awareness of the entire
history of the nation. We observe through the repetition of phrases
in the opening verses the implicit transformation of a seemingly literal historical reference into an open-ended perspective on the
entire tradition, whereby the terms juxtaposed through repetition
are joined in a figurative or metaphoric relationship, rather than in
a mere literal contiguity. The narrative history which underlies the
psalm collapses into a metaphor of simultaneity, where two separate, though related elements, derived from different vantage points
within the historical narrative, are juxtaposed as if they were simultaneous and equivalent.

Such a transformation of discourse does not become fully apparent, however, until verses 3 and 4:

3 The sea looked and fled,
   Jordan turned back.
4 The mountains skipped like rams,
   the hills like lambs.

Commentators generally agree that the phrase "The sea looked and
fled" refers to the crossing of the Red Sea in Exodus 14; whereas the
next phrase, "Jordan turned back," refers to the later crossing by the
Israelites into the promised land, described in Joshua 3–5.[7] The historical narrative of this second crossing over includes a conscious
awareness of a pattern of repetition, as indicated by the repeated
use of the same phrase for crossing over in Joshua which had earlier been used in Exodus.

Other allusions to the history of the nation are superimposed in
verse 4 – "The mountains skipped like rams, / The hills like lambs"
– although the literal, historical reference is far less explicit. No
event which could be thus described is found anywhere in the
narrative of either Exodus or Joshua, except in one crucial instance:
the revelation of the Lord to Moses on Mount Sinai. This occurs as

a volcanic explosion and earthquake, described in Exodus 19:18: "And Mount Sinai was wrapped in smoke, because the Lord descended upon it in fire; and the smoke of it went up like the smoke of a kiln, and the whole mountain quaked greatly." Verse 4 of Psalm 114 contains an allusion to the revelation at Sinai. Yet the tone and manner of the verse are totally at odds with that epiphany, due to the simile of the dancing rams. The reference to lambs in the second phrase, furthermore, suggests the carefree, joyous, pastoral activity of newborn animals in springtime.

Such imagery does not evoke divine revelation and epochal events in the history of the nation, but rather the regularity of seasonal change and the rituals of renewal which celebrate such change. In contrast to the wilderness setting of Sinai, the allusion to the skipping of rams and young lambs suggests patterns of life within the secure pastoral culture achieved for Israel only after crossing the river Jordan. At the same time, through a contrastive and opposite figurative allusion, both the rams and the lambs call to mind rituals of sacrifice which play a central role in the Bible. The most familiar instance is found in the testing of Abraham (Gen. 22:13), when a ram is substituted for his son Isaac. Equally appropriate, however, would be the sacrifice of the newborn lambs in the celebration of Passover (Exod. 12). Even to this day such sacrifice of young lambs commemorates the liberation of the people of Israel from bondage in Egypt. This ritual itself, however, may derive (so scholars point out) from an even more ancient seasonal festival, celebrating the return of spring through the sacrifice of the first-born of the flock.[8]

Such latent intertextual resonances in the first half of Psalm 114 effect a figurative transformation within the narrative portion of the text. A perspective is opened up on the historical tradition recalled through this narrative in such a way that by duplication and repetition of phrases, disparate and increasingly indeterminate elements from this tradition are conflated. This process of juxtaposition and conflation may best be described as a technique of intentional allegoresis. Such crossing over – in the strict etymological sense of the term *metaphor* (from the Greek "to carry over") –

occurs within the text of the psalm as it moves from phrase to phrase and from verse to verse. A hermeneutical strategy of composition thus begins to emerge, which may affirm the fourfold structure of meaning outlined by Dante in a way he never intended.

We have already moved in our discussion of verses 1 to 4 from the first to the second level of meaning, from the literal to the metaphoric. The third level is established in verses 5 and 6, where the preceding narrative is repeated nearly verbatim in the form of direct questions:

> 5 What ails you, O sea, that you flee?
>   Jordan, that you turn back?
> 6 O mountains, that you skip like rams?
>   O hills, like lambs?

The tense of the verbs also shifts from past to present, effecting a generic transformation of the discourse of the psalm from narrative to direct address. What does such a shift imply?

This form of dialogue, involving direct address by speaker and audience, to the text by the reader, constitutes the moral or ethical level of meaning in the psalm. Past significance becomes present meaning and is acknowledged as such by the form of the language. Commentaries usually refer the questions asked in these verses back to the anonymous psalmist, as if he were posing to himself the question of validity or authority for his own preceding narrative. I would argue instead that these questions are addressed by the reader of the psalm, specifically by the audience or congregation which recites it collectively, or by the choir which sings it, as part of the liturgy of worship. This form of implied response thus establishes for that act a communal consciousness. The act of questioning what has already been narrated as history acknowledges that the perspective established by that narrative on the historical tradition has now become present and immediate to the mind of the reader. This sense of presence or immediacy constitutes the moral level of meaning as a form of communal participation and conscious involvement in the liturgy. The meaning of history is thus reappropriated and renewed. The questions of verses 5 and 6 also acknowledge by implication that it is for us that the Jordan turns back and the mountains and hills skip. The answer to these questions at the moral level of meaning affirms the community of belief – "Yes, they do so!" – which is implicit in the very act of asking the questions.

The fourth level of meaning, which Dante in his letter to Can Grande termed the anagogical level, is the most difficult for modern readers to perceive and comprehend. For the Bible as sacred Scripture, however, this level is both necessary and essential. The psalm proclaims in its final verses that God is immediate and present:

> 7 Tremble, o earth, at the presence of the Lord,
>   at the presence of the God of Jacob,
> 8 Who turns the rock into a pool of water,
>   the flint into a spring of water.

The text thus signifies a genuine anagoge, an opening up or a leading forth into transcendence, as is appropriate to the act of worship. For the first and only time in the psalm, God is actually named as Lord (*Adon*), the God of Jacob, as if his countenance were directly revealed here before us. In his presence the congregation, in apparent sympathy with both the mountains and hills and the rams and lambs, is enjoined to tremble. In the first phrase of verse 7, if the English text offers a correct reading of the Hebrew source,[9] I take the invocation of earth to include intentionally the people and the nation that inhabit the earth, to which the faithful reader of the psalm may be assumed to belong. Such a sense of participation in this act of worship as a trembling is what I would call the hermeneutical consciousness of Psalm 114.

Verse 7 thus constitutes the climax and the fulfillment of the psalm, establishing for the anagogic stage of meaning a sense of epiphany or of divine presence. This moment is also accompanied in verse 8 by an appropriate form of reversal, a peripety or even perhaps a figure of conversion. This turn of thought enables the psalm in its final verse to recall again the passing over from bondage to freedom, from death to new life. Such reversal is signalled in the text by repeated reference to water within a pattern of miraculous events that contrasts categorically with the outset of the psalm. Water first was mentioned as a figure of flight or retreat before the power of God. Here allusion is made, by contrast, to the miraculous nourishment provided by God for the wandering tribes in the wilderness, when the rock was transformed into a pool and the flint into a spring.[10] This pattern of reversal in the ending of the psalm also restores the narrative discourse of appropriated history at a higher level of conscious awareness. History and ritual thus become identical. The figures of the pool and the spring also convey a genuine sense of renewal and nourishment. As readers of the psalm, finally, we all have access to this nourishment as a living act or an immediate event of the spirit, celebrated within the perspective of the liturgy as something truly achieved.

Purgatory 2

My discussion of Psalm 114 claims no authority or validity with regard to the original Hebrew of the Bible. My only purpose has been to demonstrate the legitimacy of the medieval tradition of fourfold exegesis from a reading of the psalm itself. Such a reading of the psalm makes it possible to take seriously what Dante says in his letter to Can Grande about the four levels of meaning. I now wish to outline a related reading of Dante's use of Psalm 114 in *Purgatory* 2. What I have in mind is quite different from the concerns of historical philology, which would address Dante's original design in the composition of his canto. In this regard I would mention the important scholarly essay by Charles Singleton, "In Exitu Israel de Aegypto," which is concerned with the philological and theological implications of Dante's inclusion of the psalm.[11] Singleton has virtually nothing to say about the task of interpreting this passage in terms of the traditional theory of fourfold meaning. My concern here, by contrast to his approach, is to show how the act of reading may include an awareness of tradition as it operates through intertextual resonances evoked by the text. I consider such a concern to be crucial for both literary history and critical praxis.

Two aspects of a critical reading are particularly important for defending the fourfold structure of meaning as I have defined it for Psalm 114. The first applies to the transformation of narrative as history into figurative or metaphoric discourse, which, as I argued, occurs in the first half of the psalm. Through this transformation the past becomes accessible to the conscious mind as a present structure. Such a transformation achieves what I call the reappropriation of tradition. Past significance becomes present meaning. The second aspect of my reading pertains to the shift from narrative to dialogical form in the latter half of the psalm, where question and answer in the present tense replace the past tense of recollection. Through this shift an implicit awareness of community is established for the reader, which affirms the authority of the covenant in the Bible and prefigures the model of the church as *ekklesia,* which developed in the Christian medieval tradition, based on the New Testament. For both Jewish and Christian forms of community, the validity of the historical tradition depends upon a ritual of response by readers, who participate in an act of worship which affirms a sense of God as revealed presence. Such a community of reading also requires of all readers, whether or not they choose to respond, an acknowledgment of theological truth, which is the foundation of religious faith.

An affirmation of tradition and community is thus built into the form of the psalm as religious song, insofar as it is intended to be recited or chanted as part of the ritual of worship. Initially, this would have occurred in the Temple at Jerusalem. Subsequently, the psalm was also used within the Christian church throughout the Middle Ages to Dante's own time and beyond. We need to consider briefly its liturgical context within the church year, what biblical scholars would term its *Sitz im Leben,*[12] which motivates and governs its performance in worship. This text belongs to a group of psalms, consisting of the sequence in the Psalter from 113 to 118, traditionally called the Hallel.[13] These psalms are recited together, even to the present day, as part of the Jewish pilgrimage festivals, including Passover in the spring. For the intertextual perspective of Psalm 114 in Dante's *Divine Comedy* Passover is crucial.

Centuries of liturgical practice thus stand behind the identification of text and event, as outlined in my reading of the psalm. This holds true above all for the feast of Passover as the superimposition of historical memory upon seasonal ritual. The founding event of the Jewish nation, when the people of Israel came out of Egypt under the leadership of Moses to confront their Lord, is commemorated within a celebration of the renewal of life and spirit, marked by the sacrifice of the first-born lambs for the Paschal meal. History and ritual are thus inextricably interwoven, as indicated already by the narrative account in Exodus 12 and 13, which includes precise instructions for the sacrifice and the feast.[14] Even the account in Joshua of the crossing over Jordan coincides, surely not by accident, with the season of Passover, which is celebrated immediately following the successful entry of the people into the promised land (Josh. 5:10–12).[15] In the New Testament, of course, acknowledging also an appropriate providential design, the Passion of Jesus coincides with the Passover in Jerusalem. Following the Last Supper, which is the Passover meal, Jesus and his disciples sing a hymn together before going out to the Mount of Olives (Matt. 26:30). This hymn would presumably have been the traditional Hallel, or at least part of it, perhaps including Psalm 114.[16]

At this point we may finally return to the text of *Purgatory* 2, in order to consider the liturgical background to Dante's citation of the psalm. Within the Christian church, as far back as I am able to trace it, Psalm 114 has been part of the Easter service, celebrating the Resurrection of Christ from the dead.[17] For purposes of performance within the tradition of Gregorian chant, furthermore, this psalm is assigned its own special tone, called the Tonus Peregrinus, a variant on the set tones used interchangeably for the other liturgical texts and psalms.[18] The souls in the boat which arrives at the base of Purgatory in Dante's poem are said to be singing this psalm in unison: "more than a hundred spirits," and "singing together with one voice."[19] Dante the pilgrim within the poem has just emerged from his journey through Hell at dawn on Easter Sunday. The performance of this psalm by the choir of spirits thus signifies for the pilgrim a recognition of community in celebration of Christ's Resurrection. His own poem thereby enters into the perspective of the Easter Mass and participates in it.

Commentators on *The Divine Comedy* have suggested that Dante included the performance of Psalm 114 based on his familiarity with the traditional liturgy of the Easter service in the Roman church, rather than directly from a reading of the Latin text in the Bible.[20] If this is valid, it strengthens my argument that the performance of the psalm by the souls in the boat signifies a reaffirmation of community. Dante also includes, however, a further dimension of historical allusion, grounded in the liturgical practice of the Christian church: Psalm 114 was used in Dante's Italy as part of the service commemorating the dead. The basis for this practice was a typological interpretation of the psalm from the perspective of the New Testament, whereby the Exodus out of Egypt and the crossing over into the promised land prefigure the redemption of the soul from its fallen state and its salvation through the example of Christ's death and resurrection. Within the framework of the Gospels Jesus himself becomes the Paschal lamb. The mystery of the sacraments, furthermore, is based upon the liturgical commemoration of his death and rebirth. Baptism is a "crossing over" through waters which cleanse and restore the soul. Holy Communion in the celebration of the Mass presents the bread and wine as sacramental signs of the body and blood of Christ, firstborn of the Father, who died on the cross. The burial of the dead, finally, including the singing of Psalm 114, represents liturgically the "crossing over" of the soul from the bondage of life in this world into the hope of eternal life through salvation in Jesus Christ.

In Dante's poem the souls of the newly dead make their journey literally, crossing the ocean in a boat guided by an angel from Rome through the Straits of Gibraltar on a southwesterly voyage to the mountain of Purgatory in the southern seas. Dante has purposefully superimposed these various liturgical resonances upon the psalm sung by this group of souls when they arrive. That this arrival coincides also with the dawn of Easter Sunday, commemorating Christ's Resurrection from the dead after harrowing Hell, enhances the significance of Dante's own pilgrimage along the same path through the Inferno to the mountain of Purgatory.

Based on such a reading of Dante's text within the perspective of liturgical tradition, the four levels of meaning outlined by the poet

71

in his letter to Can Grande may be applied directly to his own poem. Such application also affirms my argument concerning the validity of the traditional fourfold structure for a hermeneutics of reading. Within the narrative of the canto the literal and the allegorical levels of meaning are apparent, however complex, in accordance with intertextual perspectives established for both liturgical practice and scriptural tradition as outlined above. In ways that are quite free of biblical reference in themselves both the souls of the newly dead and the poet as pilgrim have just completed their literal *crossings over,* on the one hand by boat from Rome and on the other by foot through the *Inferno.* Psalm 114 thus refers for both the souls in the boat and for Dante as pilgrim to the crossing over from life into death and to the resurrection of Jesus on Easter Sunday, as also to the redemption of the soul through faith in that event.

The moral sense of the passage, which Dante called in his letter "the conversion of the soul from the sorrow and misery of sin to a state of grace," must be applied hermeneutically to the experience of the reader in response to Dante's poem. Here I am in agreement with the argument of Charles Singleton concerning the multiple structure of conversion as a verbal strategy in *The Divine Comedy.*[21] A crucial point, however, which is not made by Singleton, concerns the motive for this strategy, not with regard to the poet, who has already achieved his vision of God, but for his reader, who is guided through the poem by reading in the company of the pilgrim, just as the pilgrim is guided, first by Virgil and then by Beatrice, through the forms of conversion represented within the text. For Dante, as for Psalm 114, the moral sense of this conversion can be communicated to the reader as a conscious awareness through a basic dialogical structure of question and answer, statement and response, signalled at the simplest level by the poet's frequent direct address to the reader.

Similarly, I would argue that the anagogical level of meaning is only achieved by Dante's poem *for us* if the act of reading constitutes a progress or education of the mind through conversion and beyond, into the perspective of a divine vision. Within the grand design of the poem, its divine economy, as it were, such vision is projected as the ultimate goal of the pilgrimage at the far end of the *Paradiso*. Even within the *Purgatory*, whose specific goal is the redemption of fallen man in the Earthly Paradise, the recitation of Psalm 114 constitutes at best the beginning of the journey as the sun rises on Easter Sunday. Yet clearly the ultimate vision that *The Divine Comedy* seeks to communicate can only be achieved by the reader as a response to the text. In this regard the hermeneutical structure of Psalm 114 in its performance prefigures in more limited scope that sense of divine presence which the poem as a whole seeks to attain. Even here, however, precisely because of the liturgical resonances of tradition, an affirmation of theological faith in the truth of God occurs through the fourfold sequence of meaning, from literal to figurative and from ethical to anagogical, in precisely the manner which *The Divine Comedy* memorializes and seeks to convey to us as a comprehensive whole.

The Negativity of Reading

My discussion of Dante in relation to Psalm 114 may seem too esoteric for a theory of literary history and hermeneutics, although I hope I have at least demonstrated the validity of the traditional fourfold structure of meaning for the act of reading as a sequence of hermeneutical reversals. What are the implications of this argument for the act of reading? In response to this question I shall attempt a radical reversal of my own, in order to reconsider the role of tradition and community in the reading of poetry.

The singing of the psalm in *Purgatory* 2 may be argued to symbolize both the reappropriation of tradition and a community of reading, which thus interprets the biblical text through liturgical performance. The authority of both the church and Scripture stands behind Dante's use of the psalm. Yet Dante as poet also writes about this liturgical event from a cognitive and temporal distance, separated from it by memory. For Dante writing as narrator of *The Divine Comedy*, the pilgrimage into the presence of God represented by the poem has already been completed. Dante as poet, writing his poem in exile, has no community. At best he can bear witness to the idea of such community as remembered and evoked within the solitude of his poetic composition. As readers of Dante's poem there can be likewise no community *for us* apart from the capacity of the text to represent it as an imagined or fictional event. The singing of the psalm by the choir of souls in Dante's poem is thus also removed from us as event, in the same way that the Exodus from Egypt and the crossing over into the promised land are removed from the perspective of Psalm 114 through a process of historical memory. The liturgical performance of the psalm, however, by moving through its fourfold hermeneutical structure of meaning, still conveys a valid sense of presence and affirmation for those who perform it within the context of worship.

Dante's poem itself cannot achieve such a sense of presence, nor does it claim to. Any sense of immediacy in *The Divine Comedy* is established only as a poetic fiction, an aesthetic illusion, mediated through the verbal form of narrative recollection. Both the poet and his reader are necessarily separated from the events and experiences represented by the poem. Dante's *Divine Comedy* is as much a meditation in solitude as it is a poetic imitation of community and vision. As readers we must never forget, as Dante the poet never allows us to forget, that the entire poem is written in exile. The poet is removed from his native community, having been banished and rejected by it, and his entire pilgrimage, from beginning to end, occurs only in the company of the dead. Those spirits who encounter the poet-pilgrim in sympathy and support, as in the case of Virgil and Beatrice, still remain only spirits. It is a supreme paradox of literature that the poem which achieves without equal what Erich Auerbach called the representation of the real world (*der irdischen Welt*)[22] remains itself from beginning to end no more than a fiction, a vision or dream, a memory or echo, which continuously imposes upon its reader a conscious awareness of that fact. To read Dante's *Divine Comedy* and to make his pilgrimage with him is at best an act of communion with spirits of the dead, even if the language of the poem enables these spirits to represent what is real and true with a voice that speaks directly and authentically through that language. For us, as readers of the poem, even the poet has become such a spirit, regardless of his frequent claim, as the pilgrim who journeys through the poem, to be alive. I emphasize this all pervading paradox about Dante's *Divine Comedy* because there is no better example for what I mean by the *negativity of reading*.

The concept of negativity and its validity for a theory of critical reading are outlined by Wolfgang Iser in the concluding section of his book *The Act of Reading*.[23] In my response to Iser's argument, "Strategies of Reversal in Literary Narrative" (chapter 8 below), I summarize his view of negativity as follows:

Our sense of the *truth* or the *reality* of this meaning [in a literary text]…is the result of a self-projection and is in the highest sense a fiction created by the act of reading. Meaning is the *what-not*, the *not-given* or *no-thing* of the text, which thus also qualifies the construct of meaning as a valid reflection of our own identity, achieved through the act of self-alienation that occurs in the process of reading.[24]

From Iser I was led to Hegel, the grand master of negativity as a theory of cognition for Western thought, and my attention was directed in particular to Hegel's theory of negativity in Romantic art (by which he meant the entire tradition of post-Classical, medieval or Christian art, e.g., Dante's *Divine Comedy*).

In another essay, entitled "Reading the Romantic Ode" (chapter 5 below), I attempt to apply Hegel's concept, with a tentative glance at his extremely difficult discussion of negativity in the *Science of Logic,* to the hermeneutics of reading.[25] My conclusion is central to the argument here:

Negativity…describes the status of meaning [for Hegel] in conceptual or speculative thought, as constituted by the mind in its dialectical encounter with discourse. More precisely…negativity defines the necessary hermeneutical relation between a text and its meaning, which is established *for a reader* in and through the act of reading… . Negativity is the negation of the negative [as Hegel frequently asserts]. What he means by this will be apparent if we bear in mind that language itself as medium of discourse is negative, insofar as sign and signified necessarily are opposed or discontinuous. The sign is distinguished from what it signifies through the disjunctions of irony or the complexities of metaphor. The act of reading and interpretation thus constitutes the negation of this negative relationship by *positing,* or constructing, the meaning of the text through a dialectical interaction which occurs through that act. Understanding is only achieved through a characteristic transformation of thought, which Hegel terms a *sublation* (*Aufhebung*), involving a reflective turn or reversal in the mind.[26]

In Romantic art for Hegel this reflective turn imitates the fundamental mythical pattern of a death and rebirth, even if only at a symbolic level of imagined experience. It is also the pattern of conversion and crossing over, I submit, which was traced above in the texts from Dante and the Bible.

The structure of such negativity is essentially identical to the traditional fourfold structure of meaning when applied as a hermeneutical principle to the process of reading. The importance of such negativity for literary history, furthermore, will be apparent. The act of reading achieves historical consciousness, in the manner of what Gadamer in *Truth and Method* calls the "fusion of horizons."[27] This consciousness involves an intertextual reappropriation of tradition, *not* as a presence *for us* so much as an absence, which we must recognize indeed to be an absence. Finally, this process, whether or not in Hegelian terms, is identical with what traditionally is called self-reflection or self-consciousness. To understand a text, specifically in its historical and intertextual determinations, we must also understand ourselves. For this reason, incidentally, literature and the act of reading are central to education.

In order to clarify further these several points, I wish to consider briefly two characteristically "modern" poetic texts: John Donne's "Hymne to God my God, in my sicknesse" and Friedrich Hölderlin's "Remembrance." I use the term *modern* not as a period concept (which seems questionable to me), but to designate a mode of discourse in written texts. Dante's text is thus modern in this sense, especially in the manner in which it cites Psalm 114. Even the psalm itself could be called modern, insofar as it reappropriates the narratives of Exodus and Joshua. It could finally be argued that every genuine reading must be modern, because the text makes it so, obliging us to locate our interpretations within an intertextual perspective defined by our own self-consciousness.

Texts impose a radical sense of opposition and otherness upon readers, who must appropriate meaning through a process of subla-tion (*Aufhebung*) and dialectical transformation (or *crossing over*, in the sense adapted above from biblical usage and applied to the process of *metaphor*). In this regard I agree with Paul de Man in his essay "Literary History and Literary Modernity," where he defines modernity, with reference to Nietzsche and Baudelaire, as a funda-mental and irresolvable opposition between temporal or historical consciousness and a sense of the moment or the present within the act of reading.[28] "Modernity" and history are incompatible, yet nec-essary, components of all texts. The tension between them is what causes poetry continually to provoke the present as a legacy from the dead past.

The sequence of texts from Donne's "Hymne" to Hölderlin's "Remembrance," however, also traces a development in the tradi-tion of European poetry which is crucial for the emergence of what is conventionally called *modernism*. The mode of communal spiri-tual experience represented by the Psalms and so powerfully evoked by Dante when he encounters the souls of the newly dead arriving at the shore of Purgatory and singing Psalm 114 is replaced in Donne and Hölderlin by something more personal, more solitary and more secular. All trace of the liturgical tradition is eliminated, even though Donne still alludes to the trappings of religion on his supposed deathbed and even though Hölderlin evokes at least the memory of a secular festival that may serve as a subsitute for Easter and Passover. What this development implies for the act of reading and for the task of hermeneutics must still be further clarified.

Donne's "Hymne"

Apart from its use of a fixed stanza defined by meter and rhyme, Donne's "Hymne" would hardly be appropriate as a devotional text for congregational singing within the conventions of Protestant hymnody.

HYMNE TO GOD MY GOD, IN MY SICKNESSE

Since I am comming to that Holy roome,
Where, with thy Quire of Saints for evermore,
I shall be made thy Musique; As I come
I tune the Instrument here at the dore,
And what I must doe then, thinke here before.

Whilst my Physitians by their love are growne
Cosmographers, and I their Mapp, who lie
Flat on this bed, that by them may be showne
That this is my South-west discoverie
Per fretum febris, by these streights to die,

I joy, that in these straits, I see my West;
For, though theire currants yeeld returne to none,
What shall my West hurt me? As West and East
In all flatt Maps (and I am one) are one,
So death doth touch the Resurrection.

Is the Pacifique Sea my home? Or are
The Easterne riches? Is *Ierusalem*?
Anyan, and *Magellan*, and *Gibraltare*,
All streights, and none but streights, are wayes to them,
Whether where *Iaphet* dwelt, or *Cham*, or *Sem*.

We thinke that *Paradise* and *Calvarie*,
Christs Crosse, and *Adams* tree, stood in one place;
Looke Lord, and finde both *Adams* met in me;

As the first *Adams* sweat surrounds my face,
 May the last *Adams* blood my soule embrace.

So, in his purple wrapp'd receive mee Lord,
 By these his thornes give me his other Crowne;
 And as to others soules I preach'd thy word,
 Be this my Text, my Sermon to mine owne,
 Therfore that he may raise the Lord throws down.[29]

The poem reads like a self-conscious deathbed performance by an isolated mind, reflecting on its own imminent demise. This has led some scholars to argue that Donne wrote the poem when he was indeed dying, a few days before his death. I am interested here in formal and figurative characteristics of the text rather than biographical questions. A thematic opposition is established within the poem between choral song and private meditation. The former is envisioned beyond death in God's sanctuary, or "Holy roome," where the soul will be played upon as an instrument of heavenly music among the "Quire of Saints." The poem itself, however, is a form of the latter, an exercise in thought which tunes the instrument in preparation. The poem also imitates the tone of a sermon, particularly in the final stanza, where a text for the argument is offered in the manner of a moral lesson or homily. Furthermore, through direct invocations of the Lord in the last two stanzas, the poem includes the manner of a prayer as well.

Donne purposefully internalizes these conventional forms of religious discourse into a kind of inner monologue, or soliloquy. He is preoccupied with figures of the mind's own death to the categorical exclusion of all sense of audience. The solitude of reflective discourse is far more explicit and thematic in Donne's "Hymne" than Dante's *Divine Comedy*. There is no concern for any reader, not even an acknowledgment of the possibility of communication. At best our role as readers is to overhear the poem. We are intruders upon the death throes of an isolated mind. None of that congregational singing attributed by Dante to the souls arriving in the boat at Purgatory is left in Donne's language, even if hope still remains for such communal song beyond death.

The imagery of death developed in the central four stanzas, however, still participates in the biblical tradition of a crossing over into eternal life. That Donne employs such traditional imagery is not surprising in a poem so conscious of its ironic manipulation of forms. What matters for my argument is that this imagery is organized within a hermeneutical structure of self-reflection that corresponds to the four levels of meaning in biblical exegesis. It may even be argued that the perspective of the reader is included within this structure after all, through a dialectical reversal analogous to a Hegelian sublation. Donne's hymn finally opens up for us an anagogical dimension in accord with the concept of negativity. Let me outline briefly how this is achieved through the four middle stanzas.

Donne's central trope – appropriate to the age of exploration in which he lived – compares his disease to a voyage of discovery, as if westward to the new world. All literal reference is subsumed within an elaborate, even outrageous metaphor. This is represented, on one hand, in cartographic terms, where his physicians read him, "flat on this bed," like a map, and, on the other, through traditional mythological associations of the west with death. His "South-west discoverie" is defined by a pseudo-scientific Latin diagnosis containing an etymological pun on *fretum* ("strait" or "channel") and *febris* ("fever"). Recognition of this pun immediately and ironically reverses the mood of the poem from despair to joy, from death to resurrection, by imagining the flat map turned into a globe where west meets east. The voyage westward thus attains its eastward goal, through whatever straits – *Gibraltare, Magellan* or *Anyan* (i.e., Bering) – to Jerusalem, which is identified through a superimposition of separate moments in salvation history as the location of both Paradise (where Adam's tree caused mankind's fall) and Calvary (where Christ redeemed mankind on the cross). Finally, completing this narrative of shifting tropes, Donne identifies himself, with a plea to the Lord to acknowledge him so, as both the first and the last Adam. Donne here follows a theological interpretation of the Crucifixion derived from St. Paul.[30]

The hermeneutical implications of Donne's argument become apparent if we consider how his reader is gradually gathered into the perspective of the poem. First, we observe a purposeful expansion of figurative reference beyond the particular instance of the poet's own disease and death, in order to ground his statement in theological doctrine. Next, we perceive the conscious appropriation of a typological narrative, derived from a New Testament reading of the crossing over from bondage into the promised land. Donne's southwest voyage of discovery thus becomes identical with that described in Psalm 114 and celebrated by the souls arriving at Mount Purgatory in Dante's *Divine Comedy*. This continuity of tradition is affirmed regardless of the question of influence (and it seems unlikely that Donne had Dante in mind). The essential component of this tradition is the pattern of redemption or conversion through death into new life.

We may also affirm that this process of figurative expansion and appropriation includes the perspective of the reader, along with that of the dying poet, within the duality of the first and last Adam. All who include themselves in this tradition share in the Pauline identification of Christ with Adam. The use of the first person plural pronoun at the outset of stanza 5 provides formal acknowledgment of this: *we* are all implicated. The third, or moral level of meaning is thus achieved, affirming a sense of shared community, in seeming contradiction to the form of private meditation used throughout the poem. Donne's imitation of liturgical forms – prayer, sermon, and hymn – is also affirmed ironically. Readers may even apply the personal emphasis of the title retrospectively to themselves: "Hymne to God *my* God, in *my* sicknesse," where the sickness becomes a metaphor for life itself.

From this perspective the fourth, anagogic level of meaning may be intuited as a projected transcendent vision beyond the limits of the poem as meditation. The choir of saints in the holy room, making its joyful song unto the Lord, thus establishes a legitimate goal for us also, even though the poem itself remains no more than the tuning of the instrument in the antechamber for such communal song beyond. A mediation between the text of the poem and this intuited vision only takes place through what I have called the negativity of reading. Donne's "Hymne" thus affirms the validity of the traditional fourfold structure of meaning in hermeneutical terms, even though no conscious awareness of that tradition may have motivated the composition of the poem. The solitude of a deathbed meditation by the self can only be communicated through reading, i.e., through the hermeneutical transformations that constitute such negativity.

Hölderlin's "Remembrance"

The most controversial point of my argument thus far concerns the relationship of negativity, as the basic structure of reflective thought in reading, to the appropriated forms of tradition and community that texts of literature come to represent for the mind through such thought. The privacy or solitude of the reflective mind and the festivals of community which celebrate transcendent values of the spirit are simply not compatible. I acknowledge this to be the given condition of human existence. To celebrate such festive joy and to think about it cannot take place at one and the same time. Yet the language of poetry, through its ironic and negative forms of representation, can successfully mediate between these opposing extremes of joy and thought. Time itself may thus be redeemed and history may become a constructive trope for discourse. To add support on this point I wish to consider briefly Hölderlin's poem "Remembrance"[Andenken].[31]

ANDENKEN

Der Nordost wehet,
Der liebste unter den Winden
Mir, weil er feurigen Geist
Und gute Fahrt verheißet den Schiffern.
Geh aber nun und grüße
Die schöne Garonne,
Und die Gärten von Bourdeaux
Dort, wo am scharfen Ufer

Hingehet der Steg und in den Strom
Tief fällt der Bach, darüber aber
Hinschauet ein edel Paar
Von Eichen und Silberpappeln;

Noch denket das mir wohl und wie
Die breiten Gipfel neiget
Der Ulmwald, über die Mühl',
Im Hofe aber wächset ein Feigenbaum.
An Feiertagen gehn
Die braunen Frauen daselbst
Auf seidnen Boden,
Zur Märzenzeit,
Wenn gleich ist Nacht und Tag,
Und über langsamen Stegen,
Von goldenen Träumen schwer,
Einwiegende Lüfte ziehen.

Es reiche aber,
Des dunkeln Lichtes voll,
Mir einer den duftenden Becher,
Damit ich ruhen möge; denn süß
Wär' unter Schatten der Schlummer.
Nicht ist es gut,
Seellos von sterblichen
Gedanken zu seyn. Doch gut
Ist ein Gespräch und zu sagen
Des Herzens Meinung, zu hören viel
Von Tagen der Lieb',
Und Thaten, welche geschehen.

Wo aber sind die Freunde? Bellarmin
Mit dem Gefährten? Mancher
Trägt Scheue, an die Quelle zu gehn;
Es beginnet nemlich der Reichtum
Im Meere. Sie,

Wie Mahler, bringen zusammen
Das Schöne der Erd' und verschmähn
Den geflügelten Krieg nicht, und
Zu wohnen einsam, jahrlang, unter
Dem entlaubten Mast, wo nicht die Nacht durchglänzen
Die Feiertage der Stadt,
Und Saitenspiel und eingeborener Tanz nicht.

Nun aber sind zu Indiern
Die Männer gegangen,
Dort an der luftigen Spiz'
An Traubenbergen, wo herab
Die Dordogne kommt,
Und zusammen mit der prächt'gen
Garonne meerbreit
Ausgehet der Strom. Es nehmet aber
Und giebt Gedächtniß die See,
Und die Lieb' auch heftet fleißig die Augen,
Was bleibet aber, stiften die Dichter.[32]

REMEMBRANCE

A northeaster's blowing,
To me the best of all winds,
Because it promises a fiery spirit
And a good voyage to sailors.
But blow now my greetings
To the beautiful Garonne
And the gardens of Bordeaux,
There, where along the steep bank
The footpath makes its way and the brook falls
Deeply into the stream, above it though
A noble pair looks out
Of oak and silver poplar.

Still I recall it well, and how
The elmwood bends
Its broad crowns above the mill,
But in the courtyard a figtree grows.
On feastdays just there
The brownskinned women walk
Upon silken ground,
In the month of March,
When night and day are equal,
And above the slow footpaths,
Heavy with golden dreams,
Cradling breezes pass.

Yet may someone pour for me,
Filled with the dark light,
A fragrant cup,
So that I may rest; for sweet
Would be slumber beneath the shade.
It is not good
To be soulless with
Mortal thoughts. But conversation
Is good and to speak
The heart's opinion, to hear much
About days of love
And deeds which are done.

But where are my friends? Bellarmin
With his companion? Some
Are shy to approach the source;
For wealth, namely, begins
At sea. They,
Like painters, gather together
The beauty of the earth and do not
Disdain the winged war and
To dwell alone, yearlong, beneath
A leafless mast, where festivals of the city

Do not light up the night,
Nor the play of music, nor native dance.

But now the men are gone
To the Indies,
There, at the windy point of land
By the steep vineyards, where downward
The Dordogne comes
And together with the splendid
Garonne, as broad as ocean,
The stream flows forth. But memory
Is taken away and given back by the sea,
And love also seizes hold of our eyes,
But that which abides, the poets create.

   (my translation)

The occasion for this poem deserves mention in passing. It was composed, presumably in the spring of 1803, when the poet was living in the solitude of his mother's home in Nürtingen, near Stuttgart (South Germany), to commemorate his sojourn in southern France a year earlier, where he was employed as private tutor in the house of the German consul at Bordeaux. While in France he may have witnessed some local springtime festival, such as he describes in his poem: "in the month of March,/When night and day are equal," a secular equivalent to Easter.[33]

The poet presents himself speaking in response to a northeasterly breeze, which blows from his retreat in Swabia toward the southwest, the region of Bordeaux and the Garonne, carrying with it – as a greeting sent to that region by the poet – the voice which speaks the poem. An act of recollection thus commences in response to the breeze, which calls to mind that festival in southern France within its particular figurative space. Hölderlin's description assumes the characteristic of a genre painting, with paths along a river bank, a stand of trees: oaks, silver poplars, elms, and a solitary figtree growing in the courtyard of a mill.[34] The place which is thus recalled even assumes the quality of a mythical illumination, where "cradling breezes" are "heavy with golden dreams." The mind of the poet as he remembers is transported by the power of his recollective imagination into the illusion of actually being at the festival again. He asks that someone pass him a glass of wine, "filled with the dark light" of Bordeaux's fragrant vintages, in order that he may find rest: "damit ich ruhen möge." He desires slumber within the shade, as a release from mortal thoughts, and friendly discourse, which would speak the heart's opinion and hear about days of love and the performance of heroic deeds:

> . . . for sweet
> Would be slumber beneath the shade.
> It is not good
> To be soulless with
> Mortal thoughts. But conversation
> Is good and to speak
> The heart's opinion, to hear much
> About days of love
> And deeds which are done.

A strange transformation takes place in the discourse of the poem as it proceeds. What begins as a recollection of personal experience gradually becomes permeated with a quality of imaginative projection or identification. Both the setting of the festival and the activity of participating in it assume a dreamlike sense of metaphoric or ironic presence. All the more disruptive, then, is the sudden turn of the poem in stanza 4, marked by a series of questions, through which the mind recovers an awareness of its condition in solitude. The language imitates the form of a recognition, as consciousness, emerging out of reverie, asks with an acute sense of surprise and loss about departed friends: "But where are my friends? Bellarmin/With his companion?"

The name Bellarmin had earlier been used in Hölderlin's epistolary novel *Hyperion* to designate the recipient of the hero's letters, written by him in equal solitude as "a hermit in Greece" (to quote the subtitle of the novel).[35] In "Andenken" this reference to

"Bellarmin with his companion" signifies a form of communication in writing through which a discourse of the heart had earlier (in the novel) been successfully conveyed. Such form is here acknowledged to be absent, since the poet's friends are gone, sailing the seas. There, he remarks, "like painters," they gather the earth's bounty, living year in and year out before "a leafless mast," removed from the festivals of the city with its songs and native dances. Indeed, as the final stanza mentions, they have gone to the Indies, by which Hölderlin presumably meant the islands of the Caribbean, which played so active a role in colonial trade with France in the eighteenth century. These ships thus pursue and extend that same southwesterly path of discovery established at the outset by the breeze, which carries the poet's greetings from Germany to Bordeaux. It is the same geographical axis, incidentally, as that described in the texts of Dante and Donne discussed above, through which the *crossing over* takes place, both literally and metaphorically, from death through redemption to new life. The absent friends are thus gathered into the remembrance of the poem as participants in a poetic act of commemoration.

What is Hölderlin's "Andenken" trying to say? A threefold differentiation of geographical space is apparent between, first, the position of the poet in his solitary retreat in Germany; second, the city of Bordeaux at the mouth of the river Garonne, with its festivals of community; and third, the open sea, extending beyond the horizon toward the Indies, which has gathered the sailors to itself. This symbolic topography includes a corresponding distinction between activities: poetic reflection, festive celebration, and heroic action. Remembrance mediates between all three. In response to the visitation of a sympathetic breeze, the poet's mind moves from its solitude into the recollected festival, only to recognize again its isolation due to the absence of friends out at sea. The entire poem thus becomes a dynamic representation of the act of remembrance itself, advancing into an imagined presence and then retreating to a reflective solitude which commemorates the loss of all community.

The progress of modernity in the poems I have been discussing is thus completed in a kind of breakdown or failure of discourse. In

Dante the temporal and experiential distinction between the poet as narrator and the poet as pilgrim thematizes the process of reading *for us* as an advance of thought into vision. Donne internalizes this distinction as a private meditation that establishes a universal pattern of death and redemption, in which the reader shares vicariously. In Hölderlin a categorical separation occurs between the heroic voyage and the reflective retreat, which destroys all sense of community except as a poetic fiction or remembered event. The reader is thus excluded from the poem, and even the possibility of communication is denied. What is left for the poet, in effect, is a kind of pipe dream: a whistling to the wind.

Ironically, however, a reader might still find inclusion in Hölderlin's poem through its fundamental structure of negativity, which is identical to the structure of poetic remembrance itself. The traditional forms of moral and anagogic meaning are established for us in Hölderlin's poem through a categorical negation. Instead of affirming the festival as a secular Easter, the poet denies all possibility of community. The poem memorializes the loss of companionship as an irredeemable absence. Finally, the poem implies that the isolation of the mind, within which the poet's discourse takes place, is the necessary consequence of this loss and the precondition for the act of poetic remembrance itself. Remembrance thus becomes a form of mourning.

The place of the reader within the poem is identical to the state of the mind in its act of remembrance, which the poem itself represents. The final lines express in sequence with a kind of gnomic authority all three moments in this negativity of reading. The sea, as for the heroic voyagers, both takes away and gives us remembrance. Love, as within the springtime festival of the community, transfixes our eyes as a symbol of community. Yet that which *abides,* as the poem itself proves, is created by the poets:

> Es nehmet aber
> Und giebt Gedächtniß die See,
> Und die Lieb' auch heftet fleißig die Augen,
> Was bleibet aber, stiften die Dichter.

The commemoration of heroic loss, the joy of communal celebration, and the permanence of reflected form constitute together
the act of remembrance as an experience of reading. The negativity
of this process enables us as readers to participate in that which is
otherwise denied. In precisely the same way a continuity with the
tradition of the voyage as *crossing over*, extending all the way back
to the Bible, may be sustained despite a sense of irredeemable distance and absence. I would even assert that the reader of Hölderlin's
poem finally achieves an intuition of transcendence, conveyed as a
silence within the structure of poetic reflection itself, as that which
is *not* spoken by the language, like a gap or a caesura in the rhythm
of discourse, where the mind turns reflectively upon itself.[36]

The Hermeneutics of Reading

A diachronic interpretation of the traditional fourfold structure of
meaning as a model for the act of reading, such as I have attempted
here, may not be historically valid. Dante scholars may well regard
my discussion of his letter to Can Grande as a misreading. This
judgment would not bother me, provided my argument may stand
as a valid allegory for the act of reading. On this basis I propose
that each of the four levels of meaning may also be related to the
theory and practice of literary history.

The first, or literal, level pertains to the so-called "old" literary
history, specifically as defined by the historical-critical method,
which dominated academic scholarship from the early nineteenth
to the mid-twentieth century.

The second, or figurative, level corresponds to the "new" literary
history, which is concerned above all with the historicity of forms
and genres. Certainly the dynamics of continuity and discontinuity
within a text occur at the figurative level of discourse, especially
through the appropriation and transformation of traditional forms.

The third, or ethical, level – insofar as it may be understood as a
conscious interaction between reader and text, through which a
community of dialogue is established – belongs to the new
hermeneutics (which is really no different from the old hermeneu-

tics, as practiced in the great tradition of biblical exegesis). At this level of historical consciousness the reader achieves a *fusion of horizons* by reading. Through the dialectical process of reversal or sublation (in the Hegelian sense of *Aufhebung*), the mind participates in the hermeneutical form of self-reflection and in the act of self-understanding.

The fourth, or anagogic, level of meaning, finally, is incompatible with any sense of historical determination, literary or otherwise, and should be regarded as beyond the limits of criticism and beyond any other possible function of discourse. This holds true, even though (as argued) a concern for the anagogic level provides the essential motivation for all authentic interpretation, as for all critical reading.

This leads me to my second point in conclusion, which derives from the concept of *negativity* as the essential structure of reading. The anagogic level of meaning resides beyond language in a transcendent silence, which will be regarded by various readers either as the dwelling place of Being or as mere Nothingness. I believe that some anagogic principle is necessary for the concept of negativity, precisely because it lies beyond the limits of language. The structure of transformation essential to the experience of reading – whatever image we use for it: crossing over, reversal, sublation, conversion, intellectual intuition, or even the promise of the New Jerusalem – depends for its validity upon a radical sense of Otherness. Such a sense of the ideal Other provides the ultimate goal of understanding. This goal imposes an order and a limit to history, as it does also to language, literature and criticism.

Finally, let me return once more to the passage from Hölderlin's "Andenken" which served as the motto for this essay:

> But conversation
> Is good and to speak
> The heart's opinion.

What is stated here about dialogue may also be applied to Dante's use of Psalm 114 and to my own argument (via Hegel) concerning the negativity of reading. The immediate referent for this assertion is the negative condition of the poet who writes in solitude – whether it be Hölderlin as German singer in the solitude of his retreat; or John Donne as devout meditator upon his own deathbed, tuning his soul in preparation to join a heavenly choir; or Dante as poet in exile, recording the visionary pilgrimage of his *Divine Comedy*. In each of the instances considered in this essay, the poet's discourse struggles with the irreconcilable opposition between an ideal model of poetic community – for which the congregation of spirits reciting the sacred psalm in *Purgatory* 2 stands as norm – and the solitude of the poem itself, a solitude which may well characterize the scene of writing for the entire tradition of Western literature.

This opposition between community and solitude is transferred to the reader through an act of negation, in such a way as to thematize the radical ambivalence of any hermeneutical relation to the text. Hölderlin's model of conversation (*Gespräch*) must be identified ultimately with the act of reading itself, through which, if at all, the solitude of the poetic act may be translated into that reciprocal exchange between minds across language which constitutes dialogue. Not that the act of reading can ever itself achieve communal song, even if it must always aspire to such an ideal. What sustains the act of reading, however, is the constant hope that such communal song may nonetheless be possible. Reading is constituted as a negativity in and through the process of interpretation itself. Only by such endeavor may the solitude of the text be translated into the dialogical form of understanding.

Afterthought

I conclude by quoting a seminal passage from Hölderlin's Pindaric hymn "Celebration of Peace" [Friedensfeier], the poet's supreme fiction of a visionary future festival, which was only discovered in 1954:

> Viel hat von Morgen an,
> Seit ein Gespräch wir sind und hören voneinander,
> Erfahren der Mensch; bald sind wir aber Gesang.
>
> [Much from the morning onwards,
> Since we became a conversation and hear about each other,
> Mankind has experienced; but soon we will be song.]
> (91-3; *GStA*, iii, 536)

Critics have recognized that Hölderlin here offers a complex metaphor for the history of Western culture. From its beginning – "from the morning onwards" – the advance of culture has been through dialogue, or "conversation" (*Gespräch*), as an exchange of thought through the medium of discourse across the gaps of difference and conflict which separate the participating voices. The goal of this advance, like the movement of the sun through the day toward evening, is communal "song" (*Gesang*), which the hymn in its confidence about the festival to celebrate the coming Peace, proclaims as imminent: "Bald sind wir aber Gesang." Readers of poetry may still believe in the possibility of such song; but the burden of our tradition, as a dialogue from the Bible to Dante and from such poets as Donne and Hölderlin to the present, suggests that such a goal must remain always at best an anagogical projection by the mind beyond the limits of poetry and discourse. We ourselves have access to such song only through the redemptive and sublating turns of hermeneutical consciousness in the negativity of reading.

Chapter 3: The Conscience of Narrative

For Paul Ricoeur

rere regardant
–James Joyce, "Proteus," in *Ulysses*

In this essay I wish to consider an aspect of literary narrative, specifically autobiographical narrative involving the subject as first-person narrator, which I take to be of central importance for hermeneutics. By *hermeneutics* I mean here not only a general theory of interpretation but also those verbal procedures within the narrative itself whereby a reflective or cognitive awareness is conveyed to the reader of how such interpretation should proceed. Hermeneutical consciousness in narrative is essentially self-reflective.

What interests me in this form of narrative are strategies of discourse, which establish a basis for understanding beyond the limits of subjective experience and which may claim a general, universal, or even transcendent validity. The question to ask is how such narrative communicates to its reader a perspective or point of view that is not limited to the first-person narrator as subject or to the reader as the individual recipient of what is narrated, but one that they come to share in common. The basis of understanding must be acknowledged by the reader as valid within a reciprocal relationship to the subject whose life history is represented by the narrative.

The most canonical instances of such narrative are provided by texts of the Bible, such as the Books of Moses, where the central figure of the story is also the attributed narrator, including also in his narrative the code of the law with its claim to an absolute or theological truth; or the Platonic dialogues, especially where the figure of Socrates as teacher within the dialogue is also its designated narrator, as in the case of *The Republic* with its corresponding claim to authority on such philosophical ideas as justice and the theory of the state. Every reader of these texts recognizes the universality of their truth claims; how many readers also examine how such claims are validated by the narrative? I would argue that a reciprocal understanding must be established between the narrative and its reader, affirming the consciousness of a common humanity shared between the reader and the text as the basis for any universal truth. Such affirmation lends legitimacy to an authoritative system of values – based upon a model of community, timeless, universal and free of all contingencies – which constitutes the narrative as a particular history and which delimits the life of the subject as narrated by that history. It is not without hermeneutical significance for a theory of narrative that such texts have been, and continue to be, the most influential of our cultural tradition.

The Hermeneutics of Retrospective First-Person Narrative

Let me first clarify a bit further the hermeneutical structure that I have in mind. As a *theoretical* endeavor within literary criticism, hermeneutics has no validity apart from the *practice* of interpretation. On this point I am in agreement with Hans-Georg Gadamer, who, affirming a tradition in ethical philosophy that extends from Aristotle to Hegel, insists that hermeneutics is a *Praxis-Wissenschaft.*[1] According to such a notion of *praxis* for hermeneutics, theoretical reflection upon the procedures of discourse can only occur within the act of communication itself. The text invites theoretical reflection upon it by the reader in and through the act of reading. Hermeneutical theory thus results directly from the reading process and becomes an integral aspect of the experiential and cognitive forms of understanding. The hermeneutical dimension of literary

texts, which is built into the verbal structure of such texts as a conscious strategy of communication, may thus be defined in terms of
certain reflective or self-referential procedures of language. These
procedures call attention to the language itself in its communicative
functions for the reader through the act of communication.

Hermeneutical consciousness is thus imposed upon the reader as
an auto-referential dimension of the text, established in and
through the act of reading. The reader is made aware through this
process both of *what* is understood by reading the text and of *how*
the text as discourse communicates such understanding. Even more
important, the basis for understanding, as a relationship between
reader and text established through the act of reading, must be
acknowledged as reciprocal and shared in common between them,
regardless of any complexities or tensions that remain unresolved.
At the cognitive level of hermeneutical consciousness the reader
thus relates *what* is understood in the text to the *process through
which* that understanding is achieved. Gadamer's much debated
concept of a fusion of horizons (*Horizontverschmelzung*) between
text and reader, which occurs in the act of interpretation, corresponds exactly to what I have been describing here.[2]

Central among traditions of narrative in Western literature is the
genre of autobiography or self-confession, in which the life of an
individual self and the development of self-understanding are
recounted simultaneously. Both aspects of development – the
events that have occurred in the life of the individual and the
understanding of these events retrospectively – are closely interrelated in such narrative and, in exemplary instances, inseparable. I
have argued this to be the case, for instance, in an essay on Wordsworth's *Prelude* and Hölderlin's *Hyperion*.[3] As its central story or
plot, the narrative traces the advancing development of the self that
narrates it, and through the act of narration a retrospective, self-
reflective understanding is achieved for both the self and the reader.
Such retrospective narratives of the self are usually modelled upon
an individual life history, extending from youth to maturity, or
from innocence to experience – as a *Bildungsroman* or *Confessiones*.

Such works also articulate, let me emphasize, as a kind of

hermeneutical superstructure, a related process of developing awareness or self-consciousness in the narrator as a reflective response to the life history being recalled and recounted. The peculiar hermeneutical strategy that I wish to consider in this essay pertains to the designs of such a narrative upon its reader. A corresponding awareness or self-consciousness, related but not identical to that of the narrator, must also be elicited in the reader as a response to the experience of the self represented by the narrative. Such self-consciousness in the reader can only be affirmed through the act of reading if the basis for understanding is acknowledged to be mutual, reciprocal and common to both narrator and reader, however different, opposite or even contradictory their respective points of view may be.

The basis upon which such mutual recognition is established necessarily goes beyond the limits of subjectivity and imposes upon the autobiographical narrative an intersubjective dimension. In making this claim, I am indebted to a central argument introduced by Hegel in his *Phenomenology of Spirit,* concerning the ethical structure of self-consciousness, under the heading of a reciprocity between individual minds, which is termed reciprocal recognition (*gegenseitiges Anerkennen*).[4] The intersubjectivity of such hermeneutical consciousness, as I argue elsewhere in terms of the Hegelian dialectic, is the origin of that self-reflective dimension of the novel, which since Friedrich Schlegel has been called irony.[5] Such reciprocal self-consciousness, furthermore, is also a precondition for what Aristotle in his *Poetics* calls the *universal* (τὸ καθόλου, chap. 9; 1451 n5–10) and for that which in the tradition of biblical theology is regarded as the transcendent truth-claim of Scripture.

In this essay I shall outline some hermeneutical implications in autobiographical narrative, using several examples. In particular I shall try to demonstrate the validity of what might be called a hermeneutics of transcendence in two representative works from the tradition of first-person autobiographical narrative: Laurence Sterne's *The Life and Opinions of Tristram Shandy, Gentleman,* and the *Confessions* of St. Augustine. I begin with a glance at the *Divine Comedy* and shall conclude with a comment on Joyce's *Ulysses.*

The Case of Dante

Dante's *Comedy* demonstrates with unique authority a fundamental hermeneutical interrelationship between text and reader. Dante the pilgrim, the central character of the poem, travels through the poetic narrative on a visionary journey, not unlike the traditional journey of the epic hero, as in Homer's *Odyssey* or Virgil's *Aeneid*. Dante the poet, who narrates the poem – as distinct from Dante the pilgrim as character within the poem – speaks from a privileged position of retrospection or reflective awareness at a cognitive and experiential distance from everything that happens in the story. He has already made the journey and has returned to write about it *for us*. As readers we identify our act of reading the poem with the visionary journey of the pilgrim; but the goal of that journey for us is to achieve, and to share with the poet-narrator (this is his continuous promise and challenge to us), that ultimate vision of divinity which he claims to have enjoyed as a gift of grace.

Understanding *The Divine Comedy* thus depends upon our developing relationship to both Dante the pilgrim and Dante the poet and upon our response – by sharing the experience of the former and by achieving the perspective of the latter – to the poem as a theological system and as the representation of a transcendent vision, written for us so that we may also find our way toward such vision and the salvation it promises. No other work in the Western tradition thematizes so powerfully and comprehensively the theological hermeneutics of autobiographical narrative as a strategy of communication. Dante is an exemplary instance, quite apart from his status as poet. I do not suggest that he was the inventor of or even an isolated spokesman for this twofold function of the poetic self as narrator and as character; the work of Sterne and St. Augustine will offer fully comparable instances. But no other poet so authoritatively thematizes the role of the reader in a self-conscious relationship to both the poet as narrator and the poet as character simultaneously in a constantly developing, constantly varying hermeneutical form. To show how that occurs in *The Divine Comedy* would require a comprehensive interpretation of Dante's poem.

Laurence Sterne, *The Life and Opinions of Tristram Shandy, Gentleman*

The term *conscience* in my title is borrowed from a peculiar context in *Tristram Shandy,* where it assumes all but explicit hermeneutical implications.[6] In Volume ɪɪ, chapter 15, Corporal Trim fetches a book on military engineering by Stevinus to clarify a point for Uncle Toby and Walter Shandy on military fortifications. While doing so, he discovers the text of a sermon tucked between its pages. Trim is persuaded to read this text to the others as they sit with Dr. Slop in the living room of the Shandy household, while Mrs. Shandy is in labor upstairs giving birth to Tristram, the subsequent hero and narrator of the book. The sermon begins with a scriptural text taken from the ending of the Epistle to the Hebrews: "For we trust we have a good conscience."

Good conscience – bona conscientia in the Vulgate, ἡ καλὴ συνείδησις in the original Greek – signifies both a sense of right and wrong (as we use the term today) and also a more general awareness (in the sense of *consciousness*). Above all, these two senses are joined together with implications of a common ethical value as *knowledge shared with another.* I take it that such knowledge may, and indeed, in accord with the ironic strategies of Sterne's novel, does refer to the basic hermeneutical purpose of *Tristram Shandy* as narrative, as well as to the argument of the sermon read by Trim.

The sermon turns out to be the work of Parson Yorick, named (as we have already been informed in Volume I) for his Danish ancestor, the court jester whose skull is dug up in the graveyard scene of Shakespeare's *Hamlet.* The status of the sermon as text is further complicated by the fact that Sterne, himself an Anglican minister, subsequently used Yorick as his own pen name, not only in his famous *Sentimental Journey* but also in the title of his collected sermons, published in several volumes after *Tristram Shandy* had already begun to appear. The sermon read by Trim is included in this collection, itself having indeed been preached by Sterne at the cathedral in York ten years earlier, before he had begun to write his novel. It was published independently at that time under the title "The Abuses of Conscience Considered."[7] Such ironic displacement of authorship greatly complicates the status of the sermon as text within the novel, though its history also heightens its latent powers of signification when read by Corporal Trim, as if it were the quotation of a quotation. As is so often the case in *Tristram Shandy,* we cannot be certain whose voice we are meant to hear.

We need not consider the argument of the sermon in any detail here. The sermon claims that the certainty of conscience depends upon higher, more universal principles of truth and justice than mere *self*-certainty.[8] "There is an absolute necessity," argues Yorick's sermon, "to join with conscience another principle…[which derives from the teachings of] religion and morality." Good conscience is thus defined with reference not to the self alone but also to God. Quoting from the First Epistle of John, the sermon proceeds to claim that "'thou wilt have confidence towards God' – that is, have just grounds to believe the judgement thou hast past upon thyself, is the judgement of God" (II.17).

THE THEME OF MORTALITY

In what way, let me ask, would such a judgment by conscience also apply to the interpretation of an autobiographical narrative such as *Tristram Shandy* and its peculiar ironic strategies for communicating some sense of certainty or conviction about the character whose history is being narrated? In attempting to answer this question, I shall juxtapose quite arbitrarily three passages that thematize an attitude toward death and mortality, simultaneously sentimental and serious, which underlies the apparent playfulness of the novel.

The opening volume provides, first of all, an account of Yorick's death and a description of his tombstone in the local churchyard. Hamlet's famous exclamation to the skull of the court jester: "Alas, poor Yorick!" serves as epitaph. All visitors to the churchyard, we are told, see this inscription alongside the footpath and respond to it as readers, thus participating in an inherited literary gesture: "Not a passenger goes by without stopping to cast a look upon it – and sighing as he walks on, 'Alas, poor *Yorick!*'" (I.12). Immediately following this statement in the novel, Sterne inserts a black page of mourning for the dead pastor, even though Yorick does not die within the time span of the story narrated in the novel. What the narrator thus provides at the outset is a glimpse ahead to an event which will occur at an indeterminate future time after the story breaks off at the end of Volume IX but which, presumably, has already occurred when Tristram as narrator begins to write his life history.

Not by accident, furthermore, it is Yorick who speaks the last lines of the novel in casual conversation with Mrs. Shandy. She asks, in response to an incident narrated by Dr. Slop and the ser-vant Obadiah, "What is all this story about?" The parson replies in a manner which readers have always felt must also include by ironic resonance the voice of Sterne as author commenting on the novel as a whole: "A COCK and a BULL...and one of the best of its kind, I ever heard" (IX.33). We might well ask, in response to such an ironic sense of ending, why Sterne began his novel with an account of Yorick's death.

The theme of death also recurs later in the novel, totally without warning, in Volume VI, with reference to Corporal Trim and Uncle Toby. Tristram as narrator suddenly laments the loss of Trim at some unspecified future time – future, that is, to the story being narrated, though not to the act of narration. He immediately goes on to describe in even more moving terms the lamentations of Trim for Uncle Toby on the occasion – whenever? – of the latter's demise. This passage is characteristic of Sterne's sentimental powers at their best, and deserves, despite its length, to be quoted in full.

The corporal ——
—Tread lightly on his ashes, ye men of genius, – for he was your kinsman:
Weed his grave clean, ye men of goodness, – for he was your brother. –
Oh corporal! had I thee, but now, – now, that I am able to give thee a din-ner and protection, – how would I cherish thee! thou should'st wear thy Montero-cap every hour of the day, and every day of the week, – and when it was worn out, I would purchase thee a couple like it: – But alas! alas! alas! now that I can do this, in spight of their reverences – the occasion is

lost – for thou art gone; – thy genius fled up to the stars from whence it came; – and that warm heart of thine, with all its generous and open vessels, compressed into a *clod of the valley!*

——But what – what is this, to that future and dreaded page, where I look towards the velvet pall, decorated with the military ensigns of thy master – the first – the foremost of created beings; – where, I shall see thee, faithful servant! laying his sword and scabbard with a trembling hand across his coffin, and then returning pale as ashes to the door, to take his mourning horse by the bridle, to follow his hearse, as he directed thee; – where – all my father's systems shall be baffled by his sorrows; and, in spight of his philosophy, I shall behold him, as he inspects the lackered plate, twice taking his spectacles from off his nose, to wipe away the dew which nature has shed upon them – When I see him cast in the rosemary with an air of disconsolation, which cries through my ears, – O *Toby!* in what corner of the world shall I seek thy fellow? (VI.25)

Neither Trim nor Toby, of course, shows any signs of approaching death at any point within the narrative of *Tristram Shandy.* Nor do these two hobby-horsical characters in all their versatility display even the slightest hint of a consciousness of mortality, except perhaps ironically with regard to their respective war wounds, the one for Trim in his knee and the one for Toby in his groin. This sentimental attitude toward death, in both its inevitability and its banality, must refer exclusively to the sensibility of the narrator. Furthermore, this attitude depends, for its proper effect, upon a sympathetic response from the reader, a response which must include a sense of recognition and of sympathy. We are no different from Tristram in the sentimentality of our hermeneutical consciousness.

In a third instance of this theme, Sterne reminds us that all life must end inevitably in death, not only for his two favorite characters, Toby and Trim, but also for himself and indeed *for us* who are the recipients of his discourse. It is Tristram as narrator who reminds us of this, writing from a temporal perspective which also postdates the demise of Toby and Trim. I find no other explanation for the emotional power conveyed by the ironic interruption of his narrative, which occurs totally without warning, in the midst of a conversation between Toby and Trim as they walk together toward the house of Widow Wadman (ix.8). This interruption is addressed explicitly, as is much of the novel, to Tristram's intimate lady friend, whom he calls Jenny. In the silence of her receptivity she serves brilliantly as an emotional surrogate for the reader of the novel.

The passage is as follows:

> I will not argue the matter: Time wastes too fast: every letter I trace tells me with what rapidity Life follows my pen; the days and hours of it, more precious, my dear *Jenny!* than the rubies about thy neck, are flying over our heads like light clouds of a windy day, never to return more – every thing presses on – whilst thou art twisting that lock, – see! it grows grey; and every time I kiss thy hand to bid adieu, and every absence which follows it, are preludes to that eternal separation which we are shortly to make. –
>
> – Heaven have mercy upon us both! (ix.8)

Can any reader fail to share the duality of that final invocation? What other basis can there be for such a sense of inclusion, for such *empathy,* than the *conscience* of the narrative (in the precise sense of *syneidesis,* as established by Yorick's sermon from the theological tradition of the New Testament), as a *reciprocal recognition* between the text and its reader?

Tristram Shandy is notorious for the unpredictable indirections of its narrative, advancing as if it were free of either design or control. The narrator Tristram often acknowledges this, most conspicuously at the end of Volume vi, where he diagrams the progress of the narrative in each preceding volume with various zigzagging, twisted and circling lines. He concludes his survey of narrative structure, however, by promising to mend his ways, even to the extent of outlining his future course as a straight horizontal line, drawn (so he asserts) with "a writing-master's ruler." If this promise is subsequently fulfilled in Volume vii – and there is no apparent evidence that the narrator thinks it has been – then the straight line of the narrative must be signified by the journey undertaken by Tristram the narrator (*not* by the character in the novel, who never outgrows his childhood) through France in a race to outstrip death.

Many readers have felt this entire sequence to be out of place, and biographers have assembled evidence to support such a view. Sterne actually traveled on the continent in the mid-1760s for his health, from which subsequently was written *A Sentimental Journey through France and Italy by Mr. Yorick* (1768). Except for the fact that Parson Yorick, not Tristram Shandy, serves as narrator for that book, Volume VII of the novel could serve as a preliminary draft of the later travelogue. Volume VII, however, establishes a model structure for autobiographical narrative: it advances either as a straight line or as a flight from death. The validity of this account for the novel may thus be defined precisely in terms of what I call the *hermeneutical conscience* of the narrative.

THE DISPLACEMENT OF AUTOBIOGRAPHY

Despite its meandering path and its parodistic overelaboration, the narrative of *Tristram Shandy* initially follows a conventional pattern of developmental autobiography. The first-person narrator attempts to recount the moment of his conception, which may be the boldest ironic stroke of the novel, since it defies the limits of memory. He then offers an inordinately convoluted account of his birth, which involves a long, slow, difficult labor and delivery for Mrs. Shandy that extends for more than two volumes of the novel, during which the conversation mentioned earlier between Mr. Shandy and Uncle Toby takes place in the parlor downstairs, including the reading of Yorick's sermon by Trim. The story of Tristram's early childhood is rather truncated and focuses outrageously on the incident with the falling window sash and its disastrous consequences for our hero. The final episode in this developmental sequence, intended most likely as a parody of eighteenth-century treatises on education, concerns Walter Shandy's incredible document of instructions for the upbringing of his son, the *Tristrapaedia,* which would appear to be absolutely incompatible with the kind of retrospective autobiography that Tristram attempts to write. The basic ironic pattern of all this autobiographical material will be apparent to every attentive reader, as it also provides the essential counterstructure for the seemingly random and endless digressions by the narrator.

All the more striking therefore is the radical shift of focus and concern, introduced totally without warning, as a general strategy for the narrative in the middle of Volume vi. This shift, which effectively transforms the generic model of the novel away from autobiography, has not been much noted by critics of *Tristram Shandy*.

The narrator suddenly asserts: "We are now going to enter upon a new scene of events" (chap. 20). Several figures from the narrative are evoked in sequence as possible new focal points, only to be rejected: Tristram's breeches, his mother, Dr. Slop, Le Fever (the French soldier whose death has just been described), and, last but by no means least, "if possible, *myself.*" In effect the narrator of this strange autobiography thus announces rather indirectly and laconically his ironic intention to abandon *himself* as the central subject of the narrative. He hastens to add, however, an acknowledgment that this is not strictly possible: "I must go along with you to the end of the work." What he means by this, I surmise, especially on the evidence of Volume vii – shortly to follow with its account of the journey through France – is that his role as first-person narrator must continue *qua narrator,* regardless of whatever displacement may occur in the subject of narration away from himself. Such displacement, however, does indeed occur.

The final volumes of the novel focus on Uncle Toby's affair with the Widow Wadman. She is introduced at the end of Volume vi with a blank page, on which the reader is instructed to draw his own image of the lady: "as like your mistress as you can" (chap. 38). The wooing subsequently fails when Toby learns, through the indirection of Trim's surmise, that the widow is motivated by all too venal designs, since she fears that Toby's war wound has made him impotent.

Why is failure of this kind included in a narrative so preoccupied, however indirectly, with sexual innuendo? The answer is found ironically in the substitution of selfless friendship as a counternorm to sexual desire for human values. This norm is demonstrated in exemplary manner by the reciprocal courtesy and mutual generosity shared between master and servant. Toby and Trim function together through their bond of selfless friendship, like a latter-day Don Quixote and Sancho Panza. The most telling sign of their reciprocity, in contrast to all forms of erotic desire, is the ironic association of their respective war wounds with questions of sexuality. The narrative affirms that both men are functionally unimpaired in this regard, but nowhere is there any hint that sexual desire motivates their actions and their concerns.

The courtship of Toby is thus juxtaposed in the novel with the ironies of marital love between Walter Shandy and his wife, not to mention the initial focus on the hero's conception and the continuing question of his sexuality. The failure of this courtship, furthermore, assumes symbolic significance as a negative, if nonetheless comic, norm of behavior in explicit opposition to the friendship or shared humanity between master and servant. Their friendship remains completely free of self-interest. It is motivated instead by an all-pervasive sense of play, indicated by their "hobby-horse" of reconstructing battles upon the bowling green. This sense of play constitutes an implicit self-referential model within the novel for the kind of aesthetic experience which constitutes the narrative itself. Such aesthetic play as "hobby-horsing" is conveyed to the reader by the ironic freedom of the narrative. This point needs further clarification.

The displacement of the autobiographical narrative in *Tristram Shandy* away from the narrator as subject toward a model of selfless mutuality assumes formal significance for the meaning of the novel. In place of the development of the self, recollected and reconstructed by the narrator as its own history, the focus of discourse is transferred to the manners of exchange which occur between Toby and Trim as master and servant. Within the social world of the novel this exchange serves, however gradually and awkwardly, to establish a basis for ethical and social values. In itself such displacement may appear commonplace, or even banal. Nor does the novel fail to provide a broad spectrum of analogous and contrasting instances of social exchange, both within the Shandy household and throughout the seemingly endless anecdotal digressions. An unusual richness and variety to the fabric of such social value is thus established for the world of the novel.

The basis for all such exchange, not surprisingly, is verbal, specifically involving forms of interaction through dialogue. Ethical values are thus constituted by intersubjective relationships, which also extend to perspectives of response by the narrator and, implicitly, by the reader. Tristram as narrator plays a central role in this gradual displacement of the focus of narration away from himself as subject, leaving only his voice and point of view. He mediates between the substance of the narrative with its various forms of dialogical interaction and the perspective of implied response in the reader. In this way the ethical values of the narrative are translated into a hermeneutical consciousness.

Thus we come to understand our relationship to the text in explicit analogy to the friendship between Uncle Toby and Corporal Trim and the ethical values which they share. A crucial distinction remains, however, between form and content. The shift of the narrative from a subjective to an intersubjective perspective imposes upon the reader a hermeneutical awareness of the narrative as narrative, for which the story being narrated serves merely as the fictional or figurative referent.

The form of the narrative thus reflects upon its content in a manner which also implicates the reader in that which I have called – borrowing the theological concept which Sterne used from the New Testament in Yorick's sermon – the *conscience* of the narrative. This is not to claim, however, that the perspective of such conscience attains a transcendent dimension, as the sermon argued it should. Yet the pathos of the theme of mortality, which is so pervasive in the narrative, does impose an awareness of limit to human experience. The claim of the novel to convey a shared experience of humanity is thus affirmed *for us* at a level of generality through the forms of discourse. Sterne gathers the myriad aspects of the story, including all digressions, into a comprehensive and coherent figure or metaphor for the human condition.

THE ETHICS OF ENCOUNTER

This great variety of material in the narrative provides further evidence in support of my claims for the hermeneutical conscience of *Tristram Shandy*. Such evidence would include the structural delineations of plot and the interaction of characters, as well as the functions of language at the level of style and rhetoric or even grammar and syntax. Sterne offers us an abundant, indeed a uniquely variable feast of verbal riches. Two brief and seemingly peripheral incidents from the later volumes provide further evidence for the hermeneutical conscience of the novel. Ostensibly these episodes have nothing to do with each other, yet both reflect on the meaning of the narrative *for us*. They offer implicit commentary on the central formal design of the novel, to the point where they almost assume symbolic status as hermeneutical ciphers for its conscience.

The first episode occurs at the end of Volume VII, when Tristram describes an accidental encounter with a village festival during his coach tour through France (chap. 43). Leaving his coach, he approaches the villagers, and a young girl gets up in response and comes to welcome him. He calls her Nanette, apparently having later learned her name: "a sun-burnt daughter of Labour." He describes her invitation to him to join in the dancing, the drinking of wine, and the singing of rustic songs. His account of the incident concludes with a tribute to the maiden and his response to her:

A transient spark of amity shot across the space betwixt us – She look'd amiable! – Why could I not live and end my days thus? Just disposer of our joys and sorrows, cried I, why could not a man sit down in the lap of content here – and dance, and sing, and say his prayers, and go to heaven with this nut brown maid? capriciously did she bend her head on one side, and dance up insiduous – . (VII.43)

Separate contexts of reference are here superimposed upon each other – the *then* of the incident and the *now* of the narration – so that terms of invocation and celebration (*thus* and *here*) also come to signify *for us* the narrative we are reading. An invitation is thus conveyed by the narrative to ourselves, analogous to that extended by the nut brown maid to the narrator. We as readers join in a form of festivity appropriate to the narrative, a song and dance of language. In the end we also affirm, together with Tristram, the ways of the world. The fictions of the narrative stand as a model or norm, in an ethical as well as an aesthetic sense, for the common destiny of mankind. As readers of the novel we thus enter into the perspective of desire as expressed by the narrator to share in the festivals of life.

The final episode from *Tristram Shandy* which I shall consider occurs very near the end of the book, as part of the displaced Invocation to the novel, which falls between chaps. 24 and 25 of Volume IX. How far removed is such a belated position from the conventional place of invocation at the outset of traditional epic! Tristram suddenly transports us again to France, thus providing the only reprise of his journey in Volume VII during the final two volumes which follow it. He speaks *in propria persona* as narrator of his book, but he does so within the narrative context of his journey. Responding to his account of Uncle Toby's amours, Tristram asserts, "They had the same effect upon me as if they had been my own." The hermeneutical implications of this phrase *(as if)* are apparent. "Everything I saw, or had to do with," he concludes, "touch'd upon some secret spring either of sentiment or rapture." Then suddenly Sterne performs a brilliant sleight of hand as he slips into a descriptive mode of narration, instantly transforming literal reference into a self-reflective fictional form. His next remark: " – They were the sweetest notes I ever heard," seems to describe his emotions in response to his own narrative. Abruptly, however, these notes are externalized within a totally unexpected narrative context: "and I instantly let down the fore-glass to hear them more distinctly – 'Tis *Maria*; said the postilion, observing I was listening."

Who is Maria? What postilion, and where? We are left to answer these questions from the account which follows. Maria, as it turns out, is a deranged maiden, driven mad by unrequited love, like a creature from some popular ballad. She plays a melancholy song upon a pipe with what – we are told – is unsurpassed beauty.

Tristram approaches her to listen, sitting down beside her goat, even comparing himself to the animal (Sterne's wit never falters!), in a question addressed directly to the girl: "What resemblance do you find?" But the girl never speaks a word. Tristram's response to this silence begins to assume hermeneutical resonance: "I swore I would set up for Wisdom and utter grave sentences the rest of my days – and never – never attempt again to commit mirth with man, woman, or child, the longest day I had to live." He accompanies this statement with an allusion to Rabelais, whose wit he emulates, though he claims ironically in the face of this "hapless damsel" to lack such wit here.

He then takes his leave of her, which in the context of the Invocation sounds ironically like a prefiguration of the end – the end of the novel and his own end as well – anticipating the moment when the narrative will take leave of its readers. He also asserts that he hopes one day to hear her story from her own lips. This wish, ironically, is later fulfilled in *A Sentimental Journey,* when Parson Yorick encounters this same Maria near the end of Volume ii. In response to the Parson's reminder of the earlier visit she received from "my friend, Mr. Shandy," she proceeds to tell him her story.[9]

To readers of *Tristram Shandy,* however, this allusion to the possibility of future narration must remain open and indeterminate. Yet Maria surprises Tristram by playing once again upon her pipe a song which overwhelms him with sorrow: "For that moment she took her pipe and told me such a tale of woe with it, that I rose up, and with broken and irregular steps walk'd softly to my chaise." As readers of Sterne's novel we are obliged to attend its *conscience* from a hermeneutical perspective. The emotions of this song, unheard by us, are nonetheless shared through the power of empathy evoked by the narrative. Maria's song is filtered through the sensibility of the narrator as an event which he recalls. For us, as for him, however, it also assumes the status of a symbol, which signifies no less than the meaning of human existence with all its suffering and its mortality. The paradox of such symbolism for Sterne's novel resides in the fact that the song itself remains silent and unheard. As readers of the novel we nonetheless come to share an awareness of the song

with Sterne as its author, with Tristram as the narrator who recalls
it, and even as an attitude or emotion expressed by this mute, mad
girl. Maria thus takes her proper place, despite the limitations of
her role, alongside such major figures in the novel as Uncle Toby
and Corporal Trim, precisely because of the common humanity
which they share within the all-inclusive *conscience* of the narrative.

The *Confessions* of St. Augustine

Such displacement of attention away from the self as subject toward
an intersubjective norm of ethical values constitutes the central feature of what I have called the *conscience* of narrative in Sterne's
Tristram Shandy. Corresponding shifts of concern away from the
subject may be traced throughout the tradition of autobiographical
narrative in Western literature from Dante to Joyce. The implicit
model or source text for such ethical displacement is the *Confessions* of St. Augustine. The structural peculiarities of narrative in
this work also demonstrate with unsurpassed authority what I
would call a hermeneutics of transcendence. The cultural and intellectual context in which St. Augustine writes is explicitly Christian
and theological, yet his autobiography also establishes implicitly a
general of narrative discourse. In *Tristram Shandy* the universality of figurative reference remains essentially human and secular. Sterne conveyed his theology as a writer of fiction only
through the guise of sentimental irony appropriate to the role of
Parson Yorick. The example of St. Augustine – as I shall argue
shortly – indicates how a principle of transcendence applies also to
secular narrative, valid as much for Joyce's *Ulysses* as for *Tristram
Shandy,* if only by negation with regard to the limits of language
and the verbal sign.

For centuries a naive reading of Augustine's life history has prevailed, still to be found among his commentators, which insists that
the *Confessions* proper concludes at the end of Book ix, where the
narrative of that history breaks off.[10] What follows in Books x to
xiii is a series of theological reflections, explicitly concerned with
the interpretation of Scripture. Such biographical scholars claim

that these latter books were written several years later than the rest and they thus have concluded that the final books constitute a separate text. Such a reading is not only hermeneutically naive, it misses the central conviction elaborated and demonstrated by the *Confessions* concerning the theology of narrative, which motivates the autobiographical account from its opening paragraph.

The argument of the later books never addresses the function and status of language as such. Yet the categories of memory and time, which are discussed in Books x and xi, are defined in terms of the mind's consciousness of itself, as knowledge or thought. The representations of the mind's experience are necessarily and exclusively verbal.

THE HERMENEUTICS OF TIME AND MEMORY

Memoria is discussed in Book x as a power of internalization, not unrelated to Hegel's later claim for memory in his *Science of Logic*, based upon an etymological pun on the German term *Er-Innerung*, as the power of "inwardizing." The images (*imagines*) of experience and things are retained by the conscious mind, so argues St. Augustine (chap. 25), and remain accessible for creative reflection. Memory even extends to our knowledge of God, Augustine asserts, addressing himself, as throughout the *Confessions*, directly to the deity: "You dwell in my memory." This holds true, despite the fact that the mind has no direct or unmediated experience of divinity and likewise, as I would argue on the evidence of the *Confessions* as narrative, no capacity to represent such experience in language.

Time is defined in Book xi similarly as a perspective of consciousness which results from such internalization. Time consciousness depends entirely on the capacity of the mind to differentiate its experience and activity according to a threefold distinction among past, present and future. These differentia do not exist in themselves, says Augustine, but only in the mind as they are known to consciousness. The *experience* of time, therefore, involves a dynamic movement of the mind in its consciousness through these temporal modes.

Such consciousness also includes an implicit hermeneutical

dimension, as becomes apparent in Augustine's central example for such time consciousness, namely the reciting of a psalm (Book XI, chap. 28). He argues as follows:

I am about to recite a psalm that I know. Before I begin, my expectation extends over the entire psalm. Once I have begun, my memory extends over as much of it as I shall separate off and assign to the past. The life of this action of mine is distended into memory by reason of the part I have spoken and into forethought by reason of the part I am about to speak. But attention is actually present and that which was to be is borne along by it so as to become past. The more this is done and done again, so much the more is memory lengthened by a shortening of expectation, until the entire expectation is exhausted. When this is done the whole action is completed and passes into memory.

St. Augustine's argument concerning the cognitive experience of reciting a psalm, presumably from memory, may also be applied to the act of reading generally. This classical formulation concerning the dynamics of temporal consciousness in and through the reading process thus offers the basis for a hermeneutical theory of interpretation as such. The implications of the Augustinian position for modern hermeneutics deserve further study.[11]

The conclusion drawn by St. Augustine from this example is extended to an astonishing range of instances, beginning with the units of language in discourse (the sounds and syllables) and reaching finally beyond the individual mind to encompass the totality of collective experience for all mankind. No greater claim has ever been made for the all-pervasiveness of a hermeneutical consciousness. "What takes place in the whole psalm," so the text continues,

takes place also in each of its parts and in each of its syllables. The same thing holds for a longer action, of which perhaps the psalm is a small part. The same thing holds for a man's entire life, the parts of which are all the man's actions. The same thing holds throughout the whole age of the sons of men, the parts of which are the lives of all men.

Translating this assertion into a terminology which is admittedly more Hegelian than Augustinian, I would argue that both the essential structure of discourse, even at the level of grammar and syntax, and the history of redemption for the individual and for the human race as a whole, are essentially dialectical. At the same time, the act of understanding at both extremes of discourse and at all points between must be hermeneutical. The Bible, of course, constitutes the totality which Augustine has in mind, both as a text and as the representation of the world and human history, the manifestation of God's will.

These concepts of memory and time as defined in the *Confessions* – not to mention others which I cannot discuss in any detail here, such as that of *form* developed in Book xii, which justifies for St. Augustine the plurality of readings for Scripture – apply retrospectively to strategies of communication throughout the autobiographical narrative of the *Confessions*. The conceptual mode of argument in these later books is the direct outcome of the preceding narrative. Augustine's theoretical formulations reflect upon that narrative and also provide implicit directives to the reader for interpreting it. The entire story of his life is told from a position beyond the climactic moment of his conversion. From this retrospective vantage point of the author as narrator, the entire narrative is organized around those concepts of *memoria, tempus, forma.* These concepts are then discussed in the later books on the basis of the preceding narrative. St. Augustine recollects his life through the power of his memory. Its meaning *for us* is constituted by that power through the narrative.

His autobiography also proves to be an imitation of Scripture. Augustine applies the essential hermeneutical structure of salvation history to the development of his individual life as *confession.* At the outset of Book x (chap. 4) he asserts that "to such as you [God] command me to serve"– by which he apparently means the intended readers of his book – "I will reveal not what I have been but what I now am and what I still am" [non quis fuerim, sed quis iam sim et quis adhuc sim]. Such conceptualization of the self transforms the particularity of narration into a generality of reflection. The narrative of the self imposes an obligation on us as its readers to comprehend it not only for itself but also as an *exemplum* or *figura.*

With regard to such a figurative transformation of perspective and reference, crucial theological questions arise. Where are the limits of narrative and where are the limits of language, when the retrospective narration of the self in its developmental and experiential process becomes a general model for self-interpretation as *confession* addressed directly to God? I take these questions also to be essential for hermeneutics.

All sense of limit is defined by St. Augustine with reference to God as the transcendent *signifié* of his discourse. Also crucially important for the rhetorical form of his narrative, God is the intended recipient of his *confession*. As is appropriate to the theological concept of confession, the entire discourse is addressed directly to the deity. The legitimacy of narrative in the *Confessions* thus depends upon St. Augustine's faith in God as a relationship that precedes and motivates everything he writes. The central purpose of the entire work, furthermore, is defined exclusively by one ultimate transcendent goal: to affirm the author's faith in God and to bear witness to the experience on which it is based.

There is a profound paradox to this dual concern for God as both source and recipient of his confession, which directly affects the rhetorical form of the narrative. The basis for the narration is a dialogical relation between the speaker and God, defined both theologically and verbally by the rituals of confession. Yet the experiential basis for the speaker's faith lies beyond the semiotic capacity of his discourse to signify and beyond the hermeneutical capacities of his narrative to represent and to reveal.

THE HERMENEUTICS OF CONVERSION

The climactic moments of the autobiography, where the development of the self is completed and its confession fulfilled, also participate directly in this paradox. These moments conceal and displace the meaning of the speaker's experience in a manner which imposes on the reader an obligation to respond in kind. In order to understand what the narrative describes, we must achieve, through a kind of sympathetic imitation, an intuition of that which the speaker acknowledges to lie beyond the limits of his language.

The two climactic episodes in the narrative – occurring in Books viii and ix, respectively – are the account by St. Augustine of his conversion and his account of the transcendent vision at Ostia, subsequently shared with his mother shortly before her death. These episodes have been so influential across the centuries and have assumed such an authority – second only to Scripture itself – that it is difficult for us to respond as readers with a suitable critical awareness of the narrative strategies they employ. I shall attempt to indicate briefly how each episode establishes a crucial aspect of what I call the hermeneutics of transcendence. They complement each other as two stages in the completion, transformation and final displacement of the autobiographical narrative.

The Greek term for conversion in the New Testament, introduced in the Epistles of St. Paul, is μετάνοια. This signifies, in accord with its etymology, a "turnabout," or reversal, of the mind. As used by St. Augustine in the *Confessions,* this concept is also grounded in the essential hermeneutical form of his discourse. To what extent this might also hold true for the New Testament I hesitate to say. One might indeed regard *metanoia* as a necessary prerequisite to that state of mind described as *syneidesis,* discussed above with reference to the sermon of Parson Yorick in *Tristram Shandy* under the heading of *good conscience.*

Conversion occurs in St. Augustine's narrative, at one level, as an interpretive response to Scripture, a response of the mind to the *kerygma* of the text – its power to proclaim the salvation of Christ – which affirms a common ground in faith as the basis for understanding. St. Augustine thematizes such hermeneutic implications for his own conversion, when (at the end of Book viii, chap. 12) he describes his response to the voice that he hears in the garden calling to him in his distress: "Take up and read!" [tolle! lege!]. He opens the New Testament and reads at random a passage in Paul's Epistle to the Romans (13:13–14):

Not in rioting and drunkenness, not in chambering and impurities, not in strife and envying; but put you on the Lord Jesus Christ, and make not provision for the flesh in its concupiscences.

He responds to this text by applying its message directly to himself. It speaks to him and for him, and his conversion signifies a gesture of immediate acceptance, accommodation, and affirmation in terms which substantiate as authoritatively as anything in literature what Gadamer has called the fusion of horizons. As Augustine reports:

Instantly, in truth, at the end of this sentence, as if before a peaceful light streaming into my heart, all the dark shadows of doubt fled away.[12]

The passage cited from St. Paul in itself reveals nothing. At most, it could speak to Augustine, as it does to us, as a moral command, rather like an echo of the Law. The moment of conversion occurs, however, as Augustine indicates, entirely within his mind. He responds to the text as he does due to his specific psychological and emotional state at that time. He had achieved a readiness or receptivity prior to his reading, following a lengthy development and preparation, which is manifested as a crisis of despair, tears and longing at the moment of conversion. All this is described at length in the narrative. Yet the act of reading is itself still necessary for the actual event of conversion to occur. The encounter with this arbitrarily selected passage from Scripture establishes the hermeneutical form of interaction through which the mind is truly *turned around*. He hears and he responds.

Several related episodes in Book VIII establish this twofold pattern of conversion as an act of reading. A text provides the occasion and the form of response, but understanding occurs only through an inner disposition of the mind, which has been achieved prior to the encounter.

Augustine's friend Alypius, for instance, who attends him in the garden where the conversion takes place, immediately after the event reads the passage in Romans which immediately follows the passage read by Augustine and himself similarly undergoes conversion. Augustine also tells us that, just before reading the passage from St. Paul, he remembered the story he had been told by Ponticianus of his conversion with several others at Trier, when they read together a book about the life of St. Anthony, an Egyptian monk.

This encounter with Ponticianus is narrated by Augustine several chapters earlier (Book VIII, chap. 6), when a discussion occurred about the writings of St. Paul. Ponticianus there describes the impact of the book of St. Anthony on one of his friends as a "tossing about on the waves of his heart" [volvit fluctus cordio sui] whereby "he was changed within" [mutabatur intus]. Augustine then asserts that the encounter with Ponticianus "turned me back upon myself" (chap. 7). His description of the experience is astonishing:

You, Lord, took me from behind my own back, where I had placed myself because I did not wish to look upon myself. You stood me face to face with myself.[13]

This series of responses to the reading of texts leads inevitably to the reader of Augustine's own confessional narrative and the question of its intended effect. His account bears witness to the experience of his own conversion by reading for the sake of those who may correspondingly be affected and transformed by *their* reading of him. The text itself, however, can provide no more than the occasion for such an event by those who have already come to that internal state of readiness and need, which alone can effect the appropriate response. Conversion thus results from a predisposition in the mind of the reader.

THE HERMENEUTICS OF VISION

St. Augustine's account of his conversion at the midpoint of his *Confessions* has served ever since as an authoritative exemplum for a theological hermeneutics in accord with St. Paul's concept of *metanoia*. Less influential, though equally crucial for my argument concerning the form of interpretation, is another famous passage in the following book, where Augustine describes a moment of visionary revelation which he shared with his mother soon after his conversion and shortly before her death (Book IX, chap. 10).

The hermeneutic implications of this passage provide yet further support for my supposition that the basis for understanding in autobiographical narrative must transcend the limits of the individual subject. The categorical displacement of narrative by theological reflection, which occurs throughout the remaining books of the *Confessions,* leading finally to Augustine's exegesis of the account of Creation in Genesis, is directly motivated by the transcendent vision achieved in Book ix and by the fact that this vision was shared with another and communicated between them. The exemplary form of the relationship demonstrated between St. Augustine and his mother is further heightened, intentionally so, by an implicit analogy to the relationship between Jesus and Mary in the Gospel narratives.

Augustine's account of this vision in his narrative as a reciprocal response shared with another thematizes the event *for us* as his readers, in such a way that a hermeneutical participation in that vision through our reading is also demanded from us. The form of narration and reflection through dialogue, which Augustine and his mother share, is applied directly to our relation with his text, even if the transcendent vision itself remains beyond the limits of language for them as well as for us. The entire passage deserves careful study; I shall limit myself here to a few details only.

Augustine describes the moment of shared vision, first of all, as an ascension of their minds together, "into themselves:"

We ascended higher yet, by means of inward thought and discourse and admiration of your works, and we came up to our own minds.[14]

Then, immediately and automatically, they transcend themselves and enter into the domain of Wisdom (*sapientia*), which is eternal, "by which all things are made" [per quam fiunt omnia ista] and "which itself is not made" [et ipsa non fit]. Following this, they "turn back again to the noise of our mouths, where a word has both beginning and ending" [et remeavimus ad strepitum oris nostri, ubi verbum et incipitur et finitur]. They are thus once more able to speak of what they saw, though now once more at a remove from it. What they say together – apparently speaking in full unison with one another – is said to be not their own words but those which are received from God.

God alone speaks, not through such things [as were made by him] but through himself, so that we hear his Word, not uttered by a tongue of flesh, not by an angel's voice, "nor by the sound of thunder," nor by the riddle of a similitude, but by himself whom we love in these things, himself we hear without their aid.[15]

Finally, after relating the speech thus spoken together by them in response to their mutual transcendent vision, Augustine asserts directly to his reader: "Such things I said, although not in this manner and in these words" [Dicebam talia, etsi non isto modo et his verbis].

We are obliged to acknowledge a hierarchy of transformations, which are said to have occurred in the writing of the text. These establish a structure of mediation between the silence of vision and the indirect, inadequate representation of that vision in language at several levels of response and remove from the vision itself. We thus enter into a relationship with Augustine's text across these several levels of verbal displacement. Only through a process of negation and denial, which emphasizes *that which is not,* both for the text and for its reader, can St. Augustine describe and represent his visionary experience.

A skeptic might therefore wish to reject the whole vision as a fiction or a fraud, or at least as a pious illusion. Such a deconstructive reading would constitute an act of bad faith, which might be justifiable in itself but which, within the communicative strategies of the *Confessions* as a whole, I regard as hermeneutically dishonest. The text establishes structures of interrelationship for the reader, which stand in opposition to the transcendent meaning they are intended to convey. Our response as readers, however, is conditioned by this point in the narrative to accommodate itself to the form of confession, for which at the highest level the relationship between Augustine and his mother provides an exemplum. To deny the validity of his vision would be to deny the validity of their relationship, which would also necessarily undermine the structures of discourse that convey the relationship to us as an implicit "dialogue of one" (John Donne's phrase).

Only through such dialogical form is it possible for us as readers to participate in the experiential process described by the text. The proper hermeneutical response to St. Augustine's text requires the acknowledgment of this hierarchy of formal projections and displacements as a function of the negativity of discourse (Hegel's term). The strategies of the narrative impose on us an obligation to enter into a vicarious participation in his discourse, so that – by analogy, or a sense of similitude, or through an imaginative reconstruction – the transcendent vision which St. Augustine asserts that he shared with his mother must be affirmed by us.

Consider the long description which fills the penultimate paragraph of the chapter. A single sentence extends for more than a full page, which is characteristic of St. Augustine's syntactical exuberance in its most dynamic and forceful performance. The strategy of the sentence is to project the behavior of some human being, whoever (*cui*) might experience what Augustine had shared with his mother. An extended catalogue of circumstances and conditions follows, all of which constitute negative instances in contrast or opposition to the authentic vision. The catalogue begins with a series of things that would have to fall silent – "the tumult of the flesh," "the images of earth, and of the waters, and of the air," "the heavens," and even "the very soul itself" [sileat tumultus carnis, sileant phantasiae terrae et aquarum et aeris, sileant et poli et ipsa sibi anima sileat] – so that out of such silence "God alone speaks" and "we may hear his own Word." (I have here skipped over a further sequence of negative qualifiers.) Then follows a survey (cited above) of those who do *not* utter this Word – "not uttered by a tongue of flesh, nor by an angel's voice, 'nor by the sound of thunder,' nor by the riddle of a similitude" [non per linguam carnis neque per vocem angeli nec per sonitum nubis nec per aenigma similitudinis].

Such a hypothetical person as this "cui" opens up the possibility that such experience, even *per contrarium*, be conveyed also to us as readers of the text. At the same time, this catalogue of negatives establishes a corresponding sense of incommensurability between the available language of descriptive reference for human discourse and the Word of God as alone eternal and transcendent Wisdom (*sapientia*). Such Words of Wisdom neither St. Augustine nor his readers can utter or comprehend.

The passage concludes in the form of a question and answer, which thematize the hermeneutical implications of St. Augustine's narrative in terms that defer appropriately to the authority of Scripture as the only valid basis for interpretation. "Would it not be this: 'Enter into the joy of your Lord'?" [nonne hoc est: Intra in gaudium domini tui?]. This statement alludes to a question asked by Jesus concerning the Kingdom of God (in Matt. 25:21). Again, Augustine asks, "when shall this be? When 'we shall all rise again, but we shall not all be changed'?" [et istud quando? an cum omnes resurgimus, sed non omnes inmutabimur?]. The biblical reference here is to St. Paul's prophecy of the Last Judgment (in 1 Cor. 15:51). How appropriate for the negative hermeneutics of this extended quotation of what had been spoken together by St. Augustine and his mother, that the sentence concludes with such citations of Scripture!

These brief comments indicate tentatively and partially how the dynamics of St. Augustine's sentence elaborates the central paradox of a hermeneutic consciousness. It is indeed a sense of *conscience* – in the full theological sense of *syneidesis,* as discussed above with reference to Sterne's *Tristram Shandy* – that defines the form of reciprocal intersubjective consciousness between the reader who reads and the text that is read. We could document in even greater detail the elaborate dialectical structure of this passage at the level of its syntax. The act of reading in this case involves a twofold process of opposing concerns: on the one hand, a form of participation and inclusion within the context of the visionary experience, described and evoked from an implicitly reciprocal and dialogical perspective, as it was shared at the time between Augustine and his mother; and, on the other, a process of concealment and exclusion imposed upon the reader by the language, which keeps us at a distance from that vision and reminds us continuously that we are unable to share it with them.

The mediations of language, both as silence and as utterance, thus participate in a structure of negation that systematically displaces the experience of transcendence. The most effective resolution, finally, to the perambulations of this sentence is the dialogical form of question and answer, directed to the authority of Scripture, which affirms both the promise of the Kingdom and the prophecy of the Last Judgment. Then, finally, even this intertextual allusion is displaced by the narrative context into the perspective of a recollected past event, which offers the promise of fulfillment only at an indeterminate future time.

Summary and Conclusion

The path of reading is roundabout and indirect, leading the speculative mind upon a long, uncertain journey apparently without end. To move from Sterne's *Tristram Shandy* to the *Confessions* of St. Augustine is itself an ambitious exercise in comparative reading for the historical imagination. Far more difficult is the task of reflection and comprehension itself, which is also far more crucial to the aims and needs of criticism. Only through such endeavor can the experience of reading be thematized and comprehended. At the end of this inquiry into such master texts of our intellectual tradition, looking back across the terrain surveyed, I must acknowledge the limitations of my own vision. What has emerged from these various explorations and clarifications is no more and no less than what at this juncture appears to be just so *for me*. This must suffice for an essay in criticism. Whether other readers will agree with these readings of *Tristram Shandy* and the *Confessions* is a question for them to decide.

The original point of departure for my inquiry into literary hermeneutics was the concept of self-consciousness (*Selbstbewußtsein*), developed within German philosophical idealism from Kant through Fichte to Hegel, specifically as this concept has been reinterpreted in our own time with reference to these philosophers by such theorists as Hans-Georg Gadamer and Dieter Henrich. Henrich's authoritative argument concerning Fichte's "original insight,"[16] alongside a provocative critical statement by Geoffrey

Hartman entitled "Romanticism and 'Anti-Self-Consciousness,'"[17]
led me to explore the limits of autobiographical narrative in the
work of Hölderlin and Wordsworth.[18] Such an inquiry into the
poetics of Romanticism resulted in the conviction that the certainty
(*Gewißheit*) of the spirit in its movement toward absolute knowledge (Hegel's formulation for conscience as *Gewissen* in the
Phenomenology of Spirit) is offset by a fundamental uncertainty, or
even indeterminacy, of the self within poetic forms of language.
The moments of deepest insight in poetry are totally incompatible
with the cognitive and reflective procedures of self-knowledge.

By subsequently writing several essays on hermeneutical theory,
specifically on metaphor and irony in Romanticism, I was able to
move beyond a preoccupation with subjectivity in self-consciousness.[19] Hartman again provided valuable guidance in his seminal
essay "From the Sublime to the Hermeneutic,"[20] as did Gadamer,
from a more comprehensive philosophical context, in his various
explorations of hermeneutical strategies in Hegel,[21] as also in his
seminal work on Plato. These two philosophers constitute the primary source for all dialectical theory and practice in the Western
tradition.[22] Interpretation can only proceed, as I came to realize,
through an intersubjective, dialectical interaction between text and
reader in the act of reading. On this point I also learned from
Wolfgang Iser in his book *The Act of Reading,* particularly with
regard to the role of opposition and transformation as constitutive
of this hermeneutical interaction, which he discusses under the
headings of "structured gaps," negation, and the Hegelian concept
of negativity.[23] In direct response to Iser's argument I was led to
consider the hermeneutical implications of *reversal* as a central
communicative strategy in all narrative discourse.[24] This device
may be identified both with Aristotle's notion of *peripeteia,* applied
to the structure of representation in narrative emplotment, and
with St. Augustine's narrative of *conversion* as a mode of participation and response by reading.

Only from this vantage point with regard to strategies of reversal
in narrative has it been possible to bring together in the argument
of this essay the concepts of *conscience* and *conversion* from Sterne
and St. Augustine. These central concepts of *syneidesis* and *metanoia*

ultimately lead back to the New Testament as a common source. What do these essential presuppositions imply for a general theory of hermeneutics?

The central focus of argument in this essay concerns the relation of reflectivity to the displacement of autobiographical narrative away from the subject. The essential structure of hermeneutical consciousness – indicated in my title as the *conscience* of narrative – involves a reflective interaction between text and reader in such a way that this structure achieves cognitive and thematic status for the reader. And the reader must recognize it. The narrative thus conveys to its reader a full awareness of what the structure of communication through reading involves. In both complex instances discussed above – *Tristram Shandy* and the *Confessions* – the meaning of the book is established in and through the reader's awareness of a dynamic, developing relationship with the text. Understanding thus depends on the knowledge of how the act of reading implicates the reader in a structure of interrelationships which *in its very form* as verbal communication establishes, as figura or exemplum, that intersubjective, ethical certainty indicated by the motto of Yorick's sermon, itself borrowed from the Epistle to the Hebrews: "For we trust we have a good conscience."

In both *Tristram Shandy* and the *Confessions* the structural displacement of the autobiographical narrative away from the subject, away from the developing life history of the author-narrator, also involves the reader's own developing relationship to the narrative. On the one hand, through this displacement the story itself – regardless of its truth claim or the realism of its account – is thematized as a fictional form, in the broadest sense of *fiction* as creative, or *poetic,* construct. The narrative comes to be perceived as a kind of *analogia entis* for our lives. It represents a structure of human value which is exemplary, yet which depends for its validity upon our response to the act of reading. On the other hand, alongside this thematic awareness of the fictionality of the narrative discourse, the reflectivity of hermeneutical consciousness in the reader achieves the recognition that the ultimate referent for the narrative discourse remains indeterminate and beyond the limits of signification. The narrator as subject submits to this awareness of indeterminacy by allowing the displacement of the narrative to occur. The success of that displacement as ironic structure of communication depends on the reader's willingness to participate in it to an equal degree. We share in the emptying out of the sign, so that the narrative as verbal structure communicates to us an understanding which, in accord with the necessary dialectical form of negativity, replaces all subjective certainty of the self with a genuine ethical concern for an indeterminate and unknown otherness.

The tone and the style of presentation in these two books is, of course, radically different. *Tristram Shandy* depends upon the sentimentality of its wit and the *Confessions* upon the theology of its faith and piety. Yet both works manifest an identical hermeneutical form, whereby the narrative imposes on the reader through patterns of negativity an awareness of that which the narrative cannot express directly and which thus cannot be communicated to us with any authority or authenticity. What cannot *itself* be known in each case is the transcendent *signifié*: death in *Tristram Shandy* and the vision of God in the *Confessions*. All we have from the narrative, despite St. Augustine's insistence to the contrary about his shared vision and the Word of God which spoke to him, are figures of similitude, which finally subsume within themselves the totality of the autobiographical narrative as fiction or figura. The reader thus achieves self-understanding only in and through a relation to such fictional or figural forms of narrative. Explicit reference is made to an ultimate concern, shared between reader and narrative, for that which cannot be directly expressed and thus cannot actually be known. The concept of a fusion of horizons as the basis of hermeneutical consciousness thus collapses into an enigma which remains unresolved.

Coda: "Proteus" in Joyce's *Ulysses*

I began this chapter with several paragraphs on the ethical structure of hermeneutical consciousness, followed by a brief glance at Dante's *Divine Comedy*. Having now attempted this further statement about the essential paradox of autobiographical narrative for such understanding, I conclude with a similar brief glance at an episode from Joyce's *Ulysses*. The monologue of Stephen Dedalus in the "Proteus" chapter demonstrates a reversal and a displacement of narrative perspective away from the narrator as subject, corresponding in many ways to everything I have described above. As he walks along the shore of Sandymount, Stephen reaches a point of outer limit where the incoming tide forces him to turn back to the land:

> He stood suddenly, his feet beginning to sink slowly in the quaking soil. Turn back.
>
> Turning, he scanned the shore south, his feet sinking again slowly in new sockets.

This figure of reversal and return for Stephen's reflective journey occurs at the very end of the chapter. A backward glance provides him with a sign or signal of encounter, which prefigures the larger patterns of relationship to be established later in the novel, when Stephen finally meets Leopold Bloom in the Nighttown episode. This meeting, of course, recapitulates the mythical pattern of encounter between Telemachus and Odysseus, the reunion of the son and the father, in Homer's *Odyssey*. Stephen sees the ship Rosevene sailing into Dublin harbor. This ship, within the intertextual resonances that Joyce has superimposed upon his narrative as a symbolic repetition of its Homeric source, signifies the eventual homecoming of the father for the son who seeks him:

> He turned his face over his shoulder, rere regardant. Moving through the air high spars of a threemaster, her sails brailed up on the crosstrees, homing, upstream, silently moving, a silent ship.

The question which would deserve further consideration with

regard to *Ulysses,* in line with the directions of inquiry pursued in this essay, is how this pattern of reversal and displacement in narrative, the dynamics of encounter and vision for the self, relates to those structures of reading and hermeneutical response described in this essay under the headings of conversion and conscience, *metanoia* and *syneidesis*? To address this question with reference to Joyce's *Ulysses,* as indicated also in response to Dante's *Divine Comedy* at the outset, would require another essay, in which this modernist novel would serve as countertext in its hermeneutical implications to both the *Confessions* of St. Augustine and Sterne's *Tristram Shandy.* Such brief allusions to Dante and Joyce at the beginning and end of my argument are intended to suggest the directions that further critical inquiry into the *conscience of narrative* might take as it has developed and is manifested throughout the tradition of Western literature.

Chapter4 : The Poetics of Self-Consciousness

For Dieter Henrich

Γνῶθι σεαυτόν! Nosce te ipsum! Know thyself!

This familiar dictum, a command from the gods to mankind, is as old as Western thought; no particular historical era can claim such a concern for self-knowledge as uniquely its own. Pope's famous couplet from his "Essay on Man" speaks for the entire tradition:

> Know then thyself, presume not God to scan;
> The proper study of Mankind is Man.[1]

Maynard Mack refers this thought back to Pascal, whose *Pensées* Pope is known to have read: "La vraie science et le vrai étude de l'homme est l'homme."[2] One commentator on Pope called this "the oldest dictum of logic or philosophy on record."[3] Pope also knew, no doubt, that this saying, both commonplace and venerable, however well expressed in his couplet, derived from a complex Stoic tradition originating with the ancient inscription at Delphi, the sources of which were lost in legend even for the writers of Classical Greece.[4]

Coleridge also had Delphi in mind when he responded late in his life and late in the Romantic era to the passage from Pope – as I. A. Richards suggests[5] – by composing an untitled poem with a motto from the eleventh Satire of Juvenal, which also cites the Delphic tag: "E caelo descendit Γνῶθι σεαυτόν."[6] Coleridge offers a mocking reversal of Pope's dictum:

Γνῶθι σεαυτόν! – and is this the prime
And heaven-sprung adage of the olden time! –
Say, canst thou make thyself? – Learn first that trade; –
Haply thou mayst know what thyself had made.
What hast thou, Man, that thou dar'st call thine own? –
What is there in thee, Man, that can be known? –
Dark fluxion, all unfixable by thought,
A phantom dim of past and future wrought,
Vain sister of the worm, – life, death, soul, clod –
Ignore thyself, and strive to know thy God![7]

Ipse cognoscere. The phrase has meant different things to different writers at different times. The ancient oracle at Delphi, as Wolfgang Schadewaldt emphasizes in an essay concerning the Greek concept of humanity, offered a reminder to man of his mortality: "erkenne dich, Mensch, als Sterblichen, in deiner Sterblichkeit."[8] Juvenal had less exalted concerns in mind, asserting that human beings should know what is appropriate to being human: "noscenda est mesura sui spectandaque rebus / in summis minimisque."[9] The background of Pascal's statement was theological, in accord with the implicit systematics of his Christian faith. For Pope the proper study of mankind is defined more exclusively within the human realm, in the spirit of eighteenth-century Enlightenment thought. The ironic reversal imposed by Coleridge thus makes a more absolute claim for the self. Yet there is a paradox contained in his text, indicated by the question: "Say, canst thou make thyself?" I take this paradox to be central for Romantic poetry. Self-consciousness is only achieved by an act of self-creation. Poetry provides the norm for such creative activity, and through poetry the limit of consciousness is attained, whether that yields knowledge of the self or of God. The development of a poetics based upon this Romantic view of self-reflective creativity in the work of Friedrich Hölderlin and William Wordsworth will be explored in this essay.

"Subjectivity or self-consciousness," so Harold Bloom remarks in the introduction to a collection of critical essays, "is the salient problem of Romanticism."[10] This judgment derives from an apparent concern among contemporary critics of Romantic poetry for what Bloom there defines as "the dialectic of consciousness and imagination." One critic who takes this dialectic seriously is Geoffrey Hartman, whose essay "Romanticism and 'Anti-Self-Consciousness,'" included in Bloom's anthology, explores the dilemma of self-consciousness among poets who looked to the poetic imagination as a counterforce to nature on behalf of the mind. We may also associate the imagination with that power which, again citing Coleridge, would *make* the self. "Self-consciousness cannot be overcome," argues Hartman with regard to the views of Shelley, Keats and Blake, "and the very desire to overcome it, which poetry and imagination encourage, is part of a vital, dialectical movement of 'soul-making.'"[11]

This dialectic in Romantic poetry finds a theoretical basis, as Hartman also acknowledges, in the arguments of the German Idealist philosophers, notably Fichte, Schelling and Hegel, concerning that condition of self-reflection which they term *Selbstbewußtsein*. Fichte above all was aware of a fundamental paradox in self-consciousness, upon which Hegel later founded his dialectical method. These teachings were an important point of departure for the German Romantic poets, notably Hölderlin, who were concerned, as were Wordsworth and Coleridge in England, with the role of the self in poetry.

In an essay concerning Fichte's "original insight," Dieter Henrich surveys the development of a theory of self-consciousness in Fichte's philosophy in terms that emphasize this essential paradox.[12] In order to avoid the vicious circle of traditional theories of self-reflection from Descartes to Kant, so argues Henrich, Fichte defined the self in his *Wissenschaftslehre* as an active force, a power which "posits," or creates, the conditions of its own consciousness. What the self can know of itself is thus its own activity as agent of knowledge. What the self knows of itself is the process of its own experience. "Ichbewußtsein ist Tatbewußtsein," says Henrich. "Knowledge is the result of the self's act of positing itself."[13] Self-consciousness, in Fichte's own definition of 1801 (*Wissenschaftslehre,* cited in Henrich), is "an activity [of the self] which includes an eye that sees" [eine Tätigkeit, der ein Auge eingesetzt ist (25)].

Both vision, or intuition (*Anschauung*), and reflection, or concept (*Begriff*), are united within the self as an organic whole. The *eye* of self-consciousness, asserts Henrich (26), is not like an ornament for the body but more like the heart for life. The process of experience is hence defined dialectically by Fichte as a reciprocal interaction (*Wechseltätigkeit*) between these two capacities within the self. "Selbstbewußtsein," to quote Henrich's paraphrase of Fichte, "ist die unmittelbare Wechselbeziehung von Begriff und Anschauung in einer Tätigkeit, die wesentlich von sich weiss" (32).

Particularly important for the poetics of self-consciousness is the fact that such self-knowledge, as Fichte defines it, always involves an act of recognition (*ein Wiedererkennen*). For the self, paradoxically, can only know itself, if it is already known to itself (31). The activity of the self, through which self-consciousness is achieved, thus constitutes an act of repetition, at least at the level of reflective cognition. But this paradox extends even further, for the ultimate basis, or ground, or source, for such self-knowledge is not contained – so argues Fichte – within the self at all. The origin of selfhood is the Absolute, or Being, or God. Self-consciousness not only manifests the self to itself, but also establishes a direct cognitive relationship to the transcendent source of its existence (39). Such a theory of self-consciousness, as outlined by Henrich from Fichte's later philosophy, provides eloquent affirmation of the ironic paradox expressed by Coleridge in the dictum of his poem on "Self-knowledge," where he corrects the claim of Pope's "Essay on Man": "Ignore thyself, and strive to know thy God!"

Wordsworth and Hölderlin

Wordsworth and Hölderlin have rarely been considered together, even from the broadest perspectives of European Romanticism. Though they knew nothing of each other, analogies and similarities in their lives and work may be readily demonstrated, as in a comparative study by Walter Silz.[14] Deeper affinities in their lyrical *oeuvre* were explored tentatively by Paul de Man, particularly with regard to the problem of temporality for poetic experience.[15] No consideration has yet been given, however, to striking parallels of autobiographical narrative form in Hölderlin's epistolary novel *Hyperion* and Wordsworth's epic *The Prelude*. Only recently has the role of self-consciousness in these narratives been discussed by respective critics of either work.[16]

Both poets were fundamentally concerned with the problem of self-consciousness as outlined above. This concern greatly influenced their conception of poetry and its function, especially with regard to the use of a reflective, autobiographical narrative. Both *Hyperion* and *The Prelude* constitute programmatic attempts, consciously modelled on the example of Rousseau's *Confessions*, to achieve a comprehensive understanding of the self through a poetic reconstruction of personal experience. Wordsworth and Hölderlin were both aware, though to differing degrees, of idealist theories of self-consciousness: Hölderlin from his association with Fichte and Schiller in Jena (not to mention his study of Kant and his close friendship with Schelling and Hegel!); Wordsworth at least indirectly from his friendship with Coleridge, who became increasingly familiar with German philosophy (including Fichte and Schelling).[17] In the mature work of both poets – notably in Wordsworth's *Prelude*, which constitutes his supreme achievement in a self-reflective mode, and in the mature odes and elegies of Hölderlin (which cannot be considered here)–the dialectic of consciousness and imagination in Romantic poetry finds its most authoritative and most eloquent voice. The present argument is intended to suggest how a more comprehensive study of the poetics of self-consciousness in their respective work might proceed.

Hyperion and *The Prelude* are basically dissimilar in outward appearance. The tradition of the sentimental epistolary novel, which Hölderlin adapted from Rousseau and Goethe, had little to do with the norms of epic emulated by Wordsworth on the model of Milton's *Paradise Lost*. Neither tradition was primarily suitable to poetic autobiography. Goethe, to be sure, had established in *The Sorrows of Young Werther* an emphasis on the aesthetic sensibility of his hero, yet Hölderlin was the first to use an epistolary narrative for the recollective reconstruction of individual subjective experience. Wordsworth, as his catalogue of rejected themes for an epic narrative in Book One of *The Prelude* makes clear, only selected his subject matter, the growth of his own poetic mind, by default.

What these two works share above all is the self-reflective role of their respective narrators. Through this device primarily is achieved the developing self-consciousness of each. The manner in which this self-consciousness is achieved constitutes the central poetic significance of both works. This holds true despite the obvious difference that Wordsworth speaks in *The Prelude* more or less in his own voice about his own life, whereas the narrator of Hölderlin's novel is a fictitious character, an eighteenth-century Greek patriot living in solitude as a "hermit," who writes letters about his past life to a friend in Germany named Bellarmin. The character of Hyperion assumes important autobiographical qualities which reflect Hölderlin's own growth to poetry. These resemblances go deeper than simple analogies between Hyperion's story and events in the poet's own life. The autobiographical mode of both these works needs to be acknowledged at the outset, quite apart from their respective generic traditions. Self-consciousness thus assumes a central significance for both the subjective content and the reflective narrative form in both works.

Hyperion and *The Prelude* are both presented through retrospective narrative. The story to be told in each case has already taken place in its entirety before the telling of it begins. The narrator calls to mind his own experience, tracing the growth of his spirit and offering reflective comments on this growth from the perspective of his narrative. Also similar is the role of the intimate friend to whom the narrative is addressed: Bellarmin in the one case and Coleridge in the other. The friend provides a rhetorical focus for the narrator, who attempts to convey to him an understanding of how and why he has come to be what he is. The reader thus comes also to share the position of the friend, participating vicariously in the process of reflective recollection.

Most important is the development which occurs in the perspective of the narrator in the course of his narrative. An evolution of attitude or transformation of mood takes place in both works through the accumulation of reflective responses. The process of recollection involves an expansion of the narrator's point of view, leading ultimately to a comprehensive awareness of himself in and through his own development. To narrate the growth of his mind thus includes also a growth in his understanding of how that growth occurred. The ultimate standpoint of the narrator, therefore, which is intended to be shared by both the friend who is addressed and the implied reader of the work, consists of a security and tranquil-lity of mind, sustained by the achievement of its own self-consciousness and the communication of that self-consciousness to another. This state of mind, which in terms of Fichte's philosophical theory would best be called an "intellectual intuition" (*intellektuelle Anschauung*), constitutes the highest level of reflective understanding for each work.[18]

Such self-fulfillment is not without a sense of paradox, however, which corresponds to the claims of a general theory of self-consciousness. This is due in large measure to a pattern of uncertainty or incomprehensibility in those particular experiences recollected through the narrative in both books, which are regarded by the respective narrators as the climactic moments of their existence. These experiences involve various sorts of self-transcendence and the loss of self-control. At the time when such moments occurred, as both works emphasize, no clear understanding was achieved about what was happening, or how, or why. Also implicit to both narratives is the sense that such experience involves a failure of the subjective will, a defeat of the conscious mind. This theme of defeat is stronger in *Hyperion,* which ultimately affirms a tragic view of life, in contrast to the all-pervasive sense of harmony and peace that concludes *The Prelude.* The self thus becomes the agent or instrument of a higher power, which transcends the individual life and which remains for that self ineffable. The result may be disappointment, error, suffering or loss; or equally the outcome may be joyous, ecstatic or even epiphanic. These moments achieve within their respective narratives the intimation of a universal power beyond the limits of consciousness. They constitute spots of time, which are felt to be eternal. Only through the poetic act of recollection and narration, however, can the conscious mind attempt to comprehend such moments of higher intuition. Such comprehension is necessarily conditioned and defined by the dialectic of self-consciousness. The retrospective narrative, which traces the growth of the poet's mind, thus becomes also the recollection of experiences that go beyond the limits of understanding.

It has often been remarked that Romantic poetry in essence is a poetry about poetry; more specifically it is a poetry which represents and reflects upon the poetic process itself. This holds true for both Wordsworth and Hölderlin, as especially for *The Prelude* and *Hyperion,* in a very precise sense. For both these poets the act of recollection or remembrance is identical with the poetic process. Poetry may thus be understood as the act of retrospection by the poetic self upon itself and as the re-creation in language of privileged moments of experience, which characteristically go beyond the limits of thought and knowledge. Insofar as *The Prelude* and *Hyperion* are motivated by such concerns, they become more than just autobiographical narratives about the growth of the poet's mind. These are poems about the self-reflective process of poetic experience as such. The self-consciousness, which they thus achieve for both the poet as narrator of his life story and for the reader as recipient of that story, establishes also an implicit poetics or theory of poetry. The structure of the narrative is defined by the dialectical tension between the reflective role of the narrator and the kinds of experience, moments of vision or spots of time, which constitute the climaxes of that narrative. This dialectical tension corresponds precisely to the reciprocity between concept and intuition, which Fichte, according to Dieter Henrich, ascribed to self-consciousness. Critics of Romantic poetry, such as Bloom, Hartman and de Man, have emphasized the importance of this dialectic above all else as constitutive of Romantic poetry, whether or not they had Wordsworth or Hölderlin explicitly in mind. My point in this essay goes one step further with regard to the challenge of understanding this dialectic. The poetics of self-consciousness depends upon the paradox of its own inherent irreconcilability. Romantic poetry always strives to resolve this dialectical tension within a comprehensive existential vision, but always, whether it knows it or not, fails. In that failure may reside such poetry's greatest hermeneutical powers. More needs to be said on this point, based on evidence summoned from the texts themselves.

Hyperion, oder der Eremit in Griechenland

In the course of *Hyperion* the narrator speaks at intervals about his state of mind at that particular stage in the telling of his story. By juxtaposing several instances of such reflective comment we may observe, in schematic outline at least, the evolution of self-consciousness in the novel. Corresponding evidence may then be assembled from *The Prelude*.

Hyperion's initial mood is confused and changeable. This vacillation is conditioned, on the one hand, by his recent experiences in Germany, based on a trip to that country just prior to the commencement of his narrative, which he begins after returning in solitude to Greece. His account of that trip is not given until the very end of the novel. On the other hand, he writes in immediate jubilant response to the sight of his native Greece, which has now become the setting for his spiritual hermitage. In the opening letters a rapid fluctuation of mood occurs between these extremes of joy and regret. The narrator emphasizes that reflection and recollection destroy every pleasure which the sight of his homeland provides. Reflection and vision are thus completely at odds, and the narrator is incapable as yet of reconciling them in any way:

My whole being falls silent and listens when the delicate swell of the breezes plays over my breast. Often, lost in the wide blue, I look up into the ether and down into the sacred sea, and I feel as if a kindred spirit were opening its arms to me, as if the pain of solitude were dissolved in the life of the Divinity.

   . . . On this height I often stand, my Bellarmin! But an instant of reflection hurls me down. I reflect, and I find myself as I was before – alone, with all the griefs of mortality, and my heart's refuge, the world in its eternal oneness, is gone; Nature closes her arms, and I stand like an alien before her and do not understand her.[19]

At the beginning of the second part to Volume I, Hyperion moves to the island of Salamis, where he leads a life of rustic simplicity. Here the narrator emphasizes the constancy of his contentment. His mood of tranquillity, which corresponds to the peaceful landscape around him, provides a source of strength for continuing his tale:

As Jupiter's eagle listens for the songs of the Muses, so I listen for the marvelous, unending euphony in me. Undisturbed in mind and soul, strong and joyous and smilingly serious, I play with Fate and the Three Sisters, the holy Parcae. Full of divine youth, my whole being rejoices over itself, over all things. Like the starry sky, I am calm and moved. (37)[20]

Later on, near the beginning of Volume II, after describing his separation from Diotima, Hyperion speaks with authority about the value which the telling of his story has assumed for his developing understanding of himself and for his ultimate peace of mind. He emphasizes the resolution of all conflict, an acceptance of life, and a corresponding tranquillity of mood:

Why do I recount my grief to you, renew it, and stir up my restless youth in me again? Is it not enough to have traveled *once* through mortality? why do I remain still in the peace of my spirit?

It is, my Bellarmin! because every living breath that we draw remains dear to our heart, because all the transformations of pure Nature are part of her beauty too....Dear Bellarmin! I was quiet for a while; like a child, I lived under the still knolls of Salamis, oblivious to mankind's fate and striving. Since then much has changed in my eyes, and now I have peace enough in me to remain quiet when I look at human existence....I think that even my letters should suffice to show you that my soul is becoming more and more still every day. (84)[21]

The final instance of such reflective comment by the narrator occurs immediately after Hyperion quotes the letter from Notara, which describes the death of his beloved Diotima. Asserting the security of his spiritual repose, even while remembering such great sorrow, he now declares himself reconciled to all suffering as a necessary aspect of life itself. This proves to be his ultimate wisdom:

> So Notara wrote; and you ask, my Bellarmin! how it is with me now, while I tell you of this.
>
> Best of friends! I am at peace, for I want nothing better than the gods. Must not all things suffer? And the more excellent, the more deeply! Does not sacred Nature suffer? O my Divinity! that you could mourn as you are blissful – that was long beyond my understanding. But the bliss that does not suffer is sleep, and without death there is no life. (125)[22]

These instances of self-reflection in the narrator document the evolution of a constancy out of his changing moods. This process is offset by moments of climactic experience, in which he loses all conscious awareness of himself, whether this occurs in joy or in sorrow. One instance of the former is Hyperion's meeting with Diotima in the garden of Notara, when he first declares his love to her. The ecstasy of that moment, he asserts, created a gap in his existence: "Es ist hier eine Lüke in meinem Daseyn. Ich starb, und wie ich erwachte, lag ich am Herzen des himmlischen Mädchens" (*Hyp* 1: 128.4–5; *GStA* III: 72). The opposite extreme of experience occurs at the point of Hyperion's suicidal despair in Volume II, when he throws himself into the naval battle at Tschesme, expecting to be killed. After being wounded and barely escaping with his life, he lies for six days in a deathlike coma. He reports this experience to Bellarmin: "Mein Leben war, wie eine Nacht, von Schmerzen, wie von zükenden Blizen, unterbrochen" (*Hyp* 2: 61.11–12; *GStA* 3: 125).

Careful analysis of the structure of *Hyperion* reveals a purposeful interplay, indeed a dialectical sequence of such opposite states of mind, ranging from the extremes of experience recollected in the narrative to the narrator's reflective comments on them. The structure of experience is basically cyclical, like the sequence of the seasons, moving from joy to sorrow.[23] The structure of reflection, however, advances, as indicated by the passages cited, from an initial rapid fluctuation of mood to a final tranquillity and security of vision. Through the emergence of a reflective understanding of life, achieved by narrating his story, Hyperion learns to accept and affirm the entire range of variant moments, which constitute that story, and to integrate them all into a comprehensive vision, which regards all loss and all sorrow as part of an ultimate and essential order. The novel concludes with images of resolution and harmony:

"Like lovers' quarrels are the dissonances of the world. Reconciliation is there, even in the midst of strife, and all things that are parted find one another again.

"The arteries separate and return to the heart and all is one eternal glowing life." (133)[24]

This concluding passage has solicited totally opposite interpretations from the two most authoritative critics of *Hyperion*, specifically with regard to the role of the reflective narrator. The entire passage is printed with quotation marks at the end of the last letter of the novel (as Hölderlin himself presumably intended it to be in the original published edition).[25] Just prior to this statement the narrator describes a unique moment of revelation which occurred for him one day during his visit to Germany, when he was alone with himself in nature. "It was the fairest noonday I have known," so he asserts [Es war der schönste Mittag, den ich kenne].[26] In response to "an incomprehensible desire" (*ein unbegreiflich Sehnen*), he is visited – so he reports – by the spirit of the dead Diotima.[27] Her voice seems to speak to him in a way which remains unexplained:

"Diotima," I cried, "where are you, oh, where are you?" And it seemed to me that I heard Diotima's voice, the voice that cheered me in the days of happiness –

"I am with my kindred," she cried, "with your kindred, whom the erring minds of men know not." (132)[28]

In response to this epiphany, or moment of communion, in a manner which corresponds precisely to earlier moments of ecstasy in his experience, Hyperion reports that he was "seized by a mild fright" and his "thought slumbered within" [Ein sanfter Schreken ergriff mich und mein Denken entschlummerte in mir]. He cried out to this "dear word from holy mouth," so he asserts, when he again awakened, calling it a "riddle" and asking how or if he comprehends, or grasps, or understands (*fassen*), that word: "O liebes Wort aus heil'gem Munde,...liebes Räthsel, fass' ich dich?" He then describes how he looked back once more into the cold night of men, shuddered and wept for joy, that he was so blessed, and spoke words – so it now seems to the narrator – "but they were like the roaring of a fire, when it flies upward and leaves only ashes behind:"

> Und Einmal sah' ich noch in die kalte Nacht der Menschen zurük und schauert' und weinte vor Freuden, daß ich so seelig war und Worte sprach ich, wie mir dünkt, aber sie waren, wie des Feuers Rauschen, wenn es auffliegt und die Asche hinter sich läßt – . (*Hyp* 122, 15–18; *GStA* III: 159)

Hyperion's final celebration of life in all its contradictions, which constitutes this final speech, follows immediately. The novel then abruptly ends with a statement by the narrator: "So dacht' ich. Nächstens mehr."

On the basis of the past tense of this last line, as well as the implications of the quotation marks, Lawrence Ryan argues that Hyperion's concluding revery was uttered in direct response to his visitation by Diotima's spirit and thus represents an unreflected statement by the character within the narrative, *not* by the reflective narrator at a distance of time.[29] It would be, in other words, an expression of Hyperion's experience of ecstasy but not the product of his self-conscious reflection. The final truth of the novel is found, for Ryan, in Hyperion's comment to Bellarmin about his state of mind after he reports the letter concerning Diotima's death (quoted above).[30]

Friedbert Aspetsberger offers an interpretation which totally contradicts Ryan's view.[31] The concluding passage, he argues, despite its quotation marks, was not uttered at the time of the visitation. Whatever may have been said at that time – and the narrator only *thinks* he spoke at the time ("wie mir dünkt") – was lost like the flames of the fire which leaves only ashes behind. Thus, for Aspetsberger, the quoted speech is a "reconstruction" by the narrator of those lost words, the product of a "creative reflection," in accord with the definition of poetic language as *schöpferische Reflexion* in Hölderlin's later theoretical essays.[32]

Both these interpretations are valid to a degree, but neither takes adequately into consideration the purposeful confusion here introduced by Hölderlin between the experience of the character Hyperion and his subsequent reflective narration of it. This confusion may be regarded as an attempt to fuse the two perspectives. The speech is certainly the product of a re-creative reflection (as is, indeed, the entire novel) – as Aspetsberger argues[33] – but it is also a fully accurate re-creation of the hero's revery in immediate response to his visitation – as Ryan would have us believe. I would also go a step further to suggest that the entire experience as presented to us in the final letter of the novel serves as a paradigm for the poetic process itself, as it applies both to the composition of *Hyperion* and to Hölderlin's subsequent practice as a poet.

The origin of poetry is the experience of ecstasy or inspiration, here represented as a visitation by the spirit of Diotima, now transformed by death into Hyperion's Muse. Only for such experience is the poetic vision, or intuition, authentic. The motive for writing the poem is found in the immediate response to this experience, as indicated with regard to the novel by the fact that Hyperion apparently returned to Greece immediately after this experience of communion, in order to start writing his letters to Bellarmin (as Aspetsberger emphasizes).[34] But the process of poetic composition must be reflective, involving the re-creation of the original experience by the poetic mind in and through its state of self-consciousness. Only in this way can the self achieve comprehension of itself in its act of experience, in accord with the definition of self-consciousness. The fact that the novel concludes with the narration of this event in Hyperion's life suggests that here, in comprehending *this* experience, the novel achieves fulfillment and completion.

The end of *Hyperion* thus corresponds precisely to Fichte's notion of "intellectual intuition." Yet the ultimate basis of truth for that which is expressed about the experience remains inexplicable, as the theory of self-consciousness would argue that it should. We are not expected to believe that Hyperion merely speaks from his own conviction at the end of the novel, however valid that conviction may be *for him*. What is understood and expressed by his speech is the ultimate truth of the novel as a whole. To comprehend this has been possible only through the re-creative, reflective process of narration from beginning to end, and it is comprehended not only by Hyperion, but also by his friend Bellarmin and, implicitly, by us as readers of the novel. Corresponding to the fiction of Diotima's spirit, speaking to Hyperion from a separate realm beyond life, we are expected to believe that the ultimate meaning of the novel is derived from a source beyond the limits of the hero's self, revealed to him initially in a moment of ecstasy and finally re-created and comprehended through the reflective process of the narrative. Such affirmation may be regarded as the supreme fiction of the poetics of self-consciousness.

"INTELLECTUAL INTUITION"

Hölderlin's *Hyperion* is in the broadest sense a novel about a poet, a form of fiction which in German is given the generic label *Künstlerroman*. In many ways this work anticipates the sort of fictional autobiographical narrative undertaken in our century by James Joyce in *Portrait of the Artist as a Young Man*. The subtitle used by Wordsworth for *The Prelude*, furthermore, could equally apply to Hölderlin's novel: "Growth of a Poet's Mind." It has been remarked, for instance by Lawrence Ryan, that the character Hyperion emerges from Hölderlin's novel as the poet, potentially, which the author himself was shortly to become.[35]

More to the point of this essay is the extent to which this novel also develops an implicit program for poetry, specifically through the evolution of self-consciousness in the process of narration. This occurs, as argued just above, through a series of self-reflective comments by the narrator concerning the events of his own life history, which trace a development in his own perspective on that history through the act of communicating it in letters to his friend Bellarmin. This sequence of letters thus constitutes a remembrance of things past across an experiential gap of time, undertaken from a position of cognitive solitude in which the narrator now lives as "hermit in Greece."

One question that we still need to address is the extent to which the text of the novel offers any evidence or provides a demonstration concerning the poetic process itself, specifically insofar as this would involve a self-reflective creative (or re-creative) activity on the part of the central character. The only actual poem cited in the novel, as readers have always noted, is the song of destiny which Hyperion sings near the end, his "Schicksalslied." This relatively simple but powerful lyric has come to be one of Hölderlin's most famous poems, above all due to the choral setting with orchestra composed for it in the latter part of the nineteenth century by Johannes Brahms. This poem, however, is not the work of Hyperion himself, since he remarks that it had been taught to him once by Adamas, the mentor figure who appears briefly near the outset of the novel. We must look elsewhere for the implicit praxis of Hyperion's poetics.

Early in the second book of Volume II, Hyperion quotes a letter he has received from his beloved Diotima, after he has left her to join the rebellion of the Greeks against Turkey (in the war of Russia against Turkey in the 1770s, viewed by Hölderlin as preparatory to the struggle of Greece for independence). She accuses him of making her into his muse, a role which now causes her much anguish: "Hyperion! Hyperion! hast du nicht mich, die Unmündige, zur Muse gemacht?" (*GStA* III: 130). This role had been implicitly affirmed by her – so we may argue in retrospect – during the visit made by Hyperion and Diotima to Athens at the end of Volume I. At that time, when they witnessed the sad ruins of the ancient culture which constituted the glory of Classical Greece, Diotima herself defined the challenge which Hyperion must face as his future destiny. Her words constitute the climactic message of the novel's first volume:

Hyperion! I think you are born for higher things. Do not misjudge yourself!...You must shoot down like the beam of light, you must descend like the all-refreshing rain, into the land of mortal men, you must illuminate like Apollo, shake and animate like Jupiter, or you are not worthy of your heaven. (72)[36]

Hyperion, she asserts, must become the educator of his people: "Du wirst Erzieher unsers Volks, du wirst ein großer Mensch sein, hoffe ich" (III, 89). She thus views his mission with regard to the impact his work will have on the people. Such a conception of the effect of art upon culture indicates Hölderlin's own commitment to the program of *aesthetic education* outlined by Schiller for the future of German culture in his *Briefe über die ästhetische Erziehung des Menschen,* published in 1795. This program was familiar to the poet from his sojourn in Jena during the first half of that year, when he was for a time in near daily contact with Schiller. Such aesthetic education for a people and a culture could only be achieved, so Schiller argued, through the power of art and poetry to transform and enlighten the mind. In this regard Hölderlin was of one mind with Schiller, and Diotima in her appeal to Hyperion speaks for both.

Diotima also describes in images of natural creation the explicit response that she hopes Hyperion's poetic work will elicit from the people:

They must arise, they must come forth, like young mountains out of the ocean when their underground fire drives them....All must be changed! From the root of humanity the new world shall spring! A new divinity shall rule over them, a new future brighten before them. (73)[37]

Hyperion himself, speaking with the voice of Hölderlin's own vision of a future possibility for culture through the power of art to transform humanity, concludes the first volume of the novel on a climactic chord of hope:

You ask for men, Nature? You complain, like a lyre on which only that brother of chance, the wind, plays because the artist who imposed order on it has died? They will come, your men, O Nature! A rejuvenated people will rejuvenate you, too, and you will be as its bride, and the old union of spirits will renew itself in you.

> There will be but *one* Beauty; and man and Nature will be united in *one* all-embracing divinity. (74)[38]

The key to this future of culture is the concept of *rejuvenation* (*Verjüngung*), which Hölderlin no doubt derived from Herder's theories of cultural history. The ideal goal for such renewal, as indicated in the final sentence cited here, may be defined as a universal state of *beauty*, where nature and humanity will be united once again, as at the origin of culture, within a single, all-encompassing, and thus revealed, divinity.

Nothing of all this is achieved, of course, within the novel. In the second volume Hyperion suffers categorical disillusionment with his fellow Greeks, when they resort to plunder and greed during the war, which they supposedly have entered in order to achieve the political liberation of their nation. Hyperion himself is wounded and almost dies during the battle of Tschesme (5 July 1770), which occurs at the end of the first part of the volume. Diotima subsequently dies, apparently of a broken heart, and his revolutionary comrade in arms, Alabanda, leaves Hyperion for other causes on other shores. By the time he sings his "Song of Fate" Hyperion is thus utterly alone and forsaken, in a mood which corresponds precisely to the radical split between the ideal realm of the gods and the relentlessly destructive fate of mankind expressed by the song:

> Ihr wandelt droben im Licht
> Auf weichem Boden, seelige Genien!
> Glänzende Götterlüfte
> Rühren euch leicht,
> Wie die Finger der Künstlerin
> Heilige Saiten.
>
> Schiksaallos, wie der schlafende
> Säugling, athmen die Himmlischen;
> Keusch bewahrt
> In bescheidener Knospe.
> Blühet ewig

Ihnen der Geist,
   Und die seeligen Augen
      Bliken in stiller
         Ewiger Klarheit.

Doch uns ist gegeben,
   Auf keiner Stätte zu ruhn,
      Es schwinden, es fallen
         Die leidenden Menschen
            Blindlings von einer
               Stunde zur andern,
                  Wie Wasser von Klippe
                     Zu Klippe geworfen,
                        Jahr lang ins Ungewisse hinab. (3: 143)

[You move above in the light
   Upon a soft ground, blessed geniuses!
      Radiant breezes of the gods
         Touch you lightly,
            Like the fingers of a musician
               Sacred strings.

Free of fate, like a suckling
   Babe asleep, breathe the heavenly ones;
      Chastely preserved
         In a modest bud
            The Spirit blossoms
               Eternally for them,
                  And their blessed eyes
                     Gaze eternally
                        In silent clarity.

But to us is given
   No place for rest,
      They dwindle, they fall,
         The suffering mortals,

> Blindly from one
> Hour to another,
> Like water hurled
> From cliff to cliff
> Yearlong downward into uncertainty.]

(my translation)

Subsequently, Hyperion undertakes a journey to Germany, where the behavior of the people – the author's own countrymen, who include the implied readers of the novel – elicits the famous *Scheltrede* near the end of the novel (III: 153ff.). The people to whom this diatribe is addressed include, of course, the author's own countrymen, as also presumably the implied readership of Hölderlin's novel. This polemical diatribe against the Germans established Hölderlin's fame as a poet during the nineteenth century, such as it was, more than anything else he had written. What happens to the poetics of self-consciousness through all these events in the novel?

One answer to this question may be found in the visitation of Diotima's spirit to Hyperion, which occurs in the final letter, considered briefly above.[39] We are meant to regard this experience, I believe, as a model for poetic inspiration. Such a moment of spiritual communion is grounded in a tradition which extends back through such parallel instances of inspiration as that of Dante and Petrarch by the spirits of their respective dead beloved women, Beatrice and Laura. Ultimately, Hölderlin also had in mind no doubt accounts of poetic visitations by the Muses in antiquity, notably as described by Hesiod for himself on Mount Helicon.

More specifically, we should regard the words spoken by Hyperion in response to this visitation as a model for the act of poetic creation itself. This speech of response ends the novel and, as argued, demonstrates how the cognitive distance between immediacy and reflection, between experience and memory, between intuition and comprehension, may be resolved through the creative power of poetic discourse. Particularly instructive in this regard is the image of a consumption by fire (cited earlier), with which

Hyperion as narrator introduces his response:

Und Einmal sah' ich noch in die kalte Nacht der Menschen zurük und schauert' und weinte vor Freuden, daß ich so seelig war und Worte sprach ich, wie mir dünkt, aber sie waren, wie des Feuers Rauschen, wenn es auffliegt und die Asche hinter sich läßt – (III: 159)

[And *once* more I looked back into the cold night of men, and shuddered and wept for joy that I was so blessed, and I uttered words, I think, but they were like the roar of fire when it flies up and leaves the ashes behind –] (132–33)

This image suggests that his reconstruction of these words – the text that concludes Hyperion's final letter to Bellarmin – must resemble at best the ashes left behind after the flames of his living discourse in response to Diotima's spirit have dissipated.

And what is actually stated in Hyperion's text, quoted as if verbatim from the words uttered at that moment? The passage consists of a sequence of discrete short paragraphs, eight in number, which seem to function like separate stanza units in a kind of prose poem. Following the text in German and English translation, I shall paraphrase them briefly, indicating several rhetorical features of interest:

1) "O du, so dacht' ich, mit deinen Göttern, Natur! ich hab ihn ausgeträumt, von Menschendingen den Traum und sage, nur du lebst, und was die Friedenslosen erzwungen, erdacht, es schmilzt, wie Perlen von Wachs, hinweg von deinen Flammen!

2) "Wie lang ists, daß sie dich entbehren? o wie lang ists, daß ihre Menge dich schilt, gemein nennt dich und deine Götter, die Lebendigen, die Seeligstillen!

3) "Es fallen die Menschen, wie faule Früchte von dir, o laß sie untergehn, so kehren sie zu deiner Wurzel wieder, und ich, o Baum des Lebens, daß ich wieder grüne mit dir und deine Gipfel umathme mit all deinen knospenden Zweigen! friedlich und innig, denn alle wuchsen wir aus dem goldnen Saamkorn herauf!

4) "Ihr Quellen der Erd'! ihr Blumen! und ihr Wälder und ihr Adler und du brüderliches Licht! wie alt und neu ist unsere Liebe! – Frei sind wir, gleichen uns nicht ängstig von außen; wie sollte nicht wechseln die Weise des Lebens? wir lieben den Aether doch all' und innigst im Innersten gleichen wir uns.

5) "Auch wir, auch wir sind nicht geschieden, Diotima, und die Thränen um dich verstehen es nicht. Lebendige Töne sind wir, stimmen zusammen in deinem Wohllaut, Natur! wer reißt den? wer mag die Liebenden scheiden? –

6) "O Seele! Seele! Schönheit der Welt! du unzerstörbare! du entzükende! mit deiner ewigen Jugend! du bist; was ist denn der Tod und alles Wehe der Menschen? – Ach! viel der leeren Worte haben die Wunderlichen gemacht. Geschiehet doch alles aus Lust, und endet doch alles mit Frieden.

7) "Wie der Zwist der Liebenden, sind die Dissonanzen der Welt. Versöhnung ist mitten im Streit und alles Getrennte findet sich wieder.

8) "Es scheiden und kehren im Herzen die Adern und einiges, ewiges, glühendes Leben ist Alles."

So dacht' ich. Nächstens mehr.[40]

[1] "O you," so I thought, "with your gods, Nature! I have dreamed it out, the dream of human things, and I say, Only you live, and what they who know no peace have attempted and conceived melts away from your flame like beads of wax!

2) "How long have they done without you? oh, how long have their tribe abused you, called you and your gods common, your living gods, your silent, blissful gods!

3) "Men fall from you like rotten fruits, oh, let them perish, for thus they return to your root; so may I, too, O tree of life, that I may grow green again with you and breathe your crown about me with all your budding twigs! peacefully and devoutly, for we are all sprung from the same golden seed!

4) "You springs of earth! you flowers! and you woods and you eagles and you brotherly light! how old and new is our love! – We are free, we are not narrowly alike in outward semblance; how should the mode of Life not vary? yet we love the ether, all of us, and in the inmost of our inmost selves we are alike.

5) "We too, we too, are not parted, Diotima, and tears for you understand it not. Living tones are we, we sound together in thy harmony, Nature! which who can undo? who can part lovers? –

6) "O Soul! Soul! Beauty of the World! indestructible, ravishing one! with your eternal youth! you are; what, then, is death and all the woe of men? – Ah! those strange creatures have spoken many empty words. Yet from delight all comes, and all ends in peace.

7) "Like lovers' quarrels are the dissonances of the world. Reconciliation is there, even in the midst of strife, and all things that are parted find one another again.

8) "The arteries separate and return to the heart and all is one eternal glowing life."

So I thought. More soon.]⁴¹

1) The speaker begins in a mode of intimate direct address to Nature and her gods (*du…mit deinen Göttern, Natur!*). He asserts that his dream of human affairs (*von Menschendingen den Traum*) has now been completed (*ich hab ihn ausgeträumt*). Is this perhaps an allusion to the substance of the novel as a whole, although strictly speaking *before* he has begun to write? On this basis he now asserts to Nature that she alone truly lives: *[ich] sage, nur du lebst.* Such affirmation contrasts with those who are referred to as not at peace (*die Friedenslosen*). Whatever these have induced and devised (*erzwungen, erdacht*), so asserts the speaker, it now melts away like pearls of wax (*wie Perlen von Wachs*) from Nature's flames. Would these flames be identical to those attributed to his words?

2) How long has it been, so asks the speaker, still addressing Nature, that these others (*sie*) have denied you (*dich*)? How long has it been that this mob (*Menge*) has abused and mocked you, called you common, along with your gods, who live and are blissfully silent? These questions seem to recall the radical dualism of the "Schicksalslied," as they also suggest how alienated the speaker has become from mankind as a whole.

3) In a general assertion that also echoes Hyperion's "Schicksalslied" (*Es schwinden, es fallen / Die leidenden Menschen*), human

beings are said to fall from nature like rotten fruit. "Let them go under (*untergehen*)," he exclaims, so that they return to nature's roots. Would Hyperion include the death of Diotima within such a return? The speaking self, by contrast, returning to the form of first person pronoun singular, asserts that he thus achieves new growth and ripens again (*ich grüne wieder mit dir*), addressing the tree of life (*o Baum des Lebens*). He breathes about its crown with blossoming branches, peacefully and inwardly (*friedlich und innig*), using imagery of an all-pervasive and reciprocal spirituality. "For we all grew forth," so he adds, "from the same golden seed!" Such affirmation may signify the process of rejuvenation, which had earlier been envisioned for the effect of art upon culture.

4) The next stanza consists of a series of apostrophes addressed to various living agencies in nature: "you streams of the earth, you flowers, you forests and you eagles, and you, fraternal light!" All these powers are said to share a love with the speaker, which is both old and new, as indicated by the use of the first person plural pronominal adjective (*unsere*). "We are free," he asserts in language which may also reflect the political idealism of aesthetic education: not merely in some fearful external sense (*ängstig von außen*), but inwardly in [our] inmost being (*innigst im Innern*) we are equal and alike. "Why should not," he asks of this plurality, "the ways of life (*die Weise des Lebens*) change? For we all of us love the aether." This sense of a shared existence, achieved through a general transformation and renewal, where the speaker joins these several agencies of nature in a common new life, affirms what appears to be the spiritual basis for his address to Diotima. But is it the cause of or the response to the visitation of her spirit?

5) Only now in the fifth stanza, more than halfway through the sequence, and then not once again in the entire prose poem, is the name Diotima mentioned. That name occurs through direct invocation by the speaker in a statement formulated by an emphatic first person plural pronominal subject: *auch wir,* which asserts that the lovers are not separated: *Auch wir sind nicht geschieden.* The process of death appears thus to have achieved a new and higher life in a common spirit. "The tears which mourn your loss do not

understand," he continues, "since we are [now become] living tones (*lebendige Töne*), tuned together into your harmonies (*in deinem Wohllaut*), Nature!" Given this shared condition in what appears to resemble a musical form, so the speaker continues, "who could tear that [i.e., nature's harmony?] apart? who could separate those who love (*die Liebenden*)?" The stanza concludes with a dash, indicating, I surmise, a sense of climax or cognitive reversal within a moment of sustained silence, perhaps where a degree of hermeneutical affirmation is to be achieved.

6) The next stanza appears to continue this invocation of Diotima's spirit through direct address. She is not explicitly named, however, but only described by epithet as "Soul" (*Seele*) and as "the Beauty of the World" (*Schönheit der Welt*). "You, who are indestructible and exquisite" (*du unzerstörbare! du entzükende!*), he goes on, "you, with your eternal youth, *you are* (*du bist*)!" Where else does Hölderlin use such an absolute sense of the verb "to be"? It appears to affirm an existential condition beyond all human limits, beyond all mortal time. In this sense the speaker then asks, "what is death and every woe of mankind (*alles Wehe der Menschen*)?" With an exclamation of grief (*Ach!*), separated from his preceding question by another dash, he then asserts that many empty words (*viel der leeren Worte*; in contrast to those words which are here being uttered?) have been used by "those strange creatures" (*die Wunderlichen*; i.e., human beings in general?). "Everything happens," so he concludes, "out of desire (*Lust*), yet everything ends in peace."

The final two stanzas consist of short general statements, which express what must be regarded as universal truths, free of all rhetorical delimitation without reference either to the speaker or to Diotima, neither to nature and the gods nor to the rest of mankind. The prose poem thus concludes in the manner of a gnomic wisdom, affirming whatever has been achieved by the preceding sequence. These statements thus constitute a form of poetic truth, resulting directly from the process of intuitive self-reflective response articulated by the prose poem as a whole.

7) "The dissonances of the world are like lovers' quarrels: reconciliation occurs in the midst of strife and everything separate comes together again."

8) "The arteries divide from and return to the heart, and everything is one, eternal, glowing life."

Did ever a novel end in this way? Is it even possible for devoted
readers of Hölderlin as a poet to understand what is being said here?
I submit that this passage, however challenging and powerful as
visionary utterance, remains essentially incomprehensible in itself.
Only the novel as a whole can provide an adequate context for
interpreting Hyperion's words, according to a principle of aesthetic
unity in diversity, which Hyperion himself defines through a quotation from Heraclitus that is used by Plato in his *Symposium*: "*hen
diapheron eauto* (das Eine in sich selber unterschiedne)" (III: 81).
Even the context of the novel as a whole, however, will not clarify
the motives and strategies which underlie the complex rhetorical
shifts and turns of this poetic sequence. Indeed, Hölderlin's later
poetry provides the best frame of reference for the complex dynamics of mood and tone which occur in this passage. It may be argued,
for instance, that the elegy "Menons Klagen um Diotima," first
drafted about a year after *Hyperion* was completed, constitutes a
fully realized poetic structure according to a complex poetological
principle of composition, which Hölderlin labelled *Wechsel der
Töne* – a structure for what in the prose of *Hyperion* is only the raw
material for poetry.

Hyperion's poetic utterance in this final letter of the novel thus
serves implicitly as a model for his entire project of writing, as it
also defines the motive in the novel for the recollection of his experience in narrative form. This project of reflective autobiography
only commences after this spiritual visitation with its singular poetic response has already occurred, even though that visitation by
Diotima and the poetic response of Hyperion define the ultimate
goal toward which the narrative as a whole aspires. Poetry thus
becomes an act of re-creation or repetition from a cognitive, temporal and experiential distance on the actual event. In this way as
well – like the ashes left behind after the fire of the words spoken in
response to the vision has consumed itself – the text becomes the

vehicle for a self-conscious mode of poetic thought, which the
novel seeks to communicate to its reader, symbolized by Bellarmin,
the designated recipient of Hyperion's letters. In this regard, I
would argue that Hölderlin's novel also thematizes a specific
hermeneutical challenge for the form of its narrative in general.
Admittedly, once this challenge has been recognized by a reader it
may still require an exercise in philosophical reflection to understand the implicit poetics of the novel, which strains the limits of
what such a narrative can convey.

Two specific aspects of this concluding prose poem in *Hyperion*
define the essential paradox which I would ascribe to the poetics of
self-consciousness. These aspects of the passage are also responsible, I surmise, for the disagreement outlined earlier between
Lawrence Ryan and Friedbert Aspetsberger concerning the cognitive and temporal perspective from which the narrator concludes
the novel.

First, there is the apparent contradiction between the speaker's
claim that *at that time* he spoke words without knowing consciously
what he was saying. In this regard, the image of the roaring of
flames – "wie des Feuers Rauschen" – which leave only ashes
behind offers a singularly appropriate commentary on this contradiction. The *text* of his utterance as the representation in writing of
what he then spoke, in contradistinction to the act of speaking the
words themselves, thus resembles more the ashes than the flame.
The utterance itself constitutes a spontaneous, immediate and fundamentally unselfconscious mode of discourse. Yet simultaneously,
the cognitive stance of the narrator, who quotes his own speech
verbatim within the reflective account of Diotima's visitation and
his poetic response to it, constitutes a heightened degree of self-
consciousness *for the novel,* and hence also *for Bellarmin* and *for us*
as the intended readers of the novel. Our task is thus to achieve a
self-conscious reading of this supposedly un-self-conscious text.
This is the first aspect of the novel's paradox.

The second aspect relates directly to the first, as cause to effect.
We cannot know what actually constitutes Hyperion's experience of
communion with the voice and spirit of the dead Diotima. No hint

whatsoever is provided by the text of the novel concerning even the possibility that the dead may still communicate with the living. Nor is there at any point in the entire novel any other experience remotely resembling this event. Are we to believe that either the narrator or the author of the book could expect the reader to accept this visitation as actual, real or true? We must assume that the origin of the voice is either external to the character Hyperion or internal to his own mind. On one hand, it would thus originate within nature, or else be transcendent in a theological sense, located beyond all determinations of place in some afterworld; or, on the other hand, it would have to be an illusion or a fiction, the result of a projection or externalization by the character's own inner mind, perceived by him *as if* it were speaking from above. This is the second sense of paradox which the episode conveys.

Such radical ambivalence is central, I would argue, to the role of inspiration in Romantic poetry. It may also reflect a fundamental indeterminability for Romanticism with regard to any authentic experience of the transcendent or the divine, either in the form of an epiphany or through an act of communion among spirits. Hölderlin was no doubt aware of this ambivalence when he chose to end his novel in this way. He was certainly also aware of the larger theological implications of such ambivalence, as much of his later poetry makes abundantly clear. The Christology of such hymns as "Friedensfeier" and "Patmos" could provide eloquent evidence on this point.

The poetics of self-consciousness, as argued at the outset of this essay, always includes such a sense of paradox or ambivalence. Vision and reflection are simultaneous to such poetry, and yet they remain incommensurable with each other. Intuition (*Anschauung*) and concept (*Begriff*) must somehow coincide within a verbal figure of capable imagination, which confounds all reason as it also affirms an authentic mode of being for the self-conscious mind. Nor is it possible for the language of poetry to achieve such tropes of self-conscious visionary utterance, as in the case of this concluding passage in *Hyperion,* except through an act of recollection or re-creation, repetition or re-cognition. Poetic vision and spiritual communion in Romantic poetry may thus be possible only through the hermeneutical function of verbal forms, which establish authentic modes of experience through fictional means.

No reader of *Hyperion* would wish to argue that any of its writing measures up to the subsequent achievement of Hölderlin's later poetry. This would also hold true for the prose poem of Hyperion in the final letter. Neither do we emerge from our reading of the novel with anything approaching a fully articulated theory of poetry. The poetics of this novel remains at best implicit. The model for poetry which it offers derives from the context of the narrative as a whole, particularly through the cognitive and hermeneutical resonances of retrospection established by the epistolary form and the temporal and experiential distance sustained between narrative and event. The poetics of self-consciousness in *Hyperion* is thus achieved only in and through the form of the narrative itself. Hölderlin's novel thus becomes, at least implicitly, as Wolfgang Binder argued, using a notoriously obscure abstraction from Hegel's *Science of Logic*, the working model for "a consciousness of the consciousness of consciousness" [ein Bewußtsein vom Bewußtsein des Bewußtseins].[42]

The Prelude, or The Growth of a Poet's Mind

The Prelude offers a vast range of pertinent material for a discussion of the poetics of self-consciousness. The selection of evidence must necessarily be somewhat arbitrary. Critics have often acknowledged that Wordsworth develops an implicit poetics in the course of his autobiographical epic, especially with regard to his definition of poetry as "emotions recollected in tranquility."[43] Attention has been addressed especially to the reflective role of the poet as narrator.[44] So far as I am aware, however, it has not generally been recognized that a significant development of self-consciousness also occurs in the perspective of the narrator upon his own life history as the telling of it proceeds. Here a remarkable similarity to *Hyperion* may be perceived.

The poet-narrator's self-awareness is often articulated in *The*

Prelude through the central figurative motif of the journey. This motif is applied both to the course of the poet's life and to the advance of his poem. To compose a poem is to undertake a mental journey of discovery. This journey of self-discovery in *The Prelude* only achieves clarification of its purpose and its proper path as it proceeds. Three instances of this motif may be considered here, all involving a pattern of rustication. The poet departs from the society of men in favor of the open country and the pleasures it provides. In each of these examples the *mode* of poetic travel is fundamentally different. The sequence of all three defines a developing consciousness in the narrator, though only implicit, of the dialectical process of poetic recollection.

The first example (in Book 1) is a narrative description of an actual walk – at least it is presented as such – and the poet's immediate response to that experience. The passage proceeds to describe a failure of spontaneity and the temporary loss of direction and purpose. As the result of this failure and loss the poet discovers that retrospection is the only appropriate mode of progress for his poem.

The second example (from Books 7 and 8) exhibits a conscious juxtaposition in the poet's mind of present condition and past experience, in such a way that a comparative value system is established between them. This frame of reference enables the poet to adjust and correct his mood, indeed to renew himself, through his mental ability to travel across time through memory. This passage serves as an instance of antithetical thought, as distinct from the third example, which demonstrates true dialectical thinking.

In this final example (from Book 10) the mind of the poet goes beyond the mere juxtaposition of separate temporal frames of reference to achieve a multiple and diverse perspective on experience. His mind can thus move freely both forward and backward in time from an independent vantage point, which enables him to comprehend or intuit the totality of his life. The developing path of the poet's journey thus involves much more than linear progress. His mind moves progressively toward a liberation of consciousness, a freedom of thought back and forth dialectically across the temporal range of his remembered experience.

We shall consider each of these three instances in turn.[45]

1) The very beginning of the poem presents an eloquent description of liberation and escape. The poet has left the city and now walks, "Free as a bird" (9), through the countryside. This opening passage conveys a mood of joy in response to the visitation of a breeze. The encounter elicits or inspires in the mind of the poet an awareness of that "correspondent breeze," which constitutes for Wordsworth the source of poetry.[46] His initial song is thus spontaneous and immediate, apparently without reflective distance.

The poet as narrator subsequently comments on just this quality of the event, which the opening of the poem locates as a quotation from that time:

> Thus far, O Friend! did I, not used to make
> A present joy the matter of a song,
> Pour forth that day my soul in measured strains
> That would not be forgotten, and are here
> Recorded: to the open fields I told
> A prophecy: poetic numbers came
> Spontaneously to clothe in priestly robe
> A renovated spirit singled out,
> Such hope was mine, for holy services.
> (46–54)

Coming to rest at last in "a green shady place" (62), the poet conceives the initial goal of his journey:

> . . . choice was made
> Of a known Vale, whither my feet should turn,
> Nor rest till they had reached the very door
> Of the one cottage which methought I saw.
> (71–74)

Yet this inspiration fails him, and his sense of direction is quickly lost:

> . . . the harp
> Was soon defrauded, and the banded host
> Of harmony dispersed in straggling sounds,
> And lastly utter silence!
> (96–99)

This incident, reported by the narrator from his past, may also be applied to the present purpose of his poem. The poet himself does not make this connection, nor is he yet aware at all what that purpose might be. Only later in Book 1, when he first looks back upon the journey of his life, does the present journey of his poem begin to move forward. He invokes the river Derwent, heard by him in his infancy, when it flowed past his birthplace. With a backward glance from his present perspective toward that place and time, he asks about the purpose of its call. Even then, he asserts, it gave:

> Amid the fretful dwellings of mankind
> A foretaste, a dim earnest, of the calm
> That Nature breathes among the hills and groves.
> (279-81)

The river also, here as elsewhere in the poem, symbolizes the path or journey of his life. Its sound communicates, as it flows past, the intuition of a higher power, which also guides the poet. At this point Wordsworth introduces a reflective dimension to his narrative, which quickly commences the recollection of his past life from childhood to maturity. We must assume, of course, that Wordsworth as author knew from the first what he was doing in constructing the opening of his poem in this way. The poet-narrator, however, does not yet know why his story can only advance toward its goal by first turning back to the remembrance of childhood, in order then to trace the growth of his own mind. There is a studied ignorance of ends and means to the narrative at this point, which suggests that the narrator still lacks all reflective self-consciousness.

2) By the end of Book 7 the poet has come to accept his journey through retrospection as the proper course for his poem. This is indicated when the negative effect of describing his residence in

London is corrected through the redemptive power of memory. Book 8 purposefully looks back to his earlier life in the country for its retrospective lesson, as indicated in its title: "Love of Nature Leading to Love of Mankind." In this instance of a backward turn to the narrative, however, the narrator is very much aware of his purpose. The poem can only achieve a comprehensive understanding of his life and growth through such reflective and recollective turns and returns:

> . . . though the picture weary out the eye,
> By nature an unmanageable sight,
> It is not wholly so to him who looks
> In steadiness, who hath among least things
> An under-sense of greatest; sees the parts
> As parts, but with a feeling of the whole.
> (731–36)

This "under-sense" of the whole is referred by the narrator to his condition in London at that time. He was only aware of what he valued in life through contrast with the place in which he dwelled: "The Spirit of Nature was upon me there" (766). This statement is formulated, however, as a general truth, which applies equally to the perspective of his narrative. The poet's retrospective eye affirms a wisdom achieved through the act of retrospection itself. The final lines of Book 7 are spoken in the narrative past tense, but they also contain a purposeful resonance with the narrator's developing state of self-consciousness as he works his way through the poem.

> The soul of Beauty and enduring Life
> Vouchsafed her inspiration, and diffused,
> Through meagre lines and colours, and the press
> Of self-destroying, transitory things,
> Composure, and ennobling Harmony.
> (767–71)

This quality of "composure" and intellectual "harmony" defines the reflective state of mind, which has now been achieved by the poet-narrator.

3) Such wisdom is ultimately affirmed as an active power for the poet, based upon a sense of place (if not explicitly of self). This power is affirmed when the poet reports his response to the news of Robespierre's death at the end of Book 10. Imagery of the journey pervades the passage. The poet's recovery of joy occurs as much from an awareness of his place upon that journey, as from the news of the event itself:

> ... beneath a genial sun,
> With distant prospect among gleams of sky
> And clouds, and intermingling mountain tops,
> In one inseparable glory clad,
> Creatures of one ethereal substance met
> In consistory, like a diadem
> Or crown of burning seraphs as they sit
> In the empyrean.
> (516–23)

The poet is walking along the sea in a place associated with his childhood, as indicated by the sight of the grave of his former teacher, William Taylor (530 ff.). Here Wordsworth meets some travellers with the news from France. His initial response is jubilation, expressed in a speech which prophesies a golden time to come. The poet-narrator then quotes verbatim the words he uttered at the time, indicated by his use of quotation marks (lines 578–89). He then interrupts himself, as indicated by the use of a dash (after line 589), so as to shift his perspective back to the recollection of the event:

> "Come now, ye golden times,"
> Said I forth-pouring on those open sands
> A hymn of triumph: "as the morning comes
> From out the bosom of the night, come ye:
> Thus far our trust is verified; behold!
> They who with clumsy desperation brought
> A river of Blood, and preached that nothing else
> Could cleanse the Augean stable, by the might

Of their own helper have been swept away;
Their madness stands declared and visible;
Elsewhere will safety now be sought, and earth
March firmly towards righteousness and peace."
(578–89)

He then concludes the Book by juxtaposing the account of that experience with the memory of much earlier experiences which he enjoyed at that same place in childhood:

when – ...a joyous band
Of schoolboys hastening to their distant home
Along the margin of the moonlight sea –
We beat with thundering hoofs the level sand.
(597–603)

The impetus of Wordsworth's "hymn of triumph" (580) in response to the news of Robespierre's death was prophetic, looking forward to the happy era which he then believed would result from it. The perspective of his narrative, however, is directed backward into the past, and the conclusion thus joins the joy of an even earlier time from the poet's childhood with the joy anticipated for the future in response to the event he is remembering. Time present, time future and time past are thus united by the narrative according to the conscious design of the narrator. What we are meant to perceive here is a comprehensive awareness of relationship and coherence, which only the power of self-consciousness can achieve. The path of retrospection, which began for Wordsworth as an apparent accident in Book 1 and developed into an awareness of comparative value in Book 7, has here become a conscious mode of thought which controls the structure of the narrative itself. The juxtaposition of temporal frames of reference indicates a sense of totality with regard to the entire range of experience being recalled. This range of temporal references enables the poet-narrator to join the parts of his narrative together into a comprehensive whole within the coherent perspective of his own developing self-consciousness.

It might well be argued that the philosophical implications of this narrative structure in *The Prelude* are far less explicit for a discussion of the poetics of self-consciousness than was the case for Hölderlin's *Hyperion*. This would correspond to a general difference between English and German Romantic poetry, as has been emphasized by Geoffrey Hartman.[47] This contrast also reflects a basic difference between the two poets themselves. That Wordsworth nonetheless intended such a development in his own self-consciousness as narrator to be perceived with regard to his growth as poet may be argued by comparing two passages addressed to Coleridge, taken from the beginning and the end of *The Prelude* respectively. The first passage occurs at the end of Book 1, describing the poet's expectation that his narrative will affirm the value of self-recollection for his subsequent poetic career:

Meanwhile, my hope has been, that I might fetch
Invigorating thoughts from former years;
Might fix the wavering balance of my mind,
And haply meet reproaches too, whose power
May spur me on, in manhood now mature,
To honourable toil.
(620–25)

At this point the poet speaks prospectively, looking ahead to the completion of his poem and the meaning it will have for future labors. Near the end of Book 14 a corresponding passage occurs, where the poet looks back over his completed poem, recalling those earlier expectations, which he feels have now been achieved:

And now, O Friend! this history is brought
To its appointed close: the discipline
And consummation of a Poet's mind,
In everything that stood most prominent,
Have faithfully been pictured; we have reached
The time (our guiding object from the first)
When we may, not presumptuously, I hope,
Suppose my powers so far confirmed, and such

My knowledge, as to make me capable
Of building up a Work that shall endure.
(302–11)

Such security and confidence in the poet's professed sense of himself, though based on the authority of his poem, may somewhat strain credibility for his readers. Much of the latter part of Book 14 sustains a similar sense of fulfillment. The poet also includes dimensions of moral and psychological affirmation along with his claim for poetic success. Wordsworth celebrates a state of happiness and repose enjoyed in the intimacy of his spiritual home. He expects to share this ideal of community with his friend Coleridge and with his sister Dorothy. Appropriate mention is also made of his wife, who is to be included, and his benefactor Calvert and his brother John, both recently dead, who are thus beyond reach. Wordsworth here appears to have lost sight of a fundamental paradox which accompanies self-consciousness. Such self-knowledge inevitably isolates the mind from any communal happiness and repose, except as a poetic or utopian dream.

"SPOTS OF TIME"

The dialectical tension which is necessary for a poetics of self-consciousness cannot be so easily resolved as Book 14 implies. Sufficient proof that this holds true is provided by Wordsworth himself. His poem elsewhere offers persuasive evidence against happiness and repose in those climactic moments of his own narrative which he labelled "spots of time." These moments from his past retain for him "a renovating virtue" from the retrospective distance of his narrative :

A virtue, by which pleasure is enhanced,
That penetrates, enables us to mount,
When high, more high, and lifts us up when fallen.
(12.216-18)

Critics have correctly considered the description of these incidents to constitute the true poetic greatness of *The Prelude.* A brief review

of three such passages – the experiences recalled from early youth
in Book 1, the crossing of the Simplon Pass in Book 6, and the
ascent of Mount Snowdon in Book 14 – will affirm their importance for the dialectic of consciousness and imagination, described
earlier as essential for the poetics of self-consciousness.

1) In the sequence of incidents, which fills much of the latter half
of Book 1 (305–570), the narrative is presented consistently in the
past tense. In each instance the poet recalls from childhood memo-
ries a manifestation of natural, if not supernatural, power, represented as it was perceived and experienced at the time it occurred.
Qualifications are introduced to the narrative, however, which differentiate the perspective of the narrator from that of his childhood
through terms of appearance or similitude. The poet thus implicitly
acknowledges that his experience of these powers involved a measure of assumption or projection on his part at the time.

In the bird-snaring episode, for instance, the relation of the
child to the natural setting is qualified repeatedly by the term
seemed:

> ... I was alone,
> And *seemed* to be a trouble to the peace
> That dwelt among them [the moon and stars].
> (315-17; my emphasis)

> [I was] almost (*so it seemed*)
> Suspended by the blast that blew amain,
> Shouldering the naked crag, ...
> (333-35; my emphasis)

> ... the sky *seemed* not a sky
> Of earth –
> (338–39; my emphasis)

More striking is the qualification introduced to the description
of the boat-stealing, where the huge cliff uprears its head "*as if* with

voluntary power instinct" (379; my emphasis). The description of the apparition as it continues to emerge from behind the hill further sustains this sense of appearance:

> . . . and still,
> *For so it seemed,* with purpose of its own
> And measured motion like a living thing,
> Strode after me.
> (382–85; my emphasis)

The assumptions of the fearful child are apparently no longer shared by the narrator; yet the experience is reported precisely because of those assumptions.

Similarly, in the skating episode, where the descriptive narrative is otherwise presented as a matter of fact, a sense of appearance is introduced at the end. The effect when the skater suddenly stops short in his glide includes a sense of the world in motion:

> . . . yet still the solitary cliffs
> Wheeled by me – *even as if* the earth had rolled
> With visible motion her diurnal round!
> (458–60; my emphasis)

Such attributions of semblance, finally, are also ascribed to the child's experience of a general relationship to nature. We sense in the poet-narrator a continuing sympathy, yet clearly he no longer shares the same perspective:

> . . . even then I felt
> Gleams like the flashing of a shield; – the earth
> And common face of Nature spake to me
> Rememberable things; sometimes, 'tis true,
> By chance collisions and quaint accidents
> (Like those ill-sorted unions, work supposed
> Of evil-minded fairies), . . .
> (585–91)

The value of such remembered experiences from childhood is measured for the mature poet in the act of remembrance itself.

The predominant mode of narration for these episodes remains literal and factual, as if it were a strictly historical account. Wherever the voice of the narrator intrudes in its present adult perspective, it does so in order to affirm the truth of those assumed powers. This may be perceived, for instance, in the rhetorical force of the poet's question to the river Derwent concerning its supposed purpose for the child, when it called to him as it flowed past: "Was it for this ...? For this, didst thou, / O Derwent! ..." (269, 274–75). The attribution of purpose to nature in the boat-stealing episode is similar in its affirmation: "... and so she [Nature] dealt with me. / One evening (surely I was led by her) ..." (371–72; 1805).

Far more important for the rhetorical structure of the narrative throughout this sequence are various general statements by the narrator in the present tense, which provide transitions between the separate accounts of the incidents. The narrator invariably affirms the sense of relationship which he felt – or remembers having felt – at the time of his experience. This is true especially of the passage between the bird-snaring and the boat-stealing episodes:

> Dust as we are, the immortal spirit grows
> Like harmony in music; there is a dark
> Inscrutable workmanship that reconciles
> Discordant elements, makes them cling together
> In one society. How strange that all
> The terrors, pains, and early miseries,
> Regrets, vexations, lassitudes interfused
> Within my mind, should e'er have borne a part,
> And that a needful part, in making up
> The calm existence that is mine when I
> Am worthy of myself! Praise to the end!
> Thanks to the means which Nature deigned to employ;
> Whether her fearless visitings, or those
> That came with soft alarm, like hurtless light
> Opening the peaceful clouds; or she may use
> Severer interventions, ministry
> More palpable, as best might suit her aim.
> (340–56)

He emphasizes the volition or purposiveness, which he attributed to Nature, and still affirms with a sense of gratitude, communicated to him through these experiences. Even more forceful is his direct invocation of these powers in the passages which follow the boat-stealing and the skating episodes, respectively:

Wisdom and Spirit of the universe!
Thou Soul that art the eternity of thought,
That givest to forms and images a breath
And everlasting motion . . .
(401–4)

Ye Presences of Nature in the sky
And on the earth! Ye Visions of the hills!
And Souls of lonely places! can I think
A vulgar hope was yours . . .
(464–67)

The narrative account of these incidents maintains a degree of ambiguity, which allows us to question the objective truth of these attributed powers, at the same time that the narrator affirms their continuing reality *for him.* The value of these experiences for his subsequent career as poet still depends upon that sense of purpose in Nature, felt to be true at the time and now remembered by the narrator in accord with that feeling. Whether or not Wordsworth so intended it, this ambiguity corresponds to the paradox of self-consciousness with regard to the source or origin of its intellectual intuition.

2) The most famous reflective interruption in *The Prelude* occurs in Book 6. After describing his disappointed expectations for an experience of the sublime when crossing the Simplon Pass, Wordsworth invokes the imagination, "that awful Power" (594), which he holds to be responsible for such expectations. Hartman has argued persuasively that this interruption, made by the narrator from the present perspective of his narrative, constitutes a radical correction of that earlier, more conventional notion of the sublime, which was disappointed when the poet crossed the Alps. It would also correct,

presumably, the earlier attribution of an objective power to nature, which we just considered with regard to the incidents of Book 1. Hartman offers this passage in Book 6 to demonstrate conclusively that Wordsworth ultimately came to regard the poetic imagination as an autonomous power, the basis for his poetic vision.[48]

For the poet-narrator of *The Prelude* this conviction emerges, apparently, by surprise:

> Imagination! lifting up itself
> Before the eye and progress of my Song
> Like an unfather'd vapour: here that Power,
> In all the might of its endowments, came
> Athwart me; . . .
> (525–29; 1805)

The effect of this seizure, as Hartman argues, is a liberation of the poetic mind from all natural conditions and an affirmation of the infinite and eternal in and for itself:

> Our destiny, our being's heart and home,
> Is with infinitude, and only there;
> With hope it is, hope that can never die,
> Effort, and expectation, and desire,
> And something evermore about to be.
> (604–8)

Problematic to me, however, is the relation of this interruption by the narrator to the descriptive passage which follows it, presenting his descent on the far side of the pass. This passage is justly famous as a poetic tour de force, representing the life of nature at complete odds within itself. In his essay on "The Intentional Structure of the Romantic Image," Paul de Man pointed out how this language of oxymoron and contradiction appears to be a purposeful rejection by the poet of the earthly setting it describes, in favor of a higher realm, another nature beyond the earth:[49]

> ... The immeasurable height
> Of woods decaying, never to be decayed,

The stationary blasts of waterfalls,
And in the narrow rent at every turn
Winds thwarting winds, bewildered and forlorn,
The torrents shooting from the clear blue sky,
The rocks that muttered close upon our ears,
Black drizzling crags that spake by the wayside
As if a voice were in them, the sick sight
And giddy prospect of the raving stream,
The unfettered clouds and region of the Heavens,
Tumult and peace, the darkness and the light –
(624–35)

It is important to observe that Wordsworth here maintains the temporal reference of his narrative to that experience of descent in the past. The affirmation of apocalypse and eternity, which proceeds from this description of nature, thus remains an intuition attributed to his response at the time. Even the figure of semblance, which was characteristic of the narrative in Book 1, is here reintroduced to define his sense of a higher power.

[These]
Were all like workings of one mind, the features
Of the same face, blossoms upon one tree;
Characters of the great Apocalypse,
The types and symbols of Eternity,
Of first, and last, and midst, and without end.
(636–40; my emphasis)

Hartman implies that the narrator as he writes this account of the crossing of the Alps, interrupting himself in the midst of it to comment from his present perspective, corrects the assumptions that he made in immediate response to the experience.[50] The description of the imagination would thus be interpreted as a contradiction of his sense of apocalypse and eternity in response to the landscape of his descent. My own view would be that this discrepancy of perspective does not define alternatives, especially in the juxtaposition of "infinitude" (605) and "Eternity" (639). A dialectical correspondence is established through the disjunction of the narrative between the two separate temporal frames of reference and the two apparently contradictory attitudes of the poet.

This dialectic of vision and reflection, intuition and concept, corresponds precisely to the dynamics of self-consciousness, represented in the language of poetic recollection. In this regard the ambiguity of time frame and perspective in this passage corresponds precisely to the words of Hyperion in Hölderlin's novel in response to his final vision of Diotima, which was discussed earlier. Just what the implications of this dialectic may be for the poet-narrator's developing comprehension of himself through the composition of his poem becomes apparent in the final book of *The Prelude*, when the ascent of Mount Snowdon is described.

3) The Snowdon passage at the beginning of Book 14 is generally regarded as the visionary climax of the entire *Prelude*. M. H. Abrams has described this episode as a theodicy of the mind in nature, which affirms what he takes to be the poem's ultimate humanism, its "comprehensive myth of mind," achieved by Wordsworth through that peculiar generic mode which Abrams labels "crisis-autobiography."[51] I shall survey the passage briefly with regard to rhetorical distinctions already applied to earlier passages discussed above.

The narrative mode of recollection in the past tense dominates consistently from the start of the account (line 11 on). The initial vision of open landscape with the moon shining upon a sea of mist is located entirely within that experience:

> For instantly a light upon the turf
> Fell like a flash, and lo! as I looked up,
> The Moon hung naked in a firmament
> Of azure without cloud, and at my feet
> Rested a silent sea of hoary mist.
> (38–42)

The rift, or "fracture in the vapour" (56; 1805), through which the poet heard the sound of waters below, "roaring with one voice" (60),

was called in the earlier version the place where "Nature lodg'd /
The Soul, the Imagination of the whole" (64–65; 1805). The revised
text emphasizes more emphatically that subsequent reflection "in
calm thought" (65) – which occurred at the time, in immediate
response to the vision – led him to regard this as an image or
emblem of the mind:

> . . . it appeared to me the type
> Of a majestic intellect, its acts
> And its possessions, what it has and craves,
> What in itself it is, and would become.
> There I beheld the emblem of a mind
> That feeds upon infinity, that broods
> Over the dark abyss, intent to hear
> Its voices issuing forth to silent light
> In one continuous stream; a mind sustained
> By recognitions of transcendent power,
> In sense conducting to ideal form,
> In soul of more than mortal privilege.
> (66–77)

This statement is offered as an account of the poet's meditation
at the time. We may wish to question, however, whether this poetic
representation of the experience is not also filtered through the
medium of remembrance, in such a way that the poet-narrator has
in effect re-created the event in accord with what he remembers of
it in his present state of self-consciousness. In this regard Wordsworth's description of his vision on Mount Snowdon would correspond precisely to Hyperion's account of his final vision of Diotima
in Hölderlin's *Hyperion.*

Specific temporal reference is presently abandoned, however, in
order to describe in general terms the relation of this power
embodied or manifested in nature to those kindred spirits, those
"higher minds," who are able to respond to this power and to comprehend it:

> . . . The power, which all
> Acknowledge when thus moved, which Nature thus
> To bodily sense exhibits, is the express
> Resemblance of that glorious faculty
> That higher minds bear with them as their own.
> (86–90)

These "higher minds" reside presumably with the poets in their self-reflective wisdom, and that "glorious faculty" must be none other than the imagination, celebrated in Book 6 as an autonomous power and here affirmed through a vision of its objective manifestation. We may even surmise an implicit allusion to the hermeneutic program of *The Prelude* itself and the response intended from its reader.

Wordsworth also emphasizes the capacity of those possessed of this faculty of imagination to respond to such a vision through a creative act of recollection:

> This is the very spirit in which they deal
> With the whole compass of the universe:
> They from their native selves can send abroad
> Kindred mutations; for themselves create
> A like existence; and, whene'er it dawns
> Created for them, catch it, or are caught
> By its inevitable mastery,
> Like angels stopped upon the wing by sound
> Of harmony from Heaven's remotest spheres.
> (91–99)

These "kindred mutations" are the products of poetic re-creation. They are the poems produced by the self-conscious imagination. Just such a creative response as is here described was also at work in the creative act which produced the poet's account of his experience on Mount Snowdon. The achieved expression of his reflective response to that vision constitutes the ultimate fulfillment of his purpose in composing this autobiographical poem.

The poetic imagination is represented by Wordsworth as fundamentally ambiguous in its influence. Particularly felicitous in this regard is the juxtaposition of active and passive verb forms in the passage just quoted: the poets "catch it, or are caught by it" (96). The imagination is a reciprocal power, manifesting itself both externally through nature and internally to the responding self. In this reciprocity it is truly transcendent, infinite and eternal (recalling the description presented in Book 6), providing

> . . . fit converse with the spiritual world,
> And with the generations of mankind
> Spread over time, past, present, and to come,
> Age after age, till Time shall be no more.
> (108–11)

More than a theoretical doctrine put into verse is at work here, more than the celebration of an idea in the language of the emotions. A precise image of completion and fulfillment is thus achieved for the poetic project which motivated *The Prelude* from the outset. Beginning with the poet's spontaneous response to the visitation of the breeze in Book 1 and extending through the creative recollection of his entire spiritual growth as poet until this final moment of achieved self-comprehension in the account of his ascent of Mount Snowdon in Book 14, *The Prelude* constitutes an all-encompassing poetics of self-consciousness for the comprehending mind.

Most important here is the fundamental ambiguity between external and internal sources for this creative power, which includes the poetic identification between the vision of that power as experienced by the poet and its verbal representation within the poem. The temporal distinction between narrative event, recollected from past experience, and the act of narration, with its reflective awareness of the experiencing self in its achieved self-consciousness, is here overcome to such a degree that the response of the poet at the time may be considered identical to the expression of it in the present perspective of the narrative. This corresponds exactly to the fusion of perspectives which I argued to take place in the final letter of Hölderlin's *Hyperion*. The dialectical tension between vision and reflection is not permanently resolved, not even for *The Prelude,* as indicated above all by the moralistic and psychological excess of Wordsworth's final claims in the concluding section of Book 14. Yet a moment of ultimate affirmation, corresponding precisely to the German notion of "intellectual intuition," is here achieved by Wordsworth in a manner which remained unsurpassed in the poetry of English Romanticism.

The Poetics of Self-Consciousness

Comparative study of the poetics of self-consciousness in *Hyperion* and *The Prelude* demonstrates fundamental similarities of concern between the two poets. Given the influence of contemporary idealist philosophy on their respective thought, which is direct and all-pervasive in Hölderlin's case, though only indirect and mediated through Coleridge for Wordsworth, this similarity also has historical significance for the development of poetry during the Romantic era. Yet the comparison itself remains somewhat unbalanced and could all too easily ignore equally fundamental differences in temper and attitude between the two poets. One obvious difficulty for such a comparative study is the contrary position of each work in the respective careers of the poets.

The Prelude is Wordsworth's crowning achievement, as most modern critics would agree, his poetic masterpiece, whether or not Wordsworth himself was ever fully aware of this. His autobiographical epic, despite its great length and complexity, also constitutes the most comprehensive and systematic instance of that kind of programmatic, conversation poem that M. H. Abrams has called the "greater Romantic lyric."[52] In a sense the epic scope of the poem, competing intentionally with *Paradise Lost* in the canon of English literature, results from a sustained externalization of the inner life of the mind in a manner essentially identical with the practice of the Romantic ode. As first developed by Coleridge in such conversation poems as "The Aeolian Harp," "This Lime-tree Bower my Prison," and "Frost at Midnight," and subsequently applied by Wordsworth to his own work, with an acknowledged debt to

Coleridge, in such a poem as "Lines Composed a Few Miles above Tintern Abbey," this genre achieved its programmatic fulfillment during the early years of the nineteenth century in Wordsworth's "Ode: Intimations of Immortality" and Coleridge's "Dejection: An Ode." *The Prelude* emerged from this complex evolution in the lyric as an almost unique form of subjective epic in the conversational mode. Within the history of English Romantic poetry in general *The Prelude* finds its proper place as the crowning achievement of both the era and its leading poet.

Hyperion, by contrast, was Hölderlin's apprentice work, the tentative exercise of a young writer just discovering his own poetic idiom and testing his personal vision against the norms of public discourse that prevailed in Germany at the time. His novel was first conceived while the poet was still a student at the Seminary in Tübingen and was completed about five years later, well before any of his mature poems were composed.[53] Much of what Hölderlin subsequently expressed in poetry may already be perceived in embryonic form within the novel, as has often been acknowledged. But Hölderlin's importance for European literature nonetheless derives far more from his odes, elegies and hymns than from his epistolary novel. There is a distinct programmatic quality to *Hyperion,* as I have argued, which is not without an appropriate parallel in Wordsworth's epic poem. The fulfillment of Hölderlin's poetic destiny, however – his mature song, as he himself emphasized in the short ode "An die Parzen"[54] – still lay ahead of him, and only in these later poems would the program of the novel be completed.

To identify the hero-narrator Hyperion with the poet whom Hölderlin himself later became is problematic in many ways, not only because fiction and biography become confused. Yet we may still agree with Lawrence Ryan in his claim, cited above, that Hyperion emerges from his autobiographical narrative on the threshold of that career in poetry which his author was about to achieve.[55] For the sake of balance this comparative study of the poetics of self-consciousness in Wordsworth and Hölderlin should thus also consider the later poems of the German poet, but such a study would require a separate monograph in itself.

A further complication for such comparison would be the fact that Hölderlin himself also developed a very intricate and abstruse theory of poetic structure based in large part on the philosophical theory of self-consciousness, specifically in response to the teachings of Fichte. Nor did Hölderlin fail to test his theory of "tonal modulation" (*Wechsel der Töne*) in his poetic practice, as the work of Ryan, among others, has demonstrated authoritatively.[56] Wordsworth, by contrast, was far less suited by temperament and intellect to systematic theorizing, perhaps to the benefit of his poetry. He participated informally in the development of a theoretical poetics through the work of his friend Coleridge, and he assimilated that theory to his poetic practice more implicitly and intuitively than was the case with Hölderlin. He also drafted several programmatic statements about poetry in the prefaces he published with the collections of his poems, starting with the second edition of *Lyrical Ballads* in 1800. But these prefaces, however important, do not constitute a coherent poetics that can measure up to Wordsworth's achievement as a poet.

It would be inappropriate in the present context to attempt even a brief and superficial survey of Hölderlin's theory of poetic structure. His concept of modulating tones, probably derived in part from contemporary theories of music, depends upon the dialectical interaction of those verbal components in a poem that articulate emotive and existential attitudes of mind, various kinds of feeling, and attitudes toward the world. Basic genres of poetry – epic, tragic and lyric – are also constituted, so Hölderlin maintained, by such experiential modes, which he labelled, as he did the tones themselves, according to a tripartite developmental model of the self: the naive, the heroic and the ideal stages of thought. The norm of intellectual intuition, which defines the climax or high-point of the poem, is defined as a moment of silence in the sequences of discourse. In terms which derive equally from musical theory and from philosophical speculation this climactic moment is said to occur as a gap or caesura in the poetic rhythm of thought, within which the totality of the poem is felt and understood. This

sequence of dialectically alternating tones within the verbal structure of the poem also establishes, so Hölderlin argued, a twofold
cycle of reflectivity, through which the self-consciousness of the
poem is realized as a repetition or recollection of thought.

All these ideas, outlined in the important though extremely
complex essay-fragment "Über die Verfahrungsweise des poetischen
Geistes,"[57] deserve more consideration within the European context
of Romanticism than they have yet received. Striking affinities of
dialectical structure might be demonstrated, for instance, in several
media of thought and in the praxis of several art forms, ranging
from the philosophical arguments of Hegel to the orchestral com-
positions of Beethoven. Criticism has as yet been disinclined to
attempt a comparative project of such scope and complexity.

Particularly challenging, in the light of the argument developed
in this essay concerning the poetics of self-consciousness, would be
a detailed analysis of Hölderlin's great elegy "Menons Klagen um
Diotima." This poem originated, as I suggested earlier, from the
scene of conflict between language and vision which is articulated
in the concluding letter of *Hyperion*. I would argue that the elegy
was initially conceived *not* from an autobiographical concern (as
usually argued), following Hölderlin's traumatic separation from
Suzette Gontard in Frankfurt, but as a conscious reworking of the
final speech of the novel. The poem dramatizes as a sustained
monologue of the self the encounter between Hyperion – now
renamed Menon – and the spirit of the dead Diotima. The language
of the poem in its tonal sequence articulates a self-reflective process
whereby tragic suffering and loss is transformed into an ultimate
affirmation and a joyful prophetic promise for a future life. This
sequence through a twofold cycle of reflection corresponds precisely
to Hölderlin's theory of tonal modulation. The developmental form
of self-consciousness, which unfolds through the language of the
poem, recapitulates in complex and as yet unrecognized ways the
self-reflective role of Hyperion as narrator of his life story in the
novel, struggling to salvage the ruins of a wrecked existence
through the re-creative poetic act of remembrance.

The struggle of the mind to recover in thought what has been irretrievably lost through experience in the world is the central pre-occupation of Hölderlin's later poetic work. Poets, he tells us in the elegy "Brod und Wein," are like priests of the Winegod, travelling as solitary pilgrims from country to country in the cultural darkness, trying to keep alive the memory of an absent God.[58] Like St. John the Divine on the island of Patmos, composing his vision of Revelation, with whom the poet identifies himself in his great hymn on that subject, or like a medieval monk in his cell, meditating on Holy Scripture, the poet seeks to reconstruct, interpret and sustain a living relationship through language with a transcendent source of the spirit, which has departed from the realm of human existence.[59]

Nothing comparable to such philosophical and theological endeavor may be found in Wordsworth's later poetry, particularly in those endless cycles of occasional poems, written from the contentment of his retirement within the rural life of Grasmere, a contentment that the poet celebrates and anticipates at the end of *The Prelude*. Hölderlin's own retirement at about the same time resulted, by contrast, from a complete and irreversible mental breakdown. In this regard the German poet stands in pathetic contrast to the Englishman. The final phase of Hölderlin's poetic work consists of short rhymed lyrics, which he composed for visitors during the several decades spent in his tower over the river Neckar in Tübingen. These benign and seemingly mindless ditties document the collapse and failure of all self-consciousness. The passivity of thought expressed in these poems extends far beyond the tedium of Wordsworth's retirement poems. Yet prior to his final breakdown Hölderlin composed a series of hymnic drafts and fragments, where moments of vision and illumination flash like the lightning of storms in the night. These texts, which have only recently begun to receive serious attention, extend the limits of self-consciousness beyond thought and beyond all verbal form in a manner and to a degree that remains without parallel in European literature.

Late Coleridge and the Poetics of Despair

The basic paradox of self-consciousness in poetry was clearly for-mulated by I. A. Richards nearly sixty years ago in his book *Coleridge on Imagination.* He outlines two alternative doctrines with reference to the source of poetic vision. His formulation may still serve as introduction to a Romantic poetics.[60] According to one view, which might be called *realist,* "the mind of the poet at mo-ments, penetrating 'the film of familiarity and selfish solicitude,' gains an insight into reality, reads Nature as a symbol of something behind or within Nature not ordinarily perceived." The opposite view, which would be *idealist,* claims that "the mind of the poet creates a Nature into which his own feelings, his aspirations and apprehensions, are projected."

Traditionally, Fichte has been associated with the latter position, especially with regard to his concept of the Absolute Self. Recent studies – notably the essay by Dieter Henrich cited at the outset – suggest that the *Wissenschaftslehre* was never intended to be so restrictive or exclusive in this idealist sense. The poetry of Words-worth and Hölderlin, by contrast, was traditionally associated by critics with the realist perspective, though never with reference to the challenge of self-consciousness. An all-encompassing presence of nature in their poetry was also associated both with pantheism, through the influence of Spinoza, and with primitivism, through the influence of Rousseau. For more than a century criticism tend-ed to regard Wordsworth and Hölderlin as poets of nature. Here also recent arguments have demonstrated that the position of both poets is not so one-sided. Studies of Wordsworth by Hartman and de Man, among others, might now persuade a reader to relocate the poet in the opposite camp. This shift of perspective derives above all from arguments for the autonomy of the poetic imagination in his poetry. Philosophical criticism of Hölderlin, correspondingly, has demonstrated with increasingly persuasive arguments that the earlier view of the poet as a devout celebrant of a mystical aether must be revised due to the crucial role played by Hölderlin in the development of idealist philosophy between Fichte and Hegel.

My own argument in this essay has tried to delineate above all a fundamental ambiguity between these realist and idealist alternatives in the poetic process of "soul-making" for both poets. The poetic construction of the self through the recollective presentation of its dialectical encounters with the world involves at one and the same time both the projection of the mind upon the world and an insight or intuition into the reality of the world. The former perspective would regard the poetic construct of self-consciousness to be a kind of *fiction*, the autonomous creation of the subjective imagination; while the latter would locate the *truth* of self-consciousness within some higher dispensation or revelation derived from an absolute or transcendent source.

That both these judgments may be equally valid for Coleridge was recognized by Richards in his book on the imagination several decades before the problem was addressed by other scholars of English Romanticism. He cites, for instance, Coleridge's image of the Eolian Harp (in the poem of that title) as an instance of such ambiguity.[61] Wordsworth's notion of a "correspondent breeze" in the mind of the poet, which responds to the visitation of an actual breeze in nature (as described at the beginning of *The Prelude*), provides another example of this productive ambiguity. M. H. Abrams later traced the implications of this image in a seminal essay which uses the image as its title.[62] Richards also acknowledges a need, even in the poets themselves, to give preference to one or the other of these alternative views. This need, I would argue, is also central to the poetics of self-consciousness. The mind cannot comfortably tolerate such paradox. But "it is the privilege of poetry," so Richards concludes, "to preserve us from mistaking our notions either for things or for ourselves. Poetry is the completest mode of utterance."[63]

As stated earlier (at the end of the first section), Romantic poetry always strives to resolve the dialectical tension between vision and reflection, or intuition *(Anschauung)* and concept *(Begriff)*, into a comprehensive existential image of humanity. The attempt to achieve such a comprehensive resolution, as a moment of truth or a spot of time, or as an intellectual intuition, defines both the triumph and the limitation of a poetics of self-consciousness. These moments of reconciliation in language can be no more than a semblance or a simile of the thing itself. The climactic visions and revelations of self-reflection in Romanticism function only as poetic fictions or figures of a capable imagination. In the poetry of both Wordsworth and Hölderlin, as demonstrated above, such moments of visionary climax fulfill splendidly by intention and design the exact conditions of such absolute reconciliation. Yet these moments do not in truth resolve the central paradox of self-consciousness. The all-pervasive dialectical tension within the language of poetry between vision and reflection can at best be only suspended within a momentary feeling or transitory intuition, communicated by the poem to its readers through specific self-conscious strategies of hermeneutical sympathy or resonances of reciprocal interrelationships. These are perceived as moments of silence beyond the limits of language, which – as Hölderlin argued in his theoretical essays – function like the gaps or caesurae in the rhythms of thought (*Rhythmus der Vorstellungen*), where the mind responds through an act of reciprocated re-cognition.[64] Since the reality of poetic experience is necessarily conditioned and defined by language, these moments of intellectual intuition beyond the limits of language can only be achieved within the realm of aesthetic feeling as events constituted by the mythical or poetic imagination.

The successful communication of such visionary experience constitutes both the triumph and the failure of Romanticism. The ultimate affirmations of art also define its necessary limits. Contrary to the programmatic claims of aesthetic and cultural theories, as in the case of Schiller's *Letters on the Aesthetic Education of Man*, art failed to achieve any corresponding transformation of life. The poetic celebrations of festival feeling, as Hölderlin put it, where "art celebrates mythically the festivals of life,"[65] could not claim to fulfill the programs of an aesthetic education, except within the privileged domain of thought or idea. The visions of poetry always look elsewhere for their reality, toward a transcendent realm, located either in the remote past through memory and recollection as a time lost or in an indeterminate future through prophetic anticipation and promise as a time still to come. The event itself is not ever, nor can it be, here and now.

The impulse toward apocalypse in Romantic poetry thus ends invariably in disillusionment and even despair. Hölderlin's collapse into madness and Wordsworth's long decades of tedium in retirement bear eloquent witness to such failure. Abundant instances from other Romantic poets and artists come also readily to mind. When in the history of human thought and culture have such apocalyptic expectations led to such categorical collapse and despair? Coleridge's late poems, for instance, not often regarded as a major achievement in the period, provide a characteristic and hauntingly eloquent instance. Brief consideration of two such poems will serve to conclude this essay on the poetics of self-consciousness.

Coleridge's poem "Limbo" (1817) evokes a realm of poetic vision, where souls like ghosts dwell in a strange state of purgatorial dread, awaiting ultimate annihilation:[66]

> The sole true Something – This! In Limbo's Den
> It frightens Ghosts, as here Ghosts frighten men.
> Thence cross'd unseiz'd – and shall some fated hour
> Be pulveris'd by Demogorgon's power,
> And given as poison to annihilate souls –
> Even now it shrinks them – they shrink in as Moles
> (Nature's mute monks, live mandrakes of the ground)
> Creep back from Light – then listen for its sound; –
> See but to dread, and dread they know not why –
> The natural alien of their negative eye.

Subject to the destructive power of this Demogorgon (presumably an allusion to Plato's *Timaeus*),[67] which serves like a poison "to annihilate souls," such a place assumes an awesome quality of negation for vision itself, in terms which are central to the creative activity of the poetic mind: "The natural alien of their negative eye."

Coleridge even denies to this den of Limbo the validity of time and space as coordinates for experiencing this "sole true Something":

'Tis a strange place, this Limbo! – not a Place,
Yet name it so; – where Time and weary Space
Fettered from flight, with night-mare sense of fleeing,
Strive for their last crepuscular half-being; –
Lank Space, and scytheless Time with branny hands
Barren and soundless as the measuring sands,
Not mark'd by flit of Shades, – unmeaning they
As moonlight on the dial of the day!

Coleridge here conjures up the image of a landscape by night –
"barren and soundless as the measuring sands" – in terms which
radically negate such a landscape of vision as had been viewed by
Wordsworth when he ascended Mount Snowdon in the dark of
mists and moonlight. Indeed, the moonlight is here denied all
power of illumination whatsoever, as if the human eye perceived it
only in the obliterations of daylight. In this poem negation thus
extends even to that source of light for the poetic mind which has
been associated with illuminations of divinity throughout the tradition of Western literature. The final book of Wordsworth's *Prelude,*
which, though unpublished at the time, was nonetheless known to
Coleridge from the reading his friend had provided for him from
the manuscript, constitutes only the last and most immediate
instance for such a figure of transcendence.

"Limbo" then goes on to speak of a solitary old man:

But that is lovely – looks like Human Time,–
An Old Man with a steady look sublime,
That stops his earthly task to watch the skies;
But he is blind – a Statue hath such eyes; –
Yet having moonward turn'd his face by chance,
Gazes the orb with moon-like countenance,
With scant white hairs, with foretop bald and high,
He gazes still, – his eyeless face all eye; –
As 'twere an organ full of silent sight,
His whole face seemeth to rejoice in light!
Lip touching lip, all moveless, bust and limb –
He seems to gaze at that which seems to gaze on him!

Nowhere is the paradox of self-consciousness expressed so force-fully as in this passage, where a blind old man intent on seeing – "his eyeless face all eye" – provides an overwhelming image of the futility and the fiction of transcendent vision. Such gazing by an eye which cannot see upon that heavenly orb which does not shine provides a categorical indictment of everything that Romantic poetry sought to affirm. The blindness of the old man may symbol-ize the reflectivity of the poetic mind itself. Though blind and with-out sight, he is still attentive to that heavenly object, which, though moon-like, does not illuminate, yet nonetheless appears to reflect his unseeing gaze back upon him. Intellectual intuition is thus reduced to such a reciprocal act of non-vision between both the subject who gazes and the object which is gazed upon: "He seems to gaze at that which seems to gaze on him!"

Another figure from another late poem by Coleridge, which is strikingly similar to the old man in "Limbo," deserves consideration here. Entitled "Constancy to an Ideal Object,"[68] the exact date of composition is uncertain, but its mood of reflective elegiac despair suggests close proximity to "Limbo." Here Coleridge evokes the fig-ure of a rustic woodman, who perceives in the mists of early morn-ing the so-called Brocken-spectre, known to Coleridge from his visit to the Harz mountains in 1799, when he was living in Ger-many.[69] This spectre symbolizes that "ideal object" to which the poem is addressed. The woodman, like the old man in "Limbo," provides correspondingly a model for the poet and his claim to the constancy of self-consciousness. He also serves as a fugitive from the characteristic rustic landscapes so often depicted in Words-worth's poetry, where the poet encounters lonely shepherds, solitary reapers, country beggars, or crippled leech-gatherers. These figures of rustic solitude always represent for Wordsworth essential human qualities in himself, which constitute his own poetic genius. Coleridge indeed must have had his friend explicitly in mind, recalling that precise correlative visionary experience on Mount Snowdon, which is evoked in the last book of *The Prelude*. Critics have noted this parallel,[70] suggesting that Coleridge by intention provides a grim corrective to those characteristic moments of vision or spots of time in Wordsworth, which constitute the highest achievement of English Romantic poetry.

Coleridge's counter-image to Wordsworth is as follows:

> . . . Such thou art, as when
> The woodman winding westward up the glen
> At wintry dawn, where o'er the sheep-track's maze
> The viewless snow-mist weaves a glist'ning haze,
> Sees full before him, gliding without tread,
> An image with a glory round its head;
> The enamoured rustic worships its fair hues,
> Nor knows he makes the shadow he pursues!

This image offers implicitly a disturbing answer to the question asked in that other late poem by Coleridge, "Self-knowledge," cited at the outset of this essay: "Say, canst thou make thyself?" Should we be disturbed to think of the poet in his quest for self-conscious-ness as an "enamoured rustic," worshipping the "fair hues" of a sha-dow which he himself has made? At this late stage in his career, at the far end of the Romantic era, Coleridge indeed meant it to be so.

Yet we may also bear in mind with regard to this image of the Brocken-spectre, whether or not Coleridge intended it, a powerful analogy from Plato's *Republic*. In the famous allegory of the cave (Book VII) the images perceived as reality in human life are ex-posed as mere shadows projected from the reflected light of a fire against the wall of the cave. Characteristic of a Romantic poetics of self-consciousness, the poet himself becomes the source, the creator of such shadow-images, which he perceives before him in the mists of morning, whether or not he comprehends them to be only a projection of himself.

Coleridge thus calls into question the very possibility of any higher, transcendent source for such spectral vision. Yet Plato also provides a further corrective here, as Coleridge well knew, with regard to the notion – eminently Platonic in itself! – of an "ideal object." Those who seek to interpret and understand the shadows on the wall of the cave must first have freed themselves from the chains of sense-perception, in order to journey outside the cave into the higher realm of ideas, where they perceive the true reality in the light of the heavenly sun. Those who return into the darkness of the cave with such transcendent visions understand the shadows of reflected light and are called philosophers. The poetics of self-consciousness imposes precisely such a philosophical mandate as a hermeneutical contract for its readers, that they understand the shadow-images of the poem, its fictions and its figures, to be mere projections of the subjective mind. The only basis for such understanding, however, must be the knowledge of some higher realm, whether it be located outside the cave or within the reflective mind, where that "ideal object" resides, to which the poet is "constant."

Coleridge's "Constancy to an Ideal Object" corresponds exactly to the devotion of the poet in Hölderlin to the spirit of the dead Diotima, both in the final letter of the novel *Hyperion* and in the later elegy "Menons Klagen um Diotima." The radical difference between the two poets is found in the complete absence in Coleridge of that visionary moment of communion achieved in Hölderlin. Contrary to the prophetic promise with which Hölderlin affirms his vision of the dead beloved as basis for the hope of new life, even though he knows *as author of the poem* that his vision is only a poetic construct, the only outcome for Coleridge's poem is existential despair. That ideal object which, like Diotima for Hyperion or Menon, has been lost or taken away is not recovered at all by Coleridge's reflective meditation, except through a radical negation, which exposes the fictions of the poetic mind to be no more than that.

"Why shouldst thou remain," he asks in a question addressed directly to this ideal object,

> The only constant in a world of change,
> O yearning Thought! that liv'st but in the brain?
> Call to the Hours, that in the distance play,
> The faery people of the future day –
> Fond Thought! not one of all that shining swarm
> Will breathe on thee with life-enkindling breath,

> Till when, like strangers shelt'ring from a storm,
> Hope and Despair meet in the porch of Death!

The ideal object is here acknowledged to be a "yearning thought," which "lives but in the brain," and the projection of that yearning (presumably in the fictional world of the poem) is peopled with faery figures of a future day, none of whom, we are told, can breathe with life, until a strange encounter may take place between hope and despair. Such a meeting between these dread personae, Hope and Despair, even if it can only occur "in the porch of Death," affirms still further the essential paradox of self-consciousness. That this meeting cannot occur in the everyday world of human existence is not surprising, though the programs of Romanticism had once seemed to hope not only for such a meeting, but even for an ultimate reconciliation within a utopian dream of harmony or eternal peace.

Coleridge cannot deny his fascination with the thought or idea of such a meeting, the dream of a reconciliation beyond reality, as he continues to explore the full ambiguity of his imagined scene:

> Yet still thou haunt'st me; and though well I see,
> She is not thou, and only thou art she,
> Still, still as though some dear embodied Good,
> Some living Love before my eyes there stood
> With answering look a ready ear to lend,
> I mourn to thee and say – 'Ah! loveliest friend!
> That this the meed of all my toils might be,
> To have a home, an English home, and thee!'

A bitter irony is conveyed in these words of mourning addressed to the ideal object, accompanied by a sense of nostalgia for domestic harmony and joy. Personified as a woman, though identified also with abstractions, such as Good and Love, this object of the poet's constancy is defined by a paradox, which may be directly related to the fundamental challenge of the poetics of self-consciousness: "She is not thou, and only thou art she." These lines would also seem to constitute a reluctant, yet bitter parody of Wordsworth's all-too-optimistic celebration of home and friendship at the end of *The Prelude*. Coleridge affirms the value and the need for such an ideal of place and relationship, as well as his longing for its realization, even to the point where he identifies the ideal object of his poem with that spiritual sense of home, which only poetry could affirm. Yet an overriding consciousness that such ideals are only dreams or poetic fictions prevails.

The alternative to an imagined domestic bliss and intimacy is expressed, in the lines which follow, through a purposeful allusion to Coleridge's own earlier lyrical ballad, "The Rime of the Ancient Mariner," as critics have noted.[71] The terms of this alternative condition for the mind are far more frightening to contemplate:

> Vain repetition! Home and Thou are one.
> The peacefull'st cot, the moon shall shine upon,
> Lulled by the thrush and wakened by the lark,
> Without thee were but a becalméd bark,
> Whose Helmsman on an ocean waste and wide
> Sits mute and pale his mouldering helm beside.

The poem affirms that this vision of peace at home, thematized by such emblems as the cot, the moonlight and the singing of thrush and lark, must also signify the ideal itself as concept. Otherwise even such a scene of rural pastoral would have no other meaning than that absolute desolation and solitude defined by the mariner, that helmsman "mute and pale," who drifts upon the infinite and lifeless ocean. The mariner's journey thus becomes a symbol also for the futility of the poetic quest to realize and sustain the ideal object of the mind.

Keeping in mind this highly ambivalent model of constancy to an ideal object, we may return to the text of "Limbo." That poem concludes with an even more categorically negative counter-image to its own earlier figure of the blind old man, gazing in his reciprocally eyeless communion upon the orb of the moon:

> No such sweet sights doth Limbo den immure,
> Wall'd round, and made a spirit-jail secure,

By the mere horror of blank Naught-at-all,
Whose circumambience doth these ghosts enthral.
A lurid thought is growthless, dull Privation,
Yet that is but a Purgatory curse;
Hell knows a fear far worse,
A fear – a future state; – 'tis positive Negation!

Puzzling lines indeed! Coleridge seems to deny to his Limbo precisely that paradoxical image of reciprocal gazing which would seem most appropriate to it, where the walls surrounding its space symbolize a prison house for the self. How does poetic self-consciousness relate to such a "Purgatory curse" – "dull Privation" imposed upon "a lurid thought"? That it involves a sense of spiritual confinement within the surrounding walls of "a spirit-jail" is apparent. Yet we may assume that the kind of thought associated with such a place, "lurid" and "growthless," would *not* hold true for poetry, even for a poetry of despair such as this. The curse of Purgatory as this state of "dull Privation" may thus be interpreted as an absolute isolation of the poetic mind, which precludes the possibility of all communication with any other mind, specifically with an implied reader. The poetics of despair thus negates even the possibility of a hermeneutical consciousness.

Yet Coleridge allows himself a further thought beyond the dilemma of Limbo, looking ahead toward a future state of even greater fear, which he identifies as Hell. It is "the mere horror of blank Naught-at-all," where all reality and all value collapse into a radical nihilism. What might result from such "positive Negation" – how paradox is heaped yet further upon paradox! – is not stated or even imagined. The poem simply breaks off at this point, as if all further statement would be in vain. What can we make of such an ending?

Coleridge anticipates with this poem the kind of absolute negation for thought and existence, which we associate with such writers later in the nineteenth century as Georg Büchner, Charles Baudelaire and Friedrich Nietzsche. A lineage is thus established within the decline and collapse of European thought on the way from Romanticism to Modernism, which employs, however metaphorically as poetic figures of its advance, the traditional imagery of Purgatory and Hell. The prospect for the future of art is grim indeed. Yet Coleridge's fear is also grounded in the central conviction inherited from the era of his own growth to poetry, the era of a high Romanticism shared with his friend Wordsworth at the turn of the eighteenth to the nineteenth century and, although unknown to him, shared also with such a poet as Hölderlin. The poetics of self-consciousness in Romanticism is thus the gateway through which the spirit of nihilism first emerges in modern European thought.

The poetics of self-consciousness originated in a program of high hope for the future of human culture. It ended in defeat and despair. The history of Romanticism thus includes the early recognition of a crisis and tragedy for European culture and thought, the implications of which remain as significant for readers today as they were for the poets of that time. Nor does the ultimate collapse of this program for renewal and affirmation entirely annihilate the genuine poetic achievement of such works as *Hyperion* and *The Prelude.*

The history of self-consciousness in Romanticism thus also includes its own unavoidable negation, where the recognition of defeat and failure accompany the hope for affirmation and fulfillment, if only within the specific aesthetic domain of art. It is the process of a dialectical reversal without any option of a Hegelian "sublation" (*Aufhebung*). We may adapt Coleridge's formulation from "Constancy to an Ideal Object" to describe this radically ambivalent outcome in European thought. Hope and Despair meet, "like strangers shelt'ring from a storm" – the storm of history and the crisis of modernity – within the protective space of poetry and art, which is revealed to be a self-defeating prison-house of the mind.

Hölderlin in His Tower

Eloquent witness to such an outcome, even if it remains only a hypothetical prospect from the viewpoint of a defeated mind, is found in one of Hölderlin's short rhymed poems, composed during the long years of his isolation and mental derangement. These lines provide an appropriate conclusion to this essay. They were written as a gift for the carpenter Zimmer, in whose home the poet lived, located in the tower above the Neckar river, in a section of the old city walls of Tübingen. Hölderlin's tower still survives as a landmark in the city where the poet had studied in the Protestant Seminary, along with Hegel and Schelling, and where he eventually died in his seventy-fourth year after nearly four decades of an existential night (*Umnachtung* is the euphemism used by German scholars). The poem is preserved only in a letter written by Zimmer to Hölderlin's mother in April 1812, describing how the poet composed it in response to an incidental comment by the carpenter. Hölderlin had showed him the picture of a temple, perhaps an image from ancient Greece, symbolizing the era celebrated in *Hyperion* as the ideal of humanity. Hölderlin suggested, so Zimmer wrote, that the carpenter ought to build such a structure with his wood. Zimmer answered that he had to work for his living, he was not so fortunate as the poet, who could live his life in *philosophical repose*. "Alas, I am but a poor man," replied Hölderlin: "Ach, ich bin doch ein armer Mensch." Thereupon he took a pencil and wrote the following lines on one of the boards from the carpenter's shop:

> Die Linien des Lebens sind verschieden
> Wie Wege sind, und wie der Berge Gränzen.
> Was hier wir sind, kan dort ein Gott ergänzen
> Mit Harmonien und ewigem Lohn und Frieden.

> [The lines of life are various,
> Like pathways and like the mountain borders.
> What we are here, a god can there fulfill
> With harmonies, eternal recompense and peace.][72]

Chapter 5: Reading the Romantic Ode

To the students in Comparative Literature
at the University of Toronto,
who helped me to clarify the hermeneutics of form

The true content of romantic art is absolute inwardness, and its corresponding form is spiritual subjectivity, with its grasp of its independence and freedom.
–Hegel, *Aesthetics*

Form is universal; content is contingent, accidental, occasional: *gleichgültig.*[1] Such a statement reflects idealist theory, as formulated notably by Hegel, both in his argument about the language of Spirit in its self-certainty (in the *Phenomenology of Spirit*) and in his concept of Romantic art (in the *Aesthetics*). In both instances Hegel is concerned with a problem of communication, specifically the problem of understanding what is said or written from a perspective that is more than subjective, that is authentically interpersonal, general or universal. Such a perspective, argues Hegel, is only established by the *form* of language:

Whoever says he acts in such and such a way from conscience, speaks the truth, for his conscience is the self that knows and wills. But it is essential that he should *say* so, for this self must be at the same time the *universal* self. It is not universal in the *content* of the act, for this, on account of its specificity, is intrinsically an indifferent affair: it is in the *form* of the act that the universality lies. It is this form which is to be established as actual: it is the *self* which as such is actual in language, which declares itself to be the truth, and just by so doing acknowledges all other selves and is acknowledged by them.[2]

In normal human discourse such verbal form is constituted by structures of grammar and syntax and also pertains to more general aspects of style and rhetoric that govern language usage. Communication depends upon the ability of the audience to recognize and interpret the form of what is stated. In the verbal arts, and especially in poetry, form also includes conventions of organization, such as meter and rhyme, which reflect techniques of the poetic medium that, from the perspective of normal discourse, are completely artificial. Hegel addresses such poetic form under the heading of Romantic art – by which he means the entire post-Classical, Western or European, medieval or Christian tradition – as an *absolute negativity* of every particular.[3] What Hegel means by negativity in relation to the hermeneutical function of verbal form will be further addressed in the argument of this essay.

The true subject of what Hegel calls Romantic art is spiritual, transcendent, as its goal is the affirmation of divinity,[4] but the medium of Romantic art is limited and artificial, hence utterly incompatible with this subject or goal. The experience communicated by such art thus involves a complex process of transformation, which Hegel describes in terms of the Christian myth of sacrifice and rebirth. Through this process all particularity of the self is dissi-pated and a true spiritual subjectivity is achieved.[5] The act of communication thus involves a kind of intuition or feeling that is completely at odds with the arbitrary and artificial substance of art. Hegel describes this process with biblical images traditionally applied to mystical vision:

This subject-matter, by being purely external material, carries with it at the same time the character of being indifferent and vulgar, and only attaining worth of its own if the heart has put itself into it and if it is to express not merely something inner but the heart's *depth of feeling*, which instead of fusing with the external appears only as reconciled with itself in itself. In this relation, the inner, so pushed to the extreme, is an expression without any externality at all; it is invisible and is as it were a perception of itself alone, or a musical sound as such without objectivity and shape, or a hovering over the waters, or a rising tone over a world which in and on its heterogeneous phenomena can only accept and re-mirror a reflection of this inwardness of soul. (*Aes,* 1: 527)[6]

In poetry, concludes Hegel, such spiritual qualities pertain above all to the lyric, where "spirit and mood" (*Geist und Gemüt*) speak through the form (*Gebilde*) to spirit and mood.[7]

To the casual student of English Romanticism – by which conventionally we refer to the poetry of Coleridge and Wordsworth, Keats and Shelley (among others), at the end of the eighteenth and beginning of the nineteenth century – Hegel's theory of Romantic art, and specifically his concept of form in language as the basis of meaning as a universal, will seem obscure and irrelevant. It is the purpose of this essay to demonstrate that the opposite is the case. Hegel's theory provides an orientation for criticism in terms of what I would call a *hermeneutics of form,* applicable to the entire European tradition of literature, for which the so-called Romantic ode will serve as convenient instance. I do not intend, however, to explore in detail the implications of Hegelian theory at this time. Two points only from the context of Hegel's argument should be emphasized as sufficient prerequisite for the discussion of the ode which follows:

1) The concept of form releases criticism from its traditional preoccupation with the role or the voice of the poet within the poem, often identified in psychological or existential terms with the actual author. The concept of *negativity,* furthermore, in accord with recent semiotic theory concerning the fundamental discontinuity in language between the sign and what it signifies,[8] avoids the corresponding preoccupation of criticism with concepts attributed to Romanticism, such as the symbolic or imaginative fusion between subject and object or the organic unity of the poem. Hegel's view of universality and negativity was originally conceived in conscious opposition to competing Romantic theories, as in the work of such contemporaries as Schelling and the Schlegels, concerning the nature of symbols and the poetic imagination.[9] What underlies

Hegel's approach is a dialectical theory of experience and self-reflection in language, which correlates directly to the act of reading and interpretation. The Hegelian dialectic is essentially, if only implicitly, a hermeneutics, as I have argued elsewhere.[10] The act of interpretation occurs through a dialectical and self-reflective inter-action between reader and text, involving what Hegel calls the process of internalization or recollection (*Er-Innerung.*)[11]

2) A hermeneutical response to the form of poetry, as constitu-tive of what Hegel calls tone or mood, achieves for the reader an intuition or feeling of that which in an explicitly religious, Christian-Platonic context Hegel calls *Spirit*. The most important passage for this view, also cited by Hans-Georg Gadamer in support of his hermeneutical theory in *Truth and Method*,[12] occurs in the intro-ductory paragraphs on "Revealed Religion" in the *Phenomenology of Spirit (PhG,* 523–24; *PhS,* 455–56). For us (*für uns*),[13] argues Hegel, the works of art from the past are like beautiful fruit, broken off the tree on which they grew and lived and transmitted to us by a friendly destiny, as if a servant girl were to offer such fruit to us at a banquet. All that we possess of such works is "the veiled recollec-tion" (*die eingehüllte Er-Innerung*) of the reality in which they lived and blossomed and ripened. Our task is *not* to enter into the actual life of these works – that is forever lost to us – but "to possess an idea of them in our imagination." Yet interpretation as reflective recollection nonetheless achieves more than the original life that has been lost precisely because of our self-conscious understanding.

Hegel concludes:

But, just as the girl who offers us the plucked fruits is more than the Nature which directly provides them – the Nature diversified into their conditions and elements, the tree, air, light, and so on – because she sums all this up in a higher mode, in the gleam of her self-conscious eye and in the gesture with which she offers them, so, too, the Spirit of the Fate that presents us with those works of art is more than the ethical life and the actual world of that nation, for it is the *inwardizing* (*die Er-Innerung*) in us of the Spirit which in them was still [only] *outwardly* manifested; it is the Spirit of the tragic Fate which gathers all those individual gods and attributes of the [divine] substance into one pantheon, into the Spirit that is itself conscious of itself as Spirit. (*PhS,* 455–56)[14]

The germ of Hegel's later theory of Romantic art, with its herme-neutical implications, is contained in this passage.

Theory of Poetic Form

In his discussions of language and art Hegel consistently accepts the traditional distinction between form and content. In doing so he shares a conventional terminology current in his own time and likewise affirms a central conviction in Western philosophy, derived through scholastic thought from Plato and Aristotle, concerning the relation between *forma* and *materia*.[15] Such a distinction is valid for literary criticism only to the extent that a text conveys to its reader a hermeneutical awareness of itself *qua form* with regard to intentional generic characteristics. The legitimate function of form in poetry always depends upon its recognition by readers. Such recognition does not involve descriptive systems and categories, such as those used in the natural sciences (e.g., *species* and *genus* in biology), so much as it involves a perceived correlation between the particular and the universal, much in the manner of the relation established by Kant between the phenomenal and the noumenal in his Transcendental Analytic,[16] or the intuition of an *eidos,* as argued by Plato, through the recollective power of the soul. Plato's notion of *anamnesis* may thus be regarded as a recognition of form based upon a quality of being, which, according to Plato's myth of the soul in the *Phaedrus,*[17] is prior to existence and consciousness. In the terminology of modern hermeneutics such a recognition of form is constituted by what Gadamer calls the horizon of expecta-tion (*Erwartungshorizont*).[18]

A sonnet, whether by Petrarch or Shakespeare, Baudelaire or Rilke, imposes upon its reader the expectation that it will be recog-nized as a sonnet. This recognition of generic form is necessary if the poem is to be understood *qua sonnet.* All particulars of content and theme, occasion and point of view will be indifferent to such a recognition of generic form. The sonnet can be *about* anything at all, so long as it fulfills the demands of its form. This point is expressed with particular vividness in a short novel by Anthony Burgess entitled ABBA ABBA. The title refers both to the rhyme scheme of the octave in the Petrarchan sonnet and the cry of Christ to the Father as he is dying on the cross. In the novel the poet Keats, while he is dying of consumption in Rome, dreams about the sonnet and the possibility for an artwork of the future:

> It came to him thus that the sonnet *form* might subsist *above language,* but he did not see how this was possible. Language itself was perhaps only a ghost of the things in the outer world to which it adhered, and a ghost of a ghost was a notion untenable totally. And yet it seemed that two men, of language mutually unintelligible, might in a sense achieve communication through *recognition* of what a sonnet was.[19]

The act of communication through a recognition of form at a level above language as a system of signs constitutes what I would call the *hermeneutics of form.*

In an important essay concerning poetic form in the sonnets of Wordsworth, J. Hillis Miller emphasizes a crucial ambiguity in the word *form,* already contained in the Greek term τύπος (*typos*), an ambiguity that is endemic to Western metaphysics.[20] On the one hand, form is an abstract principle of origin or priority, as in the case of Plato's *eidos* or Aristotle's formal cause, which preexists the work and to which the work as phenomenon refers or which it embodies. Form is thus the transcendent *signifié.* On the other hand, form is itself the external shape, the outward appearance, the achieved object, *morphé* or *Gestalt.* Miller attributes such a radical ambivalence of form to Wordsworth, focussing on the paradox of the "still heart" in the sonnet "Composed upon Westminster Bridge." Miller's own position on this issue is indicated by a brief allusion he makes to the *deconstruction* of metaphysics attempted by such philosophers as Heidegger and Derrida.[21] According to this position the priority of form, as well as the concept of an origin, or *Ursprung,* of meaning, is at best a fiction. Meaning is only generated, or constituted (so Miller argues), through the arbitrary interplay of elements or signs within the achieved form (i.e., *Gestalt*) of the work.

The position here outlined by Miller, though he does not acknowledge the fact as such, is a hermeneutics of form. The act of constitution, or – to use the *terminus technicus* of phenomenology, as developed in the work of Ingarden or Vodička – *concretisation*,[22] occurs through the interaction between text and reader in the process of interpretation. For hermeneutics the paradox of form may be restated in terms of Gadamer's concept of a fusion of horizons, achieved through the act of interpretation (*wm, 289–90; tm, 306–7*): the one sense of form precedes the act of reading and the other is the consequence of it. Wolfgang Iser, in his book *The Act of Reading*, uses the terms *Vorstellung* and *Gestalt*, adapted from the vocabulary of phenomenological and psychological theory, to describe the relation of meaning to text as, respectively, either prior to or posterior to the act of reading.[23] In itself such a distinction is not new to hermeneutics. In an important passage from the *Confessions*, St. Augustine describes the process of reciting a psalm using similar terms.[24] Augustine distinguishes between memory (*memoria*) and expectation (*expectatio*) as a changing awareness in the mind of the reader (or reciter) with regard to a prior knowledge or consciousness of the psalm as a whole, from which the act of recitation proceeds.

Crucial for understanding the Romantic ode as genre is the distinction assumed here between the meaning, or *Gestalt*, of a poem, achieved through the act of reading, and the text itself as articulated verbal structure. The relation between these two aspects of the poem depends upon a sense of difference which can only be mediated through the act of interpretation. Such a concept of meaning departs radically from the traditional Classical norm of coincidence or identity between form and content, where the beauty of a work of art is argued to consist in a unity or all-pervasive harmony of the parts into an apprehended whole. A corresponding unitary view of art as organic form is familiar from Romantic theory, where the traditional distinction between body and soul is applied to the substance of the work of art as the manifestation (*phenomenon*) or the appearance (*Schein*) of a spiritual content. Of particular relevance here is Hegel's famous definition of Beauty (in his lectures on *Aesthetics*) as "the sensual manifestation of the Idea" [das sinnliche Scheinen der Idee].[25] According to such a view, the poem is like a living plant, which manifests an inner life through its external *shine*. Goethe argued that poetry should possess an *inner form*; Novalis maintained that the meaning of poetry should be a mystical inwardness (*Innigkeit*); and Coleridge asserted that the poetic imagination could achieve a coalescence of subject and object.[26]

In hermeneutical theory this familiar view is replaced with a dialectical principle of interaction between opposite and incompatible elements. In Hegel this dialectical principle is most apparent in his concept of the negativity of Romantic art. Negativity, in accord with definitions in Hegel's *Logic*,[27] describes the status of meaning in conceptual or speculative thought, as constituted by the mind in its dialectical encounter with discourse. More precisely – though Hegel nowhere makes this point explicitly – I would argue that negativity defines the necessary hermeneutical relation between a text and its meaning, which is established *for a reader* in and through the act of reading. Hegel frequently asserts that negativity is the negation of the negative.[28] What he means by this will be apparent if we bear in mind that language itself as medium of discourse is negative, insofar as sign and signified are necessarily opposed or discontinuous. The sign is distinguished from what it signifies through the disjunctions of irony or the complexities of metaphor.[29] The act of reading and interpretation thus constitutes the negation of this negative relationship by *positing*, or constructing, the meaning of the text through a dialectical interaction which occurs through that act. Understanding is only achieved through a characteristic transformation of thought, which Hegel terms a *sublation* (*Aufhebung*), involving a reflective turn or reversal in the mind.[30] The meaning of the Romantic work of art *for us* is thus called by Hegel an *absolute negativity*, in essential accord with his theory of absolute knowledge in the *Phenomenology of Spirit*. Understanding for Hegel is achieved through a conflictual recognition of Spirit in its Self-certainty.

The Romantic Ode as Genre

The dilemma of Romantic art, as formulated by Hegel, concerns the relation of transcendence as its motive or claim to the absolute as criterion of knowledge. Traditionally this dilemma is referred to by the artist as a crisis or challenge for the imagination. It applies equally to the conviction that the basis of understanding may achieve more than a subjective validity. How can the vision or experience communicated by a poem be more than personal and individualistic? How can the language of poetry represent a reality which is more than a fiction or a dream? Romantic theory attributes to the poetic mind in its *negative capability* (to use a term from Keats) the capacity to affirm a universal truth through its visionary powers as if through an act of faith. Hegel, by contrast, substitutes the authority of the philosophical mind for such naive faith, whereby the visionary powers of art and poetry are displaced by the self-reflective dimensions of conceptual thought. My reading of the Romantic ode as a poetic form or genre will resist both the claims for transcendence in Romantic theory and the criterion of the absolute in Hegelian philosophy as the basis for understanding. Following the argument of Gadamer concerning the nature of hermeneutical experience (*hermeneutische Erfahrung*), which itself derives in large measure from Hegel, I shall argue that the Romantic ode as form or genre is constituted as a dialogical structure through the communicative function of its discourse.[31]

In response to a historical study of the ode as genre in English literature by the German scholar Kurt Schlüter, Geoffrey Hartman has outlined a view of the Romantic ode as a conscious displacement of discourse from the primacy of vision to the secondary role of mediation.[32] In his seminal essay "From the Sublime to the Hermeneutic," Hartman's revisionary view of Romanticism derives in part from Hegel's concept of the *negative* in the *Phenomenology of Spirit,* specifically with regard to the text as a trace (*vestigium*) of the Spirit.[33] Such a sense of poetry as mediation also provides the basis for a revised literary history, developed from the perspective of interpretation and historical consciousness.[34] Romanticism, even in the narrower sense appropriate to the English poets, is defined by Hartman in Hegelian terms with reference to the "westerly drift" of the European imagination. The language of poetry retreats from the bright light of epiphany into the twilight zone of the *Abendland,* where divinity can only be intuited as absence through the medium of dream or reverie. Hartman accepts Schlüter's central hypothesis that the ode always looks to the cult hymn as model and source, seeking to affirm the presence of divinity through communal celebration. How such a model may be affirmed in the negative context of the modern, secular world needs further clarification.

The Romantic ode thus stands in opposition to its traditional model in a perspective of belatedness. The old quarrel between the ancients and the moderns, which formed the background for the original distinction between Classical and Romantic art in German theory,[35] is revived implicitly in the use of the ode as form. The Romantic ode is characterized by a nostalgic or elegiac sense of distance from the conditions of festive or epiphanic presence that it seeks to celebrate. This distance may be attributed, on the one hand, to a failure of human institutions, like the church and the theatre (which originally were one), to sustain an authentic sense of community. As Hölderlin asks in his elegy "Brod und Wein," with reference to the vision of Classical Greece as ideal norm for such festive community, which he has evoked in the central stanzas of the poem:

> Aber wo sind sie? wo blühn die Bekannten, die Kronen des Festes?
>   Thebe welkt und Athen; rauschen die Waffen nicht mehr
> In Olympia, nicht die goldnen Wagen des Kampfspiels,
>   Und bekränzen sich denn nimmer die Schiffe Korinths?
> Warum schweigen auch sie, die alten heilgen Theater?
>   Warum freuet sich denn nicht der geweihete Tanz?

> [But where are they now? where do they blossom, well-known, the
>   festival's crowns?
>   Thebes is withered and Athens; do the weapons no longer resound
> In Olympia, nor golden chariots in the games of combat?

> And the ships of Corinth are no longer wreathed with flowers?
> Why are they also silent, the ancient sacred theaters?
> Why does consecrated dance no longer rejoice?][36]

The belatedness and solitude which pervade the Romantic sensibility also derive simultaneously from the retreat of divinity beyond the reach of human experience. Such an absence of the divine constitutes an essential condition of modernity. This sense of loss may be interpreted metaphorically or psychologically as the departure of a glory from the world or as the collapse of the natural sublime. It may also be represented mythologically and historically – again as in Hölderlin's "Brod und Wein" – as the actual departure of the gods from the earth when the festival of the ancient world came to an end:

> Aber Freund! wir kommen zu spät. Zwar leben die Götter,
>   Aber über dem Haupt droben in anderer Welt.
> Endlos wirken sie da und scheinen wenig zu achten,
>   Ob wir leben, so sehr schonen die Himmlischen uns.

> [But, my friend! we have come too late. True, the gods still live,
>   But above our heads, up there in another world.
> Endlessly they are active there and seem little to care
>   Whether we live, so very much do the heavenly spare us.]
> (109–12)

The form of the Romantic ode reflects this cultural and historical shift from the sublime to the hermeneutic in two important ways. Both may also be symptomatic of written texts, where the cultic celebration of communal festivals is replaced by the act of reading. First, the song of the community, represented by the Greek chorus, becomes the private meditation of the exegete, and the place of interpretation is shifted from the religious festival to the solitude of the study. The form of the ode acknowledges this, implicitly at least, even if its fiction continues to deny it. Hölderlin again provides the most striking image for the solitude of interpretation in his Pindaric hymn "Patmos," where the modern poet is represented in a condition analogous to the medieval monk in his cell, like St. Jerome or Martin Luther, testing his vision against the *milder light* of scripture, in preparation for the day when God's transcendent brilliance will once again be directly revealed as a new dawn for culture and history.

> Wenn aber, als
> Von schwellenden Augenbrauen
> Der Welt vergessen
> Stillleuchtende Kraft aus heiliger Schrift fällt, mögen
> Der Gnade sich freuend, sie
> Am stillen Blike sich üben.

> [But when, as if
> From rising eyebrows
> Forgotten to the world
> Silent illuminating power falls from holy scripture, may
> They, rejoicing in its grace, test themselves
> Upon its silent gaze.][37]

Second, as a consequence of this awareness of poetic vision as merely subjective and inward, the poem must defend itself against the possibility of denial and rejection by the reader, who has the power to deconstruct its witness and deny the truth of divinity in its absence. The skeptical judgment of modern criticism declares the constructs of the imagination to be mere fabulae or fictions. The poet knows this to be so and seeks to achieve a viable form for the successful communication of his vision, despite such a negative relation to his intended readership.

The Romantic ode thus plays with figures of ambivalence, applied to itself through patterns of negation, as if to expose its celebratory gestures as mere imaginative projections, thus preventing the consequences of such denial by preempting them. To quote yet once more from Hölderlin, the poet's plea at the end of the elegy "Stutgard" is characteristic of the self-reflective mode that such a discourse of denial assumes, thematizing the solitude of the poetic process as an all-pervasive challenge for the hermeneutics of the poem:

>   – O kommt! o macht es wahr! denn allein ja
>   Bin ich und niemand nimmt mir von der Stirne den Traum?
> Kommt und reicht, ihr Lieben, die Hand!
>
>   [– Oh, come! oh, make it true! for I am
>   All alone and will noone lift this dream from my brow?
> Come and reach out, dear friends, your hands.][38]

To whom is the poet's plea addressed other than to his readers, who are thus acknowledged to be absent from the place and the event of poetic vision, as its god also is absent? The poet's plea here signifies nothing other than the main task of hermeneutics, namely to establish a sense of community through the act of reading, through the work of interpretation, and to translate through appropriate ironic reversals the poem's thematic doubts about the truth of its vision into an affirmation of its specific poetic form. The negativity of the poem thus serves as the source of its authority in the act of communication. The dialogical form across such gaps and discontinuities of difference establishes the only legitimate basis for an effective interaction with the reader as the necessary basis of understanding. Despite the poet's urgent devotion to his creative vision, the poem only succeeds as communicative discourse through such a conflictual, self-reflective recognition of its inherent negativity.

The exercise of close reading which follows seeks to demonstrate the validity of a concern with the hermeneutics of form in ways that also affirm the central convictions of Hegel's theoretical definition of Romantic poetry. The choice of Coleridge's ode "Dejection" was motivated in part by a longstanding fascination with this supreme exemplar of the ode as self-conscious poetic genre in English Romanticism. Coleridge's ode was also chosen in preference to the somewhat more fully programmatic odes and elegies or the Pindaric hymns by Hölderlin, such as "Dichterberuf," "Brod und Wein" or "Der Rhein," composed at virtually the same time as "Dejection." Hölderlin was too close to Hegel and Idealist philosophy to be trusted as a neutral representative of European Romanticism – however supremely great his poetic achievement! – and Coleridge's ode will be more accessible to readers unfamiliar with German.

Coleridge's "Dejection: An Ode"

> Late, late yestreen I saw the new Moon,
> With the old Moon in her arms;
> And I fear, I fear, my Master dear!
> We shall have a deadly storm.
> *Ballad of Sir Patrick Spence.*

I

Well! If the Bard was weather-wise, who made
    The grand old ballad of Sir Patrick Spence,
    This night, so tranquil now, will not go hence
Unroused by winds, that ply a busier trade
Than those which mould yon cloud in lazy flakes,   5
Or the dull sobbing draft, that moans and rakes
Upon the strings of this Æolian lute,
      Which better far were mute.
    For lo! the New-moon winter-bright!
    And overspread with phantom light,   10
    (With swimming phantom light o'erspread
    But rimmed and circled by a silver thread)
I see the old Moon in her lap, foretelling
    The coming-on of rain and squally blast.
And oh! that even now the gust were swelling,   15
    And the slant night-shower driving loud and fast!
Those sounds which oft have raised me, whilst they awed,
    And sent my soul abroad,
Might now perhaps their wonted impulse give,
Might startle this dull pain, and make it move and live!   20

II

A grief without a pang, void, dark, and drear,
    A stifled, drowsy, unimpassioned grief,

Which finds no natural outlet, no relief,
    In word, or sigh, or tear –
O Lady! in this wan and heartless mood,   25
To other thoughts by yonder throstle woo'd,
    All this long eve, so balmy and serene,
Have I been gazing on the western sky,
    And its peculiar tint of yellow green:
And still I gaze – and with how blank an eye!   30
And those thin clouds above, in flakes and bars,
That give away their motion to the stars;
Those stars, that glide behind them or between,
Now sparkling, now bedimmed, but always seen:
Yon crescent Moon, as fixed as if it grew   35
In its own cloudless, starless lake of blue;
I see them all so excellently fair,
I see, not feel, how beautiful they are!

III

    My genial spirits fail;
      And what can these avail   40
To lift the smothering weight from off my breast?
      It were a vain endeavour,
        Though I should gaze for ever
On that green light that lingers in the west:
I may not hope from outward forms to win   45
The passion and the life, whose fountains are within.

IV

O Lady! we receive but what we give,
And in our life alone does Nature live:
Ours is her wedding garment, ours her shroud!
    And would we aught behold, of higher worth,   50
Than that inanimate cold world allowed
To the poor loveless ever-anxious crowd,

Ah! from the soul itself must issue forth
A light, a glory, a fair luminous cloud
    Enveloping the Earth –   55
And from the soul itself must there be sent
   A sweet and potent voice, of its own birth,
Of all sweet sounds the life and element!

V

O pure of heart! thou need'st not ask of me
What this strong music in the soul may be!   60
What, and wherein it doth exist,
This light, this glory, this fair luminous mist,
This beautiful and beauty-making power.
   Joy, virtuous Lady! Joy that ne'er was given,
Save to the pure, and in their purest hour,   65
Life, and Life's effluence, cloud at once and shower,
Joy, Lady! is the spirit and the power,
Which wedding Nature to us gives in dower
   A new Earth and new Heaven,
Undreamt of by the sensual and the proud –   70
Joy is the sweet voice, Joy the luminous cloud –
    We in ourselves rejoice!
And thence flows all that charms or ear or sight,
   All melodies the echoes of that voice,
All colours a suffusion from that light.   75

V I

There was a time when, though my path was rough,
   This joy within me dallied with distress,
And all misfortunes were but as the stuff
   Whence Fancy made me dreams of happiness:
For hope grew round me, like the twining vine,   80
And fruits, and foliage, not my own, seemed mine.
But now afflictions bow me down to earth:

Nor care I that they rob me of my mirth;
    But oh! each visitation
Suspends what nature gave me at my birth,   85
    My shaping spirit of Imagination.
For not to think of what I needs must feel,
    But to be still and patient, all I can;
And haply by abstruse research to steal
    From my own nature all the natural man –   90
    This was my sole resource, my only plan:
Till that which suits a part infects the whole,
And now is almost grown the habit of my soul.

VII

Hence, viper thoughts, that coil around my mind,
    Reality's dark dream!   95
I turn from you, and listen to the wind,
    Which long has raved unnoticed. What a scream
Of agony by torture lengthened out
That lute sent forth! Thou Wind, that rav'st without,
    Bare crag, or mountain-tairn, or blasted tree,   100
Or pine-grove whither woodman never clomb,
Or lonely house, long held the witches' home,
    Methinks were fitter instruments for thee,
Mad Lutanist! who in this month of showers,
Of dark-brown gardens, and of peeping flowers,   105
Mak'st Devils' yule, with worse than wintry song,
The blossoms, buds, and timorous leaves among.
    Thou Actor, perfect in all tragic sounds!
Thou mighty Poet, e'en to frenzy bold!
        What tell'st thou now about?   110
        'Tis of the rushing of an host in rout,
    With groans, of trampled men, with smarting wounds –
At once they groan with pain, and shudder with the cold!
But hush! there is a pause of deepest silence!
    And all that noise, as of a rushing crowd,   115

With groans, and tremulous shudderings – all is over –
  It tells another tale, with sounds less deep and loud!
    A tale of less affright,
    And tempered with delight,
As Otway's self had framed the tender lay, –   120
      'Tis of a little child
      Upon a lonesome wild,
Not far from home, but she hath lost her way:
And now moans low in bitter grief and fear,
And now screams loud, and hopes to make her mother hear. 125

VIII

'Tis midnight, but small thoughts have I of sleep:
Full seldom may my friend such vigils keep!
Visit her, gentle Sleep! with wings of healing,
  And may this storm be but a mountain-birth,
May all the stars hang bright above her dwelling,   130
  Silent as though they watched the sleeping Earth!
    With light heart may she rise,
    Gay fancy, cheerful eyes,
  Joy lift her spirit, joy attune her voice;
To her may all things live, from pole to pole,   135
Their life the eddying of her living soul!
    O simple spirit, guided from above,
Dear Lady! friend devoutest of my choice,
Thus mayest thou ever, evermore rejoice.

The English Romantic ode is not easily defined with any precision. There are no fixed formal criteria of meter and rhyme, as in the sonnet; nor are the thematic concerns expressed in the ode necessarily different from those which occur in other kinds of poetry, such as the conversation poem or even the lyrical ballad. It may be argued with some confidence that Keats achieved the most authoritative and self-conscious exempla of the genre in those several odes composed near the end of his brief career, which include explicit generic notations of the ode in their titles. A similar mastery of generic form is indicated in those poems by Shelley where a designation of genre is included in the title, as in his "Ode to the West Wind." At the same time it could be argued that an earlier poem such as "Mont Blanc," which lacks such a generic designation in the title, may also be regarded as an ode.

More difficult is the question of when precisely the ode as form was first established within the historical context of English Romanticism. I would argue that Coleridge deserves credit for this achievement, namely in his poem "Dejection," which he published with the generic subtitle "An Ode" in the *Morning Post* on October 2, 1802, coincident with the wedding of his friend and fellow poet Wordsworth to Mary Hutchinson.[39] This judgment is complicated by various conflicting historical data. It is generally acknowledged that Coleridge's poem was conceived in part as a response to the draft of what later became the opening stanzas of Wordsworth's single all-important contribution to the genre, "Intimations of Immortality." Based on later evidence from Wordsworth himself, it may be deduced that his great ode was not completed until early 1804 and that he did not achieve a conscious awareness of generic form for the poem until that time, almost certainly based on the example of Coleridge's published ode. Wordsworth first published his ode in 1807, including it in a collection of his poems. At that time it was given the simple generic title "Ode," and was accompanied by the Latin motto *Paulo majora canamus,* which is the opening phrase of Virgil's famous Fourth Eclogue.[40]

The history of reciprocal influence between the two poets for their respective work in this genre extends even further. The final version of Coleridge's "Dejection," slightly revised from the text of 1802, was published only in 1817, contained in his collected poems entitled *Sibylline Leaves.* This collection was undertaken by Coleridge at the time he was working on his *Biographia Literaria,* partly in response to the important edition of Wordsworth's poems that appeared in 1815. In that volume the "Immortality-ode" was placed in a separate, clearly privileged position, as was the case in all subsequent editions of Wordsworth's collected poems. Even to this day the ode claims a unique status in the body of the poet's work, independent of the various groupings by sensibility that the poet developed for organizing his poetry, under such headings as the "Affections," "Fancy" and "Imagination."[41] I would argue for the history of reception that a programmatic awareness of the ode as genre for English Romantic poetry within the public domain of letters was only achieved by the appearance of these odes in the collected poems of Wordsworth in 1815 and of Coleridge in 1817. Shelley and Keats composed their programmatic odes in the years 1819 and 1820, presumably motivated in part by a direct response to the respective texts in this genre by their precursor poets. Both of the younger Romantics had been reading their Wordsworth and Coleridge attentively.[42]

Despite such complexities of historical and bibliographical data, Coleridge deserves credit for originating the English Romantic ode. This point should be emphasized above all because of the notoriety achieved in recent decades by a document directly related to "Dejection." I refer to the verse letter addressed by Coleridge to Sara Hutchinson, which is dated April 4th (1802). Coleridge, as is now well known, had developed a complicated, secret and essentially hopeless emotional attachment to this woman, the sister of Wordsworth's fiancée. He wrote the verse letter at a time when the Hutchinson sisters were staying with Wordsworth and his sister Dorothy at Grasmere, while Coleridge resided with his family nearby in Keswick. The verse letter, untitled and without numbered stanza divisions, constitutes a draft for what subsequently became the ode "Dejection." It is in every sense an occasional utterance, containing, as critics have noted, considerably more personal, autobiographical allusions than does the published ode. The verse letter was never published by Coleridge, and the manuscript survives in the Wordsworth papers at Dove Cottage. It was first made public by Ernest de Selincourt in 1937 and subsequently discussed by Humphrey House in his Clarke Lectures on Coleridge's poetry and by the Canadian scholar George Whalley in his biographical study of Coleridge and Sara Hutchinson.[43] The source text for "Dejection" would be of no concern to the present argument were it not for the fact that several scholars have expressed the opinion in recent years that the verse letter is superior to the ode as a poem.[44]

Such a preference for the draft text of the verse letter reflects a preoccupation among scholars with the poet's biography. A tendency has developed to read the poems as documents for the biography, giving priority to those passages which are most personal and intimate. From this perspective it is argued that the material omitted from the verse letter in the published ode, much of which pertains to the poet's private life, needs to be included somehow if the ode is to be properly understood. For the argument of this essay such a position is untenable; nor is the generic claim which the subtitle of "Dejection" establishes for the ode *as ode* compatible with any consideration of the poet's personal affairs, as Coleridge himself well knew. Biographical material is of no interest whatsoever for a discussion of the ode as poetic form. Valuable support on this point is provided by I. A. Richards with explicit reference to "Dejection" in an essay he published late in his life entitled "Coleridge's Other Poems."[45] Richards asserts that biographical information about how a poem came to be written will be of no use in telling us how to read it. Nor do we need to consider what sort of person Coleridge was in order to interpret "Dejection."

I would go one step further. No amount of speculation concerning Coleridge's actual attitude or state of mind when he wrote this poem will be of any significance whatsoever for the hermeneutics of form. This includes any consideration of his surreptitious love for Sara Hutchinson and his presumed distress, or state of *dejection,* with regard to his domestic situation as he composed the verse letter. The poet as speaker, or agent, within the ode should not be identified with the actual author Coleridge, just as the unnamed "Lady," mentioned several times in the final text as intended recipient of the ode, should not be identified with Sara Hutchinson.[46] A hermeneutics of the Romantic ode can only begin at that point where all preoccupation with the life and thought of the poet is abandoned.

STRUCTURE OF THE ODE

The basic form of the ode is dialogue. "Dejection" affirms this, developing the technique of Coleridge's earlier conversation poems, in a manner comparable to the structure of dialogue in the odes of Horace or the eclogues of Virgil. The ode thus stands as discourse in conscious contrast to earlier models of community for poetic song – e.g., the choral hymns of ancient Greece, intended to be performed as part of the public religious festivals, or the forms of celebration established by the Psalms of the Old Testament for collective use by congregations of the faithful in worship. Within the text of the ode any sense of authentic community is replaced by a rhetorical exchange between formalized personae, the poet, who speaks as agent in the poem, and his lady, who is intended to hear as its recipient. Such a dialogical relationship is also modelled on the European love lyric, notably in traditions of songs and sonnets from the Middle Ages to the Renaissance and beyond. Appropriate also to the ode as form in "Dejection" is the sense of occasion that defines the role of both poet and lady. The situation depicted in the poem determines both emotional attitude and psychological response. Character thus functions as an artifact of discourse and is subject to strategies of communication. We relate as readers to both the poet as speaker and to his lady as intended recipient. Indeed the ode demands that we recognize its essential structure as implied dialogue and adjust our response as readers accordingly.

In order to read the ode from a perspective beyond the subjective limits of character, we must be aware that its form depends upon an ironic contrast between incompatible points of view. The attitude of the speaker, characterized by his dejection, stands in opposition to the conviction expressed in the central stanzas, that a transcendent intuition may be achieved in direct response to the external events and situation in nature. This intuition is personified implicitly, as patron divinity or Ideal of the poem, under the name of Joy. This state of being or existential condition is also attributed to the lady as her nature, in radical contrast to the poet. Her innocence or purity of soul opposes his state of dejection, which is the result of experience and self-consciousness. To understand the ode does not require that the reader identify with either persona, the dejected poet or the joyful lady, but depends rather upon our recognizing a dialectical differentiation between them both as the essential motive for the discourse addressed by the one to the other. The ode can only make sense to its readers if a corresponding sense of difference is conveyed through the sequence of contrasting moments that constitute the syntagmatic axis of the text. The ode establishes a rhythm of opposing attitudes or contrasting moods, which are never fully integrated and resolved. The supreme achievement of "Dejection" as discourse, despite all the proponents of organic form who have attacked the poem for a lack of unity or coherence of sensibility, is to affirm that cognitive form of communication in language which Hegel termed the *negativity* of Romantic art and which the poet Hölderlin, looking to the example of the Horatian ode for the composition of his own poems, labelled variation of tones (*Wechsel der Töne*).[47] A fundamental hermeneutic tension of negative discontinuity is never abandoned in "Dejection," nor ever allowed to resolve itself into a false sense of completion or resolution.

Once we have differentiated the perspective of our own response as readers from the subjective position of the poet-speaker, the essential structure of the ode as a sequence of varying moments becomes apparent. A principle of concentric frames is employed, which locates the description and interpretation of the weather (in stanzas I and IIb and in VII, respectively) as frame surrounding the introspective self-presentation of the poet-speaker (in IIa–III and in VI). At the center of the ode (in IV and V) the celebration of Joy as intellectual and experiential ideal is expressed in quasi-philosophical terms. The poet's direct address to the lady (first introduced in stanza II) is fully established as a form of dialogue in the central stanzas, only to return at the end of the poem, like a coda, through a categorical shift of reference (in stanza VIII) away from the poet himself toward the lady, who is imagined in a state of bliss, sound asleep, at a safe distance from the storm that holds the poet captive. Each unit of the poem is organized around a crucial tension of opposing elements, which, though they vary from unit to unit, remain unresolved throughout. It will be instructive to outline briefly these patterns of opposition.

The descriptive sections of the ode (stanzas i and ii, 31–36; stanza vii) juxtapose an apparently objective representation of the nighttime landscape, contrasting the deceptive repose of nature at the outset and the violent storm at the conclusion, with a poetic interpretation of these scenes. In the first instance this interpretation by the poet derives from the traditional popular ballad "Sir Patrick Spence," well known from Percy's *Reliques*, a stanza of which is used as motto for the ode:

> Late, late yestreen I saw the new Moon,
> With the old Moon in her arms;
> And I fear, I fear, my Master dear!
> We shall have a deadly storm.[48]

The authority of the ballad, as anonymous statement of folk wisdom from the tradition, provides the basis for a prophecy concerning the storm to come due to the sight of the new moon cradling the old moon in its arm. In the latter instance, the poet intuits a tale of warfare and violence, which he claims to hear in the sound of the storm. This tale is also modelled implicitly on the ballad tradition, telling about "the rushing of an host in rout" (111). Such a sense of heroic military clash is followed by a sudden interlude of silence, when the intuited tale shifts to a "tender lay" (120), which was originally attributed in the verse letter to Wordsworth. This is an apparent allusion to the poem "Lucy Gray," contained in the second volume of *Lyrical Ballads* (1800). (Subsequently in the published version of the ode, this literary allusion was shifted to a more neutral and public source, Thomas Otway, author of the tragedy *The Orphan,* one of the most popular plays of the eighteenth-century London stage.)[49] This metaphoric tension between the objective depiction of natural activity and the poetic interpretation of it is crucial for the supposed doctrinal claim of the ode and its dialogical structure. The central premise of the ode is that a reciprocal correspondence exists between the inner life and mood of human beings and the external conditions of nature: "in our life alone does nature live."

Within the self-analytical passages of "Dejection" (stanzas IIa and III; again in stanza VI) a more conventional dialectical opposition is developed with explicit reference to the poetic persona. This may also indicate a conscious imitation of Wordsworth, particularly in the opening stanzas of what became the "Immortality-ode," to which Coleridge is argued to have been responding, even when composing the initial verse letter.[50] In the first instance a tension of spatial opposition is developed, involving an incompatibility of mood between the poet's dejected state of mind – "A grief without a pang, void, dark, and drear" (21) – and the visual beauty of the night sky, which is described with particular eloquence:

And those thin clouds above, in flakes and bars,
That give away their motion to the stars;
Those stars, that glide behind them or between,
Now sparkling, now bedimmed, but always seen:
Yon crescent Moon, as fixed as if it grew
In its own cloudless, starless lake of blue. . .
(31–36)

As the poet asserts concerning the clouds, stars, and moon: "I see, not feel, how beautiful they are!" (38). In the later passage the opposition is temporal, involving a contrast within the self, almost archetypal for the poetic psychology of Romanticism, between a former, privileged state of mind, endowed at birth by nature with a "shaping spirit of Imagination" (86), and the poet's present state of existential solitude, where a reflective, introspective power of thought, which prevents all living, creative interaction with nature, has become "the habit of my soul" (93). What must be recognized by the reader is that this opposition in the self applies only to the poet-speaker as agent or persona, *not* to the poem as a whole.

In the central section of the ode a strategy of generality affirms *for us* (in Hegel's sense) the doctrine of Joy. The poet speaks throughout in a dialogical plural. The poet's statements are explicitly addressed to the Lady, as indicated by a sequence of epithets.

The pronominal *we* of this discourse, however, extends beyond the poet and his lady, to gather into itself the perspective of the reader as well. Such a rhetoric of universal affirmation lacks the kind of hermeneutical conflict or tension which occurs elsewhere in the ode. A dialectical sense of difference is nonetheless implied for the context in which the doctrine of Joy is uttered. This difference is crucial for defining the appropriate response of the reader. We need to recognize that the doctrine of Joy, proclaimed at the center of the ode, is incompatible with the evidence presented by the rest of the poem. The poet emphasizes, and will emphasize again, that *he* no longer has access to such Joy. This claim has led biographical critics to assume, not only that Coleridge here denies for himself any further access to the creative power of poetry, but also that the poem itself, in which this statement is made, must therefore be about the inability or failure of the poet (i.e., Coleridge as the author of "Dejection") even to compose this poem successfully! The inappropriateness of such a judgment should be sufficiently apparent from any consideration of what I have termed the hermeneutics of form. How strange an aberration of literary criticism to pass such a negative judgment on the founding text of the English Romantic ode, simply because the poetic persona within that ode depicts – with a supreme ironic eloquence! – the failure of its own poetic imagination.

Even more important for the hermeneutics of form, the validity of the doctrine proclaimed in the central stanzas may be called into question by the evidence provided at the beginning and at the end of the poem, in the description of natural process. The crux of this doctrine occurs at the outset of stanza iv:

> . . . we receive but what we give,
> And in our life alone does Nature live:
> Ours is her wedding garment, ours her shroud!
> (47–49)

Such a theory of spiritual correlationship between nature and the self could be applied to the poet's own use of traditional tales, borrowed from the popular ballad and theater, to interpret the

phenomena of nature. Insofar as the figurative analogy between tale
and natural event holds true – as it clearly does for the motto borrowed from "Sir Patrick Spence," predicting the storm that subsequently does indeed occur – then such a doctrine of correlation
would seem to hold true. Yet the explicit attitude of the ode toward
such popular tradition goes directly contrary to the doctrine.
Coleridge's "Dejection" shares with the earlier *Lyrical Ballads* a
respect for the language of people and the poetry of the popular
tradition. Both the ballad "Sir Patrick Spence" and Otway's play *The
Orphan* are derived from such tradition, whether or not *we* would
concur with the use made of them by Coleridge. The poetry and
language of nature is considered to be the authentic product of a
higher spiritual dispensation, like the gift of imagination which the
poet claims to have received from nature at birth. The authority of
these traditional tales provides the justification for the poet's use of
them as a projection of meaning upon the events of nature. In
truth, however, this authority only derives *from* nature, as the
source of natural wisdom. This contradicts the doctrine of Joy proclaimed in the central section of the ode. The traditional tales about
nature only prove that the meaning of *our life* derives *from nature,*
despite the opposite claim in the passage quoted from the ode. Such
implicit contradiction is crucial for understanding the hermeneutics of form in "Dejection" and in the Romantic ode generally.

Only the lady remains, finally, as a mute symbol for the Joy proclaimed as doctrine by the poem. Her role in the ode, especially in
the final stanza (VIII), where she is invoked in her innocent sleep as
final focus of the Ideal, resembles that of the sleeping infant in
Coleridge's earlier conversation poem "Frost at Midnight." A silent,
unconscious, pre-verbal persona serves as the passive recipient of
the poet's statement. *As such* (in the sense of Hegel's *an sich*) the
lady in "Dejection" represents an ideal state of being which stands
against the negativity of the ode itself. Such a contrastive role for
the Lady is affirmed in stanza VIII where the poet invokes a spiritual blessing upon her from the powers of "gentle Sleep" (128). The
irony of such a blessing becomes apparent when we contrast the
role of this "simple spirit" (137) as dialogical referent, silent and

absent, indeed unconscious and sound asleep, with our own role as readers and interpreters of the ode. We enter into our own dialectical relationship with the text, which is the very opposite of simple, naive and unreflective – as in the case of the sleeping Lady – and which follows the example of the poet in his discourse, working through the paradoxes and aporias of *dejection.* The effect of the poet's invocation of the Lady *for us* must therefore be a sense of categorical difference between her positive role in the ode as projected Ideal, blessed by the spirit of nature, and our own negative relation to such blessing, sustained by a self-conscious awareness that this poetic Ideal does *not* hold true for ourselves. Such a consciousness of difference may be the basis for the poet's own state of *dejection,* but for his readers it is the basis for a hermeneutical understanding of the poem.

THE DOCTRINE OF "JOY"

The dialectical tension established by the hermeneutical form of "Dejection" corresponds exactly to the metaphoric, or ironic, structure of Romantic poetry, as defined by Hegel's theory of negativity. More important for the present argument, which looks both to Hegel's theory of the dialectical form of self-consciousness and to theories of reflectivity in modern hermeneutics, notably in Gadamer and Paul Ricoeur,[51] I would conclude that the true purpose of dialogical form in such a poem as Coleridge's "Dejection" is to establish a verbal model, like the image of a mirror or an eddy, for the processes of thought itself. These dialectical forms symbolize the mind's own act of self-reflection in and through the process of reading and interpreting the poem. Several particular images used in the ode provide further support for this argument.

The initial image in the motto of the ode, borrowed from "Sir Patrick Spence," describes the old moon resting in the lap of the new moon. Critics have interpreted this image with reference to a passage in the verse letter, subsequently deleted from the ode, where Coleridge recalls an evening spent with Sara and her sister Mary, when he rested his head on Mary's lap, felt her hand on his brow and Sara's eyelash on his cheek.[52] He calls this remembered experience *Joy* and contrasts it with his present state of solitude, where he can only feel his own hand upon his brow. A more sophisticated reading of the image, without recourse to the verse letter, is offered by I. A. Richards,[53] who points out that the "phantom light" of the old moon, seen as a sphere above the "silver thread" of the new moon, derives from the reflected light of the sun shining upon the earth. By seeing such earth-light we do indeed "receive but what we give" (47), except for the ironic fact that the light of both the moon and the earth derives from the absent sun. The source of vision is, in effect, transcendent. The image of the old moon cradled by the new moon thus provides an instance of a transcendent illumination, as is emphasized with reference to Coleridge's Neoplatonism by Reeve Parker in his book *Coleridge's Meditative Art.*[54] I would argue in addition that this image also demonstrates the form of self-reflection as an implicit auto-referential metaphor for the hermeneutical structure of the ode itself. The new moon's cradling of the old moon constitutes the reflection of a reflected light back upon itself. Essentially the same procedure is enacted by the reflective thought of a reader in response to the dialectical form of the ode. In sympathy with the essential negativity of transcendence in Romantic art, as defined by Hegel in his *Aesthetics,* such a figure, or metaphor, represents an intuition of the Spirit in its self-consciousness. We should not forget that the poet-speaker in "Dejection" responds to what he sees in the night sky, recalling the old traditional ballad of "Sir Patrick Spence," by correctly prophesying a storm.

A corresponding image of reflectivity and reciprocity is introduced at the end of the ode, perhaps as a conscious correlative of the new moon cradling the old at the beginning. The privileged status enjoyed by the Lady is described as a harmony that she enjoys with all things that live: "Their life the eddying of her living soul!" (136). Such reciprocity, admittedly idealized with reference to the Lady as recipient of the poem, may be interpreted in terms of the doctrine of poetic Joy developed in the central section of the ode. Just as the Lady is invoked in the final line to affirm the possibility that such a state of mind may endure: "Thus mayest thou ever, evermore rejoice" (139), so also does the doctrine of Joy in stanza v receive its climactic affirmation in an image of reciprocal dialogical exchange in the reflexive voice, a kind of spiritual *eddying* of sympathetic souls: "We in ourselves rejoice!" (72).

This model of interrelationship may further be applied to the imaginative interaction between mind and nature, which is symbolized by the images of *cloud* and *voice* in the passage immediately preceding: "Joy is the sweet voice, Joy the luminous cloud" (71). Poetic form is the veil of the spirit, perceived as enveloping the earth: "A light, a glory, a fair luminous cloud" (54). From the soul itself, in essentially the same kind of eddying movement, a sweet and potent voice is sent forth as a sound which itself has been received from nature, like the wooing song of the throstle mentioned earlier (26): "Of all sweet sounds the life and element!" (58). An intentional ambiguity of transcendence is contained in this attribution to nature of "strong music in the soul" (60) and a "fair luminous mist" (62). An ambiguity of source and recipient, active and passive at one and the same time, is made explicit in the epithet used to describe this power as "beautiful and beauty-making" (63). This ambivalence of creation and reception imposes an ironic mystification on the question of spiritual origin. Yet the image of *rejoicing* as a reciprocal eddying applies explicitly to the dialogical relationship articulated within the ode between the poet and his lady, despite the radical contrast emphasized in their respective states of mind. By figurative analogy, finally, the image of *eddying* may be extended to include the hermeneutical interaction between the text and its reader. Such an ambivalent form of reflectivity with regard to the origin or source of meaning is exactly appropriate for a poetic theory of the sign and the hermeneutical process by which it is understood.

A further aspect of "Dejection" worth consideration is the fiction of a transcendent referent for the metaphoric or ironic discourse of the poem. Few readers of the ode will fail to notice the distinctive use made by Coleridge of the Eolian harp, or "Æolian lute" (7), an image that calls to mind the earlier poem on this subject, "The Eolian Harp" (1796). This instrument, which produces music from the force of the breeze, contributed to the central preoccupation of English Romantic poetry with what Wordsworth called the "correspondent breeze" of poetic inspiration.[55] The wind that blows is like the spirit that moves, and the song that results from the harp is considered to be a symbol for authentic inspiration, as if the poet's mind were also moved by a heavenly muse. In "Dejection" this symbolic theme is subjected to a twofold irony. At the outset of the poem the poet rejects the sound of the Aeolian lute – "Which better far were mute" (8) – because the "dull sobbing draft" (6) of the breeze fails to correspond to the poet's dejected state of mind, or at least that is what the poetic persona claims to be the case. He longs instead for the coming storm, because the heightened song it will produce from the lute may then truly send his soul abroad, as it had so often done in the past:

> And oh! that even now the gust were swelling,
>   And the slant night-shower driving loud and fast!
> Those sounds which oft have raised me, whilst they awed,
>   And sent my soul abroad,
> Might now perhaps their wonted impulse give,
> Might startle this dull pain, and make it move and live!
> (15–20)

The second irony occurs in stanza VII, where the actual effect of the storm, once it has arisen, upon the lute is described as a "scream /Of agony" (97–98). Coleridge thus rejects the Aeolian harp in favor of a more appropriate instrument for this inhuman sound, namely the natural landscape itself, imagined to be the proper setting for a fairytale of the sublime:

> Bare crag, or mountain-tairn, or blasted tree,
> Or pine-grove whither woodman never clomb,
> Or lonely house, long held the witches' home . . .
> (100–2)

The wind itself is invoked as a transcendent power, an awesome, if overwhelming spirit, performing its role upon the stage of a grandiose theater:

> Mad Lutanist! who in this month of showers,
> Of dark-brown gardens, and of peeping flowers,
> Mak'st Devils' yule, with worse than wintry song,
> The blossoms, buds, and timorous leaves among.
>   Thou Actor, perfect in all tragic sounds!
> Thou mighty Poet, e'en to frenzy bold!
> (104–9)

The role of the poet as speaker or voice is here ironically reversed, and his task within the dialogical form of the poem now corresponds exactly to our own as readers. He must listen, apprehend and interpret the meaning of the wind from the sound of its howling. This he proceeds to do, as mentioned earlier, in terms of models or sources from traditional tales and poetic legend.

Reeve Parker argues persuasively that Coleridge applied sources from the Miltonic sublime to both instances of his projective reading, the clashing of armies in conflict and the wailing of a lost child. The tale of battle "of an host in rout" (111) may recall the war in heaven when the rebellious angels fell, described in *Paradise Lost*.[56] The cry of the lost child, initially derived from Wordsworth's "Lucy Gray," as all critics acknowledge, may also include a conscious allusion, both as parallel and contrast, to the Christ child as described by Milton in his "Nativity ode":

> It was the winter wild
> While the heaven-born-child
>   All meanly wrapped in the rude manger lies.

The birth of the child, to cite Parker, "is associated with a sacramental stillness in the wake of a raving storm."[57] The most important significance of this evidence for my argument concerns a hermeneutical irony in the poet's interpretive response to the silence of the storm as a child lost in the wilderness. The imposition of a poetic tale from the tradition includes an implicit, figurative self-reference to the ode itself. Parker also quotes an important parallel passage in a letter written by Coleridge to Thomas Poole in February 1801,[58] where he speaks of his desire to have his friend with him for a talk: "to the Tune of this Night Wind that pipes its thin doleful climbing sinking Notes like a child that has lost its way and is crying aloud, half in grief and half in the hope to be heard by its Mother."59

The hermeneutical implications of these intertextual borrowings for a reading of "Dejection" are apparent. Our own response to the text of the ode may be compared to the poet's interpretive act within the poem in response to the sound of the wind. The tale which is thus attributed to the storm involves loss, isolation, agony and even death, all these in valid parallel to the poet's own dejection. Yet the act of interpretation in which we are engaged as we read the poem, analogous to, yet different from, the poet's interpretive response to the storm, provides a more positive, affirmative model of meaning. The hermeneutics of form involves a dialogical relation of interaction, which includes both ourselves as readers and the poet-speaker as witness and exegete of a natural event. The most authoritative description for that relationship is still to be found, as argued above, in the exact midpoint of the ode, where the poet affirms a mutual poetic recognition that is shared between himself and his Lady: "We in ourselves rejoice!" (72) The reader enters a corresponding relationship to the text of Coleridge's poem, so that even the catastrophe of a tragic loss by figurative analogy to the wailing of the storm may be *sublated* (*aufgehoben,* in the Hegelian sense) hermeneutically into the form of a reciprocal interaction. More needs to be said on this point.

TRANSFIGURATION AND DISPLACEMENT

> But hush! there is a pause of deepest silence!
>   And all that noise, as of a rushing crowd,
> With groans, and tremulous shudderings – all is over –
>   It tells another tale, with sounds less deep and loud!
>   A tale of less affright,
>   And tempered with delight,
> As Otway's self had framed the tender lay,
>   'Tis of a little child

> Upon a lonesome wild,
> Not far from home, but she hath lost her way:
> And now moans low in bitter grief and fear,
> And now screams loud, and hopes to make her mother hear.
> (114–25)

The tale of the lost child, whose voice the poet claims to hear in the momentary calm of the storm, plays a crucial role in the structural organization of the ode. The poet's interpretation, not of a sound but of the absence of sound, constitutes a climactic instance of poetic transformation through the projection of inner, human value upon an external, natural event. Ironically, despite the doctrine of poetic projection proclaimed in the middle stanzas, this intuited tale affirms the validity both of the poetic tradition as intertextual resource, providing the means or medium for interpretation, and of nature as the source or origin of meaning. Through intertextual allusion, implicit to the tale of the lost child, the theme of poetic transformation assumes significance for the ode, both as story, or plot, and as hermeneutical form. Coleridge's initial source text, Wordsworth's ballad "Lucy Gray" from the *Lyrical Ballads,* demonstrates in its final stanzas how this transformation is conceived poetically in response to the wind and with reference to the lost child:

> – Yet some maintain that to this day
> She is a living child;
> That you may see sweet Lucy Gray
> Upon the lonesome wild.
>
> O'er rough and smooth she trips along,
> And never looks behind;
> And sings a solitary song
> That whistles in the wind.

Readers of "Dejection" have correctly perceived that the shift of reference in stanza VII from the tale of the noisy host in rout to the silence of the lost child constitutes a critical moment of climax and reversal for the ode as a whole. That the theme of solitude and *dejection* is here transformed into an emblem of poetic *Joy* has been felt but not explained, due to the preoccupation of critics with the figure of the poet in the poem and with the autobiographical significance of the ode in relation to Coleridge's life and thought.[60] The transformation of concern achieved by this moment of reversal, or *peripeteia* (in the Aristotelian sense), constitutes a dialectical sublation (in the Hegelian sense of *Aufhebung*). It is the climactic turning point in the structure of the poem as a whole. All personal, subjective concern, above all with reference to the poet-speaker as emotional agent of the ode, is displaced into the hermeneutical form of the language itself. The reader must attend to the shifts of focus and intensity in the ode, as the structure of thought moves through a sequence of rhythmic turns and variations, as if the poem were music. The language thus constitutes what Hegel in his discussion of Romantic art calls *tone* or *mood* (*Gemüt*),[61] through which the *inner Spirit* of the work is expressed.

The poet as agent and persona of the poem virtually disappears from the last two stanzas of the ode, retreating into the language as voice, or point of view, or as author of its rhetorical form. Only once briefly, in the opening line of stanza VIII, does the poet reappear as first person subject, reiterating the stance of a solitary vigilant, which was established at the outset: "'Tis midnight, but small thought have I of sleep" (126). His vigil is contrasted with the image of his Lady at peace and asleep, which occupies the central focus for the remainder of the poem. The figure of the lost child at the end of stanza VII displaces the poet as subject and establishes, as a substitute for the poetic self, a surrogate pattern of experience at the rhetorical climax of the poem. The theme of solitude and dejection is thus carried to its furthest limit in the image of agony and the prospect of death as a soul lost in the storm. In association with Wordsworth's "Lucy Gray," the figure of the child may be interpreted as a tragic victim or indeed as a sacrifice to the destructive power of nature. Yet the voice of the child, whether moaning or screaming, is in fact no more than the sound of the wind, or rather the momentary silence of that sound, which the poet overhears.

For us, it is true, as readers of the poem the voice of the child is not actually heard, but only mediated through the story alluded to by the poet. This tale of sacrifice and death is mediated through the poet's interpretive response to the wind. In association with the figure of the Christ child in Milton's nativity ode – even if this remains only a latent model for the transformation which takes place in "Dejection" – the sacrifice of the child also includes a sense of renewal and rebirth. This holds true even in a strictly naturalistic context, where the wind as *spiritus* serves as an emblem of the Spirit as power of divinity, constant and eternal through all changes of weather. The poetic tale attributed to the wind as voice, even in its momentary silence, does not make this mythical pattern explicit, but the formal structure of the ode as a sequence of tones and varying mood nonetheless affirms such a pattern as the movement of thought, which constitutes the hermeneutical consciousness of a reading. In this regard Coleridge's "Dejection: An Ode" affirms exactly that universal, dialectical drama of the Spirit that Hegel attributes to the absolute negativity of Romantic art.

In the *Aesthetics* Hegel discusses this theme of spiritual death and rebirth in Romantic art. In a complex passage containing one of his most brilliant theoretical insights into this aesthetic tradition, Hegel also defines the implicit basis for what I have termed the hermeneutics of form:

In romantic art death is only a perishing of the *natural* soul and *finite* subjectivity, a perishing (related negatively only to the inherently negative) which cancels nullity and thereby is the means of liberating the spirit from its finitude and disunion as well as spiritually reconciling the individual person with the Absolute. (*Aes,* 1: 523)[62]

Hegel's formulation derives, of course, from Christian theology with regard to the death and resurrection of Jesus. The immediate context to which Hegel alludes is the medieval tradition of representing this Christian mystery in the media of art, above all in religious painting. The philosophical significance of such art works for Hegel, however, resides precisely in the cognitive *form* of the experience they convey. Even in a strictly secular, naturalistic context, this hermeneutical form may claim a universal validity. Its affirmation by Coleridge's ode provides a case in point. The figure of death is negated, transformed, sublated into the experience of a new life – "vita nuova," to use the title that Dante assigned to the collection of sonnets celebrating his love for Beatrice, a love which is ultimately transformed through her death into a higher spiritual realm. Such an experience of transformation and renewal of spirit constitutes the motive and the goal of Romantic art. Hegel proceeds to address explicitly the concept of negativity in art in a passage that deserves to be quoted in full, despite its length:

In the romantic outlook death has the significance of negativity, in the sense of the negation of the negative, and therefore changes all the same into the affirmative as the resurrection of the spirit out of its mere natural embodiment and the finitude which is inadequate to it. The grief and death of the dying individual reverses into a return to self, into satisfaction, blessedness, and that reconciled affirmative existence which spirit can attain only through the killing of its negative existence in which it is barred from its proper truth and life. Therefore this fundamental principle does not merely affect the fact of death as it comes to man from the side of nature; on the contrary, death is a process through which the spirit, now independent of what negates it externally, must itself go in order truly to live. (*Aes*, 1: 523–24)[63]

Hegel's argument should not be applied to Coleridge's "Dejection" as if the ode intended consciously to delineate such an action as Hegel describes. No common ground between the two authors exists by conscious design at the level of subject matter or content. At issue is the *form* of the ode and the kind of hermeneutical response it elicits. A twofold displacement of perspective is demanded from the reader, the first involving the displacement of the poet-speaker as subject and the second transforming the attributed tale of the lost child into a figure or metaphor for the kind of experience conveyed by the ode. The basic form of this experience, as all readers of "Dejection" must intuit, nonetheless affirms the life of the spirit, even if understood in strictly naturalistic terms, through a process of catastrophe, reversal and renewal at the level of poetic form. The tale of the lost child introduces a figurative analogy for this process, shifting the focus of the poem away from the poet as agent and subject. The poetic doctrine of Joy expressed in the central stanzas is also implicitly affirmed through the act of interpretation by the poet, whereby the momentary silence of the wind is referred to the voice of the lost child. With regard to the poet this interpretation must be viewed as a conscious fiction, a statement of personal opinion at best, based on an arbitrary sense of analogy. Such a reading can be no more than merely subjective, a poetic fantasy or a waking dream in response to the wind, which can evaporate as quickly as the weather can change. *For us* as readers of the ode, however, this interpretation by analogy may also be seen as a component in the formal design of the poem as a whole, a strategy of the plot, which signifies the kind of reflectivity that we ourselves must achieve in order to understand the hermeneutics of Coleridge's ode.

The pattern of sacrifice and renewal thus establishes finally a figure of self-reflection for the act of reading. This structure of experience is communicated to us as a dialectical pattern of discourse, quite independent of character or action, the self of the poet or the situation in which he finds himself in any literal, mimetic or representational sense. What we understand from our reading is therefore not the tale of the lost child as such (*an sich*), nor the particular attitude or point of view of the poet as subject, but rather an image or a figure for what Hegel calls the Spirit in the form of its own self-reflection (*an und für sich*), in and through the language of the poem. Nor does such understanding allow for any naive or unconscious fusion of perspective or horizon, either as a coalescence of life and soul or as a communion of the spirit. The final benediction addressed to the lady as the ideal recipient of the poet's concern, programmatically excludes us, as it also does the poet, from the utopian optatives with which the poem concludes:

> May all the stars hang bright above her dwelling
> > Silent as though they watched the sleeping Earth!
> > > With light heart may she rise,

> Gay fancy, cheerful eyes,
>   Joy lift her spirit, joy attune her voice;
> To her may all things live, from pole to pole,
> Their life the eddying of her living soul!
>   O simple spirit, guided from above,
> Dear Lady! friend devoutest of my choice,
> Thus mayest thou ever, evermore rejoice.
> (130–39)

The Lady is clearly idealised by such devotion and such bless-
ings. She sleeps through the storm and will awake, so the poem
suggests, in a state of complete harmony, at peace with herself and
the world. Joy will inspire her and give music to her voice, so that
her life will move at one with all things that live, "guided from
above" by some higher destiny or benevolent divinity. Were such an
existence to be realized, it would reconcile the individual with that
which Hegel in his *Phenomenology of Spirit* terms the Absolute
Spirit. Such affirmation of the Ideal, however, is only achieved within the scope of the poem as a negative norm, against which we
measure our understanding of the poem, as does the poet also from
the perspective of his continuing vigil in solitude. The condition of
life and thought that pervades the whole of "Dejection" is a self-
conscious awareness of dialectical difference and existential conflict.

Keats and Shelley

The hermeneutics of form in the Romantic ode deserves a book-
length study.[64] Critical principles and concepts developed from the
experience of reading and the reflective response to such experience
must be defined with reference to formal strategies of discourse in
the poems themselves. Within the limitations of an essay no more
can be offered than a few examples which suggest how a more comprehensive study might proceed. The necessary critical instruments
are not yet available with sufficient conceptual clarity and authority
to sustain such a hermeneutical reading in more than tentative and
experimental ways. This holds true above all for such a seminal

work from the canon of English Romanticism as Coleridge's "Dejection," which has traditionally been interpreted exclusively from the subjective perspective of the poetic persona within the poem. Nor has the definition of the genre yet been freed from such extrinsic criteria as occasion and chronology of composition. Recent discussion concerning the original verse letter offers proof on this point. Virtually every discussion of the ode traces its genealogy from text to text within the arbitrary limits of a national tradition. No attempt has yet been made to assess the formal features of poetic language within this genre as they affect the specific communicative strategies employed.

Traditional literary histories invariably discuss Coleridge's "Dejection" in relation to Wordsworth's "Intimations of Immortality," usually with regard to questions of priority in their respective histories of composition. The odes of Shelley and Keats, correspondingly, demand consideration with reference to the odes of Wordsworth and Coleridge as precursor texts. The question of influence thus becomes as important as the question of generic function. A history of the English Romantic ode is thus constituted as a sequence of texts by these poets; yet the ode as genre demands a broader European perspective on the complex tradition of imitations based on classical models, notably from Horace and Pindar. Such a sequence of interpretations within a single national literature yields a sense of linear development for the history of the ode as generic form. The hermeneutics of that form requires a reflective awareness of the communicative strategies of the ode and of the reading experience in general.

For the purpose of such a hermeneutics the argument of Hegel in his *Aesthetics* concerning Romantic art is invaluable. The hermeneutics of the Romantic ode is constituted through the complex dialectical process of appropriation that Hegel terms *negativity*. A hermeneutics of reading frees the text from all concern with the poet's motives, biographical or psychological, as it also liberates the voice that speaks through the poem from any personal or subjective determination in time or place. This holds true, even though the poem may originally have been composed by the poet with very specific allusions to such temporal and local particulars in mind. The fundamental truth of all hermeneutical consciousness resides within the mind of the reader as a dynamic interrelationship with the text, constituted by and mediated through the communicative strategies of its language. Historical understanding is thus achieved through the act of reading, as an imaginative relationship between past and present, between the poem as artifact and its meaning *for the reader* in present experience. Any external reference to contexts beyond the verbal configurations of the poem, defined by historical circumstances from the poet's life and time, thus become subordinate to such a hermeneutical understanding. Precisely this self-reflective interrelationship between reader and text is what Gadamer in *Truth and Method* defines as the consciousness of the history of effect (*Wirkungsgeschichtliches Bewußtsein*). Traditional literary history has ignored such a consideration for understanding as irrelevant to its specific concerns.

Hermeneutical theory addresses the modes of interaction that occur between texts and readers in and through the act of reading. Such concerns are fundamentally incompatible with traditional academic literary scholarship. The voice of the poet has always been discomforting for scholars in the academy, as the voice of the prophet has been for exegetes in the church. Yet the experience of reading, at least in our own literary culture, remains the most powerful stimulus for the education of the mind. Why else should literature be included in the curriculum of our universities? Both Plato and Hegel placed the disciplines of reading at the center of their respective philosophical projects for education. The dialectical process of appropriation and reflection, which occurs through the encounter with texts, is more essential for humanistic study than all the procedures of scholarship and literary research as they have developed within the modern tradition of our universities. The Romantic ode provides a paradigm for the incompatibility between the values of poetic experience and the temporal-spatial determinations that make up our traditional sense of history. As Hegel asserted in his theory of Romantic art, the only legitimate aim for understanding should be the free communication of the spirit, as an act of re-cognition across the abyss of difference. Understanding is achieved despite the artifice and the limitations of the medium through which such communication takes place. Precisely this conflict of mediation, thematized in poetry through formal strategies of language, is worked through and resolved by the hermeneutical processes of reading. The alien, or negative, medium of the work is translated into a living, positive presence of mind. Precisely this process of translation occurs according to what Hegel calls *negativity*. An awareness of how this conflictual process plays itself out in the act of reading a specific poetic text is what I mean by the hermeneutics of form.

The challenge of reading remains full of promise. The possibilities for a hermeneutics of the Romantic ode invite renewed study of even these poems, so familiar in the canon of English literature that they often seem to have been read to death. In concluding the present essay, as an outline for future exploration, several tentative directions for a hermeneutical reading of odes by Shelley and Keats may be attempted. I shall address a few particulars in two of the most familiar texts in the canon, "Ode to the West Wind" and "Ode to a Nightingale." There are, of course, significant differences between these two poems, which reflect the poets' different sensibilities.

Both odes were composed in 1819, and both were written – as scholars affirm – under the influence of the collections recently published by Wordsworth and Coleridge, the *Poems* of 1815 and the *Sybilline Leaves* of 1817, which contain the two great precursor odes. I shall consider these two later odes by the younger poets with specific regard to three aspects of the hermeneutics of form: the structure of the stanza, the role of the poet-speaker, and the reflectivity of the reader's response.

Keats and Shelley both employ strict metrical stanza forms of their own devising. For each poet this form is derived from the European tradition of the sonnet. In each of these odes, though in very different ways, the stanza functions as a crucial unit of discourse. The particular formal features of this unit can be quickly described in each case.

Keats wrote sonnets throughout his brief career but must have felt for his purpose in composing an ode that he needed a shorter and more varied metrical form as stanza. He abbreviated and modified the sonnet structure from fourteen to ten lines, employing a quatrain with alternating rhyme (*abab*) and two tercets with responding rhyme (*cde–cde*). This stanza form and rhyme scheme is observed throughout the eight stanzas of the "Ode to a Nightingale." Iambic pentameter is used, with some rhythmic flexibility, for all ten lines of the stanza, excepting only the third from last line, which has only three stressed syllables in iambic meter. Such a truncated line presumably derives from the practice of Coleridge and Wordsworth in their odes, where in stanzas of varying length and varying rhyme scheme a norm of iambic pentameter is also varied by occasional shorter lines. Such a principle of variation may well have been introduced by Coleridge and developed further by Wordsworth as a conscious adaptation of the artificial conventions of metrical response in the tradition of the English Pindaric ode. At any rate it is apparent that Keats in all his odes of 1819 consciously modified his own practice in composing sonnets and established a clear sense of the stanza as a separate unit of discourse.

At the level of form, furthermore, the odes of Keats could be regarded as modified sonnet sequences in miniature. A principle of organization is thus established that is neither strictly lyrical, or expressive, nor narrative, or dramatic. For interpreting these odes it is important to recognize the essential reflectivity of the individual stanza form. Nothing even approximate to a narrative line of discourse is employed in the Keatsean stanza. Within the "Nightingale-ode" alone the structure of statement in each of the eight stanzas includes a significant turn or subdivision after the initial quatrain (with the single exception of stanza v, where the imagined communion with the song of the bird in its dark grove occurs). In a number of instances Keats employs a principle of repetition, elaboration or variation as a device that heightens the sense of rhetorical artifice and figurative self-consciousness. Such formal procedures also occur across the individual stanzas as autonomous units of discourse, where the theme of one stanza will be further developed in the next through a technique of allusion or contrast. Such an *echo-effect* is particularly apparent in the final stanza, which begins by repeating the word with which the preceding stanza ends ("forlorn!"). The distinction between quatrain and tercets also corresponds to a principle of variation between lyrical and narrative modes of discourse, where thought moves from self-expression to self-reflection. Wherever repetition and variation occurs, a sense of heightened consciousness or implied reflectivity on the part of the poet-speaker is included. Keats also arranges his lines by indentation to demarcate the distinction between quatrain and tercets, the only variant being the single shorter line, which is indented more than all the other lines.

Shelley imposes on his ode an even more elaborate and sophisticated metrical form for the stanza, involving a subtle blending of sonnet and terza rima, the latter derived from Dante's *Divine Comedy*. Each stanza consists of four tercets with a concluding rhymed couplet. Iambic pentameter is maintained strictly throughout, as is Dante's characteristic interlocking rhyme scheme. The tercets and concluding couplet are also separated by spaces on the printed page. Each stanza thus contains fourteen lines, constituting in effect an independent sonnet. The concluding rhymed couplet recalls the convention of the Shakespearean sonnet with its epigrammatic closure, though the syntactical and rhetorical structure of statement in each stanza also observes an approximate division into octave and sestet according to the Italian sonnet tradition. In the eighth or ninth line – i.e., the second or third line of the third tercet – in all five stanzas of the ode, a significant break or shift of statement occurs. Only in the final stanza is there a departure from this norm, where the shift is displaced, seemingly out of balance, to the middle of the second tercet.

Each of the opening three stanzas consists of elaborate forms of direct invocation to the wind, where the body of statement through the four tercets consists of figurative attributions, focussed on quasi-mythical settings of natural activity: the blowing of dead leaves and seeds across "the dreaming earth" (10) in the first; the clouds that cover the sky in the second, with their Dionysian frenzy of storms – "Like the bright hair uplifted from the head / Of some fierce Maenad" (20–21) – and a sense of the vault of heaven as "the dome of a vast sepulchre" (25); and in the third the imagery of ocean waters – "the blue Mediterranean" (30) and "the Atlantic's level powers" (37) – which as in a fairy tale constitutes a separate mythical space even beyond nature that is also affected cataclysmically by the force of the wild wind. Only in the concluding couplet of each stanza is the central plea of the poet expressed as prayer directly to the wind, that it may hear the poet's call. Each of the three stanzas ends with the identical imperative: "oh, hear!"

No other ode in the English Romantic tradition demonstrates so precise a sense of formal organization as Shelley's "Ode to the West Wind," where features from the entire European tradition of the lyric are incorporated within a sequence of sonnets in terza rima. Shelley demonstrates throughout a highly sophisticated and self-conscious use of structural and rhetorical procedures. Like Keats, though in his own manner, he employs a principle of variation between narrative, or mythical, and lyrical, or invocational, modes of discourse. Such a heightened sense of form has often been noted by critics – more often for Shelley than for Keats – but rarely has such a sense of form been referred to the interpretive procedures involved in reading the odes, least of all to conscious hermeneutical strategies of communication.

Few poems in English have received so much attention and commentary as these odes. How many generations of students have been assigned them for memorization at school? Almost without exception, however, the assumption behind every reading, whether explicit or not, is that the reader should enter into an identity of perspective with the poet-speaker and thus share his vision through a sustained meditation in response to the object of the ode, whether nightingale or wind, as expressed through the language of the poem from its beginning to its end. And how rarely does any question arise concerning the place occupied within the odes by the poet himself as persona. The consensus of criticism would seem to be that the odes of Keats and Shelley convey above all an intimate sense of inner experience or vision that may be referred to the poet himself. Various discussions of Keats in recent years seem to agree that the life of the poet is essentially indistinguishable from his poetic work.[65] Similarly, celebrations of Shelley as a visionary poet, following periods of either abuse or neglect at the hands of critics, assume that his poetry communicates above all a sense of the inner life of the poet himself, a life of the mind which enjoys a singular, privileged, transcendent vision.[66]

My own concern with the hermeneutics of form is, as stated earlier, programmatically opposed to any biographical reading. Nor do I accept any criterion of subjective or personal reference for these poems. The role of the poet-speaker within the poem is constituted exclusively by strategies of language and statement. It is the task of the reader to separate and differentiate the response conveyed by the text from the role of the speaker as such.

This preoccupation with the poetic self is not without basis in the language of the texts themselves. Far more consistently and authoritatively than is the case with Coleridge's "Dejection," or even Wordsworth's "Intimations of Immortality," the language of these poems is organized in such a way as to express the self, its nuances of mood, perspective and attitude, and above all its development and transformation of feeling and response as the statement of the ode proceeds. In the one case, the poet listens to the nightingale and responds to its song; in the other, he responds to the force and movement of the wind as it blows through the autumnal landscape. For a critical understanding of each ode it is necessary that a reader achieve a perspective of conscious difference and distance from that of the poetic persona within the poem. We should resist identifying with the speaker and the sensibility articulated in direct relation to the nightingale and the wind. Through such an exercise in critical differentiation, it is possible to discover the implicit dialogical form of discourse that underlies these quintessential instances of Romantic lyric.

"ODE TO A NIGHTINGALE"

The focus of discourse in Keats's ode moves through subtle shifts of sight and sound as the poem proceeds, delineating a spatial relationship between the listening poet and the singing bird. In stanza VII he speaks of "magic casements" (69), which open out upon the realm of "faery lands" (70). In effect the poet looks and listens through such a threshold or window to the world outside, just as likewise the poet in Coleridge's "Dejection" stood at the window of his cottage looking out upon the natural scene "by yonder throstle woo'd" (26). The surface of the text thus may serve figuratively as such a border or line of demarcation between the inner realm of the poet's mind and the outer realm of nature, in which the singing bird is located. The poet's thought and the power of his imagination move back and forth across that point of mediation as the poem proceeds. Here within, for instance, is the realm described in detail of suffering and mortality in stanza III, the realm of human activity and experience, which the reader shares with the poet merely by being human. What constitutes such human suffering above all, contrary to the claim often made by critics that Keats was acutely aware as he wrote the poem of his own approaching death, is the process of thought itself, which the language of the ode articulates and thematizes: "Where but to think is to be full of sorrow / And leaden-eyed despair" (27-28). There without, by contrast, is located the mysterious, dark grove in which the bird sits and sings, "the forest dim" (20), evoked at the end of stanza II and imagined as the setting of a communion to which the poet's thought moves in stanza IV and which becomes the stage of an encounter "in embalméd darkness" (43) in stanza V, delineated by the natural flowers and fragrances of an ideal space.

To move beyond the prison house of the self into a communion with the song of the bird, involving a mental state of ecstasy or drunkenness, as if the poet truly received the "draught of vintage" (11) that he requests in stanza II, is in reality an event of the poetic imagination, which flows "on the viewless wings of Poesy" (stanza IV). The movement of the ode is thus defined as a journey of the mind out of itself into an imagined communion with the natural source of song, where it is surrounded by the exotic aromas that characterize the mysterious, dark grove. Such communion is represented in the central section of the poem *as if* it were an actual event. For us as readers such a procedure can at best be conveyed as a verbal construct of the poetic imagination, a form of displacement for the self beyond itself, *as if* it were inspired to take flight by the music of its Muse. Yet equally the consequence of such self-transcendence is acknowledged to be oblivion, the annihilation of consciousness and all thought, as well as vision. The movement of the poetic mind in response to the nightingale's song is a kind of figurative death. This fact is recognized by the poet in stanza VI, where he looks back upon the setting of his imagined communion as if it were a spiritual tomb: "Now more than ever seems it rich to die, / To cease upon the midnight with no pain" (55-56).

Yet merely to express an awareness of such consequence, where communion signifies oblivion for the mind, demands the reestablishment of conscious awareness in the self, which thus becomes self-conscious through a reflective separation and opposition between the mind and the object of its thought and experience. A fundamental reversal occurs for the dynamics of poetic thought in the movement from stanza V to VI. The poet can only think about his own death in contrast to the singing bird, which is acknowledged to be timeless and immortal. A temporal contrast is also introduced between past and future as filtered through the mind in forms of memory and prediction, where the bird's song is imagined in stanza VII as having once been heard "by emperor and clown" (64), indeed even by the sad heart of Ruth, whose tale we know from the Bible, when she longed for home in an alien land.

Through the use of hypothesis and negation, projected into an imagined future time – "still wouldst thou sing" (59) – the categorical separation of self from Other is achieved and affirmed. The bird in its singing and the poet in death are differentiated by a subjunctive mood, where a distinction is also established between the temporal and the eternal, the former being the realm of change, suffering and death, the latter the realm of poetry and song. Such differentiation is proclaimed at the outset of the final stanza like the tolling of a funeral bell, heard in the very sound of the word *forlorn*, which concludes stanza VII and is repeated like an echo at the outset of stanza VIII: "Forlorn! the very word is like a bell / To toll me back from thee to my sole self!" (71-72). The cycle of poetic experience thus completes itself, when reflective thought truly recalls the poet to himself and imposes a sense of distance and separation from the power which first motivated his ode, namely the song of the nightingale itself. Three times he calls out his "Adieu!", as if the bird itself were retreating, flying away to some further valley until its song is lost from sound.

Yet we know full well, as does the poet also, that the failure of this communion with song is actually imposed by reflective thought, achieved as necessary consequence of the dialectical movement of the ode through its circular path of imaginative projection and reversal. The poem concludes with questions addressed by the poetic self to itself, to which the answers are already implied by the movement the poem has completed: "Do I wake or sleep?" The music of the bird's song has fled; the drowsy numbness with which the poem began, as if in a dream or a state of intoxication, has been replaced by the full recognition of the self in its autonomous, self-conscious state, from which alone such questions can be formulated.

No reader of Keats's "Nightingale" will fail to observe at some level of awareness that the structure of the ode is defined by the experience within the poet's mind resulting from his response to the bird's song. As I have suggested, that structure is essentially dialectical, moving from solitude to an imagined communion and back to a solitude of self-reflection at a higher level of thought and self-understanding. This movement also proceeds spatially, as if through a magic casement and back again, from the subjective mind outward into the mysterious, dark grove in nature, where the song of the bird originates, then backward to the position of the self through an act of re-cognition that also differentiates the self from the Other, according to a temporal contrast between the process of suffering and mortality and the constancy of eternity. This structural pattern, whether it was only intuitive with Keats or derived from his program of *negative capability,* as formulated in his letters to friends, constitutes the intentional figure of his poetry. It is a metaphor for the dynamic movement of poetic thought. The advance of the poet's discourse from imaginative fusion to reflective self-awareness provides the key to the ode's own self-reference.

A reading of "Ode to a Nightingale" according to the hermeneutics of its form, however, can go one step further than anything the persona of the poet is capable of expressing directly within the poem. This step has not been generally recognized by the many critics of Keats. An attentive reader will refer the reflective awareness achieved by the poet-speaker within the poem to the reader's own response to the poem. An exact analogy prevails between the poet's relationship to the song of the bird and our own relationship to the language of Keats's poem. As I suggested earlier, the figure of a magic casement as threshold that must be crossed through the power of the imagination applies also to the functions of discourse through the sequence of eight stanzas as discrete stages in the process of verbal communication by reading. We also reenact this movement of the mind as we read the poem. The medium of the language performs for us – or rather conveys to us as experience – a corresponding dialectic through engagement and re-cognition. Our journey of thought through the poem is parallel to that of the poet in response to the nightingale and is conditioned precisely by and articulated step by step through the sequence of statements stanza by stanza.

At the same time we recognize a crucial distinction between the experience of the poet and that of the reader, which lends a specific privilege to the poetic as distinct from a hermeneutical consciousness. The singing of the bird is beyond language, located within nature as a pure music, which is also affirmed to be timeless and beyond change. The poet in response to this music composes his ode in language, articulated through the specific formal structure of statement stanza by stanza. This verbal form is ultimately dependent upon temporal and personal experience and reflects the specific human qualities that define the poetic persona within the poem as mortal and subject to human existence. The reader, finally, participates in the poetic event expressed by the poem only vicariously through reading, at the level of a hermeneutical response to the language of the poem. A hierarchy of priority and authenticity is thus established for the ideal of poetic meaning in relation to song that may resemble the well-known view of poetic mimesis presented in Book x of Plato's *Republic*. What we receive as readers of Keats's ode remains necessarily two degrees removed from the object of the poet's response. The reality of the nightingale's song is accessible to us only through the poet's witness to it in language. All we can know about that song is what the poem says about it. What the ode conveys to us therefore is defined by this verbal structure of mediation. The poet responds to the bird's song by interpreting it for himself in language. The most that we as readers may attain is subject to our own interpretive response to the language of the ode as a reflected medium, which evokes and interprets, but cannot itself convey directly, that song. For us the nightingale remains silent and beyond access.

Ours is a subordinate destiny, derived from the text as imitation of the event. Once we recognize the inevitability of such a hierarchy, the consequence *for us* will be apparent. The dialectical process of the poem, which may reflect an actual experience for the poetic self, remains for the reader at best a fictional construct in language, which can only imitate and refer to that which it is not. In this regard the final lines of the poem acknowledge implicitly the singular poignancy of a hermeneutical consciousness, which we have come to share with the poet, but where we remain always dependent upon the language through which the poet speaks to us. His questions to himself are thus also questions for us, and the answers to them, as negations of vision and song, are all too apparent: "Was it a vision, or a waking dream? / Fled is that music: – Do I wake or sleep?"(79-80).

"ODE TO THE WEST WIND"

In the "Ode to the West Wind" Shelley conveys a sophisticated sense of the cult hymn, above all as this is defined by the tradition of ancient Greek choral lyric. To conceive of the wind as a divine spirit is a virtual commonplace in Romantic poetry. As parallel we need only recall the role of the storm and its personification as mythical power in Coleridge's "Dejection." What makes Shelley's ode distinctive as a tour de force in the Romantic era is the manner in which the central figure of the wind as divine power is integrated into the structure of the poem as a whole. Not only does the form of the ode fuse the tradition of the Renaissance sonnet sequence and the terza rima of *The Divine Comedy,* whereby the idolatry of the Petrarchan love poet is superimposed on the spiritual devotion of Dante in his epic poem, but the formality of statement, at the levels of both syntax and rhetoric, extends the theme of invocation into the style of the poet's language at every point. No other poem in English, with the possible exception of Keats's "To Autumn," so categorically focuses all sense of context on the mere invocation of the poet's intended object. The entire poem is constructed upon the role of the poet's voice as it calls out to the invisible and indifferent force of nature, which constitutes its subject.

Everything in the opening three stanzas is devoted to figurative and rhetorical elaboration, accumulated around the central, repeated invocations of the wind. Mythical attributions are constructed and explored to the point where secondary, subordinate clauses implicate their own narratives of dramatic significance. Otherwise the poet's statement consists of no more than the threefold appeal to the wind, that it may hear his call. In a manner quite opposite to the scene described by Keats in his ode, the energy of poetic utterance in Shelley originates entirely within. Keats builds his discourse on the imagined movement of his own mind toward communion with the song of the nightingale in its dark grove. Shelley, responding to the wind as it blows, constructs his elaborate images of what the wind does and where it dwells through a principle of rhetorical overdetermination, almost as if such excess of attribution were a condition for catching the wind's attention. What the poet seeks above all is to make his voice heard, to elicit a response from the indifferent force of the wind. On the one hand, such a stance is suitable to his supplication by prayer and appeal; yet on the other, there is undeniably a sense of competition involved, where the poet's voice tries to match the wind itself by its own powers of descriptive attribution.

In the fourth stanza the focus of attention shifts toward the poet-speaker, through a strategy of retrospection and recapitulation. The self of the speaker is contrasted with the natural objects described in stanzas I to III as the victims of the wind's power: the leaf, the cloud, and the wave. This self-reflective turn to the discourse of the ode is achieved through negation and the assertion of a condition contrary to fact. The pattern of syntax is also constituted by the poet in a manner that recalls the technique in so many of Wordworth's poems, including the opening sections of the "Immortality-ode," where the blissful circumstances of the poet's youth are recalled – as also occurs in Coleridge's "Dejection" (stanza VI), presumably following Wordsworth's example. The poet in Shelley's ode contrasts his former visionary self-confidence, *as if* he then could have truly vied with the wind itself for speed and power, with his present abject condition of "sore need" (52).

The paradox of this analogy between himself and the wind continues in the main clause of the stanza. The poet acknowledges that his poem, as prayer, is directed toward the wind in the absence of that inspired state represented by those objects that have been enumerated as the victims of the wind, i.e., "a wave, a leaf, a cloud!" (53), not to mention his former self. What he now seeks to achieve through his poem is that the wind may *lift* him also as it does those others. The implicit consequence of such desperate pleading is failure. The verbal form of the poet's reflection and negation makes the futility of his prayer all too apparent. He suffers as a victim of life, bleeding upon its thorns (as he asserts, 54), a victim of time, burdened by "a heavy weight of hours" (55). Such images convey a sense of categorical failure to the poet's prayer, which sustains his own imagined sense of death.

The reflective turn of the ode in stanza IV thus imposes a sense of futility upon the rhetoric of appeal in the opening stanzas. The poet knows full well that he is a victim of life and time, and that the wind in its sublime force remains supremely indifferent towards him. The final stanza in no way diminishes this sense of defeat. Yet Shelley discovers an ironic link to his failed prayer by proposing as a substitute for himself his *song* as object of the wind's inspiring power. In Coleridge's "Dejection" (near the end of the ode) the poet imagined a landscape to be the appropriate instrument for the

power of the storm, displacing the Aeolian harp, which was screaming in agony from so strong a wind. Coleridge then projected upon
that landscape an imagined story of tragic conflict, which came
finally to focus upon the cry of a child lost in the wilderness. The
wind of the storm in "Dejection" thus served as the vehicle for a
voice, as if it were the cry of a lost child. The poet in Shelley's ode
goes further than Coleridge did, by making that voice his own, even
though dissociated from himself, at least hypothetically, through a
subordinate and alternative plea to the roaring wind.

Essential to the solution that the poet achieves in Shelley's ode is
a categorical differentiation between the voice of the poet, as it
speaks through the poem and hopes to become the instrument for
a sublime music, and the poet himself as living human being. Even
more important for the hermeneutics of the ode is the implication
that this distinction is only achieved through the verbal act of
reversal and self-reflection, which confronts and acknowledges the
poet's mortality. According to this distinction the poem becomes a
kind of offering to the divinity of the wind, which is legitimized
implicitly by the self-sacrifice and death of the poet. Such a transformation and differentiation fulfills the fundamental pattern of a
tragic plot, appropriate to the aesthetics of Romanticism.

Far more significant for a hermeneutics of form, however, is the
heightened awareness indicated by the shift of focus in the final
stanza of the ode. The poem itself as achieved form serves as an
instrument or vehicle for the voice of the poet, which is no longer
merely a human subject or the individual self. The imagined identification of poetic spirit with the wind as Divine Spirit, expressed in
the climactic line at the center of the final stanza, followed by an
emphatic exclamation – "Be thou, Spirit fierce, / My spirit! Be thou
me, impetuous one!" (61-62) – must be understood in terms of
such displacement. The final passage of the ode provides explicit
affirmation of this identification by reintroducing those objects
affected by the wind, which were listed in the opening stanzas, to
serve as metaphors for the words of the poem itself:

Drive my dead thoughts over the universe
Like withered leaves to quicken a new birth!
And, by the incantation of this verse,

Scatter, as from an unextinguished hearth
Ashes and sparks, my words among mankind!
Be through my lips to unawakened earth

The trumpet of a prophecy!
(63-69)

We note the cadence of intensification in this sequence of appeals. The poet's thoughts will be driven through the world as if they were the dead leaves, fallen from the boughs. Shelley thus combines a traditional metaphor for the souls of the dead as leaves blown upon the wind, which was used by Virgil in *Aeneid* vi and by Dante in *The Divine Comedy,* with an implicit though familiar pun that identifies the language of poetry as printed text upon the "leaves" of a book with such dead leaves blown by the wind. The utterances of the poem as voice, however, are also to be carried like the ashes and sparks from a fire, to ignite those who receive them and set them metaphorically to a spiritual burning. The language of the poem thus becomes itself the "unextinguished hearth." Finally, through the lips of the poet, as if he himself were speaking, the West Wind itself will become "the trumpet of a prophecy," presumably to awaken the entire sleeping earth. Leaves, sparks, tones: all of them carried abroad by the Divine Spirit, are thus substituted for the objects affected by the wind that were cited at the outset: leaves and seeds, clouds, and the voice that awakens "the blue Mediterranean."

The power of retrospection thus provides at the end of the ode a commentary and interpretation of the descriptive material at the outset, which was introduced initially as a rhetorical elaboration, accompanying the poet's prayer to the wind. In the full cycle of the ode we learn how precisely the wind may be both "destroyer and preserver" (14). The reader can now perceive this material to constitute a mythical action, which is identified ultimately with the poem itself through self-reference at the end. All sense of mimetic realism gives way to a form of prefiguration for that process of communication by the poem, which is affirmed at the end to be an instrument of Divine Spirit. The imagery of death contained in these opening stanzas – "pestilence-striken multitudes" (5) and "dark wintry bed" (6), "the dome of a vast sepulchre" (25) and the fear, the trembling, the despoiling (41–42) – may also be understood to anticipate the poet's later sense of his own mortality (stanza iv).

From the final perspective of the poem in stanza v we may impose yet a further implication to these figures, in the manner of a latent hermeneutics, with reference to the process of communication as the poem is read. To read is to be driven, "like ghosts from an enchanter fleeing" (3), and also to be awakened as from a dream by a clarion call; it is to enter into the frenzy and the ecstasy of the "fierce Maenad" (21), and to see the visions of "old palaces and towers" (33). Even the opposition of seasonal cycles, where winter and spring are contrasted thematically in terms of life and death (in stanza i) – an opposition that reappears in the final question of the ode – may be referred to this paradoxical transformation of the self into poetic form, which is now seen to include the reader as well as the poet.

To read Shelley's ode is to undergo such transformation, much in the manner of a symbolic death and rebirth, whereby the meaning is conveyed as a prophecy, which affirms *for us* no more and no less than the presence of the Spirit, involved from the outset as the "wild West Wind" that blows through it. In accord with such a reflective, hermeneutical response to the text, we may affirm the comment concerning the imagined audience of the ode at the end, as "mankind" upon the "unawakened earth." If the poet's final appeal to the wind as the force that is to blow through his own words has any validity, then we who read his words should respond, as he hopes, with a sense of inspiration and new life. The final question asked by the poem must therefore be addressed ultimately to ourselves as readers of the ode. An understanding of the poem must also include the sense that we as its readers serve to fulfill its prophecy. The winter of the West Wind is to be transformed through ourselves, as we are – or should be – transformed by our reading, into spring. Just as the final questions of Keats's "Ode to a Nightingale" were argued to include the implied response of the reader to the poem, so also the famous query with which Shelley's ode concludes must depend upon the reader for its answer.

Poetic Genre as Hermeneutical Form

What is the status of the Romantic ode as a poetic genre? This question cannot be answered definitively on the basis of a few close readings of texts. Nor is the canon of such texts at all definitive. The only serious omission from my argument in this essay regarding the English tradition is Wordsworth, specifically his "Immortality-ode," which has been mentioned several times as a constitutive text for the genre, at least as important as Coleridge's "Dejection." But what of other languages and other national literatures? Could there be a common ground between these English poems and the comparable and essentially contemporaneous odes by German poets, such as Goethe or Hölderlin? I could well imagine that a careful reading of "Harzreise im Winter" by the former or of such odes as "Dichterberuf" or "Der blinde Sänger" by the latter would lend further support to the argument of this essay concerning the English odes. My own conviction, based on a comparative study of the poetics of self-consciousness in Hölderlin's novel *Hyperion* and Wordsworth's autobiographical epic *The Prelude*,[67] is that these two master poets of the Romantic era have a great deal in common, though for reasons that are difficult to explain. To introduce their work in the genre of the Romantic ode to the present essay would require at least as much expansion of the argument as has already been achieved. Such an endeavor of critical reading must be left for another occasion.

Yet the question of genre still remains. For present purposes, by way of conclusion, perhaps a few tentative general remarks may be offered, based on the reading of the three odes by Coleridge, Keats and Shelley attempted above. The evidence from these texts may not be definitive, but no one would question the representative status within the canon of English Romanticism that these three odes may claim. What qualities do they share?

In a certain sense each of these odes may be described as a poem of occasion, somewhat in the manner of the *Gelegenheitsgedicht* developed by Goethe. None of these occasions involves, however, anything more than a confrontation with nature by the isolated poetic self. The Romantic ode is essentially antisocial, even though it is committed to a model of dialogue through its use of direct address and invocation. The occasion that inspires the poem involves a form of spiritual encounter, where a momentary and even unexpected visitation for the poetic self by a force or power of nature causes the effusion of a meditative discourse, which constitutes the ode. The existential condition of the poet assumes quasi-archetypal status. Coleridge in "Dejection" positions himself at the window of his cottage, looking out upon the natural landscape in the darkness of evening and night. Keats defines his position exclusively with reference to the song of the nightingale, which captivates him in some unspecified position from a mysterious and dark grove of nature, also during the night. Where precisely the poet stands and how he might have come there is a matter of absolute indifference to the poetic persona in "Ode to a Nightingale." In the case of Shelley the setting or context for the song is even more abstract, lacking all sense of position and place. Apart from the fact that the wind is blowing and that it is the season of autumn with approaching winter, we have no idea where the poet is located and what circumstances may have led to his encounter with the wind. This kind of poetry may thus be regarded as a private meditation on an existential encounter with the agencies of external nature. Nowhere in the entire European tradition of the ode, least of all in the literature of Classical Greece or Rome, would the ode as poetic form have been used for so specific and idiosyncratic a purpose. In this regard we may justifiably consider the Romantic ode to be the product of a fundamental transformation of the traditional genre.

The second most striking feature of the Romantic ode results from the peculiar formal procedures of its discourse. The poem

consists of a sequence of complex stanzas, organized by certain figurative and rhetorical utterances, which all relate to the poet's internal state of mind in response to the encounter with nature that
motivates the whole. In simplest terms, thinking of the procedures
established by Hegel in his *Phenomenology of Spirit,* we may
describe such a formal sequence of statements as a dialectic of
thought. The mind of the poetic persona moves through a series of
moments, externalized in varying forms of expression, whereby an
evolution of consciousness and understanding is achieved. There is
no linearity to this development, nor any sense of a logical or ratio-
nal progression from one moment to another. The advance of the
mind in its experiential process fulfills one or another of a variety
of patterns consisting of an interaction between the self and its
transcendent Other. Such development does not in any sense constitute a coherent action, as in the plot line of a drama or a novel,
but delineates instead the emergence of a confident and secure
self-consciousness, an inner conviction of thought, which is the
result of this interaction. The goal of the ode would thus appear to
be a form of self-certainty, if not a kind of existential wisdom,
where at least the essential issues for the individual self have been
clarified.

In each of these three odes, however, this dialectical development
of thought may be defined by a sense of conflict and difference,
where the mind recognizes a fundamental failure to achieve and
sustain a unity or even a sense of reciprocity with its Other over a
sustained period of time. I have discussed this pattern of conflict
and difference in relation to Hegel's notion of negation as a necessary stage in the dialectical process of thought. In each of the odes
negation is most clearly defined by contrast to an explicit norm, or
Ideal, which is established in relation to the object in nature
encountered by the poet. This Ideal proves to be an inaccessible
object of desire for the poetic self except through a symbolic pattern of sacrifice and death. The existential condition of the mind is
thus categorically differentiated from its Ideal. The circumstances of
life cannot be fully reconciled with the desire for fusion or coalescence with that ideal object.

In Coleridge's "Dejection" the Ideal is defined in the central stanzas as a doctrine of Joy in quasi-metaphysical and spiritual terms, where the inner life of the mind and the external life of nature are asserted to be interdependent. The poetic self, however, recognizes that its own existential condition remains imprisoned within the parameters of that state of mind that is termed *dejection* by the title of the poem. In "Ode to a Nightingale" the poet responds to the song of the bird by imagining a transcendent motion beyond himself into a state of communion with the song as the ideal of a natural poesy. Immediately upon imagining such a mystical fusion within the setting of song, however, the poet acknowledges that this union would only be possible if the self were to be annihilated and destroyed. The poem ends with a sense of separation and loss, like the awakening from a dream. Shelley's ode, finally, articulates his intellectual and existential response to the wind in such a way that his own mortality, his suffering and inevitable death, are recognized to be the necessary precondition for any identity between his own voice as poet and prophet and the universal force of nature symbolized by the West Wind. Even if such a sacrifice is therefore affirmed and desired, it remains beyond the limits of language and conscious thought – in other words, beyond the limits of what the poem can represent and express as actual experience.

The essential pattern of transformation for the self, finally, which is symbolized by the pattern of death and rebirth, also imposes in each of these odes a fundamental displacement of concern beyond the subjective limits of the self. This displacement could be regarded as failure for the individual self, but within the larger context of the ode as discourse such a transformation of perspective is necessary in order to affirm the larger ethical vision of the poem. A model of human value is established in terms that are universal and thus shared also by the reader as a hermeneutical consciousness, achieved in direct relation to the poem through the act of reading and interpreting it. The ode thus affirms an intersubjective, dialogical structure through its discourse, whereby the failure to realize the Ideal as Joy, or as song, or as the prophecy of a universal power, is compensated for through a sense of implied community in and through the language of the poem. Such a sense of community corresponds exactly to that which Hegel terms the *negativity* of Romantic art.

My own reading of these three odes has suggested that just such an interrelationship through difference may constitute that quality of human existence and self-consciousness that offsets the failure to affirm the Ideal as a living reality. We may all aspire to the condition of Joy in song, as do these poets, but the state of being to which we are bound simply by our common humanity is that of dialogue and difference. All three odes implicitly acknowledge this alternative as a positive option through that which I have called the hermeneutics of form. Not the situation that is described by the poem and not the inner state of mind represented by the poetic self, but rather the dynamic structure of the language itself, through which the dialectical experience of the poem is expressed and communicated to a reader, provides the central message and lesson of the Romantic ode. What is affirmed at the end, in contradistinction to the Ideal that was perceived and desired, is the condition of discourse itself, which we all may share and which conveys even through a sense of conflict and difference a legitimate poetic basis for common understanding.

Hegel and the Romantic Ode

One final question should be asked with regard to the conceptual procedure of my argument in this essay, even if no answer can be attempted at this time. What is the legitimacy of Hegel's theory of Romantic art for a discussion of these odes by English poets? The issue is to locate a common ground between poetic theory and practice, such that the various discontinuities of language and method, of cultural context and historical position, all these and other considerations might be reconciled with each other. It is essentially a question of how Hegel's philosophical aesthetics may be applied to poems that he could not possibly have known by poets in a world that was essentially very different from the one inhabited by the philosopher. Hegel himself would have welcomed such use of his theory, as he believed that everything that falls within the scope of human experience may be subject to the conceptual claims of a philosophical system (such as his own).

The scope of the lecture course on *Aesthetics* at the University of Berlin, delivered at four different times during the years from 1819 to 1831, indicates a confident ambition to subsume all forms of art in all the different media from all cultures and epochs. The application of his theory of Romantic art to poems by English authors, who were either his contemporaries, as Wordsworth and Coleridge were, or a generation younger, as were Keats and Shelley, would only have confirmed Hegel's confidence about his conceptual insights. Nor is it without historical interest for a delineation of Romanticism, as we currently use the term to refer to European cultural history in the early nineteenth century, that the emergence of the English Romantic ode in the public domain coincided almost exactly with the beginning of Hegel's public career as philosopher in Berlin. Yet the proof of legitimacy must still reside with the use we choose to make of Hegelian concepts for a critical reading of the poetic texts today.

One approach to the theories of Hegel would be to trace their development within the context of European Romanticism in the broadest possible sense, of which this philosophy is an integral part and to which it also responds, however problematically. The discussion of Romantic art in the *Aesthetics* is the product of a complex and continuous development in theory, which extends back at least to the 1790s in Jena and Weimar, to the origins of Idealism and Romantic literary theory in response to Kant and Goethe (among others) in the writings of Schiller, the Schlegels, Schelling, Novalis, Hölderlin (among others) and even Hegel himself after his arrival in Jena in 1801.

Another approach would be to address in more general terms the intimate and necessary relationship between poetic practice and theoretical or conceptual thinking about poetry in an era where the interface between poetry and philosophy was closer and more complex than at any time since the Classical era of ancient Athens. This was certainly the case in Germany, though the direct relevance of philosophy for the English Romantic poets, with the exception perhaps only of Coleridge, who was familiar with some of the Germans, is more difficult to prove. Much remains to be done in this field of inquiry, where traditionally the scholars of literature and the historians of philosophy have had little to say to each other.

Ultimately the question that matters most for my argument concerns the concept of a hermeneutics of form as such. Hegel himself never used the phrase, and it might well be argued that I have developed this idea entirely on my own, though admittedly under the direct influence of Hegelian notions – such as the universality of form, the dialectical structure of thought as a dynamic interaction between self and other, reversal and opposition as the basis for reflective recognition, and negativity as the essential structure of reading and interpretation. My views reflect primarily the tradition of philosophical hermeneutics in the twentieth century, above all in the work of Hans-Georg Gadamer. Gadamer, of course, was himself profoundly influenced by Hegel, as he was also by many other philosophers from Plato to Heidegger, but the explicit use of Hegel for hermeneutical theory in *Wahrheit und Methode* can be demonstrated from crucial moments in the argument, as I have tried to do elsewhere.[68]

Finally, the question must remain open: how does a hermeneutical theory of the ode relate to the actual practice of the Romantic poets who created this genre? The only answer to this question must come from readers of the poems themselves, not from the poets and not from the philosophers. Responsibility for insight concerning the hermeneutics of form resides quite properly with ourselves. Hegel provides at best a convenient conceptual focus for an interpretive reading that, I believe, may ultimately stand on its own. The further implications of a hermeneutics of form for the study of poetic works and for the theory of literature in general must therefore be left open to further inquiry.

Chapter 6 : The Temporality of Selfhood

In memory of Paul de Man

The poem must stand as a metaphor for an intellectual intuition.
–Hölderlin

The status of theory in literary criticism has never been so exalted.
The present era is preoccupied almost to a fault with methodology
and basic principles in the study of literature. Earlier assumptions
about the history and the forms of literature are now called into
question by a radical reconsideration of all critical concepts.
Among these concepts *metaphor* assumes a prominent place, both
because it is central to literary language and poetic structure in
several ways and because the term itself has a complex history
within the field of literary criticism and theory. Yet all theory is
dependent, I believe, on historical conditions, and every critical
concept emerges from a process of historical development. For this
reason a theory of metaphor must be grounded in the history of
literary practice in order to serve in any way the needs of practical
criticism.

No scholar has devoted more effort with more erudition than
René Wellek to the study of central terms and concepts in criticism
with regard to their origin and history of usage. In a number of
important essays Wellek has demonstrated the crucial importance
of history for the concepts of literary theory.[1] Such historical study
provides an analogue to the history of literature itself. Complications arise, however, from the interaction between theory and
practice in every historical period. The practice of poets rarely

261

corresponds to the theories of criticism, even where the same individual may engage in both activities.

The history of metaphor in the Romantic era offers a case in point. The importance of metaphor in Romantic poetry has long been recognized by scholars in the field. Theories of metaphor that were contemporary to this poetry, however, whether or not the term itself was used consistently, do not necessarily correspond to what the poets were doing. What we need is a history of literature which takes the interaction of theory and practice into account. The following essay attempts a preliminary consideration of such interaction with regard to metaphor in Romanticism. I limit my discussion to selected theoretical texts, primarily German, but I am concerned throughout with the validity of these theories for the interpretation of Romantic poetry in general, especially as regards the use of metaphor.

Theories of Metaphor

Any discussion of metaphor in Romantic poetry must first acknowledge an apparent discrepancy between the views of modern critics and the views of the Romantic writers themselves. Metaphor, or imagery – whatever term is used for the figurative resources of poetic language – has often been discussed by the critics of Romanticism, as may be seen even in the titles of various essays.[2]

Yet within the body of poetic theory that emerged in the Romantic era, especially in Germany, traditional terms for the figures of discourse, including metaphor, are generally avoided. This reflects a marked hostility at that time toward the entire tradition of rhetorical theory. From Aristotle and Quintilian in antiquity to the handbooks of rhetoric produced during the later eighteenth century, metaphor had been regarded exclusively as a kind of verbal ornament. This at least was the reputation of the term itself within the tradition of rhetoric as understood by writers during the Romantic period. For such poets as Goethe and Wordsworth, verbal ornament, tropes and figures of speech were associated with the modes of artifice in Neoclassical poetry that they radically opposed.

Modern criticism enjoys a broader perspective on metaphor and a greater freedom of usage in its conceptual terminology. In large measure this is a heritage of Romanticism in its revisions of Classical rhetoric. We benefit from a transformation in poetic practice, which has led to a systematic reformulation of traditional critical terms from Classical theory, in order to accommodate the practice of poets in the Romantic and Modern era. A discussion of metaphor, as we now use the term, with reference to the theory and practice of Romanticism thus requires its application to poetic attitudes and techniques that were often explicitly opposed to metaphor, as the term was understood at that time.

Modern theories of metaphor have shifted attention away from rhetorical figures of speech toward modes of interaction – "crossing over" and "transgression"[3] – within larger and more fundamental structures of discourse. Poetic metaphor has thus come to be defined by the interaction between separate frames of reference in a text, in such a way that traditional distinctions between literal and figurative meaning no longer apply. At least since I. A. Richards's *Philosophy of Rhetoric* in 1936, with its now idiosyncratic substitution of the terms *tenor* and *vehicle* for the literal and figurative components of a trope, the language of poetry as such has been argued to be fundamentally and necessarily metaphoric.[4] Richards's view of metaphor derives in large measure from Romantic theory, in particular from Coleridge's concept of the *imagination*.[5] Especially important for Richards's notion of poetic interaction – often cited by Richards himself – is the passage in chapter 14 of the *Biographia Literaria*, where Coleridge describes the imagination as an integrating (or "esemplastic") power, which blends, fuses, balances and reconciles the separate and often opposing parts of a poem into a coherent unity of whole.[6]

A corresponding view of the poetic imagination as a principle of integration for the disparate elements of verbal structure developed in German Romantic theory. Schelling's notorious (if incorrect) etymological definition, which was also known to Coleridge,[7] provides a convenient focal point for the discussion that follows: "The splendid German word *Einbildungskraft* means in fact the power of 'forming a unity' (*Ineinsbildung*), from which in truth all creation derives."[8] It is characteristic of such theoretical pronouncements in the context of German philosophical Idealism concerning the poetic faculties of the mind that the term *metaphor* does not occur.

The validity of relating modern theories of metaphor to Romantic theories of the imagination was first demonstrated for me by Paul Ricoeur.[9] Looking back to the definition of metaphor provided by Aristotle in the *Poetics* under the heading of style (*lexis*, 1457b6–33), Ricoeur argues that metaphor – analogous to what Aristotle at a more comprehensive level of poetic structure terms "plot," or *mythos* – participates in the most essential function of poetry as Aristotle views it, namely the representation or imitation of human action.[10] Metaphor thus assumes both a structural and a mimetic function for poetic language. The integration of disparate elements is validated by the mimetic or referential function, so that metaphor appears to derive its truth or reality from its relation to the action represented. Some contemporary theories of metaphor, the linguistic and semantic approaches in particular, often ignore or even deny this referential aspect.[11]

Romantic theories of the imagination, by contrast, retain this essential duality of concern for both structure and reference (as will be argued shortly). I do not intend – nor did Ricoeur – to imply that Aristotle and the Romantics are interchangeable. My approach to Romantic theory, however, which is undertaken in the spirit of Ricoeur's inquiry, will apply to Romantic theory an insight into the function of metaphor derived conveniently from Aristotle. The reconciliation of opposites, which constitutes the essential quality of the poetic imagination for the Romantics, is closely related to the capacity of poetry to express, reveal, represent or *refer to,* whatever it stands for, or *means.* In the argument that follows, I attempt to demonstrate that such a coincidence between *poiesis,* as *Ineinsbildung,* and *mimesis,* as *representation* (the German term would be *Darstellung*), is indeed central to both the theory and the practice of Romantic poetry, whether or not the Romantics called it metaphor.

Romantic Theories of Poetic Language: The Role of Schiller

In order to define the place of metaphor in Romantic theories of poetry, we must first consider Romantic attitudes toward the function of language in poetry. The evidence at first seems disappointing, despite important developments at that time in the philosophy of language and the establishment of linguistics as scientific endeavor, through the work of such theorists as Vico, Rousseau, Herder, the Schlegels, Humboldt and Hegel.[12] Discussions of poetry rarely include a concern for language, except as a cultural artifact or a medium of expression. Poetry tends to be discussed with regard to its ethical value for mankind or its experiential value for the individual mind.

To offer one convenient example among many, we may consider the familiar argument of Wordsworth in his preface to the *Lyrical Ballads* (2d ed.) of 1800. The poet's avowed purpose, he asserts, is to speak "the real language of men in a state of vivid sensation" and to impart pleasure, both in kind and quantity, which is appropriate to poetry.[13] We are accustomed to regard the claims of this document – especially if we heed Coleridge's later critical assessment of it[14] – as somewhat contradictory in relation to the way in which Wordsworth's poetry actually is written. The real language of men is understood in the preface according to norms of social usage, derived from the rustic simplicity and authenticity of style in the ballad tradition, which Wordsworth was imitating in many of his poems and which were familiar to the poet from actual experience in his native Lake District.

But such models can hardly accommodate the complexities of ironic perspective and tone of voice that actually occur, as every reader knows, in the language of the poems included in *Lyrical Ballads*. Wordsworth's most famous pronouncement in the Preface is that poetry should consist in the "spontaneous overflow of powerful feelings." He does qualify this assertion by acknowledging also that the poet must know what value these feelings are to convey.[15]

He must have "thought long and deeply"; the lyrical overflow of feeling can only proceed through a "recollection of emotion in tranquillity." The language of poetry is here deduced entirely from assumptions about its function. Wordsworth is concerned, in a manner characteristic of all the Romantic poets, with the personal experience that underlies his poetry and with the effect his poems are to have upon their readers. Nothing at all is said in the preface that would indicate any concern for metaphor whatsoever.

We best approach Romantic metaphor more indirectly with reference to the preoccupation of eighteenth-century aesthetics with those aspects of art and poetry that were termed the beautiful and the sublime. Particularly important for my purpose are the theoretical essays written by Friedrich Schiller during the last decade of the century. A convenient focus in this regard is provided by a series of letters that Schiller wrote to his friend Körner in 1793, outlining an essay he planned to write (but never did), to be entitled *Kallias, or on Beauty.*[16]

Schiller's position is defined in contrast to the earlier views of Burke and Kant, which he criticizes as too subjective, since they address primarily the effect of beauty upon the beholder. Schiller proposes a more objective theory, where beauty is defined primarily as an internal, formal aspect of the work of art itself. His definition, subsequently reformulated in 1795 for publication in the *Letters on the Aesthetic Education of Man,*[17] is that "beauty is the appearance of freedom" [Schönheit ist Freiheit in der Erscheinung].[18]

Two important ambiguities are contained in this definition, both of which ultimately pertain to the role of metaphor in poetry as it is implied in Schiller's theory. The term *appearance* (*Erscheinung*) first indicates *semblance* (*videtur*), that which only seems to be, but it also signifies, in what may be the most crucial pun in the aesthetic theory of German Romanticism, *manifestation* as phenomenon (*lucet*).[19] The argument of the letters to Körner in 1793 indicates clearly that Schiller initially intended only the former sense of the word.[20] By 1795 in the *Letters on Aesthetic Education,* however, Schiller was fully aware of this ambiguity, though he associated the latter sense of *Schein* with Beauty as the ideal of art. (I will return to this point.) By the end of the decade, due especially to the Neoplatonic leanings of such theorists as Schelling, the shift of preference in Romantic theory toward Beauty as *manifestation* was complete: the view of art as mirror of nature had changed to the notion that it *shines* like a lamp.[21] The definition of ideal beauty proposed later by Hegel in his lectures on *Aesthetics* (published in 1835) merely affirms what had by then become a commonplace in Romantic theory. Beauty in art is defined as "the sensual manifestation of the idea" [das sinnliche Scheinen der Idee].[22]

The second ambiguity in Schiller's definition occurs in the term *freedom*. On one hand, freedom in art is understood as an aesthetic condition intrinsic to the work itself, a state of balance, harmony and repose, where no part conflicts with any other. In this sense artistic freedom constitutes an essential structural or formal feature of the work. On the other hand, however, freedom in art also has ethical and even political implications. In this sense the ideal of Beauty in art represents a condition of human existence in accord with social, political and cultural norms. Such freedom is a condition of the self, understood either individually or in relation to some social group, with which presumably both the reader and the author may identify. Equally, however, as in political drama or the novel of society, freedom may signify a collective ideal, which is represented through the work of art as a utopian goal or as imagined reality. Within the work of art, therefore, we may *seem* to be *free,* and this constitutes the aesthetics of beauty as ideal.

In this latter sense of freedom in art Schiller was indebted to an important dictum contained in Paragraph 59 of Kant's *Critique of Judgement* (1790), entitled "On Beauty as a Symbol of Morality."[23] In the *Letters on Aesthetic Education,* however, Schiller also pays eloquent tribute to the other more internal, aesthetic quality of freedom, as, for instance, in the celebration he offers of the Classical bust of Juno Ludovisi.[24] By thus establishing an intentional ambiguity between the ethical and the aesthetic values of art, Schiller set in motion a development in literary theory that quickly assumed profound significance for Romanticism. What initially in Kant had been restricted to a principle of analogy – where the relation of beauty to ethical values is understood as a fiction or artifice – ultimately became, for such a theorist as Schelling, a doctrine of identity – where the internal structure of the poetic work is argued to represent, embody and reveal the most fundamental qualities and values of the human spirit.

These ambiguities in Schiller's definition of beauty provide the basis for a Romantic theory of poetic metaphor. Important also for such a theory in Schiller's aesthetics is the claim for an intimate relationship between the beautiful and the sublime. The latter term signified for Schiller, as for eighteenth-century aesthetic theory in general, the capacity of art to communicate an experience of the infinite or the transcendent.[25] Particularly important for the association of the sublime with the beautiful is a statement in the fourteenth of the *Letters on Aesthetic Education.*[26] In the context of a discussion concerning the experiential processes of the human mind, Schiller admits that his concept of freedom – reintroduced in the central section of the *Letters* under the influence of Fichte's *Wissenschaftslehre*[27] – is an ideal norm beyond the possibility of actual realization in political and social existence. Freedom is here defined as a reciprocal balance between two opposing forces or impulses (*Triebe*) of the mind: the urge for form (*Formtrieb*) and the urge for substance (*Stofftrieb*).[28] In its broadest implications this dichotomy may be referred to the conventional distinction between thought and emotion, respectively. Aesthetic experience is defined in the next letter as a combination of these two urges to constitute through their reciprocal interaction a third impulse, the urge for play or "play-impulse" (*Spieltrieb*). Aesthetic experience is defined exclusively in terms of such a reciprocal interaction between *form* and *substance.*

Beauty, we recall, is for Schiller the appearance (*manifestation*) of freedom. In this context such freedom is the result of a perfect balance or harmony between these opposing forces in the self. Beauty is thus described as "living form" (*lebende Gestalt*),[29] a phrase which when applied to the work of art combines its referential and its structural aspects, signifying also the coincidence or union of the ethical and aesthetic functions of art. The *play-urge* as described by Schiller is essentially identical with the creative faculty of the mind, which otherwise is called the *imagination* (*Einbildungskraft*) by theorists from Kant and Fichte to Humboldt, Schelling and others, and also corresponds to the definition offered by Coleridge in his *Biographia Literaria*.[30] The concept of a reciprocal interaction between thought and emotion, furthermore, also corresponds to that capacity of poetry described by Wordsworth in his preface to *Lyrical Ballads*, which was mentioned above, whereby thought and feeling are united through the recollection of emotions in tranquillity, so that the "spontaneous overflow of powerful feelings" combines with the exercise of reflective thought.

The passage that is crucial for an implicit theory of metaphor in Schiller's fourteenth letter deserves full quotation:

Should there, however, be cases in which he [man]…were to be at once conscious of his freedom and sensible of his existence, were, at one and the same time, to feel himself [as] matter and come to know himself as mind, then he would in such cases, and in such cases only, have a complete intuition of his human nature, and the object which afforded him this vision would become for him a symbol of his *accomplished destiny* and, in consequence (since that is only to be attained in the totality of time), serve him as a manifestation of the Infinite.[31]

Aesthetic freedom is here asserted to be an ideal, which, if realized, would provide man with a complete intuition (*Anschauung*) of his humanity.[32] The object that might afford such a vision of self-fulfillment would be a Symbol of man's "accomplished destiny." This object is not explicitly identified as a work of art or as a poem, though clearly the meaning that the object conveys corresponds precisely to that quality of Beauty which is subsequently described as *living form*.[33] The entire statement, however, is formulated in the subjunctive mood of a condition contrary to fact. This indicates that such an ideal object cannot, in Schiller's opinion, actually be achieved. The final phrase of the passage also emphasizes a sense of infinite limit by asserting that such an accomplished destiny could only be attained in the totality of time. Were that possible, then the work of art as Symbol of human fulfillment would indeed manifest the infinite: "eine Darstellung des Unendlichen." The beautiful, in other words, would then be identical with the sublime.

In this passage Schiller establishes the basis for a theory of art which is central to European Romanticism.[34] Not only are the beautiful and the sublime regarded as essential components of one and the same experience, but the aesthetic and ethical values of art are united within the work as well. The harmonious interaction of parts constitutes a single whole, which as Symbol manifests the infinite; beautiful feeling and nobility of thought and action are seen to be one and the same. Even more important for the present argument, the ideal of humanity is attributed to the work of art as the content or substance of its symbolic form. The work of art in its imagined ideal signifies and reveals as symbolic object the fulfillment of man's destiny.

In this statement from Schiller's *Letters,* however oblique and tentative – far more than anything in Kant's aesthetics[35] – the Romantic theory of Symbol was first formulated. Schiller's successors in the development of this theory of poetry, at least in Germany – Wilhelm von Humboldt, Schelling, Novalis, Friedrich Schlegel, Hölderlin and (above all) Goethe and Hegel – were all directly influenced by the *Letters'* argument in the years following its publication in 1795, whether or not they were willing to acknowledge their debt to Schiller. Through this development there emerged a coherent program for poetic practice, which constitutes what is meant by Romanticism.[36]

Crucial for Schiller's argument is his implicit distinction between the ideal norm of theory and the actual practice of poets. The ideal work of art, he argued, would constitute a symbol of man's accomplished destiny, which could only be achieved in the totality of time. The actual experience of poetry, by contrast, is always subject to temporal process, to change and conflict and to all the vicissitudes of human existence in history. For actual experience, the ideal of self-fulfillment can never be more than an aesthetic illusion. The status of the artwork or poem in its relation to such actual human experience may far more appropriately be described therefore as *metaphoric* than *symbolic,* though Schiller does not explicitly do so.

In defense of such a metaphoric status for poetry within Romantic theory, I wish to consider what I have termed in my title the *temporality of selfhood*. In order to clarify what I have in mind, it is necessary to define what the temporal dimensions of poetry can be and how these relate to a concept of metaphor in contradistinction to symbol.

Poetic Functions of Time and the Romantic Self

The temporality of selfhood in Romantic poetry provides a convenient, if not an exclusive, focus for defining the function of metaphor in terms of the distinction between the contextual and the referential aspects of poetic language outlined earlier with regard to the views of Paul Ricoeur. What are the temporal functions of poetic language for the structural coherence of the poem? Three separate functions for time in poetry may be readily distinguished: (1) the temporal extension of discourse, that is, the time of utterance as performance; (2) the experiential process represented by such discourse, that is, time as experienced within the poem; and (3) the location of the discourse within a conscious perspective on cultural or historical time, that is, time as self-consciousness of historical place.

The first function concerns almost exclusively the structural or formal features of the language, since every statement – as implicit speech act, if not as written text – requires that it take place within a temporal medium, from a moment of beginning to a moment of conclusion. We may measure such temporal presentation as the performative movement of the language itself, its flow or rhythm, which is often controlled, or at least arranged, by strict criteria of organization, such as meter, stanza form, grammar or syntax.

The third function of time – omitting the second for the moment – is almost exclusively referential, even where the statement of the poem is so general and abstract that it cannot be easily located within a specific temporal, or historical, situation. This aspect of temporality constitutes the impulse of poetry toward self-consciousness, even though – like Schiller's notion of an accomplished destiny – this may prove to be an ideal limit beyond the performative domain of any speech act. A reflective awareness of time and place must be included in every poem, however that may be manifested, thus contributing to what Aristotle called the *mythos,* or story, as mimetic representation. In Romantic poetry, from the occasional lyric to the philosophical hymn, the mythos includes an awareness of temporality, essentially as a sense of history.

For both these functions of time the distinction between structure and reference is fairly clear, with each concerned with either the one or the other. Difficulties begin to arise, however, when we turn to the second of the three functions defined above, namely the experiential process represented or embodied by the poem. Here structural and referential functions overlap and coincide. Yet here guidance is also provided by Romantic theory, specifically where an intentional ambiguity exists between thought and emotion, between self-awareness and self-enactment, or between what Fichte called *Selbstbewußtsein* and *Tathandlung.*[37] Indeed, the metaphoric dimension of Romantic poetry, as I have defined it in this essay, depends almost entirely upon ambiguities of temporality at this level of discourse. Metaphor is a function of the temporality of selfhood.

All readers of literature are familiar with the prototypical Romantic poet-hero. He (virtually always male) is usually preoccupied with himself and with his own subjective experience. He is possessed by a limitless existential longing that can never satisfied. He is sensitive to life, in particular to the life of nature, yet troubled at the same time by a profound sense of isolation and alienation from all human society. He is an outsider figure, striving to achieve self-fulfillment through his own devices. He is a Werther or a Faust (not to mention other figures from Goethe), a Don Juan (Mozart's or Byron's), a Eugene Onegin (Pushkin), or a Hoffmann (at least in the writer Hoffmann's ironic literary guise as Kreisler, the demonic musician), a Julien Sorel (in Stendhal's *Le Rouge et le Noir,* with some reservations), an Ishmael or an Ahab (as both are portrayed in *Moby Dick*), an Underground Man (as in Dostoevsky), a Seducer (as in Kierkegaard's *Either/Or*), or a Bohemian. Indeed, if we may assign a name to the poetic persona in their respective poetry, using for convenience the name of the author, the Romantic poet-hero is a "Novalis," a Hölderlin, or a Kleist, a Blake or a Wordsworth, a Shelley, a Keats, a Byron, or any of the host of poetic selves who are known to us in and through their poems; he is present also in the next generation, as Pushkin, Heine, Poe or Baudelaire. The list could go on and on.

The true Romantic is the self which speaks from the poem, which expresses itself in poetry and as poetry, and which thus becomes aware of itself and struggles to comprehend itself as a life in poetry, indeed as a poem, though usually a highly subjective, self-reflective, often self-absorbed poem. In this regard, Romantic poetry has always seemed vulnerable to the claim that it is too subjective, too inner-directed (or *innig,* as the Germans say), even solipsistic or narcissistic. There was a time, especially in the last century, in the wake of polemical pronouncements by such critics as Goethe, Mme. de Staël or Heine, when the label *Romantic* designated a pejorative or negative judgment. Critics of Romanticism, however, have always tended to confuse a moral judgment on this poetic – or *Romantic* – self, whether negative or positive, with a critical interpretation of the actual poems in which that self is represented. Romantic poetry has thus all too frequently been dismissed, or celebrated, as *Erlebnisdichtung,*[38] as the expression of a private, intimate, subjective mood or experience, the confessions of a "beautiful" (or a not-so-beautiful) soul or of a "justified sinner," the tales of an idiot, of an ancient mariner or of an opium eater.

Such a view of Romanticism is one-sided and ultimately wrong. Readers of representative lyrics and odes, especially in recent decades, have gradually come to recognize that the meaning of the poem is more complex than merely the sense of the self or persona that speaks or sings through it. Evidence for such complexity has also been provided by Romantic theories of poetry, although the application of such theories to the interpretation of specific poems remains a very uncertain endeavor.

Wherever we turn to the poets themselves for guidance about

the meaning of their poetry, however, we find that all concern for the subjective self is made subordinate to a much more comprehensive concern for the kind of experience that traditionally has been understood in religious terms, as a revelation, a communion, an epiphany, or a vision of the infinite, the absolute, the eternal, the divine. What Romantic poetry seeks above all to embody, represent, communicate and reveal – this was argued with authority by Hegel in his *Aesthetics*[39] – is an experience which transcends the subjective self and participates in the universal life of things. Students of Romanticism who are familiar with recent reassessments of the old clichés about the poetic self will require no further evidence for such transcendent concerns. The question before us is rather how to relate this concern to the function of metaphor in poetic language in terms of the temporal dimensions of structure and meaning.

Once again I look to the argument introduced earlier from Schiller's definition of beauty and its capacity, were it ever to be fully achieved in art, to manifest the infinite in symbolic form. Schiller's reservation, we recall, was based on his claim that the complete fulfillment of the self, its accomplished destiny, would only be possible in the totality of time. In what way might poetry contain or include such a totality? This question must be addressed both to the structural and to the referential dimensions of temporality in language. If a poem were to manifest something infinite, it would presumably have to transcend its own finite limits. It would have to point toward this something as beyond itself and somehow provide its language with the capacity to communicate a valid sense, feeling or intuition of infinity.

Here is the basic dilemma of all Romantic poetry. The temporal structure of the poem is intended to transcend itself and reveal the infinite; but the language of the poem, the situation it represents and the voice of the self that speaks through it, all are necessarily finite and limited, subject to the processes of time, human experience and human history. According to the ideal of art – as I have defined it from Schiller's theory – the beautiful and the sublime should become identical through a symbolic fusion, whereby the temporal and the infinite are united within the totality of the poem. Such a concept of symbolic form stands at the center of Romantic theory, at least with regard to the ideal norm of poetry. In practice, however, the poets themselves, who usually provide a more reliable measure than the theorists for what poetry actually does and can do, ultimately recognize that such a symbolic fusion or coalescence cannot be achieved. Some degree of tension or discontinuity always remains between the finite means and the infinite end, between the temporal structure and the transcendent goal, which poetic language and poetic experience cannot overcome. This tension or discontinuity, which could also be described in terms of *ironic* or *dialectical* structure (especially if we were to use these terms as defined by such German theorists as Friedrich Schlegel or Hegel),[40] is what I mean by the *metaphoric* – as distinct from the *symbolic* – mode of Romantic poetry.

Theories of Symbol and Allegory

This distinction between metaphor and symbol may appear to contradict a central tradition of criticism with regard to Romantic poetry. Yet the status of the symbol as a norm for Romanticism has been seriously questioned in recent years. An authoritative survey of the history of the concept is provided by Hans-Georg Gadamer in the chapter of *Wahrheit und Methode* concerning the subjectivization of aesthetics by Kant.[41] Working with the traditional distinction between symbol and allegory, Gadamer traces the impact of Paragraph 59 of Kant's *Critique of Judgment* (cited earlier) within the context of a polemic against the rhetorical tradition at the end of the eighteenth century, in favor of the spontaneous creativity of the poetic genius (*WM*, 71ff.; *TM*, 75ff.).

Particularly important for my own argument is Gadamer's assertion that Schiller was the primary recipient of Kant's application to aesthetics of the scholastic concept of the *analogia entis*, whereby the beautiful was conceived as a symbol for moral goodness: "Das Schöne is das Symbol des Sittlich-Guten." Also crucial is the emphasis placed by Gadamer on Schelling as the most eloquent and systematic spokesman for the symbol as the essential norm for all art (*WM*, 72–73; *TM*, 77–78). This didactic shift resulted ultimately in the categorical rejection of allegory as a valid mode of art through the work of such later Romantics as Creuzer, Solger and Fr. Th. Vischer (*WM*, 73–76; *TM*, 78ff.). Few theoretical judgments in literary criticism have enjoyed such a confident history as this rejection of allegory, which went unchallenged until the middle of our century.

The polarity of symbol and allegory was subsequently applied by Paul de Man, under direct influence of Gadamer's argument, to his important discussion of allegory in the essay "The Rhetoric of Temporality."[42] De Man offers a radical critique of the symbol as a norm for English Romantic poetry, proposing the concepts of *allegory* and *irony* instead. De Man's description of the Romantic theory of symbol, which essentially agrees with the German ideas discussed above, is as follows: "an intimate unity between the image that rises up before the senses and the supersensory totality that the image suggests."[43] The focus of de Man's attack is the work of M. H. Abrams and Earl Wasserman on Romanticism, for whom – as de Man argues – such terms as *symbol, metaphor* and *image* are associated with one another in fundamental sympathy with the programmatic assertions about poetry by such English Romantics as Coleridge and Wordsworth.[44] Finally, he takes these critics to task for imposing a radical subjectivity on Romanticism, which he argues to be a fundamental distortion of what Romantic poetry actually does. His polemic culminates in the following assertion about such criticism:

The relationship with nature has been superseded by an intersubjective, interpersonal relationship that, in the last analysis, is a relationship of the subject toward itself. Thus the priority has passed from the outside world entirely within the subject, and we end up with something that resembles a radical idealism.[45]

The dichotomy between symbol and allegory, which de Man interprets in accord with Gadamer and which Gadamer explains with reference to the history of aesthetic theory, corresponds closely to the distinction I have been making between symbol and metaphor. More recent essays by de Man, specifically on the theory of metaphor in Rousseau and Nietzsche,[46] indicate that his thinking about figuration in poetic language expanded over the years, to the point where both allegory and metaphor came to be regarded as subcategories for the general function of figurative language in poetry as such. De Man's later theory of metaphor would not be in disagreement with the claims of this essay.

The opposition of symbol and metaphor in Romantic theory may also be understood in terms of Schiller's distinction between naive and sentimental poetry. The basis for this distinction is a theory of cultural history, which underlies much of Romantic thought concerning the structure of historical time. From Rousseau through Kant and Herder to Schiller and the later Romantics, history is argued to move through three stages of culture, in a secular analogy to salvation history as defined by traditional Christian thought.[47] Human society, as the middle stage of culture, is located between a presumed original state of nature, where all life was in harmony with itself as part of the totality of nature, and a projected utopian future, where all life would be reintegrated, thus resolving all conflict at a higher level of consciousness into a new golden age. Early Romanticism, especially in response to the French Revolution, as M. H. Abrams has argued, was filled with "apocalyptic imaginings."[48] The era of ultimate cultural and spiritual fulfillment was thought to be at hand, when mankind would advance to the final and highest stage of culture. Poets and philosophers alike looked forward to the emergence of a universal peace, the kingdom of God on earth. *Reich Gottes* was the password exchanged by Hegel and Hölderlin when they graduated from the Tübingen seminary in 1793.[49]

Despite such hopes, which were all disappointed in one way or another, language was still understood to reflect the conditions of difference and discontinuity, which constitute the middle stage of human culture. Language in its structure and its functions thus defines our sense of temporal and historical place. This sense of place was discussed above as the third aspect of time in poetry. The motive for poetry may well be the hope of attaining unmediated vision or an intimation of immortality, but the verbal medium is always bound by temporality and thus subject to division, conflict and difference.

All the major Romantic poets were aware of the temporality of their own language in the realm of history, whether or not they accepted it willingly. In Schiller's terms, they were all sentimentalists; and norms of poetic naiveté, where subject and object can coalesce and resolve all conflict within a symbolic form of freedom, remained at best an ideal or a projection, located either in the past, at the origins of culture in a world of pastoral innocence, or else in a world yet to come, in a new golden age or the utopian *Endzeit* of human history. The recollection of what had been lost or the anticipation of what was to come could only be achieved poetically through the language of *metaphor,* that sentimental mode of discourse where emotion and intuition must interact through a dialectical opposition with reflective thought and self-consciousness. The voice which speaks in poetry can only be aware of itself within a temporal structure, just as the source for any vision of transcendence must be the mortal eye, which can only see its object by standing apart from it. Mystical communion and symbolic identity reside beyond the limits of human language.

SCHELLING'S *SYSTEM OF TRANSCENDENTAL IDEALISM*

Poetic theory is often more unwilling than poetic practice to accept limits. Critics of Romanticism have also tended to confuse the two, as if theory and practice might coincide. Even the poets have sometimes described what they would like to do in poetry as if they had actually done it. A significant contrast between theory and practice in poetry may be observed in two separate, though related, programs for art and culture that were drafted in Germany during the late 1790s, within the context of early Romantic Idealism, in immediate response to Schiller's theoretical essays. I refer to Schelling's discussion of art in the final section of his *System of Transcendental Idealism* (1800) and the essay fragments on poetic composition drafted by Hölderlin (1799/1800).

The difference between Schelling's philosophical concern for art and Hölderlin's theory of poetic structure pertains directly to the distinction between symbol and metaphor discussed above. These two friends met as students (along with Hegel) at the Tübingen seminary in 1790. Both Hölderlin and Hegel were five years older than the precocious and flamboyant Schelling, who was only two years behind them in his studies. Together they shared an initial enthusiasm for the French Revolution and for the emergence of Idealism in the philosophical work of Kant. They became convinced that art and poetry had a crucial role to play in the history of human culture. Above all, they fervently believed that a great new age of the World Spirit, for which the French Revolution and the critical philosophy of Kant were the prophetic signs, would be inaugurated by the poets and the philosophers. Indeed they considered their own destinies to be defined by such a mission. Hölderlin subsequently attempted to define for his own poetic work a principle of structure in accord with the process of poetic composition, with which he hoped to achieve the artwork appropriate for this festive new era. Schelling, as professor of philosophy at the University of Jena, at the age of twenty-five, drafted a systematic philosophy of art within a more comprehensive framework for a unified philosophical system to encompass all aspects of human existence. As the immediate follower of Fichte at Jena, Schelling proclaimed an absolute Idealism for philosophy. A brief juxtaposition of the respective positions of these two Romantic theorists, in particular with regard to the essential difference between them, will provide a convenient conclusion for the present essay.

Hegel later remarked in the introduction to his lecture course on *Aesthetics* that Schelling was the first to draft an authentic "science of art" (*Wissenschaft der Kunst*) in absolute terms.[50] Schelling did so in the concluding section of his *System of Transcendental Idealism,* not from any independent interest in art itself (as Schelling emphasizes),[51] but rather as the ideal means of resolving differences for the experiencing mind, as outlined earlier in the work, in both its theoretical and its practical activities. The work of art – so he argues – is the product of an intuition (*Anschauung*) which unites the manifestation of freedom (*die Erscheinung der Freiheit,* 281; the phrase is presumably taken from Schiller) and the intuition of a work of nature. Art constitutes an identity of consciousness and unconsciousness within the self, such that the self is also conscious of this identity: "Identity of the Conscious and the Unconscious in the Self and a Consciousness of this Identity."[52]

Such a notion of identity is central to Schelling's concept of the symbol, as indicated by his later definition of art in the *Philosophy of Art* (ca. 1804; publ. 1859), where the dichotomy of general and particular replaces that of the unconscious and the conscious: "Representation of the Absolute with absolute indifference of the General and the Particular within the Particular is only possible symbolically."[53] Extending this concept of the *Symbol* to include the entire domain of art, Schelling also develops in that later work a theory of *myth* as the necessary substance or content of all art, exemplified by Homer and ancient Greek mythology.[54]

In the second part of his discussion of art in the *System* of 1800, where the character of the work of art is discussed, the qualities associated with the beautiful and the sublime – though acknowledged to be opposed by definition – are said to coincide in the ideal work of art: "thus there is no true, objective opposition between the Beautiful and the Sublime; what is truly and absolutely beautiful is always already sublime and the sublime (if it is truly so) is also beautiful."[55] The creative power of the mind which achieves such a fusion of opposites, that "miraculous poetic power" *(jenes wunderbare [Dichtungs-]vermögen,* 295–96), is called the imagination (*Einbildungskraft*). This faculty was already discussed in the opening of Schelling's argument as essential to the aesthetic act, specifically with regard to the reflective awareness of what is "absolutely unconscious" and "non-objective": ". . . this reflectivity of the absolutely unconscious and non-objective is only possible through an aesthetic act of the imagination."[56]

Schelling also asserts that the symbolic fusion of the conscious and the unconscious in art achieves an authentic revelation, "the only and eternal revelation which there is" [die einzige und ewige Offenbarung, die es gibt] (286). Art thus manifests the Absolute, defined as the universal ground of a preestablished harmony

between what is conscious and what is unconscious: "jenes Absolute, welches den allgemeinen Grund der prästabilierten Harmonie
zwischen dem Bewußten und dem Bewußtlosen enthält" (284).

Schelling's argument is a miracle of compression and conceptual
clarity. Nowhere else is the Romantic theory of symbolism in art
stated with such conviction and authority. At the same time, however, the practical question of how art might actually achieve such a
symbolic fusion is never seriously raised. The nearest Schelling ever
comes to this question is a contrast expressed in passing between
art (*Kunst*) and what he refers to as "poesy" (*Poesie*). The latter
term appears to share the somewhat mystical, Neoplatonic overtones which dominate the opening section of Friedrich Schlegel's
Dialogue on Poetry, a theoretical work of equal authority though
less systematic conceptual clarity, published in the journal *Das
Athenaeum* in 1800.[57] Schelling's theory of art in his *System of
Transcendental Idealism* and Schlegel's concept of poetry in the
Dialogue on Poetry constitute together the high point of a Romantic
aesthetics within the so-called Jena School of Romanticism.

In actual life, as Schelling admits (282, 294ff.), both for action
and for conscious thought, such identity as he demands for art is
impossible. Freedom and necessity, conscious and unconscious
activity, are always opposed. Identity may only be approached
through an infinite progression, which in human life and in historical time is never attainable. In art, however, a point must be
achieved – so Schelling asserts – where conscious productivity is
transcended and the opposition of consciousness and unconsciousness is dissolved into a unity (283). This point of symbolic unity is
achieved through the power of *genius,* through which that aspect of
art (*Kunst*) termed poesy (*Poesie,* 287) is affirmed and realized.
Schelling offers no further explanation of how this might happen.
The power of genius is taken essentially for granted as the prerequisite for true poetry. Schelling thus advocates a theory of the creative
process in art where conscious production dissolves into a kind of
mystical communion, which is unconscious yet nonetheless accessible to experience through the work of art.

HÖLDERLIN'S THEORY OF POETIC TONES

Hölderlin was also convinced for a time that poetry might truly reintegrate the world and thus affirm an all-encompassing totality and unity through beauty. The preface to a draft version of his novel *Hyperion,* composed in 1795, the so-called "Vorrede zur vorletzten Fassung," expresses this conviction unambiguously:

> To resolve that eternal conflict between our self and the world, to bring again that peace of all peace, which passes understanding, to unite ourselves with nature into One infinite whole, that is the goal of our striving, whether we may agree about it or not.[58]

Several years later, however, in a series of fragmentary essays dealing with various aspects of poetic composition, this fundamental conviction was considerably modified in the face of practical experience. Hölderlin indicates as much in a letter to his friend Neuffer late in 1798, where he criticizes his poems for a lack of nuance and lightness, a lack of tonal differentiation, as of shadows to a light, because he avoids too much what is common and actual in life.[59]

An adequate sense of the actual was to be achieved, so Hölderlin argues in his theoretical essays, through the structural principle of what he calls "alternating tones" (*Wechsel der Töne*). This principle is outlined most fully in the longest and most impenetrable of the essays, an incomplete draft text in manuscript, which editors have entitled "Über die Verfahrungsweise des poetischen Geistes" (*GStA,* 4, 1: 241–65). Three characteristic *tones* of poetic discourse are defined, initially with regard to the basic human situations that may be portrayed in poetry and the appropriate poetic responses to them. First is the *naive,* second the *heroic,* and third the *idealistic* (243–44). The names for these three tones, arbitrary as they may seem, derive in large measure directly from Schiller's theoretical essays. In juxtaposition they also evoke a sense of analogy to the threefold developmental structure of cultural-historical time (discussed earlier), whether applied to individual experience or to the collective progress of mankind as a whole.[60]

For Hölderlin these states of mind are applied to situations and responses which constitute moments in the poetic process and are directly expressed in the language of the poem. As such they define stages in the temporality of the poetic self as it speaks and expresses itself through the poem. Even more important for the concept of metaphoric structure is the emphasis placed by Hölderlin, in elaborate convolutions of argument too complex to be deciphered fully here, upon a fundamental tension or opposition between statement and attitude, or expression and point of view, at any given moment in the poem. This opposition is described in his essay as a conflict between *Ausdruck* (or *Darstellung*) and *geistige Behandlung* (245), elsewhere as a conflict between *Sprache* (or *Kunstkarakter*) and *Grundton* (or *Grundstimmung*).[61] It is this *metaphoric* tension or conflict within the language which constitutes the actual tones of the poem. Meaning is generated, and communicated to a reader, through the interaction of these opposing elements, described in terms derived from Fichte's *Wissenschaftslehre* as a "harmonic opposition" (*harmonische Entgegensetzung*). The tonal structure of the poem as an alternating sequence of moments is thus understood to be fundamentally *metaphoric* (or *hyperbolic*; cf. *GStA*, 4, 1: 245, lines 18–19). Through this sequence of alternating moments of conflict and difference, the poem achieves its content, its substance, its truth (244–45).

To offer a sample of Hölderlin's manner of argument in the essay, I quote from the opening part of a sentence that continues through a complex sequence of qualifications for more than a page:

> ... if the mental treatment effects more of a unification in its metaphor, its transposition, its episodes, whereas the expression, the representation in its use of character, emotion, individualism, effects more of a differentiation, then the meaning is located between the two, it is distinguished by the fact that it is in opposition with itself throughout....[62]

Complexities of formulation and ambiguities of terminology indicate the difficulty which Hölderlin encountered in formulating a theory of the poetic process that would also be adequate to his own sense of its practice. Also apparent is his effort to define this metaphoric principle of alternating tones in such a way that the full range and complexity of human experience would be taken into account. In this regard poetry is to include within its dynamic *metaphoric* structure a sense of the totality of life. Yet this structure also defines a dialectical process of shifting and developing moments of opposition, which advances toward a climactic moment, or high point (*Höhepunkt*) of balance and harmony, where all opposition *appears* (*erscheint,* also in the sense of *makes manifest*) as a comprehensive and all-encompassing resolution.

In practical terms Hölderlin conceived the structure of poetry to be circular, involving a sequence of shifts or modulations (in apparent analogy to musical structure) in the metaphoric tension between the tonal components. This sequence, however, which he later referred to as the *rhythm of representation,* is interrupted and categorically reversed at the moment of climax.[63] This climactic moment of "harmonic opposition" (*das Harmonischentgegengesezte*)[64] conveys an experience akin to the catastrophe of the complex plot in Aristotelian tragedy, involving both *peripeteia* (reversal) and *anagnorisis* (recognition) simultaneously.[65] At this point of opposition and unity, so Hölderlin argues, the entire scope, or structure, of the poetic process is communicated all at once, as the intuition (or feeling) of a totality, which assumes the quality of an epiphany. "The Spirit can be felt in its infinity": [der Geist (ist) in seiner Unendlichkeit fühlbar] (249–50).

No other theoretical writing in the entire Romantic era offers such a challenge for interpretation as these essay fragments by Hölderlin. The central importance of Hölderlin's theory of tonal alternation for the role of metaphor in Romantic poetry will nonetheless be apparent. The climactic moment of opposition and reversal that he describes for the poem also involves the perfect coincidence of all three aspects of the temporality of selfhood. The sense of totality conveyed by the poem would be both contextual and referential, involving both a sense of the poem as a whole and an intuition of the world and of human existence as a whole. Indeed, what the poem conveys to a reader and affirms hermeneutically is a self-reflective sense of one's own life as a totality.

1) The rhythm of performance (the first level) gathers itself

together into a moment of all-in-oneness.

2) The self-consciousness of the experiencing mind, both of the poet as voice within the poem and of his reader as participant in the poetic process (the second level), achieves its fulfillment analogous to what Schiller termed, in the passage from his *Letters on Aesthetic Education* discussed earlier, "man's accomplished destiny."

3) A vision, or "intellectual intuition" [intellektuelle Anschauung],[66] of a cultural and historical totality (the third level), is affirmed, identical to that which Hölderlin elsewhere calls "the God of the Time" [der Gott der Zeit].[67]

The notion of a climactic moment that somehow conveys the totality of a poem's meaning, however this may be conceived for aesthetic experience, is strikingly similar in Hölderlin's and Schelling's theories of poetry. The essential difference between them emerges, however, in their respective views on the medium of art; on the language of poetry in particular. Where Schelling appears confident and categorical about the status of symbol and myth, Hölderlin is beset by the paradoxes of metaphoric displacement and the intimations of a collapse into silence. With regard to this difference I would argue that Schelling defines the ideal of Romantic art, whereas Hölderlin struggles to clarify the limitations of actual poetic practice.

Much of Hölderlin's mature poetic work, from the novel *Hyperion* and the drama *Der Tod des Empedokles* to the late elegies and Pindaric hymns, is preoccupied with conflict, failure and tragic loss, both as the experience to be expressed in poetic language and as the dramatic plot to be worked out through character and situation. Ultimately the poet himself stands at the center of such tragic action, attempting to perform as the prophet of his own self-sacrifice. The poet as vehicle of divinity must expose himself to the lightning of heaven (as argued in the uncompleted hymn "Wie wenn am Feiertage..."). Or the poet must serve as visionary, like John the Divine on Patmos (evoked in the hymn of that title), who mediates the truth of divinity through the text he produces. Like Oedipus or Empedokles, who also provided models for the poet's threatened existence, he must resist the temptation to claim the exclusive privilege of divinity for himself and his poetic work. The role of metaphor in poetry finally comes to signify for Hölderlin this process of conflict and differentiation in language, which led to a sense of tragic failure in the struggle to affirm the goal of transcendent vision. His struggle to achieve such poetry ended finally with the breakdown of his own mind. What is the lesson of his example, perhaps unique in its extreme, for the larger question of Romantic theory and for what I have termed the temporality of selfhood?

Conclusion

I argued earlier with reference to Schiller's views that the Romantic theory of poetry emerged in part from the assumption that the structure of the poem and the structure of poetic experience are essentially the same. What is represented in poetry is, in the ideal instance, that mental process which created it. A poem is the reflective demonstration of the act through which it comes to be; and the subject of poetry is the mind that produces it and speaks through it. In this way, recalling the second of the three aspects of temporality defined for poetry, we might assert that the poem represents in its structure the temporal process of its own creation in and for that poetic self which speaks through it.

If this is so, then how can poetry intuit the infinite, the transcendent, the absolute, as Romantic theory claims it should? Whatever sense of totality is achieved would have to be defined with reference to the mind that speaks through the poem and serves as the experiential vehicle for what the poem represents. For this reason it is apparent why a philosopher like Schelling required a concept of symbolic identity for his theory of art. Only within the moment of such identity could the poetic self truly claim to speak for the infinite. The question posed by such a poet as Hölderlin, however, is whether in such moments any speech is possible at all. A poet who sets out to write such a poem must depend upon some kind of divine inspiration or mystical communion if his poem is to succeed. One can begin to understand why Hölderlin came to regard

the poetic act as a heroic endeavor, verging on tragic hybris.
A poem is truly, as the title of one of his odes indicates, "Dichter-muth": "poet's boldness."[68]

In opposition to such claims for symbolic identity, Hölderlin proposed the metaphoric differentiation between the poetic self and the ultimate totality of meaning that the poem seeks to communicate. The two are not and cannot be one and the same. The language of the poem acknowledges this by distinguishing between the process of its articulation, which is temporal, dialectical, and subject to the rhythm of alternating tones, and the climactic moment of silence and reversal, the sustained gap (*Lücke*) or caesura, in the temporal process of the poem. The temporal self is thus disassociated from the transcendent moment. The one defines the language and the structure of the poem, the other its motive and its ultimate meaning. The relation between the two is essentially and necessarily *metaphoric*, in both the senses of metaphor defined at the outset with reference to Paul Ricoeur: structural or contextual, on the one hand, in that the dialectical interaction of all parts of the poem alone achieves that proper sense of *analogia entis* which constitutes the all-in-oneness of beauty and the imagination; and referential, on the other, in that the object of the metaphor, which determines its truth or validity, lies beyond the limits of language and can at best be pointed toward and intuited from the language.

In closing let me adapt for the present argument one of Hölderlin's aphoristic formulations, used as motto for this essay, concerning the meaning of poetry: "The poem must stand as a metaphor for an intellectual intuition."[69]

Chapter 7 : Platonic Dialogue and Romantic Irony

For Wolfgang Iser

The Platonic dialogue was, as it were, the barge on which the shipwrecked ancient poetry saved herself with all her children: crowded into a narrow space and timidly submitting to the single pilot, Socrates, they now sailed into a new world, which never tired of looking at the fantastic spectacle of this procession. Indeed, Plato has given to all posterity the model of a new art form, the model of the *novel* . . .

–Friedrich Nietzsche[1]

Much attention has been devoted in recent decades to the concept of irony. In large part this has accompanied a renewed interest in the writings of Friedrich Schlegel, who originated the theory of Romantic irony as key to his idea of Romantic poetry in general. The evolution of modern literature, in particular the development of the novel – from Romance to *Roman,* from Ariosto and Cervantes to Sterne, Diderot, and Goethe – was characterized for Schlegel by the emergence of a self-reflective narrative. He regarded this quality of discourse in the novel as the constitutive element of Romantic irony. "Ein Roman" – to quote one of Schlegel's most famous, seemingly enigmatic assertions – "ist ein romantisches Buch."

Scholars have traditionally discussed Schlegel's concept in contradistinction to Classical irony, which was defined throughout the history of rhetoric from Aristotle and Quintilian to the eighteenth century as a trope or figure of speech, with which one says one thing but means another. The authoritative model for such Classical irony was established from the outset by the Socratic method of argument in the Platonic dialogues. This familiar contrast between Classical and Romantic irony is reaffirmed and further elaborated in a monograph by Ernst Behler entitled *Classical Irony, Romantic Irony, Tragic Irony: On the Origin of these Concepts.* Behler's point of departure is a passage from Thomas Mann's *Der Zauberberg,* where Settembrini makes a categorical distinction between these two kinds of irony, in this way: Classical irony is "upright" (*gerade*); Romantic irony is "dissolute" (*liederlich*).[2] The former pertains, so Behler argues, almost exclusively to strategies of discourse in rhetoric, particularly through the technique of *dissimulatio;* whereas the latter concerns the intimate and self-conscious relationship between author and reader in literary narrative. Romantic irony, asserts Behler, reflects a modern attitude of mind (*moderne Geisteshaltung*), where the author steps out of his work. Such an attitude or mode of behavior in language is acknowledged to derive ultimately from the role of Socrates as *eiron* – both in the Platonic dialogues and in other instances of this type of comic character, as in the plays of Aristophanes or the treatise on character by Theophrastus. But Romantic irony is argued to emerge only in the great tradition of the European novel. On this point Behler and Schlegel appear to be in full agreement.

My own view of irony is less categorical than that of Settembrini and less historical than that of Behler. I would even question the validity of distinguishing at all between Classical and Romantic irony. At issue here is a fundamental quality of discourse, which pertains to the form and the function of literary language in general. In this regard the dialogues of Plato provide a useful model, not so much because of Socrates's role as *eiron,* but rather because this form and function become thematic to the argument of the dialogues themselves. Platonic dialogue achieves that mode of self-reflective discourse that constitutes irony for both Schlegel and Behler. The importance of this mode of discourse for literary criticism, furthermore, emerges above all in theories of narrative.

Dialogue as literary form defines the interaction between text and reader that constitutes meaning through a conscious awareness of that interaction. Irony thus provides the basis for a *hermeneutics* of reading, for which the method of the Platonic dialogues and the theory of the Romantic novel in Schlegel provide convenient and mutually compatible instances.

The Concept of Irony: Schiller and Fr. Schlegel

Several assumptions are often made about irony as a concept in criticism that imply a direct concern with the functions of language as such. First, irony derives from a conscious attempt to mediate between the various elements or aspects of discourse and a presumed totality, which constitutes the meaning as a whole. These separate aspects are acknowledged to be in conflict and mutually incompatible. A fundamental discontinuity exists therefore between the separate statements of the discourse and the overriding motive that these statements seek to convey as a whole. In Romantic theory, as in Platonic philosophy, the mediation of this conflict is defined as a dialectical process, which interrelates the parts and the whole, the particular and the general, the real and the ideal. Irony thus serves as a measure of the incommensurability of language in its attempts to integrate and unite these opposites. The form of dialogue itself demonstrates, however, that the act of mediation can only be approximate or relative, as indicated by the challenge of communicating through this dialectical process. The communicative process requires both a differentiation of voices (e.g., Socrates and his interlocutors) and an extension in time (as an implied dramatic performance).

The second assumption of irony, closely related to the first, concerns the use of language as a medium of intersubjective exchange. Discourse occurs as a speech act involving separate individuals, each with a particular point of view, located in time and circumstance. The ground for any dialogical distinction between parts and whole, particular and general, the real and the ideal, must therefore be defined by the pluralistic situation of the dialogue itself as a reflection upon the fundamental existential condition of discourse. Each speaker in the dialogue functions as a finite agent, subject to the dialectical process of argument. The medium of discourse thus demonstrates this process of intersubjective exchange, even though the ultimate purpose and meaning of the discourse lie beyond the limits of that exchange as a timeless and even universal *idea* (in Plato's sense). This basic incommensurability between situation and purpose, between context and motive, is the source of irony in the Platonic dialogues. It also defines the basis of the dialogue as a form and its function as discourse, indeed as a literary *narrative,* for its implied reader.

All our concepts of criticism depend on the contingencies of intellectual history. No terminology has absolute validity. The choice of the term *irony* by Friedrich Schlegel as a key concept in his critical theory was largely a matter of convenience, or appropriateness, or personal inclination. He picked up the term from the repertoire of traditional rhetorical tropes. A similar convenience must also have governed Plato's original choice of the term *eiron* as an attribute for the figure of Socrates in his dialogues, as when Thrasymachus in Book 1 of the *Republic* rails at Socrates with a kind of Aristophanic invective and calls him *ironic* (337a), because he refuses to give direct answers to the questions put to him.

There is yet another assumption about irony that we inherit from the tradition of theory. This assumption is expressed by Nietzsche in the passage from *The Birth of Tragedy* cited as motto to this essay. Nietzsche posits a fundamental change to have occurred in the cultural history of the West, a change in the status of language and its use in literature, for which Socrates in the Platonic dialogues serves as symptom. Socrates, so argues Nietzsche, is the helmsman of a life raft that has survived the shipwreck of ancient poetry. Nietzsche's predecessors in the history of philosophy (notably Hegel) had described this change as a fundamental transformation of poetic mythology into philosophical thought. Plato thus came to be regarded as the watershed between the ancient and the modern world, between the Classical and the Romantic (to use Schlegel's terms), between the naive and the sentimental modes of poetry, language and thought (as Schiller argued in his influential treatise on the subject). On this essential model of cultural history for Western literature and thought all the German writers and theorists of that era agree: from Kant, Goethe and Schiller through the Schlegels, Schelling, Humboldt, Hölderlin, Novalis and many others, on to Hegel, Schopenhauer and Nietzsche.

What constitutes this cultural shift? These theorists projected retrospectively an ideal of perfect, or at least fully competent, semiosis in language (which is regarded perforce as *pre-ironic*) upon an era of supposed cognitive privilege. The human mind was argued to have existed – like Adam in the garden before the fall! – in perfect union and harmony with its thought and with its world. From Winckelmann's description of ancient Greek sculpture in his *History of Ancient Art* (1764) and Kant's analytic of the Beautiful in his *Critique of Judgement* (1790) through the entire history of Romantic aesthetics, at least to Hegel's lectures on the subject in Berlin (published posthumously by his student Hotho in the 1830s), Classical poetry, mythology and art were regarded as an absolute norm for the ideal of beauty, against which the entire subsequent history of literature, art and thought should be measured. Goethe's view of the Greeks may serve as a paradigm for such an affirmation of an ideal norm.[3] Homeric epic, Attic tragedy and above all Classical sculpture were asserted to embody the ideal of man's humanity (*Menschheit*), which remains and always will remain unsurpassed in the realm of art.

Friedrich Schiller develops such a concept of humanity in conjunction with a normative theory of beauty (directly influenced by Kant and Fichte, among others) in the central section of his *Letters on Aesthetic Education* (1795).[4] Particularly revealing at the end of the fifteenth Letter is Schiller's celebration of the sculpted head of Juno Ludovisi, a copy of which cast in plaster was secured by Goethe when he was in Rome and subsequently brought back to Weimar, where it is still exhibited in Goethe's house on the Frauenplan. All opposition of form and substance, spirit and material (to borrow Schiller's own terminology), is fully reconciled and integrated in this work of art, so he asserts, communicating a sense of perfect harmony and dynamic repose, which inspires in the observer a miraculous emotion, part worship, part love, for which (he concludes) reason has no concept and language has no name.[5] A corresponding projection of such an aesthetic ideal upon a supposed historical model of discourse occurs in Schiller's discussion of the *Naive* (in his essay of that title, published – like the *Letters on Aesthetic Education* – in Schiller's journal *Die Horen* in 1795), not only with reference to a kind of poetry, but also as a presumed state of mind. Indeed, naive poetry is defined as a mode of discourse which embodies a particular natural, or innocent, state of mind. The *grace* of the Naive (*Anmut* or *Grazie* – terms also used by Schiller in his theoretical writings) manifests itself in the language of poetic genius, so argues Schiller: "the utterances of a god in the mouth of a child" [Göttersprüche aus dem Mund eines Kindes].[6]

The educated mind, continues Schiller with reference to the entire history of sign theory, crucifies its words and concepts upon the cross of grammar and logic. The sign is always heterogeneous and alien to what it signifies. The language of the naive genius, by contrast, springs directly out of thought by some inner necessity. In such privileged discourse the sign completely disappears within the thing signified, and language expresses thought in its naked purity. Tactics of concealment and indirection, which constitute the discourse of sentimental minds, must be measured for Schiller against such a norm of authentic signification. The term *irony* itself is not used by Schiller. The theoretical basis for the concept as subsequently developed by Schlegel, however, is here established with full authority. The language of the sentimental, or self-conscious, mind is characterized by Schiller in terms of a radical ambivalence, opposition or discontinuity, reflecting a state of mind that is suspended in a complex dialectical process between a concern for ideal unity and totality, which motivates it, and the contradictory situation of existence in the world, which conditions and defines it. The result of such a dialectical interaction, I would argue, is the language of irony, where thought is concealed behind the words, like the beauty of Socrates behind the mask of Silenus the satyr.

What are the implications of Schiller's distinction for the

Romantic theory of irony? A paradox arises concerning the place of Plato in Western culture and the meaning of his dialogues as a literary form. The concept of irony in Romantic theory depends on a typological model of poetic language, defined for both Schiller and Schlegel within a historical framework. The structures of discourse in post-Classical literature – i.e., the Sentimental, or Romantic, mode – are defined in opposition to the norm of beauty as the ideal of Classical art. Such a norm is affirmed in aesthetic theory without exception from Kant to Hegel and beyond. In literature the Homeric epic is usually identified with this norm because of its presumed naive objectivity and the all-inclusive harmony of its mythological world view. In his essay on the Naive, as convenient instance of this contrast between Naive and Sentimental, Schiller juxtaposes Homer and Ariosto – specifically the encounter between Glaukos and Diomedes (in the *Iliad,* Book vi) and the battle between Ferrau and Rinaldo (in *Orlando Furioso,* canto i).[7] Schiller contrasts the objective and impersonal quality of the Greek epic with the self-conscious intrusion of the poet-narrator in the Italian romance. Such intrusion by a self-conscious narrator corresponds exactly to what Schlegel came to describe as irony. Schiller even allows that the effect of both poems upon the modern reader, who is perforce sentimental and self-conscious in his perspective, may be the same: "our heart interrupts our reading and separates itself readily from its object in order to gaze into itself."[8] The fact that Homer as narrator does not intrude to offer his own comment, in the manner of a sentimental poet like Ariosto, makes us feel, says Schiller, that he is insensitive, "as if he had no heart in his breast."

Similar comments concerning the contrast between Homer and Ariosto are made at greater length by Wilhelm von Humboldt in his book-length review of Goethe's *Hermann und Dorothea,* clearly in direct response to Schiller's arguments, which were well known to Humboldt.[9] Homer as narrator is characterized by Humboldt in analogy to the plastic arts, Classical sculpture in particular (which also serves for Humboldt as norm for the ideal of beauty), whereas Ariosto is described with reference to the mood and rhythm of a piece of music or the quality of color (*Colorit*) in painting, both of

which were subsequently regarded as central criteria for the subjectivity of Romantic art, e.g., in the argument of Hegel's *Aesthetics.*

Friedrich Schlegel carried the concept of objectivity in Classical
literature far beyond Homer to indicate a presumed system or
totality of *myth,* to which all individual works bear witness. In his
"Speech on Mythology," contained in the *Dialogue on Poetry* (1800),
Schlegel speaks of ancient poetry in its entirety as "a single, indivis-
ible, and perfect poem."[10] The entire corpus of ancient literature is
thus argued, despite historical and generic differences, to constitute
a coherent system of mythology. In this regard Schlegel agrees with
the more abstract argument concerning mythology as the substance
of art, which Schelling develops in his *Philosophy of Art* (c. 1804;
publ. posth. 1859). The highest instance of such a mythology in art,
argues Schelling, is provided – not surprisingly – by the gods of the
Homeric poems.[11] Schlegel's assertion concerning this kind of totality is no less categorical than Schiller's theory of the Naive: "All
poems of antiquity join one to the other, till from ever increasing
masses and members the whole is formed. Everything interpene-
trates everything else, and everywhere there is one and the same
spirit, only expressed differently."[12] The paradox of Plato for such a
theory will be readily apparent. Remembering the critical attack on
Homer launched by Socrates through the medium of the dialogues,
we may assume that the system of myth in ancient poetry, which
Schlegel claims to be a totality, must have ended before Plato began
to write. This is certainly what Nietzsche argues in *The Birth of
Tragedy,* locating the death of tragedy somewhere between the work
of Sophocles and Euripides, when Socrates chased the god Dionysus from the stage.[13] I see no reason to question the likelihood that
Schlegel would have agreed with Nietzsche on this point.

What are the implications of such an argument for the status of
irony in literature? The concept itself as redefined within Romantic
theory depended upon such a model of cultural history. Irony
could only have emerged – so argue the German Romantics – as a
symptom of loss or failure, a post-Classical phenomenon after the
demise of myth at an irretrievable remove from the ideal of Beauty.
When applied to the function of language in literature, however,

such a view of irony has nothing to do with historical distinctions. The contrast between the ancients and the moderns, on which such theories of history depend, the contrast between Classical object- ivity and Romantic subjectivity, was essentially normative. The con- cept of irony was thus based upon a fundamental polarity of op- posing states of mind, which is not historical but categorical, like William Blake's distinction between Innocence and Experience. The development of such an argument, furthermore, may be regar- ded as part of the secularization of the biblical model of salvation history, which extends from the original fall of mankind to the final redemption and Last Judgment. Irony is an unavoidable quality of language for fallen mankind.

Such a normative model for the language of literature was grad- ually transformed, however, during the course of Romanticism, into a philosophy of history. By the time Hegel lectured on *Aes- thetics* in Berlin during the 1820s, the categories of Classical and Romantic, which were derived from the Schlegels and to which was added the Symbolic to designate the earliest (pre-Classical) stage of art, served as labels for discrete epochs in the dialectical process of history itself. The status of irony for such a history, however, remained highly problematic. The concept was incompatible with a developmental model of literature. Like the banished poets from Plato's *Republic,* irony found no place in the house of history that Hegel erected (even though in his writings Hegel himself could be regarded as a supreme master of irony, as I have defined the con- cept as a mode of discourse). Hegel attacks Schlegel's notion of irony as morally irresponsible. Such an attack seems totally inap- propriate from our present perspective. In his personal animosity toward Schlegel, Hegel confuses the theory of Romantic irony with a denial of all norms of ethical value, which Hegel believed to have occurred among the extremists of the so-called Romantic school in the decades following the emergence of Schlegel's theory.[14]

The Form of Dialogue

To pursue the Romantic theory of irony any further would require more systematic analysis of the various pronouncements on the concept by critics and philosophers from Schlegel, Solger and others on to Hegel and Kierkegaard. A number of scholars have undertaken such analyses over the years.[15] The results are disappointing, due primarily to inconsistencies in the use of the concept and the fact that such usage always depends upon assumptions, often concealed, concerning the nature of poetry, art and language itself. The validity of the term *irony* for literary theory is thus open to question, since it raises more fundamental issues concerning the form and function of narrative than it resolves. If these issues are considered for themselves, the concept of irony can serve at best as a representative instance. The present discussion therefore must be content to offer a modest prolegomenon toward a more comprehensive theory.

Application of my argument to representative examples of irony in dialogue will indicate how such a theory would need to accommodate itself to literary practice. For this purpose Schlegel's *Dialogue on Poetry* is especially appropriate, since the theory of Romantic irony is put into practice by the *Dialogue* through an act of poetic imitation, the model for which is found in Plato. Schlegel develops a sense of irony in his dialogue not by reasoned argument but through performance. The dialogue itself demonstrates as an implied narrative, indeed as a parody in part of the novel, that ironic defeat is the inevitable effect of any effort to communicate definitively a general sense of what poetry means. Critics have not recognized sufficiently the extent to which Schlegel thus employed the dialogue as form for purposes of literary imitation and self-reflective demonstration.[16]

Two points in particular bear emphasis, both pertinent also to the function of irony in Platonic dialogue. First, the structure and form of the dialogue as discourse demonstrates a fundamental inadequacy of language itself, especially written language, as the medium for communicating ultimate concerns, whether these pertain to philosophical truth (as in Plato) or to the meaning of poetry (as in Schlegel). Second, the form of dialogue itself as inter-subjective exchange establishes a thematic awareness of the dilemma of understanding, which the dialogue as a text, as an implied narrative intended to be read, conveys directly to its reader. There is thus an implicit hermeneutics to the role of irony in dialogue. In Plato the challenge of interpretation forms the basis of philosophy as *paideia* and in Schlegel the search for understanding calls the very possibility of successful communication into question. Both instances of dialogue affirm Nietzsche's assertion that this is the model of a new literary form, the form of the novel. In Schlegel, however, that model was anything but new, especially since his concept of Romantic irony derived from the great tradition of Romance (or *Roman*), from Ariosto and Cervantes to Sterne, Diderot and Goethe. To affirm a theory of the novel through the performance of dialogue became an explicit intention of his work. The high point of Schlegel's ironic performance in the *Dialogue on Poetry* is a text appropriately entitled "Letter on the Novel." My discussion of Schlegel's concern with irony in practice will further substantiate my claim that an essay on Platonic dialogue and Romantic irony can provide the basis for a theory of literary narrative.

PLATO'S DIALECTIC: *SYMPOSIUM* AND *PHAEDRUS*

Plato was the first to establish the dialogue as a separate literary form, as Aristotle already acknowledged in the *Poetics* (chap. 1, 1447b). Plato's dialogues, above all other examples, also provided the model for Schlegel's *Dialogue*. This holds true despite the availability of important instances of the form from Castiglione to Diderot, many of which share significant features in common with Schlegel. It should be noted that earlier in the same year in which he composed his *Dialogue*, Schlegel had contracted with a publisher to translate all of Plato from the Greek.[17] Although he later abandoned the project, leaving his friend Schleiermacher to achieve the standard German version of Plato on his own, there can be no doubt that Schlegel was profoundly influenced by Plato, both as a writer and as a thinker. He participated, at least indirectly, in the critical revaluation of the ancient philosopher, which took place during the Romantic era. This new assessment of Plato culminated in Hegel's discussion of his work in his Berlin lectures on the *History of Philosophy*. Through the work of more recent German philosophers, such as Nietzsche, Heidegger, and Gadamer, this tradition of a modern Platonism continues to be influential to the present day. Especially important for my discussion of Schlegel's *Dialogue* as ironic form are representative works from Plato's middle career, which demonstrate supreme mastery of dialogical form. I have in mind specifically the *Symposium,* which Schlegel must have regarded as the closest analogue to his own work, and the *Phaedrus,* where the problematics of written language for dialogical discourse are made most explicit. In order to substantiate my subsequent comments on Schlegel's *Dialogue,* I offer a brief schematic survey of the formal technique of irony in these two works.

Three aspects of narrative in the *Symposium* constitute what may be called its ironic technique, one of them controlled exclusively by the figure of Socrates as *eiron,* all of them familiar to readers of the modern novel as part of the narrator's repertoire. The first may be called a distancing or backgrounding effect; the second, a sequential juxtaposing of rhetorical units as a strategy of argument; and third, a negativity of the ineffable, whereby rhetoric is transformed into a mystery rite. Each of these derives from conventions of discourse that Plato must have expected his readers to recognize: history, oratory and drama, respectively. All three also serve intentionally the ultimate concern of the dialogue to demonstrate the educational role of philosophy. There is much more that could be said about the technique of the *Symposium* as dialogue, but these three devices offer the most conclusive evidence that Plato here created a literary form which is as sophisticated, varied and self-conscious as the novel at its best. Dialogue may even be a misnomer as generic designation for this work, since the term suggests a formal procedure of exchange, in the manner of statement and response (where the response in Plato is often thought to be a mere formality: i.e., "Just as you say, Socrates"). Yet irony also, as suggested earlier, may be too restrictive as a critical term for the narrative technique I have in mind.

Distancing, or backgrounding, is a frame technique of narrative, whereby the event to be recounted – here the banquet itself – is removed through several levels of perspective and degrees of reportage. Apollodorus tells the story to a group of businessmen, who are apparently hostile to him as a follower of Socrates. We are given indications that his narrative occurs only shortly before Socrates' death. Yet his audience is curious to hear more about this famous banquet. Apollodorus, who was not himself present at the event, which took place about fifteen years earlier, long before he came into contact with Socrates, only knows the story from Aristodemus, a fanatic follower of the philosopher at that time, who attended the banquet by accident: uninvited, barefoot and unwashed, an apparent surrogate for Socrates himself (who, we are informed, did wash and put on shoes in honor of his host Agathon, but who arrived late because he lost himself in thought along the way).

This technique of backgrounding thematizes the act of remembrance. The *Symposium* is, above all, an exercise in *memoria,* whereby Plato (who is himself as author the last in this chain of narrators) commemorates for us as the implied readers of his dialogue an image of Socrates as teacher, as lover of wisdom, as philosopher. What should be kept in mind is the unreliability of memory as the medium for narrating such a history. Apollodorus emphasizes (178a) that Aristodemus forgot many of the details and that he also can no longer remember everything he was told, even though he now has his version of it near letter-perfect (173c), since he had occasion on the preceding day to tell the story to Glaukon, Plato's brother (known to readers of the *Republic,* where he plays a central role).

The substance of the banquet itself, as all readers of Plato will recall, consists in a series of set speeches, which replace the customary drinking bout on such an occasion. In response to a proposal by Phaedrus (as reported by Eryximachus, 177bc), the guests at the feast compete with one another through a sequence of rhetorical performances in celebrating Eros, the great god of love. But Plato's purpose in representing these speeches goes beyond rhetoric. The banquet is held in honour of Agathon's first victory in the competition of tragedies performed at the annual Grand Dionysia. Discourse replaces drunkenness; speeches replace music (176e); and Aphrodite replaces Dionysus as patron deity of the feast. We are provided with a second contest, an agon of oratory, where these speeches about Love displace tragedy. Plato thus intended his dialogue as literary form to be a substitute for drama, indeed to be a preferable alternative form, as the medium of a philosophical revelation, despite the irony of that medium.

All the more appropriate therefore that Socrates, not Agathon, should win this contest. It is a triumph for philosophy, as indicated (with irony on Plato's part) by the drunken Alcibiades, who arrives late with a wreath of ivy, which he places upon the head of the satyr-like Socrates (213e). Alcibiades also offers his own speech in tribute to Love, an account of his failed homosexual relationship with Socrates, which serves as an appropriate satyricon to the contest of speeches in honor of Eros. The entire performance at the Banquet demonstrates (at least for us as Plato's readers) that Socrates himself is the true daimon Eros, offspring of Poros and Penia (according to the tale told by the priestess Diotima, which Socrates recounts), as a *philo-sophos,* lover of wisdom.

The third technique of irony in the *Symposium* introduces what amounts to an implied parody of all the rest. Socrates refuses to provide his own speech on Eros, substituting instead yet one further narrative account of an event in the past – indeed, a considerably more remote past – when as a young man he met with Diotima, priestess of Mantinea, who initiated him into the mysteries of love. His report begins as dialogue, in which Socrates for once plays the role of novice or pupil, similar to so many other figures in Plato (including the implied reader of the dialogues), who play the same role to Socrates as teacher. We may compare him to his followers Aristodemus and Apollodorus, or to young Phaedrus (here and in the dialogue of that title), also to Glaukon (Plato's brother, mentioned here, 172c, chief interlocutor of the *Republic*), and even to

Plato himself (as implied author of all the dialogues).

Yet Diotima quickly abandons dialogical exchange in favor of her own discourse about Eros as daimon, providing also an alternative to the rhetoric of speeches at the Banquet, speaking with a language which imitates the sacred mysteries. She even asserts before the climax of her speech, where the well-known and often misunderstood doctrine of the ladder of ascent by desire to the attainment of ideal Beauty is described, that Socrates himself will be unable to "grasp the perfect revelation, to which the mysteries of love lead the pilgrim, if he does not stray from the right path" (210a). Here is the ultimate irony of Plato's dialogical discourse, that it seeks to communicate a mystery beyond comprehension – beyond the grasp of Socrates, beyond access to those who recount his narrative, beyond even Plato himself as author and ourselves as readers. The truth of philosophy is conveyed only through the distancing of irony, disguised as a rhetorical set speech contained within a narrative, which is reported at four degrees of remove in time and voice.

Irony of form in the *Phaedrus,* in comparison to the *Symposium,* is less complex in structure but more sophisticated in its thematic function within the dialogue. Schlegel believed this to be Plato's earliest work and even persuaded Schleiermacher that this was so.[18] This might weaken any claim for direct influence of the *Phaedrus* on Schlegel's *Dialogue.* The importance of this seminal text from the Platonic corpus for my own argument about irony, however, may quickly be demonstrated. The *Phaedrus* employs a strategy of juxtapositions intended to lead the reader into confusion, a confusion seemingly shared with Socrates himself. Within the dramatic setting of the dialogue, beneath the plane tree on the banks of the Ilissus outside Athens, a sense of divine presence – variously attributed to the Muses (237a), to Eros (257a), to Pan (279c); or is it finally the spirit of philosophical wisdom? – takes hold of the mind, possesses it, inspires it, with a divine madness.

Students of contemporary critical theory will be familiar with the argument published by Jacques Derrida concerning the *pharmakos* of the *Phaedrus* – medicine, or recipe, or is it poison? –

the *cure* for memory, invented (so Socrates informs us) by the Egyptian god Theuth and presented to Thamus, King of Egypt. For Derrida the dilemma of *écriture* in Plato's *Phaedrus* is interpreted with reference to contemporary semiotics.[19] Socrates tells this story about how writing was invented (*Phaedrus,* 274d–275b), stating that Thamus considered writing to be a power which corrupts memory, imposing forgetfulness upon the minds of those who thus become dependent on texts for what they know. We may agree with Derrida that the problem of writing is peculiarly modern. Socrates indicates his agreement with this argument. For the philosopher, he adds, writing can only serve as a reminder for what is already known. The story of writing is told near the end of the dialogue, thus reminding Plato's reader of the specific role which writing has already played earlier in the dialogue itself. This reminder also indicates the extent to which the story of writing and the use of writing in the dialogue are intentionally and thematically ironic.

We recall, first, that Phaedrus, the young man who serves as interlocutor of Socrates in the dialogue, brings with him, concealed in his cloak, the written text of a speech that he recently heard by the orator and arch-sophist Lysias. Socrates persuades Phaedrus to read the speech. His recitation leads to confusion, thus demonstrating that a written text is useless if its author does not know what he wants to say, or indeed – as Socrates argues (237c, 238e) – if the author does not know what is true. The speech of Lysias, recited by Phaedrus, is apparent nonsense, leading Socrates to offer a speech of his own in opposition to it. Initially, he tries to defend Lysias's position on love, but with different rhetorical means. This effort by Socrates, in contrast to the confusion of Lysias as author, provides an eloquent example of "Classical irony," where the speaker does not mean what he says. But Socrates interrupts his speech before it is finished, expressing remorse for arguing what he knows is not true. To atone for his offense, in what amounts to a strategy of counter-irony, Socrates offers his famous *Palinode,* supposedly derived from the poet Stesichorus (243a), who spoke it in order to cure a temporary blindness imposed upon him by the gods for telling poetic lies. Socrates sings his song, so he claims, to ward off a similar punishment. He tells the myth of the soul as a chariot drawn by two opposing horses and guided by a charioteer who seeks to control them and to direct them upward to the realm of heaven, the original home of the soul, from which it descended into the body. This myth provides a pseudoscientific, cosmological proof for the immortality of the soul, as it also demonstrates the authentic frenzy or madness of love, which enables the soul (so argues Socrates) to grow wings and take flight upward toward the realm of ideal beauty, which is the goal of all true philosophy.

This myth of the soul also offers a model for Socrates's theory of dialectic, which he proposes as alternative to the false rhetoric of Lysias (262-66). At the same time the Palinode demonstrates the power of recollection (*anamnesis*, 249c), the capacity to remember a forgotten truth, which can only be recovered through the divine inspiration of love. Such inspiration is argued to be the necessary prerequisite for all philosophy, which thus proves (by ironic anticipation) the validity of the subsequent argument against writing in the story of Theuth and Thamos. Philosophical truth cannot be communicated, so Socrates asserts, by the argument contained in a written text. Plato's dialogue itself offers dramatic support on this point. The unique idyllic setting of the conversation and the apparent visitation of a divine madness during the performance of the Palinode demonstrate both the power of memory (*anamnesis*) and the importance of inspiration for philosophy.

Plato's thematic irony with regard to writing also extends to his own dialogue as a verbal medium. The *Phaedrus* was written by Plato as a text and was meant, if not to be published (in our sense of the term), then at least to be read. What kind of readers were envisioned for the dialogue? and what effect was such an act of reading intended to achieve? Phaedrus, the youthful interlocutor of Socrates, serves within the dialogue as the model for a student of philosophy. His encounter with Socrates provides instruction in philosophy, *not* through argument only, but also through the intersubjective experience of dialogue. Socrates demonstrates through his own performance in composing the Palinode how discourse may communicate a truth that lies beyond the limits of language and reasoned thought. In order for Phaedrus to share in this experience, he must also participate in a kind of reciprocal madness or inspiration, which is the basis of philosophical love. Such a philosophical love requires the power of anamnesis, through which the soul rediscovers the ideal, represented mythically in the Palinode as a heavenly ascent into the realm of Being. The dialogue thus demonstrates in itself the dialectical method of philosophy, achieved through the dialogical interaction between Phaedrus and Socrates, as educational exchange between student and teacher.

Yet precisely as an exercise in the teaching of philosophy, the dialogue suffers an ironic defeat in accord with its own claim that philosophy cannot be a doctrine and cannot be taught by rhetorical argument. Such a defeat is also perhaps implied within the dialogue itself, due to the apparent inadequacy of Phaedrus in his role as interlocutor. He is all too eager to accept and affirm whatever Socrates says. Is this our measure of philosophical understanding, this guileless, somewhat simplistic youth? As readers of Plato's text, we are unlikely to identify our own response with the position of unqualified affirmation assumed by Phaedrus. He must seem to us, if we have correctly understood the essential dilemma of discourse conveyed by the dialogue, to be less adequate as a student of philosophy than we take ourselves to be. Yet such assumed superiority of judgment in the reader is also part of Plato's ironic strategy. To skeptical, indifferent or alien minds the *Phaedrus* could thus be argued to fail as discourse, even if the reader accepts Phaedrus's affirmation of Socrates's argument. To the enlightened, or initiated, or educated reader, however, i.e., to those true students of philosophy for whom the dialogue must be intended (whether or not there have been or ever will be many readers of this kind), Plato's dialogue provides precisely that kind of ironic affirmation that Socrates argues to be the only positive function of written texts: it reminds us of what we already know.

SCHLEGEL'S *DIALOGUE ON POETRY*

Schlegel's *Gespräch über die Poesie* uses dialogue as literary form in ways that appear initially to be quite different from the Platonic model. This is apparent even from the title, which indicates a concern with poetry rather than philosophy. In place of the Platonic ideal as a transcendent realm of intellectual or visionary experience, Schlegel offers a semi-mystical concept of poetry as a universal, all-pervasive and dynamic power. The introductory paragraphs celebrate this power in highly metaphorical language as the primal creative force of the universe, far beyond conventional limits of art and literature, even beyond the limits of human existence:

Just as the core of the earth adorned itself with formations and growths, just as life sprang forth of itself from the deep and everything was filled with beings merrily multiplying; even so, poetry bursts forth spontaneously from the invisible primordial power of mankind when the warming ray of the divine sun shines on it and fertilizes it. (54)[20]

Poetry for Schlegel is like the spirit of God in Genesis, moving upon the surface of the waters. As the object of ultimate concern in the dialogue, however, poetry functions in a manner quite similar to the philosophical ideal for Plato as an alternative for the traditional mysteries. Schlegel's introduction emphasizes that poetry cannot be adequately described in language; it cannot even be communicated and understood. For him, as for Plato, the dialogue as form of discourse is thus committed to a dialectic of the ineffable.

Another point of contrast with Plato is the lack of any authoritative spokesman for the ultimate concern of the dialogue. Schlegel does not include a Socrates among his interlocutors. Nor does the dialogue itself make any pedagogic claims. Schlegel's dialogue is not intended as a model for education as is the case with Plato. In moving from the Classical to the Romantic, we leave the Academy and enter the Salon. Schlegel's dialogue takes place in the artificial milieu of a drawing room among a group of highly cultivated and (in Schiller's sense) sentimental friends. Characteristic of good society at the end of the eighteenth century, as also of the literary genre appropriate to it, the novel of manners, both the drawing room and the dialogue are presided over by the two ladies of the group, Amalia and Camilla, who play the role of petulant but indulgent hostesses. This has encouraged biographical sleuths to argue that the two women represent Caroline Schlegel and Dorothea Veit, respectively, and to assume that Schlegel intended to portray the kinds of social discourse which took place in the home of his brother, August Wilhelm, in Jena during the brief era when their circle of friends gathered there at the very end of the century.[21]

The discussion of poetry that unfolds during the conversation among this group of friends involves the juxtaposition of quite disparate viewpoints, none of which can claim any authority. Each of the friends is sympathetic to poetry as a common concern, but each speaks with an apparent bias and limitation of perspective. None serves, even as *eiron,* as spokesman for the truth; just as none may be identified with the implied author of the dialogue (whom we conveniently call Friedrich Schlegel). But we do have such an author for the *Dialogue* as a whole, the speaker of the introductory paragraphs, who indicates that he reports the entire conversation from memory of an occasion which actually occurred among his group of friends. In this narrator the roles of Apollodorus and Aristodemus in the *Symposium* are thus united, and, like his Platonic progenitors, he acknowledges that his memory includes a subjective, indeed an imaginative, dimension: "ich weiß nicht genau, was der Fantasie und was der Erinnerung angehört; vieles ist wirklich darin, andres ersonnen" (340; 286). But we need not look as far back as Plato for the model of such a narrator. Schlegel here adapts the convention of the novelist as reporter and editor for the role of the speaker in the introduction.

Where may we locate the irony in this dialogue by our chief theorist of the concept? Not in the stance of the characters, even less in the voice of the narrator. Neither in the manner of Socrates, nor in the eighteenth-century tradition of novelistic hero and author, is there any semblance of an ironic *dissimulatio.* The irony of the dialogue resides entirely within the exchange of opposing perspectives contained in the dialogue proper, not as an element of wit or humour, but as an indication of subjective limitation in the use of language itself. Each separate point of view asserts its own validity as representative of the assumed infinite totality of poetry. As the narrator admits:

[The present dialogue] is intended to set against one another quite divergent opinions, each of them capable of shedding new light upon the infinite spirit of poetry from an individual standpoint, each of them striving to penetrate from a different angle into the real heart of the matter. (55)[22]

The speakers are polite to each other throughout and never question the concern for poetry which they share; yet the dialogue demonstrates a peculiar lack of effective communication. None of the speakers persuades any of the others that his own particular position can claim authority, nor is it even clear to what extent each individual position is understood by any of the others. The dialogue does not resolve any of the issues it raises and answers none of the questions posed in the course of conversation. The structure of the dialogue, however authentic as dialectical exchange, is not progressive but rather tends to move in circles. Its sense of an ending, furthermore, which apparently caused Schlegel some difficulty,[23] offers further evidence, with appropriate social grace, that the entire exchange has been ironic. Amalia's final statement in the second version attempts to transform through hyperbole the drawing room of the dialogue into a pastoral garden locked into its own beauty beyond the reach of reality:

And so allow us rather to lock up carefully the beautiful garden of our modern poetry, so that we will not hear any of the offensive noise outside from the streets and from the literary market places. There we wish to wander about undisturbed and in solitude beneath the high cedars, to nourish ourselves with the fragrance of the blossoming groves of pomegranates, to linger in the pleasant paths of roses, or to feast our eyes upon the splendid fields of hyacinths. (*my translation*)[24]

Plato's use of a sequence of set-speeches in the *Symposium* provided Schlegel with a model of subjective interaction for his own *Dialogue*. A similar sequence of formal presentations by several of the friends occurs according to prior agreement, though each of the speeches – as was the case with the speech of Lysias in the *Phaedrus* – is read from a written text by its respective author. The justification for such a procedure is provided at the outset by the ladies in

the group. Feeling that something has been lacking in their conver-
sations, Amalia suggests that the friends are not sufficiently aware
how much they differ in their respective views. The result, she
asserts, is a general muddle ("die Mitteilung werde verworren").
For this reason, she proposes:

Each, or perhaps at first only one who felt most inclined, should speak
from the bottom of his heart his thoughts about poetry or about a part,
an aspect of it, or better still, write them down, so that they would have
the opinion of each in black and white. (56)[25]

Camilla adds her enthusiastic support, welcoming the prospect of
something new as a relief from their eternal arguments about literature. Her comment suggests an implicit parody of idealistic hopes
at that time for the advent of a universal peace, asserting that only a
full conflict of opinions would provide hope for such a peace: "Der
Streit, sagte sie, würde dann erst recht arg werden; und das müsse
er auch, denn eher sei keine Hoffnung zum ewigen Frieden." The
texts that are read, however, do not – as indicated above – achieve
any apparent progression of insight or even a reflective clarification
of methodology. Schlegel provides us with nothing more than a
plurality of points of view, demonstrated through an apparently
arbitrary sequence of disparate texts. No Socrates to win the prize,
and no Diotima to reveal the truth.

Here perhaps we may detect the clearest distinction between
Platonic dialogue and Romantic irony. The pedagogy of philosophical insight is replaced by a strategy of radical subjectivity, which
allows at best a kind of mystical faith in that which lies beyond the
limits of the conversation. But Schlegel demonstrates in his *Dialogue* an irony of juxtaposition, where the sequence of disparate
subjective viewpoints establishes a sense of an intuited totality *per
contrarium,* an affirmation of poetry as a whole through the very
inadequacy of the various individual and particular correlatives for
that whole. Such a strategy of irony is characteristic, I suggest, for
the language of modernity, indeed for literary narrative in general,
and especially of the novel in its various manifestations from
Cervantes, Fielding, Sterne, Goethe and the Romantics on to the

great masters of the modern era who provide the supreme fulfillment of Schlegel's theory of the novel, Proust, Joyce and Mann.

In addition to the two women, Amalia and Camilla, five male friends participate in Schlegel's *Dialogue,* four of them with prepared texts, which they read. Marcus and Antonio, who arrive late, laughing in the midst of a conversation concerning the "so-called Classical poets" of English literature (342; 289), are the last to read their texts, the one an essay on Goethe, "Essay on the Different Styles in Goethe's Early and Later Works," the other the famous discussion of the novel, "Letter on the Novel." Two others, Andrea and Ludovico, offer, respectively, a treatise on the history of literature, "Epochs of Poetry," and the equally well-known theory of mythology, "Speech on Mythology."

The last of the friends, Lothario, tends to be silent for hours, we are told (341; 287), and never allows his dignified calm to be disturbed (modelled on Novalis? or Schleiermacher?). In response to Amalia's proposal for formal presentations, however, he has promised to read something. The fact that he subsequently does not do so suggests one further strategy of dialogical inadequacy to Schlegel's work. Schlegel later corrected this failure, however, when preparing the *Dialogue* for inclusion in his *Sämmtliche Werke,* published in 1823. A new and expanded ending for the *Dialogue* gives Lothario a much more significant role. Along with a new theory of genres based upon a Christian "poetry of the spirit" (*Poesie des Geistes,* 358) – which may reflect Schlegel's own religious bias at that time – he also provides a brief summary of the arguments presented by the four other friends, which is presumably intended to have some authority.

Two of the texts, he argues, namely the first and the last, were concerned exclusively with practical aspects of the instruction and study of literature, the one looking to history as the only legitimate school of poetry and the other surveying the career of the representative poet of the era as an instance or example. Literary history and literary biography (or, to use Schlegel's own term, *Charakteristik*): these texts thus represent in miniature the two most important methods of scholarship established by Romantic criticism, which have dominated the study of literature ever since. Neither approach, needless to say, contributes in any way to the narrative technique of irony.

The two middle texts, however, relate to each other in a manner, as indicated by Lothario, which is far more central to the sense of irony established by the *Dialogue*. Both are concerned, he asserts, with "revealing the hidden root and source of all poetry and legend in the miraculous power of the imagination, whose eternal influence and creation is at home in the symbolic world of mythology or in the lore of nature, as in the view of nature."[26] Ludovico's "Speech on Mythology" thus considers the eternal operation and creation of poetry in the symbolic world of myth. Antonio, by contrast, turns his attention in the "Letter on the Novel" to "the same aspect but from another side," namely "in the eternal struggle of poetry with prosaic actuality, since poetic wit and humour are said to be nothing other than applied imagination, an indirect mode of expressing the same."[27] In the juxtaposition of these two texts we may locate the core of Schlegel's theory of irony as demonstrated by his *Dialogue*.

Both the "Speech on Mythology" and the "Letter on the Novel" offer difficulties for interpretation inherent to the respective technique of presentation with which they are concerned. This form of imitative demonstration has not been fully recognized by critics of Schlegel's *Dialogue*. Neither text achieves an argument that is either coherent or clear, yet both establish a very strong sense of audience, indeed of an implied reader, whose response to the attitude of the speaker will determine the success of its presentation. The "Speech," on one hand, employs a rhetoric of persuasion, which attempts to convert its reader to a new poetic faith, outlined as a program for the future of literature. Its evangelism rides on the force of its programmatic conviction. The "Letter," on the other hand, provides an intentional parody of the form and style of the eighteenth-century epistolary novel. What the former piece achieves by force of conviction, the latter conceals behind a wit of indirection.

Ludovico, who is referred to several times as the philosopher of the group (Lothario refers to him in the later conclusion as "unser naturphilosophischer Freund" [360] which suggests that Schlegel may have intended a parody of Schelling), preaches with a kind of apocalyptic bombast. Antonio, by contrast, the humorist of the group (should one think of Tieck in his role as the novelist among the Romantics at Jena?), subordinates all argument to strategies of convolution and accommodation, addressing himself directly, almost intimately, to Amalia, as his appropriate *gentle reader.* How does this contrast of style and manner relate to the function of irony as a fundamental mode of literary narrative? We need to consider briefly the implications of such imitative form for the respective theories of mythology and the novel, as also the effect for the *Dialogue* as a whole of juxtaposing and contrasting the two modes of discourse with each other.

Mythology in poetry is argued by Ludovico to result from the fusion of chaos and love, whereby the unifying power of the mind informs and comprehends the totality of the real world. Such a mythology is proposed for the literature of the future, where Idealism – by which is meant a systematics of selfhood, such as Fichte had provided in his *Wissenschaftslehre* – will project itself upon the world as a new Physics – on the model of Spinoza's materialism and, perhaps, the *Naturphilosophie* of Schelling – to achieve a new and infinite Realism ("ein neuer ebenso grenzenloser Realismus," 360; 315). Such a mythology would constitute an ideal fulfillment of human life and society, as well as the forms of art and poetry, not to mention language itself, as a perfect, harmonious and unified totality, a supreme system of simultaneous Idealism and Realism.

The powerful appeal of such a goal for the speaker, as well as the implied impossibility of its achievement for any sensible reader, may be traced in the tone of Ludovico's concluding remark:

It seems to me that he who could understand the age – that is, those great principles of general rejuvenation and of eternal revolution – would be able to succeed in grasping the poles of mankind, to recognize and to know the activity of the first men, as well as the nature of the Golden Age which is to come. Then the empty chatter would stop and man would

become conscious of what he is: he would understand the earth and the
sun. (88)[28]

Of interest alongside such apocalyptic hopes for the future of
poetry is the acknowledgment in passing that the closest analogue
for such a mythology, apart from the gods of ancient myth, is the
wit (*Witz*) of the great Romantic writers. In particular, Cervantes
and Shakespeare are mentioned, whose work demonstrates an art-
fully ordered confusion, a charming symmetry of contradictions, a
wonderfully perennial alternation of enthusiasm and irony, which
lives even in the smallest parts of the whole ("diese künstlich geord-
nete Verwirrung, diese reizende Symmetrie von Widersprüchen,
dieser wunderbare ewige Wechsel von Enthusiasmus und Ironie,
der selbst in den kleinsten Gliedern des Ganzen lebt," 361–2; 318–19).
Unintentionally and without further elaboration, the theory of
mythology here also anticipates the theory of the novel.

The antidote proposed by Antonio for such apocalyptic pleading
is social discourse, where a categorical sense of difference establishes
the basis of all argument. His "Letter" demonstrates precisely that
quality of the novel, its wit and humor, which makes it the appropriate counterpart to mythology. The ideal of an ultimate totality is
replaced by a principle of infinite diversity and variability. The
opening rhetorical flourish of the "Letter" demonstrates this sense
of ironic difference, where verbal structure, even at the level of syntax, reflects the dialogical modes of social interaction. The first
paragraph reads as follows:

I must retract, my dear lady, what I seemed to say yesterday in your
defense, and say that you are almost completely wrong. You yourself
admitted as much at the end of the argument, having become involved so
deeply, because it is against female dignity to come down in tone, as you so
aptly put it, from the inane element of gay jest and eternal poetry to the
thought or heavy-handed earnestness of the men. I agree with you against
yourself that you are wrong. Indeed, I maintain that it is not enough to
recognize the wrong; one must make amends for it and, as it seems to me,
proper amends for having degraded yourself with your criticism would

now be that you force yourself to the necessary patience and read this critical epistle about the subject of yesterday's conversation. (94)[29]

The subject of the letter is a recapitulation of a preceding argument, in which the lady had inappropriately taken the role of critic, which role the author of the "Letter" now assumes on the lady's behalf against herself as an imposed penance for what occurred. The reader of the *Dialogue* is thus put in the impossible position of identifying with a perspective that is being criticized against itself through a recapitulation of an argument to which there is no access. What Antonio subsequently provides, furthermore, is not so much an argument as a survey of qualities inherent to the tradition of wit, humor and arabesque in the works of Ariosto, Cervantes, Shakespeare, Sterne's *Tristram Shandy* and Diderot's *Jacques le fataliste*. The best definition that he can offer for the novel, quoted at the outset of my essay, reads like a tautology: "Ein Roman ist ein romantisches Buch" (373; 335). This assertion follows a brief discussion of *romantisch* as a "sentimental theme in a fantastic form."[30] The term *sentimental* here corresponds to Schiller's usage, indicating a reflective, self-conscious awareness of the creative tension between the ideal and the real. *Fantastic,* synonymous with *imaginative,* refers to the unifying, integrating power of poetic creation.

The work of art that would thus result, i.e., the novel, constitutes, surprisingly, a perfect analogue to the new mythology described by Ludovico. Both the romantic novel and the new mythology will take the world as it is in terms of the creative, poetic power of the mind to comprehend and affirm an ultimate totality in and through the alien, negative medium of infinite variation and difference, the medium in fact of language itself as used in literary discourse. By achieving such a correspondence of theory through such apparently opposite modes of argument and perspective, Schlegel also affirms the coherence of his *Dialogue* with reference to the narrator's quasi-mystical view of poetry, despite the apparent discontinuity and irreconcilability of subjective perspectives represented by the various friends who participate. In this way also the technique of the *Dialogue* itself is affirmed as an implicit theory of irony. Even more than this, the *Dialogue* establishes a legitimate claim, however limited its literary means by comparison to the tradition from which it derives, to be a work of literature, to be indeed a novel.

Methodological Implications

In place of a formal conclusion to my argument, several methodological and terminological problems may be mentioned, which remain open for further consideration. The texts of dialogue considered here by Plato and Schlegel provide at best an example of the direction in which further discussion should proceed. Three points deserve emphasis.

First, with regard to the concept of the novel, particularly as described by Schlegel, but also as attributed to Plato by Nietzsche (in the quotation from *The Birth of Tragedy* cited as motto to this essay): it must be emphasized that such a concept imposes an all-inclusive claim upon literature, which extends beyond the limits of any generic distinctions. This view of the novel, or *Roman,* depends, as argued, upon a theory of Modern, or Romantic, literature in contradistinction to traditional norms of Classicism. Everything written in a language that is capable of self-awareness as a medium of expression and communication must be part of what Schlegel called the novel. Such usage goes contrary to the directions of subsequent fiction. Nietzsche's assertion that the novel was first created by Plato is highly problematic to literary criticism.

Second, with regard to the concept of dialogue as a fundamental mode of literary narrative: I acknowledge a further departure from conventional usage, where the form of dialogue is associated with drama, or at least an implicitly dramatic mode of exchange between separate, discrete voices. Here I plead the authority of Plato in the instances discussed above, where dialogue as a literary form provides a model for reading as an implied pedagogy through the hermeneutical interaction between reader and text. The basis for dialogue as a literary form is thus narrative, constituted by such intersubjective, dialectical exchange.

Third, with regard to my definition of irony, denying the traditional distinction between Classical and Romantic irony, as a fundamental principle of discontinuity in the structure of literary language: it must be asked whether criticism can tolerate such an expansion of traditional usage. Contemporary semiotics and hermeneutics would demand an alternative, more comprehensive category to such irony, even if the examples of Plato and Schlegel might justify my argument. Here I plead again the conviction that all terminologies are subject to circumstance and the conditions of history. Even if irony, as understood in this essay, is finally displaced by broader categories of critical theory, the concept itself, as used historically to describe certain kinds of literary language, remains a valid subject for study. The logical consequence of a discussion of irony in Plato and Schlegel, not only as a theoretical concept, but also in relation to literary practice, may well be to abandon the term altogether. That in itself would be sufficient justification for my endeavor.

My final question concerns the limits of Romanticism, as established in the tradition of German theory outlined earlier. If ironic narrative is defined according to a principle of modernity and self-consciousness in literary language, how far back may we trace the counter-Classical? Plato is a convenient revolutionary focus, but what of his own precursors? Sophocles has long been regarded justifiably as a master of tragic irony in drama; and even Homer – if we look to the example of Odysseus as man of "many turns" (*polytropos*), not to mention elements of narrative discontinuity in the *Iliad* – may emerge as an ironist, at least the equal of any of his children, despite his reputation for objectivity and naiveté.

The norms of the Classical, as suggested earlier, may always involve the projection of an ideal upon an era of supposed privilege from a position of contrast, diminishment and remove. Nor is it valid merely to replace the dichotomy of Classical and Romantic with the distinction between an oral and a written tradition of literature. Poets have always been sentimentalists of the imagination (in both Schiller's and Schlegel's sense), and their irony of discourse results from a radical ambivalence between a longing for what is irretrievably lost (whether it be Homer's Troy or Plato's realm of the philosophical ideal) and a compensatory power of poetic creativity which succeeds, despite the limits of language, in establishing (presumably through the aid of the Muse, daughter of memory) a valid mythical or novelistic surrogate. And do we not also, as readers of literature or the audience of the poem, accept perforce the dialogical condition of the inquiring spirit as a necessary prerequisite to all understanding? In this regard the situation of literary narrative as act of communication may reflect a primal condition of the human mind upon which language itself depends.

Chapter 8 : Strategies of Reversal in Literary Narrative

In memory of I. A. Richards

For speculation turns not to itself,
Till it hath travell'd and is mirror'd there
Where it may see itself.
–Shakespeare, *Troilus and Cressida*

In this essay I shall address an issue that I consider to be central to a general hermeneutics of literary narrative. It has to do with a sense of totality. How does any reader achieve through the act of reading an understanding of the literary work *as a whole*? I shall begin by juxtaposing two quite separate models from recent critical theory: I. A. Richards's views concerning the plurality of meanings in poetry, and Wolfgang Iser's concept of negativity as applied to the act of reading. Although they agree essentially about the role of interpretation in criticism, I perceive a point at issue between them regarding the manner in which a sense of totality is achieved.

In order to broaden the perspective on this issue, I shall subsequently address the question of *reversal* as a central phenomenon in the hermeneutics of reading, referring to comments from German idealist theory, specifically in Hölderlin's "Notes to Sophocles" (1804) with regard to the cognitive implications of the moment of climax in tragedy, and in remarks by Hegel from the preface to his *Phenomenology of Spirit* (1807) concerning the form of language in conceptual thought. The tradition of literary narrative with which we are concerned must be broad enough to include both the concept of *catastrophe* as used by Aristotle with reference to Attic tragedy and the concept of *conversion* as used by St. Paul in the New Testament and by St. Augustine in his *Confessions*.

Finally, I shall turn to a particular point in Shakespearean drama, indicated by the motto above from *Troilus and Cressida*, which may also assume significance for the hermeneutics of reading. From these examples, derived from such disparate traditions and theories concerning the nature of understanding, my own discussion of the role of reversal in interpretation may yield some insight into the way we achieve through the act of reading a sense of the meaning as a whole in works of literature.

Richards on Interinanimation

The strategies of reversal with which I am here concerned pertain primarily to the interaction between a text and its reader and the degree to which a critical understanding of the text also requires a measure of self-reflection by the reader in relation to verbal patterns and structures of statement established within the text. In this regard, a reader might argue as follows: "I understand what I read because I recognize a reciprocal relationship between myself and the work, achieved through a complex, dialectical process of identification and differentiation. The meaning for me is constituted by me through this dynamic process of cognitive stimulus and response as imposed upon me by the text through the act of reading." This general proposition may be further clarified by I. A. Richards's concept of *interinanimation* and by Wolfgang Iser's concept of *negativity*.

In the collection of essays by Richards published to celebrate his eightieth birthday, *Poetries: Their Media and Ends*, the term *reversals* appears in the title of a piece discussing shifts of meaning in the use of words in popular ballads. The initial example that he cites involves a radical shift in the use of the word *white* from initial associations with love to the symbolism of death in this anonymous song:

White was the sheet
That she spread for her lover,
White was the sheet;
And embroidered the cover.

But whiter the sheet
And the canopy grander
When he lay down to sleep
Where the hill-foxes wander.[1]

Richards describes such shifts of semantic association as "inter-verbal interinanimations" (*Poetries*, 61), reintroducing a term he had used as long ago as 1936 in his book *The Philosophy of Rhetoric* to describe the essential metaphoric function of language in poetic discourse. The term was borrowed from John Donne in his poem "The Exstasie," which, according to the Oxford English Dictionary, is the only occurrence of this word in the whole of English literature. This passage from Donne often served in Richards's writing and teaching to designate the essential function of language in poetry, above all, though only implicitly, through the interaction of the text of the poem with its reader. The passage in Donne is as follows:

When love, with one another so
    Interinanimates two soules,
That abler soule, which thence doth flow,
    Defects of lonelinesse controules.
    (41-44)

The power of love invoked by Donne unites the separate souls of lovers through this activity of interinanimation so that the product of this union, "an abler soule," corrects and transcends the defects that each exhibited when alone. To apply such a doctrine of love to the act of reading may well seem farfetched. The justification in doing so for Richards derives from the exalted status that he attributes to the experience of poetry and the capacity of poetic language to signify and communicate.

Throughout his career, Richards was concerned with what he

called *the resourcefulness of words.* By this he designated a plurality of functions for words in poetry, resulting from the complex inter-action among different semantic forces, set in motion through the complex and simultaneous contexts of discourse in a poem. From the first he opposed the simplistic notion of a uniformity in usage, as in the technical terms of science, where one word would opti-mally signify one meaning. He asserts, for instance, near the end of his argument in *The Philosophy of Rhetoric* that "The full use of lan-guage [i.e., in poetry]...takes its word, not as the repository of a single constant power but as a means by which the different powers it may exert in different situations are brought together and again *with an interinanimating apposition* [my emphasis]."[2]

His book *How to Read a Page* was written in explicit opposition to the ruthless reductionism applied to all of literature by the Chicago Great Books program and proclaimed as an educational policy by Mortimer Adler in *How to Read a Book.*[3] Many years later, Richards directed similar polemics against what he termed the "vul-gar packaging view" of meaning, where – to paraphrase his sardon-ic summary – the poet is assumed to *wrap up* whatever he has to say, i.e., his meaning, in a neat and elegant verbal package, which he then presents to us as his poem. "We unwrap it, if we can, and enjoy the contents," like children enjoying presents at Christmas.[4]

The act of reading, of understanding, of comprehending, is thus modelled for Richards more on the interinanimation of love than the unwrapping of a package. Correspondingly, in his later work, Richards develops an elaborate model for communication, bor-rowed and adapted from mathematical and linguistic communica-tion theory.[5] He offers two separate diagrammatic views of this model: one, as it were, seen from the side, which outlines the com-plexities of transmission and the indeterminacy of source and des-tination in the communication process; and the other a frontal view, as if seen through the channel of communication, which dis-tinguishes various functions involved in the activity of compre-hending. These diagrams may seem somewhat arbitrary, but they dramatize the kinds of complexity which Richards attributes to the act of reading a poem.

In the first of these diagrams, Richards goes to inordinate lengths to complicate the linear model of communication with which he is working. The several stages of reciprocal exchange – selecting, encoding and transmitting, on the one hand; receiving,

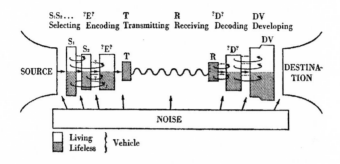

decoding and developing, on the other – are represented as circular in their movement, like gyres or revolutions of interrelationship. The distinction between the lifeless signal and the living message, furthermore, is indicated as a gradually shifting transformation from a living source to a living destination by way of a lifeless medium, like a written text. Finally, the respective positions of source and destination – which would conventionally designate the author and the reader, respectively – are left indeterminate and open-ended. The diagram virtually defeats itself through such complicating qualifiers, thus emphasizing how precarious and uncertain the entire endeavor may be.

In the lateral view of the diagram, which Richards once referred to as his mantra, a sevenfold hierarchy of distinct mental processes is defined, which are all necessary if the act of comprehending is to succeed. These levels indicate degrees of active cognitive involvement in what might be termed *hermeneutical consciousness* (though Richards never used this term and was perhaps unaware of it). The lowest level is called *Indicating*, involving the process of designating and selecting. The second level is called *Characterizing*, which would be a kind of organizing or contextualizing of data. The third level is called *Realizing*, implying the act of becoming conscious to or aware of. The fourth is *Valuing*, involving a quality of judgment about the mind's relation to what is being received. The fifth is *Influencing*, whereby an active response occurs to effect change or

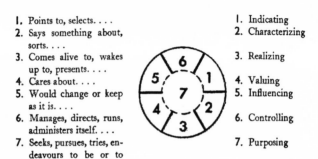

1. Points to, selects. . . .
2. Says something about, sorts. . . .
3. Comes alive to, wakes up to, presents. . . .
4. Cares about. . . .
5. Would change or keep as it is. . . .
6. Manages, directs, runs, administers itself. . . .
7. Seeks, pursues, tries, endeavours to be or to do. . . .

1. Indicating
2. Characterizing
3. Realizing
4. Valuing
5. Influencing
6. Controlling
7. Purposing

direct the outcome. The sixth is called *Controlling*, compared by Richards to the proper role of good government, imposing an order and administering the whole. The seventh, finally, is *Purposing*, through which the essential underlying motive or will involved in the whole process is realized and fulfilled. A sense of the meaning as a whole is achieved only through the active and simultaneous cooperation of all seven levels.

Readers of Richards's early pioneering work *Practical Criticism* (1929) may observe a degree of correspondence between these seven levels of activity in the act of comprehending and the categories of misreading defined in that book from the "protocols" written for Richards by his students in response to the poems they were asked to read. Equally important for the later Richards as direct influence on these distinctions is the hierarchy established by Plato in *The Republic* for the philosophical theory of justice both in the government of the individual soul and in the government of the state. The act of reading for Richards thus inherits essential aspects from this tradition of justice as it derives from Plato and may even have been implied in Plato's text with ironic reference to the verbal medium of the dialogue itself.

Despite his stature as a critic and literary theorist, Richards's general model for the act of comprehending has not received much attention. The importance of this model, however, for an implied hermeneutics of reading is beyond challenge. Equally central in all of his work is Richards's concern with the human value of literature, not only for the experience of reading but above all as an instrument for education. Despite consistent emphasis on the pluralities of meaning in literary language and the diversity of forces involved in the act of comprehending, the essential philosophical-pedagogical motive underlying his theory of meaning is never in doubt. The goal of reading is comprehension, just as the goal of education is wisdom. The only valid criterion for measuring success in both endeavors is the degree of coherence, balance and integrity, or indeed – in Plato's sense – the ultimate *justice,* whereby all competing factors are accommodated and taken into account.

Richards is committed, as a true Platonist, to the ultimate unity of ideas and thought, and equally, as a spokesman for a poetics derived from Coleridge's Romanticism, to the self as a principle of totality posited and affirmed by the poetic imagination. Poetry endeavors – as Richards often argues with conscious echoes from the *Biographia Literaria* – to reconcile opposing powers through the capacity of the mind to integrate the normal divisions of experience into opposing elements: between subject and object, between the knower and the known, indeed between the reader and the text. The unity of the poem and the totality of the comprehending mind thus become ideally one and the same. What the reader of the poem ultimately seeks to affirm through the act of interpretation is a reflective understanding of himself.

Iser on Negativity

The concept of *negativity* as applied by Wolfgang Iser to the act of reading derives from the dialectical method of Hegel's philosophy. According to Hegel's view of the human condition, the essential dilemma of the individual in history and society is that of estrangement or alienation. Human experience is thus constituted as a dialectic of opposing, fundamentally alien and irreconcilable forces. Language, as the most sophisticated instrument of thought and knowledge, provides the most elaborate and comprehensive setting for this struggle. A hermeneutics of negativity, if such a phrase may be used, introduces a model for the act of reading and the kind of knowledge that may thus be achieved, which is radically different from the concept of an integrated comprehension in the work of I. A. Richards.

Wolfgang Iser approaches the hermeneutics of reading from the perspective of what may be called an aesthetics of reception (*Rezeptionsästhetik*), which was developed under the influence of Hans-Georg Gadamer's philosophical hermeneutics by the group of literary theorists at the University of Constance in Germany. The concept of negativity is introduced at the very end of Iser's book *The Act of Reading*,[6] to designate a comprehensive criterion for defining the intersubjective relationship between a reader and the fictional text. Only through that which Iser calls the *negativity* of the text is it possible for the reader to achieve an understanding of the whole.

Iser himself would reject the notion of wholeness, or totality, as invalid for the hermeneutics of reading, in contrast to Richards's commitment to an integrated understanding. The notion of wholeness is overburdened, in his view, with Platonic and Aristotelian associations, not to mention Romantic Idealist overtones inherited in part from Hegel's philosophical project. Iser's preferred terminology is more neutral, more scientific and technological, as in such a term as *Sinnkonstitution* (*Der Akt des Lesens*, 355), which implies more or less the same criterion of meaning though with different emphasis. In addition to Iser's book, an entire volume in the series *Poetik und Hermeneutik* is devoted, as the title indicates, to *Positionen der Negativität*.[7] The choice of topic itself indicates the importance of this Hegelian concept for the hermeneutical theory of the group of literary scholars at Constance. The volume contains a great variety of contributions dealing with general questions of negation, ranging across the entire spectrum of literature and thought throughout the Western tradition. Relatively little attention is devoted, however, to the role of negativity (in Iser's sense) for the act of reading. Nor does the debt of Iser to Hegelian terminology become clear from essays in the volume, least of all from the relatively brief comments by Iser himself.

Among various sources in contemporary theory from several different fields that have influenced Iser's views concerning the interaction between text and reader, two in particular, which are discussed in *The Act of Reading,* deserve mention. The concept of *indeterminacy* (*Unbestimmtheit*), as applied to the structure of literary texts by the Polish phenomenologist Roman Ingarden, provided the basis for Iser's theory of interpretation in his essay of 1970, "Die Appellstruktur der Texte."[8] In this earlier essay Iser pursues the notion that the challenge of reading depends upon the diversity and discontinuity of the text, so that the act of interpretation involves above all a sense of uncertainty and indeterminacy, placing the reader in a position of opposition to and conflict with the semantic structures of the text. Second, from R. D. Laing and the psychoanalytical theory of communication, Iser adapts the notion of *invisible experience* in interpersonal relations – i.e., "I do not know how you experience me, and you do not know how I experience you" – to the interaction between text and reader. The reader must construct an image of what is being said on the basis of what is not said. Negativity thus emerges as a criterion of interaction for the text as a whole on the analogy of structured gaps, or *blanks* (*Leerstellen*), which occur at moments throughout and impose a challenge upon the reader to make connections and coordinate disparate moments. The principle of indeterminacy indicates that the construction of meaning always involves a conflictual, or negative, relationship between the reader and the text. Negativity thus designates a principle of totality *per contrario,* where the meaning as a whole, which is unspoken, stands in opposition to the text.

A helpful application of the concept of negativity to a particular challenge for interpretation is provided by Iser in his essay "The Patterns of Negativity in Beckett's Prose."[9] The behavior of characters in Beckett's narrative trilogy *Molloy, Malone Dies* and *The Unnamable* is discussed as a sequence of self-projections in constantly changing situations, which cause these projections to undercut themselves by exposing their fictional status. The result is a categorical denial of meaning through the unending rejection of fictions in such a way that the act of rejection itself becomes a structure of communication. A legitimate sense of the self is thus constituted ad infinitum within the finite limits of these fictions. Applying the same argument to the act of reading Beckett – whose work admittedly constitutes an extreme instance of negativity in fiction – Iser suggests that a corresponding quandary occurs for any attempt to find a meaning. We always become painfully aware that the only meanings with which we emerge from our reading of the text are those that we ourselves project upon it and that the text quickly exposes as such projections.

In the final meeting of a course on the hermeneutics of reading (presented at the University of Toronto in 1974), Iser outlined in more general terms what he means by negativity as the result of criteria within a fictional text, conceived from a stance which is not given, in such a way that the reader is obliged to produce that stance through a process of self-alienation, attempting to formulate that which remains unformulated in the text. Our sense of the meaning is thus the product of a creative act on our part as readers, fully as complex as the original creative act by which the text came to be written and achieved, in dialectical opposition to, or in negative tension with, the text itself. Our sense of the *truth* or the *reality* of this meaning – traditional terms in criticism suggesting some kind of metaphysical or ontological affirmation, which Iser would reject – is the result of a self-projection and is in the highest sense a fiction created by the act of reading. Meaning is the *what-not*, the *not-given* or *no-thing* of the text, which thus also qualifies the construct of meaning as a valid reflection of our own identity, achieved through the act of self-alienation that occurs in the process of reading.

This conclusion, paradoxically, agrees with the more traditional view of I. A. Richards (outlined above), concerning the status of the self as affirmed and made conscious to itself through the act of comprehending. The role of the literary text in its interaction with the reader in the process of achieving a hermeneutical consciousness is conceived by Iser in a radically opposite manner. In the light of Iser's concept of negativity, Richards could only be regarded as a positivist. The contrast between their respective positions concerning the construction of a meaning for the work as a whole delineates a fundamental incompatibility between a traditional and a postmodern hermeneutics.

Peripeteia and Metanoia

In his discussion of negativity Iser argues that the successful communication of the meaning as that which is not given depends upon a technique of reversal (*Wende*), whereby a dialectical sublation (*Aufhebung,* a Hegelian term) constitutes "a trace of the Not-given."[10] My own view regarding the question of reversal in literary narrative, which shares with both Iser and Richards the conviction that the reading process is essentially dialectical in nature, may best be presented with reference to the complex plot of tragedy as defined in Aristotle's *Poetics* (chaps. 10 and 11), involving what he calls *reversal* (*peripeteia*) and *recognition* (*anagnorisis*).

Traditionally, these concepts have been applied to the internal structure of drama, specifically to that climactic moment in the Sophoclean plot (looking to Aristotle's own favorite example, *Oedipus the King*) where the hero "discovers" the truth about himself and his deeds and suffers as a direct and immediate consequence of this discovery a radical reversal of status, a change of fortune, a fall. There is no doubt where and how this occurs in *Oedipus the King,* indicated by the scream of the protagonist in response to the old shepherd's words revealing who he truly is. The completion of the tragic action is achieved through this moment of discovery and reversal, the moment of *katastrophé,* literally a turning of the force of action back upon itself in such a way that its full significance is openly revealed.

Recent discussions of Aristotle's *Poetics* have acknowledged that Aristotle's concepts could also be applied to the affective dimension of tragedy (the audience's response), rather than being referred exclusively to internal aspects of plot structure. In particular arguments by the late W. K. Wimsatt, Jr., have demonstrated that Aristotle's criteria for the complex plot could also designate the appropriate response of the audience to the moment of climax in tragedy.[11] Such response involves an experience of recognition and reversal, not so much with regard to the truth about the hero (which is presumably known already to the audience of Greek drama), but rather concerning the ultimate significance of the tragic action as a whole, especially in its social and religious context. The legitimate measure of such a cognitive and reflective response, as critics of Greek tragedy have sometimes ignored, is the Chorus. In *Oedipus the King,* to pursue this example, in immediate response to the moment of catastrophe for the hero the Chorus performs its great hymn on the worthlessness of human existence, one of the supreme expressions of a tragic view of life in all literature. Such a shift in Aristotle's argument from a theory of structure to an aesthetics of reception provides the possibility, as Wimsatt was aware, for a rehabilitation of the troubled concept of *katharsis.* No longer would this category of emotional affect refer exclusively to a kind of group psychotherapy for the audience, as Aristotle apparently intended in accord with his use of the term elsewhere in his writings. The katharsis of tragedy would now signify primarily an essential and complex mode of interaction between the dramatic action and the response of the audience to it, which constitutes the true meaning of the tragedy.

Corroboration on this point is provided in an important essay by Hans Robert Jauss, Iser's colleague at the University of Constance, where katharsis is discussed as a "communicative category in aesthetic experience."[12] Jauss's argument affirms the rehabilitation of the Aristotelian category with reference to aesthetic experience in general, not just the response of an audience to tragic drama. Jauss's theory of identification between hero (or character) and reader as criterion for differentiating kinds or degrees of katharsis, however, seems problematic to me.

My own point concerning strategies of reversal in literary narrative would be that the somewhat facile distinction between verbal structure and the hermeneutics of reader response needs to be overcome. I agree with the Aristotelian argument that reversal functions essentially as an aspect of plot, though it may also be (as Jauss argues) that it has to do with establishing norms of character as well. At the same time, however, the purpose of such a strategy is only fulfilled in the appropriate response of the reader, who according to the tenets of negativity must react to what is said or done within the work through a dialectical experience of self-alienation. Only through such a transformation of consciousness can a reflective awareness of the unspoken meaning of the work as a whole be achieved. In this manner the moment of reversal places the reader in a position of suspension or surprise through a radical disruption of continuity. Such a rift, or caesura, in the rhythm of thought effects a reciprocal and opposite reaction, as if this gap in continuity were a direct call to the reader to be answered through a conscious act of recognition.

The highest instances of such strategies of reversal occur in the dialectical method of the Platonic dialogue and in the models of religious conversion in the New Testament. The interlocutors of Socrates frequently offer little resistance to the philosopher's power of persuasion – one thinks of the role of Glaukon in the *Republic* or of Phaedrus in the dialogue of that name. Yet their pattern of response provides in fact an example for the reader of the dialogue, against which the cognitive impact of Plato's text can be measured. The process of education toward philosophical understanding that takes place within the dialogue thus serves as an implied model for a corresponding hermeneutical consciousness in the reader of Plato. In the allegory of the cave (at the end of *Republic* vi), for instance, the reader identifies to the same extent as Socrates's own audience with the prisoner in the dark cave who breaks his chains in order to turn toward the sunlight of truth.

Similarly, in the parables of Jesus from the gospel narratives in the New Testament – which seem so similar to the myths of Plato in their teaching method – the reader responds, as do also the apostles to whom the parables are told, by affirming the truth of the story *for us*. The meaning of the story thus resides for the community of the faithful not so much in the moral teaching of Jesus as such, as in the response of the community to the lesson of the gospel. We ourselves are directly addressed when the teacher ends the parable with a hermeneutical signal, such as "Truly, I say unto you," or "Go, thou, and do likewise."

One of the most powerful moments of reversal in all literature, which may have profited from the example of both the Platonic dialogues and the gospel narratives, occurs in the account of conversion in the *Confessions* of St. Augustine. The author of this auto-biographical narrative, who thus also serves as his own hero, reports how he suddenly heard a voice calling to him in the garden: "Take up and read!" [tolle, lege; tolle, lege] (Book VIII, chap. 12). He responds by turning arbitrarily to a passage in Paul's Epistle to the Romans that reveals the truth of his conversion to him. So also, by implication, the reader of the *Confessions* is intended to respond to the experience of reading about this conversion by reading with a measure of sympathetic understanding. Reading in this book about the Saint's reading in the Book thus conveys a sense of dialectical reciprocity through the reflectivity of a reversal of reference, which forms the basis for our understanding.

As one last instance of such a hermeneutics of reversal, taken from the modern lyric in a strictly secular context, we may consider the powerful and surprising close to Rilke's famous sonnet on the "Archaic Torso of Apollo," which opens the *Neue Gedichte anderer Teil*: "Du mußt dein Leben ändern." Whose voice speaks these words? It is not only the poet addressing his reader, but also a voice attributed to the statue's silent eloquence: the entire surface of the fragmented stone shines like a flame or a star upon the poet in his captive state of imaginative communion. The message of the sonnet, which is thus the poet's message to his reader, results from an astonishing reversal of attribution. The light of the statue, like an oracle from the absent god, moves the poet, who thus composes his poem. What he communicates to us in the language of his sonnet is the result of a hermeneutical reversal, which we also must reenact in order to fulfill the imperative of this aesthetic truth: "You must change your life." The voice that speaks this line may thus finally be our own, addressing the "message" of the poem to ourselves in response to our reading of the poem, just as the poem is the response of the poet in language to his encounter with the divinity which is revealed to him through the sculpted stone torso. This moment of understanding as event thus assumes the status of a secular conversion. It is an illumination of the mind caused by a radical dialectical reversal that takes place through the hermeneutical encounter with the poem.[13]

Hölderlin's Concept of "Umkehr"

The concept of reversal may be further clarified by comparing two arguments from German idealist theory, which also provide unexpected insight, beyond the intention of the authors, into the hermeneutics of reading. These are, respectively, Hölderlin's "Notes to Sophocles," published in 1804 with his translations of *Oedipus the King* and *Antigone*,[14] and Hegel's comments on the language of conceptual thought in the preface to his *Phenomenology of Spirit*, published in 1807.[15] The former has been regarded by Hölderlin scholars and theorists of tragedy as a cryptic, often esoteric argument based on a profound, if somewhat intuitive, insight into Sophoclean drama. The latter has been much discussed by scholars concerned with Hegel's dialectical method, though never, to my knowledge, with reference to theories of reading and interpretation.

Both texts address, though in quite separate contexts, a principle of dialectical interaction that manifests itself within the verbal structure of discourse. In each instance, significantly, the moment of reversal that is crucial to understanding is defined with reference to *rhythm* as an overriding principle of sequential dynamics in discourse. This concept of rhythm, assuming that Hölderlin and Hegel have the same verbal phenomenon in mind, is crucial for defining the role of negativity in the reading process. These two close friends, who had spent their formative years together, initially at the Protestant Seminary in Tübingen and subsequently when they were employed as private tutors in Frankfurt, may have shared fundamental convictions about language and meaning in ways that would merit further study, despite the absence of explicit documen-

tary evidence. For the sake of brevity I shall limit my remarks to
selected passages from the two texts cited above.

In his notes to *Oedipus the King,* Hölderlin refers to the drama
as a "rhythmic sequence of ideas" [rhythmische Aufeinanderfolge
der Vorstellungen]. What he has in mind by this is clarified by a
subsequent passage, where he speaks of the dramatic action as a
sequence of discrete units that contrast and oppose each other in
their juxtaposition: the dialogue with its internal conflict, the
Chorus as opposition to the dialogue, the various complications
of formal interaction between these different parts:

> Therefore the use of dialogue in its continuous conflict, therefore the use
> of the Chorus as contrast against the dialogue. Therefore the interinvolve-
> ment – all too timid, all too mechanical and factitious in its ending –
> between the various parts, within the dialogue, and between the Chorus
> and the dialogue and the larger parts or dramata, which are constituted by
> the Chorus and the dialogue. *(my translation)*[16]

"Everything is statement against statement," he adds, "which reciprocally *sublates* itself" *(my emphasis)* [Alles ist Rede gegen Rede, die
sich gegenseitig aufhebt].

Within this complex dialectical sequence of contrasting dramatic
elements, two moments are singled out as crucial for the tragic
action and, above all, for comprehending that action.

The first of these is called the tragic *transport:* a moment within
the rhythmic sequence which is empty and disconnected ("eigentlich leer, und der ungebundenste"), like the caesura in metrics:
"das, was man im Sylbenmaaße Cäsur heißt." Hölderlin calls it the
"pure word" [das reine Wort], the "counter-rhythmic interruption"
[die gegenrhythmische Unterbrechung]. Across this gap, where in
place of the "alternation of ideas" [Wechsel der Vorstellungen] the
idea itself appears, the drama is divided into two halves against
itself, so that each part is balanced in opposition to the other:

> In this way the sequence of the design and its rhythm are divided and in
> its two halves is so mutually interrelated that the halves appear as equally
> weighted. *(my translation)*[17]

What Hölderlin means by this is subsequently revealed to be the role of the blind seer Teiresias in both *Oedipus the King* and *Antigone,* whose appearance in each play serves to interrupt the forward thrust of the action by revealing the true will of the gods. The effect of these moments of revelation, so Hölderlin argues, is to turn the rhythmic thrust of the drama back upon itself by establishing a separate, transcendent perspective upon the action, which must be integrated and resolved.

The second moment that Hölderlin singles out occurs at the climax of each drama, the moment of tragic catastrophe, the supreme moment of peripeteia and anagnorisis (as Aristotle labelled them) in the Sophoclean complex plot. It is, as Hölderlin puts it, the moment of extreme opposition in the absolute conflict between god and hero. Here, he argues, the hero forgets both himself and the god, like a traitor, though clearly in a manner which is holy. In this moment of "categorical reversal" [kategorische Umkehr], at the furthest limit of suffering, *time* holds absolute dominion: the hero is completely absorbed and obsessed by the moment, and the god is nothing but time; and both are "unfaithful" [untreu]. In this moment, time totally reverses itself, so that the beginning and the end are irreconcilable. The hero is completely caught up in this reversal and suffers the consequences of this contradiction:

In such a moment a human being forgets himself and the god and reverses himself, like a traitor, though in a holy manner. At the furthest limit of suffering, namely, nothing exists other than the conditions of time and space. At this [limit] a human forgets himself because he exists totally in the moment; the god because he exists only as time; and both are unfaithful; time, because at such a moment it reverses itself categorically and the beginning and end simply cannot be reconciled; the human, because at such a moment of categorical reversal he must follow, so that as a consequence he simply cannot be the same as at the beginning. (*my translation*)[18]

Tragic catastrophe is thus presented in quasi-metaphorical, quasi-metaphysical terms, which are admittedly difficult to relate to the action of the drama. Above all the full significance of the event as political, existential and religious revolution is emphasized in terms of the temporal, or rhythmic, process through which it is represented and comprehended: (1) by the hero in his agony of collapse, (2) by the chorus in the horror of realization and reflective response, and (3) by the audience in the totality of its katharsis.

In itself, Hölderlin's idiosyncratic discussion of Sophoclean tragedy, despite apparent echoes from Aristotle's *Poetics,* above all in his use of concepts relating to peripeteia and anagnorisis, would seem indifferent to a hermeneutics of response. That Hölderlin nonetheless had such a concern in mind could be argued from his more general theory of poetic structure, particularly as outlined in his somewhat earlier essay-fragment "Über die Verfahrungsweise des poetischen Geistes." A full elucidation of parallels between this text and the "Notes to Sophocles" would require another essay. A word may be said nonetheless about the concept of high point, or climax, in a poem as it relates to the notion of a categorical reversal.

Within the dialectical sequence of statements in poetic discourse, such a moment of climax constitutes simultaneously the extreme opposition and the complete union of the various elements which participate in that sequence. The result, as Hölderlin puts it, is that the spirit (*Geist*) of the poem, "the God of the Myth," is manifested in its infinity.[19] This moment is conveyed as a silence, a gap or caesura, and constitutes a categorical reversal in the rhythm of poetic tones. The world of the poem as totality is revealed in its particular form: "a world within the world, represented as the voice of the eternal."[20] This poetic world, this spirit, this God of the Myth, though itself unspoken and beyond the limits of language, is thus represented through the dynamics of poetic statement, through the rhythmic sequence of alternating tones (*Wechsel der Töne*). The reader must feel, or intuit, and thus comprehend, the poem as totality, just as the climactic moment in Sophoclean tragedy also manifests the ultimate truth of the drama to its audience, through reversal and recognition.

Hegel's "Speculative Sentence"

Hegel's discussion of the act of comprehension through language, in contrast to Hölderlin's existential and religious concern with tragedy, focuses upon what seems to be the simplest and smallest example of reversal in order to demonstrate the dialectical movement of thought as an abstract activity in and for itself. His well-known choice of instance in the preface to the *Phenomenology of Spirit* is called the "speculative sentence" [spekulativer Satz]. Hegel's model for such a sentence would seem at first to be a mere tautology: "God is Being" [Gott ist Sein]. As scholars of Hegel have often noted, this sentence is clearly intended as an alternative to the "sentence of identity" [Satz der Identität], which had been much discussed by Fichte and Schelling during the decade preceding Hegel's work: "I = I" [Ich = Ich].

"Conceptual thinking" (*begreifendes Denken*, also referred to as *das vorstellende Denken*) requires that the *Concept* (*Begriff*) itself be the "actual subject" [das eigene Selbst] of the thought. Hegel proceeds to analyze the grammatical structure of his sentence in conceptual terms, putting into language in his characteristically convoluted way the dialectical process through which comprehension of the Concept occurs:

[The Concept], since [it] is the object's own self, which presents itself as the *coming-to-be of the object*,...is not a passive Subject inertly supporting the Accidents; it is, on the contrary, the self-moving Concept which takes its determinations back into itself. In this movement the passive Subject itself *perishes*; it enters into the differences and the content, and constitutes the determinateness, i.e., the differentiated content and its movement, instead of remaining inertly over against it. (*PhS*, 37; *my emphasis*)[21]

Hegel here applies intentionally a fortuitous ambivalence in the term *Subject*.[22] On one hand, in accord with the traditional terminology of grammar, the subject is merely the noun that constitutes the nominative substantive of the sentence. At the same time, however, the subject is the conceptual consciousness (*Bewußtsein*) that performs the act of speculation. We may observe this performance in its self-conscious formulation in the following statement from Hegel, which needs to be quoted in full:

The solid ground which argumentation (*Räsonnieren*) has in the passive Subject is therefore shaken, and only this movement itself becomes the object. The Subject that fills its content ceases to go beyond it, and cannot have any further Predicates or accidental properties. Conversely, the dispersion of the content is thereby bound together under the self; it is not the universal (*das Allgemeine*) which, free from the Subject, could belong to several others. Thus the content is, in fact, no longer a Predicate of the Subject, but is the Substance, the essence and the Concept of what is under discussion. Picture-thinking (*das vorstellende Denken*), whose nature it is to run through the accidents or Predicates and which, because they are nothing more than Predicates and Accidents, rightly goes beyond them, is checked (*gehemmt*) in its progress, since that which has the form of a Predicate in a proposition is the Substance itself. It suffers, as we might put it, a counterthrust (*Gegenstoß*). Starting from the Subject as though this were a permanent ground, it finds that, since the Predicate is really the Substance, the Subject has passed over into the Predicate, and, by this very fact, has been sublated (*aufgehoben*); and, since in this way what seems to be the Predicate has become the whole and the independent mass, thinking cannot roam at will, but is impeded by this weight. (*PhS*, 37; *my emphasis*)[23]

As indicated in the complexities of this formulation, the process of understanding consists in two essential actions related to each other dialectically. First, the subject enters into the attributes of its predicate, literally loses itself, is destroyed (*geht zugrunde*). This content is thus indeed no longer the predicate of the subject, but is its substance, the essence (*Wesen*) and the concept (*Begriff*) of that which is being talked about. Second, as counterforce to this progression, the process of thought goes through what Hölderlin had termed a categorical reversal, referred to here by Hegel as a resistance (*Hemmung*) or a counterthrust (*Gegenstoss*). An act of recognition thus occurs whereby the predicate, into which the subject has moved as its substance, is rediscovered to be the substance *of that subject.* The characteristic sublation (*Aufhebung*) of the dialectic is thus achieved through this turning back of the concept upon itself, and the apparent loss of the subject into the predicate is corrected by its reestablishment as the ground of its substance. The activity of speculative thought is thus concluded and contained (*aufgehalten*) within the form of the statement as the conscious subject which is now known to itself. Hegel has here achieved, despite the convolutions of his own language, a description of how the dialectical process of thought achieves a reflective consciousness of itself in and through the grammatical form of language. I also submit, though Hegel may not himself have intended as much, that this description may define the basic structure of the hermeneutics of reading, whereby a reader through the process of reading a text achieves a conceptual understanding of the whole.

Further elaboration on the dialectical movement of thought is provided by Hegel a little later in the preface with reference to the concept of rhythm. The conflict between the form of a sentence and the unity of its concept, as he argues in another remarkable statement, resembles the conflict between meter and accent in rhythm:

This conflict between the general form of a proposition and the unity of the Concept which destroys it is similar to the conflict that occurs in rhythm between metre and accent. (*PhS*, 38)[24]

This conflict between meter and accent presumably refers to the distinction between the abstract schema of a given metrical form, such as iambic pentameter in a sonnet, and the specific configuration of accented or stressed and unstressed syllables by which the language of the actual utterance fills that form. He goes on to describe what he has in mind more fully, as follows:

Rhythm results from the floating centre and the unification of the two. So, too, in the philosophical proposition the identification of Subject and Predicate is not meant to destroy the difference between them, which the form of the proposition expresses; their unity, rather, is meant to emerge as a harmony. The form of the proposition is the appearance of the determinate sense, or the accent that distinguishes its fulfillment; but that the predicate expresses the Substance, and that the Subject itself falls into the universal, this is the *unity* in which the accent dies away. (*PhS*, 38)[25]

The rhythm, asserts Hegel, is the outcome of a vacillation and suspension (*die schwebende Mitte*) between meter and accent and is the unification of both. In a manner resembling such interaction, whereby a harmony between unity and difference is achieved, the form of a philosophical sentence, which is the manifestation of its determinate sense, interrelates the subject and predicate in such a way that their difference is sustained while their identity is affirmed as an all-pervasive harmony. The form of the sentence sustains a sense of difference in what it expresses, while its unity lies in the fact that the predicate expresses the substance into which the subject falls as a universal. The one is therefore like the pattern of stresses in meter – the *accent* – and the other is a fading away (*Verklingen*). The concept of rhythm for Hegel – as it is also defined in the very different context of poetry by Hölderlin – thus contains the principle of a reflective turn or reversal within itself as the determining factor in the dialectical process of language. As Hegel states in another passage from the preface, the form of the sentence must be sublated (*aufgehoben*), whereby the opposing movement of thought is expressed:

The sublation of the form of the proposition must not happen only in an immediate manner, through the mere content of the proposition. On the contrary, this opposite movement must find explicit expression. (*PhS*, 39)[26]

The return of the concept into itself must be represented: "dies Zurückgehen des Begriffs in sich muß *dargestellt* sein." This movement of thought is constituted, concludes Hegel, through "the dialectical movement of the sentence itself" [die dialektische Bewegung des Satzes selbst].

Shakespeare's *Troilus and Cressida*

The idiom of German Idealist thought does not yield either certainty or clarity in its abstract speculations about the nature of speculation. Hegel's reflections upon the language of conceptual thought and the dialectic of its turns and returns upon itself remain bound within the limits of his own convoluted discourse. His argument about the form of the speculative sentence demonstrates – perhaps as he intended, more through the dialectical reversals of his own grammar than through any sense of coherent reasoning – that thought moves toward understanding by way of a rhythmic circling back upon itself. Hölderlin provides at least the challenge of a reading that may be tested against its source in Sophocles. His claims with regard to the rhythm of ideas in tragedy and the crucial moment of categorical reversal gain credence by juxtaposition with parallel, though far less obscure, arguments in Aristotle's *Poetics* concerning the structure of the complex plot. I have argued, however, that the passages considered from Hegel about the speculative sentence and from Hölderlin about the form and the meaning of catastrophe in *Oedipus the King* may both yield related insight into the hermeneutics of reading. The only proof for the validity of this claim must derive from the experience of reading itself. The act of reading, no matter how we may define it, remains the only legitimate basis for a genuine hermeneutical consciousness.

As one last instance in support of this argument I offer a more accessible case in point, derived from one of the most challenging and peculiar scenes of dialogue in all of literature, the central scene in Shakespeare's *Troilus and Cressida* (3.3), where Achilles and Ulysses meet to address one of the crucial issues of the play. A brief consideration of the hermeneutical implications of this conversation in its several levels of irony will help bring this present essay to a conclusion.

The situation is borrowed from Homer's *Iliad*, which Shakespeare presumably knew, if not from the original Greek, or possibly translations into Latin or French, then from the English translation by his contemporary, the poet Chapman, who published his *Seaven*

Bookes of the Iliades (I, II, VII–XI) in 1598. Achilles in Shakespeare has withdrawn in anger from the field of battle, not entirely for the same insult to his honor as the removal of his prize Chryseis by Agamemnon at the outset of Homer's poem. As Odysseus comments at the council of the Greek chieftains about Achilles's frame of mind: "Kingdom'd Achilles in commotion rages / And batters down himself." (2.3.176–77) His stratagem for goading Achilles back into battle is to offer a calculated insult to his pride, persuading all the Greek leaders to pass before his tent (in 3.3) without acknowledging him. Achilles responds in dismay at the apparent demise of his prestige as a warrior. At this moment of troubled self-reflection for Achilles, Ulysses approaches him, reading what appears to be a letter that attracts Achilles's interest.

Achill.   How now, Ulysses!

Ulyss.   Now, great Thetis' son.

Achill.   What are you reading?

Ulyss.   A strange fellow here
    Writes me, that man, how dearly ever parted,
    How much in having, or without or in,
    Cannot make boast to have that which he hath,
    Nor feels not what he owes, but by reflection,
    As, when his virtues shining upon others
    Heat them, and they retort that heat again
    To the first giver.

Achill.   This is not strange, Ulysses.
    The beauty that is borne here in the face
    The bearer knows not, but commends itself
    To others' eyes; nor doth the eye itself,
    That most pure spirit of sense, behold itself,
    Not going from itself; but eye to eye oppos'd
    Salutes each other with each other's form;
    For speculation turns not to itself
    Till it hath travell'd and is mirror'd there
    Where it may see itself. This is not strange at all.
    (3.3.94–111)

The conversation continues for another hundred lines, but we may limit our discussion to this passage. The immediate purpose of Ulysses with regard to Achilles's pride is apparent. The indifference of the other Greek chieftains conveys the impression that his reputation for military prowess has been diminished by his refusal to fight. Ulysses also later makes Achilles jealous of the brutish strength of his rival Ajax, who has agreed to face Hector in a single combat. But Shakespeare has much more than such distress for reputation in mind.

The lesson conveyed by the letter that Ulysses is reading goes far beyond the specific instance of Achilles. The generality of his summary extends to philosophical abstractions about the nature of self-knowledge and self-identity. The style of this formulation has led scholars to ask who the author of the letter, otherwise unnamed in the play, might be. In a bold and suggestive essay on this question, "*Troilus and Cressida* and Plato," I. A. Richards quotes at length from *The Republic* to support his claim that, for whatever anachronistic reason, Shakespeare intends to suggest that the author of the letter Ulysses reads is indeed Plato.[27]

More important for interpreting this scene, in my view, is the manner of the verbal exchange between Ulysses and Achilles in relation to the doctrine cited from the letter, rather than the question of who might have been the author. The central criterion of identity cited by the letter is property – that which one "hath" or "owes" – not what one is or claims to be. The images used to illuminate the point about reflection, however, involve sense perception. Ulysses speaks of heat and radiation, where the "shine" of virtue is returned as "heat" upon the "first giver" by "retort" (100-1). Achilles responds with a visual image, far more familiar, where beauty in facial features is only known to the one who bears it through the eyes of others. Even more effective is the precise image of vision as such, where the eye itself cannot see itself except in its reflection from the eye of another as in a mirror. Shakespeare provides in these images of perception, as in the focus on self as property, a vivid and concrete sense of how identity as self-knowledge can only be achieved through reflection.

The form and setting of the drama, however, offers yet further demonstration of the lesson being conveyed. The exchange of dialogue between Ulysses and Achilles itself involves the pattern of reversal and reflection. Achilles first asks Ulysses what he is reading; then, when Ulysses responds, Achilles immediately interprets and affirms the truth of what the letter conveys. It is indeed Achilles who formulates the powerful statement used as motto for this essay, namely that "speculation turns not to itself / Till it hath travell'd and is mirror'd there / Where it may see itself" (109-11). The evidence of the drama, however, suggests ironically that Achilles fails to apply the point which he makes to himself. As portrayed by Shakespeare, in stark contrast to the all-comprehending Ulysses, master of speculative strategy, Achilles but little knows himself. This irony of discontinuity between what a character states and what he seems to know and understand goes to the center of the negative hermeneutics of this extremely difficult drama.

Yet there is more. The dialectic of mutual reflection that constitutes the form of conversation here extends also, not without design on the author's part, to the audience witnessing the scene. The lesson of the speculative turn may be applied both to the effect of the speeches on us, since the success of the performance is only measured by our comprehension, and also to our application of the lesson in its general formulation to ourselves and to our own understanding of ourselves. The appearance of these Homeric characters in Shakespearean guise upon the stage provides us with a complex mirror of selfhood with which to test our sense of identity *as self-knowledge* against the fabric of the play and its language as a complex mirror, which holds up an image of humanity wherein we may find ourselves reflected.

At this level of signification the scene of dialogue begins to assume general poetological and ontological implications. The conversation between Ulysses and Achilles constitutes at a higher level of abstraction an implicit theory of drama and theater, indeed a theory of poetry and art as such, in its hermeneutical interrelationship with its audience. The fictions of ancient Greek legend, which Shakespeare seems to play with so freely, thus take on an allegorical dimension, signifying no less than the meaning that their medium as drama is intended to convey. This metacritical level of response is further sustained by the fact that Ulysses is himself reading from a text, presumably holding the letter in his hand that provides the source or origin of his doctrine about the reflectivity of speculation. That letter was written by some author – whoever that may have been, Plato or anyone else (such as Will Shakespeare himself) – and for us as readers of Shakespeare's dramatic text (which is ironically the way in which this play above all has usually been received, at least until recent memory when successful productions have begun to be presented), there may finally be a sense of identification with Ulysses's words: "A strange fellow here / Writes me" (95-6).

We should also consider the enigmatic prologue to *Troilus and Cressida*, which was printed with the Quarto edition of 1609, entitled *A neuer writer, to an euer reader. Newes.* The elaborate opening sentence of this prologue deserves quotation in full without further commentary here:

Eternall reader, you haue heere a new play, neuer stal'd with the Stage, neuer clapper-clawd with the palmes of the vulgar, and yet passing full of the palme comicall; for it is a birth of your braine, that neuer vnder-tooke any thing commicall, vainely: And were but the vaine names of commedies changde for the titles of Commodities, or of Playes for Pleas; you should see all those grand censors, that now stile them such vanities, flock to them for the maine grace of their grauities: especially this authors Commedies, that are so fram'd to the life, that they serue for the most common Commentaries, of all the actions of our liues, shewing such a dexteritie, and power of witte, that the most displeased with Playes, are pleasd with his Commedies.

Conclusions

What conclusions may be drawn from the disparate evidence assembled here concerning strategies of reversal in literary narrative? Beginning with the comparison of Richards's notion of interinanimations and Iser's concept of negativity in the act of reading, the chapter has continued with a brief excursus on Aristotle, Plato, Sophocles, the New Testament, St. Augustine and Rilke to focus on Hölderlin and Hegel, juxtaposing their complex arguments about reversals in the rhythm of tragedy and in the speculative sentence. Finally, from Shakespeare's *Troilus and Cressida,* I have argued that the turn of speculation to itself might be applied also to the hermeneutics of reading. Without claiming more consistency from such a range of material than would be justified, I offer three modest hypotheses concerning the way in which we achieve a sense of totality through the act of reading a literary text.

First, the interaction – might we even speak of an interinanimation? – between reader and text in the act of reading always involves a dialectical circling between the particular, formal structures of statement in the language of the text and an awareness or intuition of the meaning of the whole, as a totality beyond the limits of what is actually expressed.

Second, the purpose or intention of a literary work is to confront and engage its reader in such a way that the sense of totality in its meaning will include a reflective awareness in the reader of an active participation or involvement in that totality.

Third, the various strategies of reversal, as they have here been described, constitute an essential communicative design at all levels of the literary text, from grammar and syntax to plot, character and idea. Through such techniques of reversal in the text an essential dialectical relation is established with the reader through the act of reading.

By means of these dialectical reversals the essentially linear sequence of statements in the text is translated through the reading process, from line to line and from page to page, into a pattern of simultaneous interrelationships – in accord with what Richards called *interinanimations* and Hölderlin and Hegel referred to as the rhythm, the *rhythm of ideas* or the *dynamics of speculation* – a reflective, dialectical circling of the mind in and through the text as a whole. The act of interpretation is essentially identical to the process of dialectical circling through the turns and counterturns of reflective thought that take place during the process of reading.

To what extent do the several theories outlined above support these hypotheses? First, in the light of arguments from Idealist philosophy concerning the "dialectical movement" of thought and language, the apparent opposition between I. A. Richards's concept of interinanimation and Wolfgang Iser's views on negativity may be resolved into a relative difference of emphasis on the twofold process of the reading experience. The real issue concerns the essential ambivalence and indeterminacy involved in the dynamic interaction between reader and text. On this point the consensus of theoretical positions assembled here offers some reassurance. The constitution of meaning *as a whole,* if this much abused notion may still serve, necessarily imposes through the act of reading a sense of ultimate concern upon thought, a concern which is open, indeterminate, boundless and presumably ineffable. Only through the dialectical process of comprehension by the reader, however, which accompanies the act of reading the text itself, may such an ultimate concern be realized and affirmed. The text as verbal structure remains by contrast fixed and determinate, closed and fully articulated. It is the task of the dialectic of reading to mediate between the text and the concern that it conveys.

Simultaneously and paradoxically, the process of opening up an awareness for such ultimate concerns also imposes an equal obligation upon the mind to turn reflectively back upon itself. The constitution of meaning in literature requires an act of self-reflection and self-validation in the reader, which corresponds to the kind of activity that Coleridge and Keats, with specific reference to the poetic act, called *soul-making.* With regard to such reflective turns of thought my argument accepts the basic premises of the Hegelian dialectic, though in ways, I hope, that would also be acceptable to I. A. Richards's more intuitive and pragmatic notion of interinanimations. The common ground between Hegel and Richards may be found in the conviction, derived from both the Platonic and the Romantic traditions of poetic theory, that literature may communicate a meaning that is transcendent.

The language of literature does not convey a meaning that could

347

in any way be described as a content, a doctrine or a message. Meaning is established as the product of the complex dialectical process of thought described by Hegel with reference to the speculative sentence as a self-annihilating movement of the subject (the mind of the reader) into the substance of its predicate (the verbal structure of the text being read). This movement is followed immediately by a categorical reversal, a return back to itself, which reestablishes the subject through self-reflection as the ground of that substance. Understanding is thus open, boundless, indeterminate, infinite, even transcendent, and what is known necessarily also affirms the cognitive and ontological role of the self as knower. The only instrument or medium for such understanding, however, the necessary and sufficient means to such reflective insight, remains the literary text itself. The poetic work serves simultaneously as a mirror to the self and as a window, which Keats in his "Ode to a Nightingale" calls "a magic casement," that opens upon a vision of what Shelley in his poetic drama *Prometheus Unbound* invokes as "The loftiest star of unascended heaven, / Pinnacled dim in the intense inane."

Postscript

Two days after completing the initial version of this essay I happened to discover the following footnote to Richards's essay "What Is Saying?":

converse is an interesting word in itself and in its relations with *convert.* The sense "talk with" is relatively recent. Dr. Johnson: "to convey the thoughts reciprocally in talk." The -*verse* element, means "turning" this way or that. The religious sense of *conversion* looks back to Plato, *Republic,* VII, 518: "The natural power to learn lives in the soul and is like an eye which might not be turned from the dark to the light without a turning round of the whole body...of which there might be an art...of turning the soul round most quickly and with the most effect." That is what education, for Plato, was to be.[28]

So also, I might add, was education to be for Richards: "a turning round of the soul most quickly and with the most effect." *Converse.* How appropriate to find so suitable a term – more so, perhaps, than *reversal* – to describe the kinds of dialectical turnabout in the act of reading that matter for the comprehending mind.

Chapter 9 : The Faults of Vision;
a Dialogue on Identity and Poetry

In memory of René Wellek, scholar, teacher and friend

It was a miracle of rare device,
A sunny pleasure-dome with caves of ice.
–Coleridge, "Kubla Khan"

SKEPTIC: What is the *identity* of a literary text? How could a text have an identity? and what would it matter for criticism?

CRITIC: As usual, you're overreacting. It seems to me that a text is about as identifiable as anything else in our culture and that the distinction of literary texts should matter to critics. Do I have to remind you that textual criticism, within the prestigious domain of *philology,* was once a most sophisticated and self-confident enterprise? Have you forgotten what used to be called "higher criticism"?

SKEPTIC: The old style of higher criticism was fine in its proper place, especially for the classics and the Bible, where editing texts and publishing critical editions could be a full-time job. We tend to take such things for granted now.

CRITIC: At least you acknowledge the legitimacy of editing texts, if only for a philology of earlier days. I hope you would also agree that the status of the text as scholarly artifact was first established by the discipline of philology, for instance in the editions of Homer by the scholars of ancient Alexandria. Behold now the splendid rows of books that fill the shelves of our university libraries, not to mention the more popular form of paperback and anthology volumes, which are supplied by bookstores to the general reader and assigned to students on the reading lists of our courses.

STUDENT : No one knows the tyrannies of a reading list so intimately as a student of comparative literature. Are you familiar with the kinds of bibliography imposed on us as recommended reading from world literature, reflecting whatever canons of taste and critical ideology may be currently in vogue, usually arranged by period and genre?

SKEPTIC: Do you maintain that the question of identity could be clarified by the role of philology, best-seller lists and the curricula of college courses?

STUDENT : Certainly not. My point would be that very few naive readers still exist. Even beginning students quickly encounter avant-garde ideas about reading. The issue of *textualité* crops up everywhere in my field these days, and we all are made to pay homage to the problem of writing, which lately has seemed an exclusively French preserve. I suppose I agree with the concern expressed by that unnamed female student of Stanley Fish at Johns Hopkins, who asked at the beginning of a course, "Is there a text in this class?"[1] The question was not so naive as it first appeared to be. Consider the byplay that Fish's book employs on that question. It reads like a calculated outrage directed against philology.

SKEPTIC: What makes you say that?

STUDENT : Let me quote from the opening statement in the preface: "The answer this book gives to its title question is 'there is and there isn't.' There isn't a text in this or any other class if one means by text what E. D. Hirsch and others mean by it, 'an entity which always remains the same from one moment to the next';[2] but there is a text in this and every class if one means by text the structure of meanings that is obvious and inescapable from the perspective of whatever interpretive assumptions happen to be in force." I think I belong among those "others" associated with E. D. Hirsch.

CRITIC : Let me offer a thought here. We need to distinguish between two separate senses of text: first, there is the verbal construct, which in our bookish culture is usually secured in print as the product of editing and publishing; and, second, there are those functions, however varied and indeterminate, that a text may legitimately serve for its readers. It seems to me that much recent avant-garde criticism, often under the vague rubric of "post-structuralism," has purposefully confused these two senses of text. Fish is an example of this. We all know that there is a difference between the sign and what it signifies (even if powerful claims have been made for subsuming both *signifiant* and *signifié* under the heading of the sign), between the medium and the message (*pace* Marshall McLuhan), or between the literary text *as a work* (*Ergon*) and the activity (or *Energeia,* to use Wilhelm von Humboldt's term) through which it is produced and disseminated. I would argue that the term *text* be limited to the former sense, as an artifact. I hold to this definition, even if we can imagine situations, for instance in oral cultures, where the fabric of language woven by a speaker (such as the Homeric rhapsode) exists only in a living relation as discourse to an actual audience. In our supposedly literate, post-Gutenberg culture, a complex relationship between text and discourse always obtains, even though the text may claim a priority, as theorists of textuality, such as Jacques Derrida, have argued. Speech acts for us would thus be a function of texts. Yet the text itself, as I am arguing, is never identical with the act of speaking. This claim would not in any way delimit the plurality of legitimate responses to a text, either hermeneutically through the act of reading or semiotically with reference to the code or system of signs which constitutes the language of a text (*langue* as distinct from *parole*).

STUDENT : Your confidence about the status of the text brings to mind a claim in current hermeneutical theory that a text must stand on its own. Gadamer has insisted that "the text stands" [Der Text steht],[3] which suggests that on this point Gadamer and Hirsch would be in agreement against the subversive strategies of Fish.

CRITIC : My own model for the ontological certainty of the text, as well as the challenge and the solace which that certainty poses for criticism, derives from the concluding lines of Hölderlin's "Patmos," where poetry is identified with Scripture as "fixed letter" [der veste Buchstab], which must be "cared for" [gepfleget] and as that which "stands" [bestehendes], which must be "well interpreted" [gut/Gedeutet]. Literature as we know it depends on such a security of texts, in order that reading, interpretation and even teaching can occur within a free and confident realm of response. Plato is perhaps the earliest and most eloquent, if also ironic, spokesman for such a security of texts. His dialogues served as the medium for his teachings as philosopher, even though the figure of Socrates as interlocutor in the dialogues participates in a scene of oral exchange in discourse. Socrates also expresses a powerful skepticism about writing (in the *Phaedrus*, 274–78); but Plato, we should remember, is only known to us as the author of his dialogues in written texts. The educational power of his writings throughout the tradition of Western culture has depended upon their capacity to communicate and instruct *as texts*.

s k e p t i c : Now we've reached the point where the question of identity becomes interesting. Do we really only mean by that term the status of the text as object or artifact, as if identity were synonymous with *individuality*, or *specificity*, or even *character*? Let me outline briefly two quite separate theoretical contexts for the concept of identity, call them the *logical* and the *psychological*, which I borrow from an elaborate and authoritative survey of the philosophical history of the term by Dieter Henrich.[4]

The logical sense of identity is familiar in philosophy as a criterion of sameness, whereby one thing is itself by definition "in itself the same." The issue of identity was first established by the ancient Greeks in terms of the verb *to be* as copula for the predication of any subject. Leibniz clarifies the essential mathematical criteria for defining the identity of any two objects, if all the qualities of one are also found in the other. The furthest limit of this tradition, amounting to an onto-theological (or would it be: theo-sophical?) mysticism, is found in Schelling's *Identitätsphilosophie*, where God is argued to be manifested in all things, much as (so Hegel argued in his famous polemical response) the night where all cows are black. I doubt that there is much insight to be gleaned here regarding the status of the literary text.

The psychological sense of identity is a more recent development, constituting a kind of special instance for the logical sense when applied to the individual self. Identity thus becomes a principle of consistency or integrity for the person, in particular as a criterion of constancy through time and change. Identity may thus be regarded as a modern substitute for the traditional concept of *psyche,* whether we look to philosophical theories of the self (as in William James, argued by Henrich to be the originator of this view of identity) or to post-Freudian psychoanalytical views (as in the so-called psycho-biographies of Erik Erikson). We are all too familiar with this concept of identity, if only as a principle of crisis.

My basic skepticism begins here. I do not believe that either of these traditional senses of identity, the logical or the psychological, can be applied to the literary text. No criterion of sameness will do, unless we rigorously exclude all concern with verbal function, in which case perhaps the mere technological capability for reproducing copies of books with exactly the same text would constitute an identity. Nor can a text in any way resemble the personality of an individual human being, except through a dubious principle of analogy, whereby the author is identified with his work. Both these senses of identity, when applied to literary texts, lead inevitably to familiar romantic mystifications, through claims either for an organic unity or for a poetic individuality. I reject both these claims and propose that we abandon the concept of identity for the literary text.

STUDENT : Wait a minute. I have a question based on my reading of the later Heidegger, specifically the difficult essay entitled *Der Satz der Identität.*[5] Heidegger there attributes to language the capacity to achieve an identity between thought and being, not only as an event in discourse, but also as knowledge, as a conscious awareness in the mind that accompanies a speech act. To signify this cognitive dimension of discourse, the self-reflectivity of speech, he introduces an etymological pun on the term for event: *Er-eignis,* where the sense of "ownness" in the root *eigen* is equated with the archaic sense of "eyeing" something in the verb *eräugnen.* Heidegger thus grounds the identity of speaking in the self-reflective movement of language itself, essentially as a dialectical or hermeneutical function (terms that the late Heidegger would not accept) of thought in and through the act of speaking. He also introduces the notion of a "leap" [Sprung] that occurs for thought within "the resonating domain or preserve" [der in sich schwingende Bereich] of language as it is spoken, whereby man and Being enter into a "belonging together" [Zusammengehören] within the "essential light" [Wesenslicht] of the event. It seems to me that Heidegger here retrieves the concept of identity as essential for language, or at least for authentic speaking and thinking, if not for the literary text as such.

SKEPTIC: Though I have little patience with such obscurity, I agree that Heidegger's oracular pronouncements belong, however obliquely, within the mainstream of philosophical thinking about dialectics and hermeneutics.

STUDENT: It has also been suggested to me that the term *Sprung* might here signify more than a leap of thought, even though the primary force of his metaphor concerns the movement of the mind through darkness, as along an uncertain forest path, into the sudden brightness of a clearing. *Sprung,* however, might also indicate a kind of break or *fault,* a gap or fissure in the totality of Being, within which thought moves, from which it originates, and towards which its inquiries strive as to a goal or end. The fault, or flaw, as in the structure of a crystal or a sculpture, would open up a perspective on that which otherwise would be concealed and self-contained. Self-reflection would thus be achieved as a distancing or an interruption in the sustaining vehicle of the mind. More specifically, with regard to language as this vehicle, which Heidegger also called "the house of Being" [das Haus des Seins], such a fault would provide the possibility of reflection through figurative rupture or the discontinuities of discourse.

SKEPTIC: This reading of the term *Sprung* seems dubious to me, yet it is an eminently Heideggerian misreading. It recalls his use of the term *rift* (*Riß*) in the earlier essay *Der Ursprung des Kunstwerks*,[6] where he discusses the cognitive structures of the work of art. Perhaps we here approach a proper sense of the violent, conflictual relation of texts, as constructs or fabrics of language, to thought, where a sense of division or separation is crucial between signifier and signified, or between message and signal. Such conflict or opposition seems incompatible with traditional notions of vision, or truth, especially in Heidegger's own sense of truth as *Unverborgenheit* (from the Greek ἀλήθεια). Yet this sense of conflict yields a crucial model for hermeneutics, in particular for the forms of language that impose interpretive responses upon the mind through the act of reading. Whether the term *rift* or *fault* is preferred seems only a question of terminology.

    C R I T I C : Well, now I've heard extreme positions on identity outlined by the two of you, based largely on the authority of borrowed philosophical arguments. I'm not persuaded that literary criticism, or even literary theory, would profit from such models, especially if we are concerned primarily with the practice of interpreting texts.

Let me outline my own position. I would maintain that the crucial criterion for any discussion of identity in a literary text derives from the nature of language itself as a system of signs and from the essential functions of discourse. Every statement in language necessarily involves two separate and simultaneous acts of mediation: on one hand, an act of representation, which establishes a relationship between the verbal code and the world to which it refers; and, on the other, an act of communication, which establishes a relationship between a speaker and an audience.[7] This twofold function of discourse will also apply to every literary text through the act of reading. With regard to such functions, identity in a strict sense is impossible, since meaning is constituted through a twofold structure of interrelationships that depend upon polarities of opposition and differentiation. The act of representation requires a distinction between the system of signs and the frame of reference (between the code of signifiers and the range of signifieds); and the act of communication requires a distinction between speaker and audience (between addresser and addressee). The text *as text* thus stands within a fourfold dynamic structure of implicit relationships, which are sustained by opposition and difference. I would be inclined to locate that "resonating preserve" of language, as Heidegger called it, within this dynamic structure; just as I would also argue that this polarity of mediations, or "crossings-over," constitutes the essential *metaphoric* dimension of poetic discourse. To be translated into such metaphoric resonance is the purpose, goal and end (*telos*) of every literary text. I fail to see how the concept of identity as traditionally defined could be applicable here.

SKEPTIC : We seem dangerously close to agreement, even if what we agree on is to deny any identity to the literary text.

STUDENT : That sounds like an admission of defeat.

SKEPTIC : Not quite. The time has come to return to the ancient Greeks. My own skeptical stance is borrowed from the spirit of Socratic inquiry, which underlies our dialogue. But we can also learn from the arguments of the philosophers.

Aristotle provides a fundamental insight into hermeneutical consciousness in that peculiar work *Peri Hermeneias*,[8] where he asserts that "spoken sounds are symbols (*symbola*) of affections in the soul, and writing (*ta graphomena*) of spoken sounds." Aristotle uses the terms *symbol* and *sign* synonymously, as in the sentence immediately following the statement just quoted, where he argues that signs (*semeia*) designate the relation between spoken words and whatever in the mind (or *psyche*) they stand for or signify. These remarks are too brief to establish a comprehensive semiotics or even a psychology of language; but a fundamental hierarchy is nonetheless clear: written words stand for spoken words and spoken words stand for thoughts, feelings or whatever within the mind. This hierarchy could be reformulated with terms appropriate to our own discussion: the text represents or signifies discourse, which represents or signifies the message or the meaning. In effect, Aristotle lends support to our challenge against the identity of the text. Insofar as the symbolizing or signifying functions of language involve a semantic differentiation or a hierarchy of figuration, the concept of identity is out of place.

STUDENT : Aristotle's hierarchy reminds me of the more familiar discussion of imitation by Plato in the *Republic*.[9] We all recall the attack against the poets in Book x, where poetry is accused of being an imitation (*mimesis*) that is two degrees removed from the truth of ideas. The painter imitates an object,

such as a couch (596c–597b), which is itself, according to Socrates'
argument, an imitation of an idea or form (*eidos*). This hierarchy of
imitations could be regarded as analogous to the hierarchy of figuration in Aristotle. The difference between them corresponds to the
basic duality of interrelationships (just outlined by our friend the
Critic) intrinsic to language in its functions as a system of signs: the
act of representation, which would be the Platonic model of mimesis; and the act of communication, which would be the Aristotelian
model of hermeneutics.

CRITIC : Plato himself may have anticipated this duality in
his use of the term *mimesis,* in a manner which suggests that
Aristotle might have been indebted to his teacher (as so often in his
work) for the hierarchy of figuration outlined in his *Peri Hermeneias.* Consider the passage in *Republic* III where the education of
the guardians is discussed with reference to stories that could be
told and music that could be performed. The term *mimesis* is used
there, not as a principle of representation, but as a criterion for
expression and response in the soul. Particularly important is the
discussion of rhythm and harmony in relation to speech (*logos*) and
the figures of diction or style (*ho tropos tes lexeos*; 400d–402e).
These attributes of music are said to follow the manner of speaking
just as speech follows the disposition, or *ethos,* of the soul (*ho tes
psyches ethos*).

STUDENT : It is also interesting to note that Plato here uses
the same term, *ethos,* that Aristotle later used in the *Poetics* to designate what is usually translated as *character* in tragedy.

CRITIC : True. But even more interesting is the claim made in
the *Republic* – a claim that has enjoyed a long history of influence –
that there is a correlation between ethical and aesthetic values
(though these are not Plato's terms) within a hierarchy of qualities:
"good speech" (*eulogia*), "good harmony" (*euharmonia*), "good
grace" (*euschemosune*) and "good rhythm" (*eurhythmia*) accompany
a "good disposition" (*euetheia*). Good disposition is defined as "the
truly good and fair disposition of the character and the mind"
(400e). There is a principle of ethical correspondence at work here,
which is developed at some length in the dialogue, that beautiful

forms in music and art, not to mention poetry and discourse as such, will be produced only by good minds.

STUDENT : The converse is also argued as a principle for what might be called aesthetic education, where the beautiful forms of art and music will have a corresponding effect upon the minds of those who respond to them. *Mousike* is offered as a model of *paideia* through its influence upon the soul by imitative (*mimetic*) response (401c–403). Could this claim be important for the question of identity?

SKEPTIC : There is no doubt that Plato's argument has been enormously influential throughout the history of Western aesthetic theory. The entire neo-Platonic and Christian tradition from Plotinus and St. Augustine through Dante to the Romantics could bear witness to this influence. The ultimate outcome of Plato's claim would be found in Schelling's *Identitätsphilosophie*, specifically in his *Philosophie der Kunst*. The legacy of Plato imposes a humanistic valorization of the arts for education. The centrality of literature and criticism in the curriculum of our universities still bears witness to this legacy. Even if it sounds like heresy, I would like to challenge its basic assumptions as misleading and, in its mystical and sentimental extremes, as downright dangerous.

CRITIC : That statement sounds rather hostile and provocative to me. Do you truly intend to reject the basic humanistic values inherent to the tradition of Plato?

SKEPTIC : Far from it. I fully agree with Plato's basic model for mimesis as a hierarchy of production and influence, of creation and reception. But I regard this model as the basis for a theory of figuration, rather than a theory of identity, whereby the creation and reception of art involves an essential process of metaphoric transformation. Modern hermeneutical theory, which is probably more indebted to Plato than it acknowledges, has demonstrated that interpretation depends upon a cognitive and reflective distance in aesthetic experience. The appropriate relationship between the mind and the work of art is that of conflict or even negation. Any principle of identity applied to the interpretation of art yields an anti-hermeneutics. Critical judgment itself depends upon such a principle of difference, or tension, or opposition.

CRITIC : You seem to be using Plato against himself, or at least your reading of the *Republic* is directed against the traditional reputation of Plato and Platonism. Perhaps your views are coloured by modern theories concerning the nature of the sign and the place of metaphor in poetic discourse, which you merely project retrospectively upon Plato.

SKEPTIC : I do not deny the influence of modern theory on my thinking, nor do I diminish the complexity of influence, which makes our own views merely another instance in the continuing tradition of Plato. But I also believe in the legitimacy of a revisionary reading of Plato's text based on whatever fresh insights we may bring to it.

CRITIC : Let me offer yet another instance of such insight specifically with regard to lyric poetry, which may throw further light on our discussion of identity. I have in mind a recent essay by the German scholar Karlheinz Stierle on identity in the lyric.[10] He develops a theory of transference or, as he puts it, *transgression* as the constitutive feature of lyric discourse. Initially he uses the term *Überschreitung* ("crossing-over") as an etymological equivalent for the Greek *metaphora,* and I surmise that *transgression* may be intended as a synonym. The implications of this term for the status of the figure seem less neutral and innocent to me, as Stierle himself seems to acknowledge, when he speaks of the lyric as "anti-discourse."

STUDENT : What interests me in Stierle's essay are the several connections he makes with related positions among contemporary theorists, especially in France. Beginning with Roman Jakobson's definition of the poetic function in his much-cited essay "Linguistics and Poetics," and referring to arguments by Michel Foucault and Pierre Macherey, Stierle proceeds to distinguish between the text as verbal structure and discourse as *praxis.* Such a speech act occurs within a specific speech community, and in accord with specific conventions and contexts of communication,[11] Stierle's notion of identity in the lyric seems to depend entirely upon discourse as event.

CRITIC : I surmise that this basic structuralist and post-structuralist distinction between verbal form and the functions of discourse is crucial for Stierle's theory of figuration as transgression. I was also struck by the privilege assigned by Stierle to Jakobson's well-known definition of the poetic function of language in that same essay. Jakobson's assertion that "the poetic function projects the principle of equivalence from the axis of selection into the axis of combination," which has always seemed a non-statement to me beyond the confines of transformational grammar, is usefully translated by Stierle into the claim that a poetic text serves to thematize its own verbal form. Jakobson says as much when he claims that the poetic function focusses on the message for its own sake. Stierle demonstrates persuasively that this focus is only achieved through a conflict between the verbal form and its communicative functions.

SKEPTIC : How does that lead us back to the question of identity?

CRITIC : Stierle's insistence on the priority of metaphor as transgression in the lyric corresponds roughly to the claims you were making with reference to Plato's hierarchy of influence and exchange in the procedures of discourse. Metaphor as transgression is essentially a challenge to the concept of identity, especially if identity is restricted (as I think Stierle intends) to a criterion of integrity or coherence in discourse as speech act or event.

STUDENT : Can you further clarify what is meant by transgression?

CRITIC : Consider the following statement by Stierle: "Metaphor in lyric poetry is not only a figure of identity, which contains in itself the appearance of divergence, but quite the opposite, the possibility of revealing what seems to be identical in its differences and thereby multiplying the primary context."[12] He says this following a reference to Boileau's discussion of the ode as *beau désordre*. Stierle offers two distinctions for what he has in mind: first, the disruption *(Aufhebung,* probably not in Hegel's sense) or the calling into question of the linearity of discourse; second, the superimposition of multiple contexts of discourse upon each other.

SKEPTIC: He also challenges the notion that there could be any literal sense, as distinct from figurative functions, in lyrical discourse. The status of both the object as referent and the subject as lyrical self is seen as problematic. Looking to the example of Rousseau and Romantic poetry, he cites the function of landscape as a symbolic image. The lyrical self is described, with reference to the tradition of Petrarch, as a construct of intersecting verbal contexts within a single moment, such that a specific, seemingly subjective mood is conveyed. The plurality of figurative discourse thus depends upon a principle of coherence projected upon the sensibility of a subject that is acknowledged, implicitly at least, to be the construct of that figurative complex. What this amounts to is a theory of reflectivity in the lyric as the direct outcome of a plurality of figurative discourse. This theory has important implications above all for the hermeneutics of reception through the act of reading. The principle of lyric transgression would thus indicate a specific formal device in the language of lyric, which imposes upon its reader a conscious awareness of that language as form and of the specific procedures through which it conveys a meaning or mood. Stierle thus challenges the concept of identity in the lyric by claiming an inherent hermeneutical reflectivity through figurative transgression.

STUDENT: I fail to understand what you mean here by reflectivity and how it might be related to lyrical figuration.

SKEPTIC: I understand your difficulty and hasten to place the blame on myself rather than Stierle. Perhaps I can indicate something of what I have in mind with reference to Hegel's concept of reflectivity in the *Science of Logic*.[13] Crucial for Hegel's project is the identification of the movement of thought with movements of language, specifically a movement of abstraction in language that constantly reflects upon itself and thus always knows what it is doing (or saying, or thinking) as it proceeds, and is capable of articulating this advancing knowledge in and through Hegel's text. The key to this process, as I see it, is Hegel's fundamental insight into the relationship between language and thought as tension or opposition, indeed as *negation* in Hegel's specific sense of the term.

The dialectical movement of thought through language is thus defined by negativity as the negation of the negative, whereby thought turns upon itself and becomes conscious of itself. This negativity of the dialectic is the basis, as I read Hegel, of thought's ability to reflect upon itself.

STUDENT : What does all this have to do with the identity of the literary text?

SKEPTIC: The figurative forms of discourse as transgression, which, as Stierle argues, constitute the poetic text, impose a cognitive task upon the reader, which is directly analogous to the negativity of dialectical thinking in Hegel. The transgressions of lyrical discourse thus impose the challenge and the capacity of reflectivity upon the mind of the reader. Such reflectivity is the basis of all hermeneutical consciousness.

STUDENT : I still fail to understand what you mean by negativity. But it does occur to me that transgression in Stierle's sense comes very close to what Heidegger referred to as the *Sprung* of discourse, either as a leap or as a fault. Perhaps Hegel stands silently behind both notions.

SKEPTIC: At any rate it should now be apparent that the forms of figuration in lyrical discourse are radically opposed to any model of visionary fusion or (to use Coleridge's term) the coalescence of subject and object, traditionally associated with Romantic theories of the imagination as the basis for identity.

CRITIC : If any of this abstruse speculation is to be valid for me, it will depend upon the outcome of specific interpretive readings. We need an example, a demonstration in practice.

STUDENT : You cannot fault Stierle on this point, since the latter part of his rich essay consists of a detailed and highly innovative reading of Hölderlin's ode "Heidelberg."

CRITIC : Of all the poems by Hölderlin, the ode to Heidelberg would seem the most accessible, as well as one of his most famous. More than any other work of literature this ode established the reputation of the city as an ideal Romantic place of fusion and perfect harmony between natural landscape and human dwelling place. As the poet says, invoking the city directly as

"Mother," he wishes to offer a gift of his "artless song" [kunstlos
Lied] to the most beautiful city of all he has seen in his homeland
because of its setting or natural location: "der Vaterlandsstädte/
Ländlichschönste, so viel' ich sah." How could Stierle's notion of
transgression in the lyric apply to this poetic tribute to a quintessential harmony?

STUDENT : Lyric transgression is located by Stierle precisely
in the tension or conflict between two fundamental generic modes
or discourses employed by Hölderlin in this poem: the idyllic mode
of celebration, addressed to the city in its essential, all-pervasive
harmony; and the dynamic, conflictual mode of personal experience or subjective memory. The lyrical self recalls a specific moment of visionary transfiguration which transfixed him once as he
crossed the bridge over the Neckar, as if by a magic power, from the
sight of the city in the full complexity of its spatial force field:
"[da] fesselt' ein Zauber einst/Auf der Brüke mich an, da ich vor-
über gieng." Stierle develops an extensive reading of the interaction
which occurs within the language of the poem between the city as
place and the poetic self as focus of experience. What seems to be
objective description proves to be the evocation of a diversity of
forces--including the river in its thrust outward onto the plain, the
ruined castle in its gravitational pull downwards into the valley, and
the rejuvenating power of nature, the sunlight, the breezes and the
fragrance of flowering shrubs along the hills. The sequence of
seemingly contrasting statements thus constitutes a symbolic reconstruction of dynamic totality. Should I summarize his argument
for you in greater detail?

CRITIC : Not at all. Let me offer instead an experiment in
critical reading, using a familiar text from English Romanticism,
which is not usually associated with theoretical questions in criticism. I refer to Coleridge's "Kubla Khan," a poem which enjoys a
reputation comparable to Hölderlin's *kunstlos Lied*. A fresh look at
this poem in the light of our discussion may prove instructive, even
for students of Coleridge. I first reproduce the entire text of "Kubla
Khan," preceded by Coleridge's prose preface to the poem.

"Kubla Khan: or a Vision in a Dream"

OF THE FRAGMENT OF KUBLA KHAN

The following fragment is here published at the request of a poet of great and deserved celebrity, and, as far as the Author's own opinions are concerned, rather as a psychological curiosity, than on the ground of any supposed *poetic* merits.

In the summer of the year 1797, the Author, then in ill health, had retired to a lonely farmhouse between Porlock and Linton, on the Exmoor confines of Somerset and Devonshire. In consequence of a slight indisposition, an anodyne had been prescribed, from the effects of which he fell asleep in his chair at the moment that he was reading the following sentence, or words of the same substance, in "Purchas's Pilgrimage:" "Here the Khan Kubla commanded a palace to be built, and a stately garden thereunto. And thus ten miles of fertile ground were inclosed with a wall." The author continued for about three hours in a profound sleep, at least of the external senses, during which time he has the most vivid confidence, that he could not have composed less than from two to three hundred lines; if that indeed can be called composition in which all the images rose up before him as *things,* with a parallel production of the correspondent expressions, without any sensation or consciousness of effort. On awaking he appeared to himself to have a distinct recollection of the whole, and taking his pen, ink, and paper, instantly and eagerly wrote down the lines that are here preserved. At this moment he was unfortunately called out by a person on business from Porlock, and detained by him above an hour, and on his return to his room, found to his no small surprise and mortification, that though he still retained some vague and dim recollection of the general purpose of the vision, yet, with the exception of some eight or ten scattered lines and images, all the rest had passed away like the images on the surface of a stream into which a stone has been cast, but, alas! without the after restoration of the latter:

> Then all the charm
> Is broken – all that phantom-world so fair
> Vanishes, and a thousand circlets spread,

And each mis-shape[s] the other. Stay awhile,
Poor youth! who scarcely dar'st lift up thine eyes –
The stream will soon renew its smoothness, soon
The visions will return! And lo, he stays,
And soon the fragments dim of lovely forms
Come trembling back, unite, and now once more
The pool becomes a mirror.

Yet from the still surviving recollections in his mind, the Author has frequently purposed to finish for himself what had been originally, as it were, given to him. Σαμερον αδιον ασω: but the to-morrow is yet to come.

As a contrast to this vision, I have annexed a fragment of a very different character, describing with equal fidelity the dream of pain and disease.

Kubla Khan

In Xanadu did Kubla Khan
A stately pleasure-dome decree:
Where Alph, the sacred river, ran
Through caverns measureless to man
    Down to a sunless sea.   5
So twice five miles of fertile ground
With walls and towers were girdled round:
And there were gardens bright with sinuous rills,
Where blossomed many an incense-bearing tree;
And here were forests ancient as the hills,   10
Enfolding sunny spots of greenery.

But oh! that deep romantic chasm which slanted
Down the green hill athwart a cedarn cover!
A savage place! as holy and enchanted
As e'er beneath a waning moon was haunted   15
By woman wailing for her demon-lover!
And from this chasm, with ceaseless turmoil seething,
As if this earth in fast thick pants were breathing,
A mighty fountain momently was forced:

Amid whose swift half-intermitted burst   20
Huge fragments vaulted like rebounding hail,
Or chaffy grain beneath the thresher's flail:
And 'mid these dancing rocks at once and ever
It flung up momently the sacred river.
Five miles meandering with a mazy motion   25
Through wood and dale the sacred river ran,
Then reached the caverns measureless to man,
And sank in tumult to a lifeless ocean:
And 'mid this tumult Kubla heard from far
Ancestral voices prophesying war!   30
    The shadow of the dome of pleasure
    Floated midway on the waves;
    Where was heard the mingled measure
    From the fountain and the caves.
It was a miracle of rare device,   35
A sunny pleasure-dome with caves of ice!

    A damsel with a dulcimer
    In a vision once I saw:
    It was an Abyssinian maid,
    And on her dulcimer she played,   40
    Singing of Mount Abora.
    Could I revive within me
    Her symphony and song,
    To such a deep delight 'twould win me,
That with music loud and long,   45
I would build that dome in air,
That sunny dome! those caves of ice!
And all who heard should see them there,
And all should cry, Beware! Beware!
His flashing eyes, his floating hair!   50
Weave a circle round him thrice,
And close your eyes with holy dread,
For he on honey-dew hath fed,
And drunk the milk of Paradise.

"Mingled Measure" in "Kubla Khan"

Σαμερον αδιον ασω: but the to-morrow is yet to come.

AS IN A DREAM : FIGURATIVELY SPEAKING

"Kubla Khan" occupies a special place among English Romantic poems. Few texts have received so much critical attention, and few of the major Romantic lyrics make so persuasive a claim for what might be called visionary or inspired discourse. Romantic poetics assigns a singular privilege to the powers of the imagination. This holds true for Coleridge above all. "Kubla Khan," however problematic its status as text, seems to demonstrate with consummate eloquence and authority that singular poetic quality. Yet precisely because of this claim as poetry and because so much is at stake for a theory of poetry to which this text bears witness, "Kubla Khan" remains a challenge for criticism. No more crucial instance comes to mind for the question of identity in poetry.

Most of the critical discussion concerning this poem addresses questions pertaining directly to Coleridge as its author. The reason for this is readily apparent. The visionary experience to which the poem bears witness derives its authenticity from the claim made by Coleridge in his prose preface that it was written in immediate response to a drug-induced slumber. This preface thus commands an interest, primarily biographical, almost equal to that of the poem itself. Little attention has been given, however, to the status of the poem "Kubla Khan" and its literary relation to the prose preface *as text.* The following remarks are intended to explore aspects of the work in this regard, quite apart from the poet's biography and the specific circumstances of the poem's origin.

Coleridge originally published the poem in 1816 within a slender quarto volume, alongside the much longer fragment "Christabel" and followed by a brief lyric, "The Pains of Sleep." This volume thus preceded by about a year the appearance of both *Biographia Literaria,* where Coleridge first proclaimed his theory of the poetic imagination, and *Sybilline Leaves,* the first comprehensive collection of his poems. None of the three poems from the 1816 volume, however, were included in either the literary biography or the collected poetry.[14] That slender volume had a considerable impact upon its first appearance, as reviews and critical comments clearly reveal. The singular reputation of "Kubla Khan" as a unique product of a drug-induced vision was thus established already during the author's lifetime and has never been seriously challenged.

In a survey of the history of critical reception for "Kubla Khan," Richard Hoffpauir reaches a peculiarly negative judgment on the poem, calling it a failure because it is "imagistically incoherent, its form is imprecise, the offered perception is vague, the emotional content is inappropriate given the subject matter, and the informing idea is foolish."[15] Such a categorical rejection of the poem, which results from little more than the personal predilections of this critic, stands virtually alone against the consensus of readers for more than one and a half centuries. Yet, ironically, Hoffpauir's essay offers a usefully succinct outline of three distinct stages in the history of reception for the poem. This survey provides persuasive documentation, whether intended or not, that critics of "Kubla Khan" have from the beginning been preoccupied with questions of the poet's biography and not with the task of interpreting the text itself.

During the first and earliest period of reception, while the poet was still living, the prose preface was accepted uncritically as an autobiographical document. "Kubla Khan" itself was regarded, in accord with Coleridge's assertion in the preface, as the aberrant product of a drug-induced slumber. The second stage, extending through the later nineteenth into the twentieth century, addressed the peculiar nature of the poet's dream vision as ground or cause for the singular poetic and musical qualities of language used in the poem. The beginnings of a critical response to the poem occurred here, though usually in very impressionistic and rhapsodic terms. The third stage, beginning in the late 1920s, has involved elaborate research into the presumed literary, cultural and historical background of the poem, based on evidence, from the then-unpublished *Notebooks,* of Coleridge's wide-ranging erudition. This research has developed into a sophisticated and high-powered industry of scholarship, whose end is nowhere in sight.

The initial stimulus for such research into sources can be located quite precisely in two important events. The first was the publication in 1927 of John Livingston Lowe's extraordinary study of sources for both "Kubla Khan" and "Rime of the Ancient Mariner" in his book *The Road to Xanadu*.[16] The second was the discovery in 1934 of a manuscript copy of the poem in Coleridge's own hand, including a slightly different brief draft for the prose preface, apparently written at a later date: the so-called Crewe manuscript, now located in the British Library. This document was discussed extensively with photographic facsimiles in several scholarly publications of the mid-1960s.[17]

Two further publications should be mentioned, each very different from the other, which provide the possibility of a further significant shift in critical attitude, enabling readers to consider the status of "Kubla Khan" as text, independent of the poet's biography, and offering the possibility of such a hermeneutical reading as I wish to propose here. The first is the book by Elisabeth Schneider, *Coleridge, Opium and "Kubla Khan,"*[18] which assembles exhaustive evidence concerning the effects of opium on the mind, in order to prove that the biographical circumstances for the origin of the poem as outlined by Coleridge in his prose preface cannot be accepted as literal truth. The second is an interpretive essay by Kenneth Burke,[19] which makes the persuasive claim that the poet's own verbal practice rather than arcane literary and historical sources (such as were assembled by Lowes in *The Road to Xanadu*) should provide the primary context for interpretation. Burke argues that, despite the original title for the prose preface to the poem, "Of the Fragment of Kubla Khan," we may legitimately regard the published text of the poem as complete and as a poetic whole. On this point I emphatically agree.

In its original publication, "Kubla Khan" was accompanied by a subtitle or indeed alternative title: "A Vision in a Dream." That dream was identified in the prose preface with a specific occasion "in the summer of the year 1797," when Coleridge claims that he "had retired to a lonely farm-house between Porlock and Linton, on the Exmoor confines of Somerset and Devonshire." Such specification is itself unusual (and has been frequently challenged by scholars as misleading or inaccurate); but Coleridge goes further to identify his dream as resulting from "an anodyne" – defined as "two grains of opium" in the Crewe manuscript – which he had taken "in consequence of a slight indisposition," resulting in "a profound sleep." At the moment when he fell asleep, so the preface continues, he had been reading the early-seventeenth-century travel book by Samuel Purchas, *Purchas his Pilgrimage,* where the palace and gardens of the great Kublai Khan are described. The very sentence in Purchas is quoted by Coleridge. During his sleep, so he goes on to assert, he composed some two or three hundred lines in a kind of trance or reverie, where "all the images rose up…as *things,* with a parallel production of the correspondent expressions, without any sensation or consciousness of effort." The text of the poem is said to be the immediate result, when, upon waking and remembering his vision, he proceeded to write down directly the words that had formed themselves in his mind. The poem thus came into existence – so the preface would lead us to believe – through a kind of transcendental dictation. The act of writing it all down, however, was interrupted by the arrival of "a person on business from Porlock" – one of the anonymous and unwitting villains of literary history – whose visit caused the memory of the dream vision and its language to fade and flee irretrievably from the poet's mind. It is a story familiar to all readers of Coleridge.

Few stories from the entire history of poetic composition can claim such immediacy and authenticity as the legend of "Kubla Khan." The poet's anodyne serves as a pharmacological substitute for divine inspiration or even original genius, as indeed Coleridge may have intended, whether or not it was only a ruse. The effect of such a claim for the bio-psychological origin of the poem, however, is to ground the vision of the poem in an extra-linguistic source, which nonetheless controls verbal production with an authority more exalted than any conventional model of semiosis. The identity of the text for "Kubla Khan" is thus displaced by the claims of the prose preface to a psychological and biochemical cause, which is literally beyond the limits of understanding. Such a fiction of origin also defeats any attempt to clarify the intertextual process of composition by tracing various obscure allusions and citations derived from Coleridge's reading. Even a study so erudite and wide-ranging as *The Road to Xanadu* cannot truly claim to resolve the essential mystery of such a drug-induced visionary creation. Once the authority of the prose preface as a reliable autobiographical document is challenged, however, the question of identity for the poem itself may be reconsidered, as it were by default.

Many of the exotic allusions which employ actual geographical place names in "Kubla Khan" may be argued, for instance, to assume a symbolic function within the poem. Kenneth Burke – to cite only one of the critics who has attempted this – pursues such an argument by establishing phonetic associations evoked by these names. Alph, the sacred river, is thus associated with the letter *alpha,* signifying a principle of origin. The Abyssinian maid, who (in the final section of the poem) is said to play upon her dulcimer, is associated with the term *abyss,* thus signifying a space which threatens to disrupt all security of ground. Mount Abora, which is said to be the subject of the maiden's song, through a slight phonetic transfer that Burke considers almost automatic, becomes the Latin term *amor.* Behind such phonetic associations, so he argues, may be perceived a myth or archetype of creation, perhaps intended as an analogue to the Biblical myth of creation and the fall of man. Many critics would perhaps agree that the poem delineates such a mythical action, whether or not these place names serve as its signal.

Burke, however, refers such action back upon the poem itself, as an analogue or an instance of such an act of creation. Such an implicit reference by the poem to itself may be regarded as a form of mythical self-reflection. Burke even identifies this capacity for poetic auto-referentiality (not his term) through symbolic transference in the language of "Kubla Khan" with what he describes as "a highly personal, *poetic* analogue of Kantian transcendentalism, which sought *conceptually* to think about itself until it ended in a schematization of the forms necessarily implicit in its very act of thinking". (209) Burke's central hypothesis concerning the meaning of "Kubla Khan" is contained in his assertion that "the poem is tracing in terms of imagery the very *form* of thinking." I regard this as a remarkable and surprising insight.

Burke's interpretation of the poem is far more productive than any attempt to ground its technique of symbolic transformation in poetic motifs and images borrowed by Coleridge from esoteric sources. This is especially true if these sources are subjected to psychological – and specifically psychoanalytical – theories of the creative process, in particular those associated with Freud or Jung. Kathleen Raine, for instance, in an essay of 1964, makes an eloquent plea that this poem, as indeed all true poetry, should be regarded as the verbalization of that *collective unconscious,* which constitutes all authentic vision and is taken somehow to be universal and shared by all mankind.[20] Identity for such a Jungian reading would thus constitute a principle of mystical union, which is just as inexplicable as the claims made for the anodyne in the prose preface.

Even more outrageous are the distortions and abuses imposed by a Freudian psychoanalytical reading of the imagery. The most conspicuous instance of such a reading occurs in Norman Fruman's book *Coleridge, the Damaged Archangel.*[21] The landscape of "Kubla Khan" is interpreted by Fruman to dramatize symbolically a sexual encounter, where various details of place are taken to be "classic symbols for primary sexual terrain" (396): the pleasure-dome, which other critics had associated with a woman's breast (producing the "milk of paradise"), is taken by Fruman to symbolize the *mons veneris,* "that deep romantic chasm which slanted / Down the green hill athwart a cedarn cover" is taken to be descriptive of the female sexual organs, and the fountain with its "swift half-intermitted burst" is taken to be a "precise description of sexual ejaculation" (398). For Fruman the poem conveys a sense of dream-image, signifying a complex cluster of sexual desires, which are attributed to Coleridge's own subconscious mind. Freud is invoked to justify such claims for a psychological reading, which goes far beyond anything claimed in the prose preface.

These samplings will indicate the diversity and the extremity of responses to "Kubla Khan," where virtually anything seems possible. A further line of critical inquiry is offered by Elinor Shaffer, who argues in her book *"Kubla Khan" and The Fall of Jerusalem* that the poem is in fact a fragment from an uncompleted larger project to compose an "oriental epic" on the fall of Jerusalem.[22] Even if that may hold true, do we not as readers have an obligation to consider the poem as published by Coleridge on its own terms, especially if the biographical line of inquiry opened up by the prose preface proves to be misleading and the question of original intention remains obscure? The issue for interpretation is not primarily biographical or psychological and cannot be defined by extrinsic considerations, such as source hunting or the possibility that some other abandoned project motivated the composition of the poem. The identity of the text must be constituted through the act of reading, and the challenge of interpreting "Kubla Khan" is essentially a question of hermeneutics. My own remarks are motivated by this conviction.

Despite the claim of the original published text to be a fragment and despite the biographical circumstances of its composition, as described in the prose preface or reconstructed by scholarly research, "Kubla Khan" can and does stand on its own as a poetic statement, complete and self-sufficient. Nor can the organization of its language be denied the status of a coherent and unified design as a conscious, or even self-conscious, work of art, despite the author's fictional denial of such design and such consciousness to himself upon the occasion of writing the poem. It may even be argued, as Kenneth Burke has done, that the verbal form of the poem opens up at least the possibility of a transcendental response (in the Kantian sense of a self-reflective or self-referential turn of thought), whereby the act of reading the poem engenders in the mind of the reader a conscious awareness of its language, both in the complexity of its design and in the dynamics of its self-reference.

The outcome of an interpretive reading – this is my central point, which has not, so far as I am aware, hitherto been made in this way – is a complex transformation of what seems to be a literal and historical description into a figurative or symbolic discourse. In this regard "Kubla Khan" serves as a paradigm for poetic discourse in general. A critical reading of the poem involves an act of recognition, whereby the poem creates in the reader a hermeneutical consciousness of the poetic function of its discourse. The identity of the text – if that term has any validity for such a reading – must be found in the dynamic process through which this hermeneutical consciousness is achieved. It includes above all a tension between vision and reflectivity, established by discontinuities of discourse within the language of the text. These discontinuities, often regarded by critics as evidence that the poem is only a fragment and therefore incoherent, impose upon the poet's descriptive statement a sense of *transgression* (in Stierle's sense) or a *fault* (*Sprung*, in Heidegger's sense): a figurative crossing-over which opens up a reflective, self-referential dimension to the poem.

AS AN EVENT: "QUIETLY SHINING"

What is the principle of organization for "Kubla Khan"? Much attention has been devoted by critics to irregularities of form, which to some might strengthen the case for the poem as visionary reverie, a speaking which does not know what it is saying, totally lacking in formal design. The stanza divisions show no formal principle of length, thus suggesting convenient demarcations of statement, as if the stanzas were paragraphs in a narrative. Yet the final stanza does indicate a significant turn in the movement of the poem, which justifies consideration of the text as if it were a composition in two movements.

The first movement focuses almost exclusively on the pleasure-dome of Kubla Khan and the exotic setting in which it is located. Certain shifts of focus and variations of tone may nonetheless be perceived, which allow the text to be arranged on the analogy of a classical sonata-allegro form in music (which I introduce only for convenience of description and shall not attempt to justify further here), as follows:

Exposition: lines 1 to 11
Development: lines 12 to 24
Recapitulation: lines 25 to 30
Coda: lines 31 to 36

A basic distinction is made throughout this movement between art and nature. The pleasure-dome is a man-made construct, exotic and elaborate, whereas the setting in which it is located is defined as a landscape, through which the sacred river flows from its source in a fountain that bursts forth from a hidden cavern or chasm to its final destination in the "sunless sea" (5) or "lifeless ocean" (28). Little attention is actually paid to the pleasure-dome itself, apart from the initial assertion that it was built by the decree of the Khan. Descriptive material in the latter part of the exposition focuses entirely upon the landscape of the enclosed space within walls and towers, which consists of gardens and forests. A sense of symmetry and order is achieved here, where verbal form appears to imitate what it describes: art encloses nature. A quality of harmony and repose is attributed to the enclosure, which yet partakes of the life and power of nature: "fertile ground" (6) is "girdled round" (7). The pleasure-dome is mentioned again in the recapitulation. There the focus, however, is not the dome itself but its shadow, reflected upon the moving surface of the river as it flows past. A displacement of concern thus occurs away from the palace of the Khan, first to the landscape that contains it and then to the surface of the river that reflects it.

The delineation of landscape remains curiously indeterminate. The river's course occupies the center in highly schematic manner, as a force ("turmoil," 17) and a sound ("tumult," 28), projected upon both origin and destination, which constitute the limit of reference for this life. In the development an exotic and momentous significance is attributed to the act of bursting forth, through which the fountain emerges from "that deep romantic chasm" (12). It is called "a savage place" (14). Several figurative associations are superimposed upon the fountain, so that it assumes a complex significance as place and event. The place is given a supernatural aura:

"as holy and enchanted / As e'er beneath a waning moon was haunted / By woman wailing for her demon-lover!" (14-16). The force of the fountain is attributed to nature as an animate if not a sentient being: "as if this earth in fast thick pants were breathing" (18). Fragments of earth thrown up by the fountain are compared to natural and rustic activity: "like rebounded hail,/Or chaffy grain beneath the thresher's flail" (21–22). This sequence of similes opens up a pluralistic perspective, more general and fantastic than the place itself. The tone of evocation is also made personal and emphatic by an exclamation: "But oh" (12); by a demonstrative: "that deep romantic chasm" (12); and by an apostrophe: "a savage place!" (14). These various verbal devices evoke a sense of design and intention to the poet's statement.

The movement of syntax is convoluted and accumulative in its rhetorical effect, as indicated by the use of repeated exclamation points and colons. Within this complex sequence, however, a spatial perspective is also established upon a middle ground, as if we ourselves were located within the pleasure-dome. This occurs through terms of position: "amid" (20) and "'mid" (23), and interruption: "intermitted" (20), enhanced by a sense of dramatic immediacy in the repeated adverb "momently" (19 and 24), which offsets the sense of temporal and historical distance in the consistent use of narrative past tense. As the poem advances from development to recapitulation, a marked shift of rhythmic cadence and phonetic patterning occurs, which resembles a kind of eddying (a favorite image of Coleridge) and which signals the movement within the poem from event to reflection upon the event. To offer one instance among many: an alliterative pattern of repeated consonants across two rhythmically balanced phrases within a single line evokes a sense of measured flow, which is attributed to the river:

Five _m_iles _m_eandering with a _m_azy _m_otion. (25)

This line introduces the recapitulation, where phrases are repeated from the opening of the poem ("to a lifeless ocean," 28, is a variant of "to a sunless sea," 5). Recognition of this repeated material thus occurs within a rhythmic and phonetic cadence of resolution and ceremonial reduction to the complex dramatic movement of the poem. A heightening of focus and accent is also achieved in the recapitulation through syntactical ellipsis and delay, so that the main subject of this continuous statement ("the sacred river," 26) assumes a sense of climax, semantically and rhythmically. The pattern of rhyme across these lines also achieves a kind of balance and interaction that complements the effect of reflective eddying: *motion – ran – man – ocean*. The movement of the language at various formal levels thus forces the mind of the reader to turn back upon itself in company with the recapitulation of statement.

The figure of the emperor is also reintroduced at the end of the recapitulation. Initially he was invoked as the originating cause for the pleasure-dome; now through a subtle shift of reference he functions as an effect of, or a response to, his creation. At the beginning of the poem his role seemed to echo that of God as creator in Genesis, causing the palace to come into being by mere decree. Now we are told that the Khan hears the voices of his ancestors communicating a prophecy of war. What does this shift of roles signify? Presumably these voices are conveyed by the sound of the river, both in the tumult of its bursting forth and in its final sinking into the lifeless ocean. The emperor thus hears a sound "from far" (29), which is interpreted as the murmuring of spectral voices. Such a response also suggests a symbolic substitution, whereby the river is associated with the course of human life from birth to death. Recognition of this substitution further opens up a sense of analogy between the role of the emperor in his interpretive response and our own role as readers interpreting the poem.

The response of the Khan thus serves as a hermeneutical signal for the task of interpretation as such. The emperor was identified initially as creator, a kind of surrogate for the author of the poem (even if that association was not explicit), and he now has been transformed into a mere recipient, a kind of auditory exegete, responding to the sounds that reach him as the effect of his own creative act. By recognizing the analogy between this shift of roles and our own hermeneutical task as readers, we also may identify the fundamental structural design of the poem as a communicative

strategy, whereby the act of reading the text accompanies the movement of the poem through a sympathetic imitation: from descriptive inquiry towards interpretive response. This shift also suggests
how we as readers may relate to the poet as author, in a relation *not*
of identity but of reciprocity, which is appropriate to the dynamic,
dialectical form of communication itself.

On the basis of this perceived relationship as communicative
procedure, we may locate in the coda a further strategy of figuration and self-referential resonance. There is a twofold focus here.
First, the "shadow" (31) of the pleasure-dome is reflected upon the
surface of the river as it flows past. To "float midway" (32) is to
attain the privileged status of symbol, where temporality is transcended or, in Hegel's sense, sublated (*aufgehoben*). Second, the
sounds of tumult from the river in the origin and completion of its
course are transformed into a "mingled measure" (33) in the manner of a musical harmony. Senses of sight and sound are thus con-
joined: presumably for the emperor, as for the poet and for the
reader of his poem. To perceive and enjoy this experience requires a
shared dwelling within that pleasure-dome as symbolic space,
which conveys both the vision of reflected resonance and the mingled measure of harmonious sound.

The poem itself thus becomes identical with this space through a
symbolic transference and the self-reflective turn of figuration. The
meaning achieved at this moment within the poem involves for
the reader an act of self-recognition, because the hermeneutical
response of the reader is included within the symbolic reference of
the poem's statement. The couplet that concludes the coda constitutes the climax and fulfillment of the poem as a whole, insofar as
it conveys to us our own experience as readers within the hermeneutical consciousness attained by our reading of the poem:

> It was a miracle of rare device,
> A sunny pleasure-dome with caves of ice! (35–36)

The poem may now be understood as *event*, in the sense intended
by Heidegger's term *Er-eignis*, both as *en-own-ment* and as *en-eye-
ment*.

What can be made of these "caves of ice"? At one level the validity of the phrase is apparent. The indeterminate copula ("it was") includes both the pleasure-dome itself and its reflected image upon the surface of the river. The mingled measure from fountain and cave is superimposed upon this ambivalence of a "resonating preserve" (Heidegger's phrase). As a symbol of art it signifies a fixed and unchanging value within a dynamic movement and a mingling of sounds: *Dauer im Wechsel* (to cite the familiar tag from Goethe).[23] Yet equally we may refer this phrase to the poem itself as artifact or verbal construct, which like a "cave of ice" is inhuman and lifeless. The image thus sustains a sense of art as pure reflectivity, an ambivalent paradigm for vision as both *shine* and *sheen* (in the dual sense of the term *Schein*, as defined by both Schiller and Hegel).[24] Here also the sense of poetry as verbal event is affirmed in Heidegger's sense of a resonating preserve: *der in sich schwingende Bereich*, where the moment is realized and known. The opposition of sunlight and ice, established by balanced phrases as a reciprocity of identity and difference, conveys the deepest paradox of what Coleridge understood to be the poetic imagination.

Readers of Coleridge will recall another symbolic image, equally powerful and precisely correlative to this, where reflected light is revealed in a fixed and frozen form. This occurs at the end of the conversation poem "Frost at Midnight" in the image of the icicle, consisting of frozen water drops, dangling from the eaves of the poet's cottage, which is seen through the window in the darkness of the night: "quietly shining to the quiet Moon."

AS THROUGH A GLASS: DARKLY REFLECTING

A critical moment of figurative transgression in "Kubla Khan" occurs at the outset of the final verse paragraph of the poem. It is a moment of categorical reversal, of disruption, disillusionment and deconstruction, of *crossing-over* in the most radical sense. Reference shifts, on one hand, to the "damsel with a dulcimer" (37), conjured apparently out of the poet's own memory; and the poet introduces himself, on the other, as first-person pronominal subject for the first time in the poem. All apparent concern with the figure of the

Khan and his pleasure-dome is abruptly abandoned by arbitrary displacement.

This transgression from descriptive subject matter to the subjective self was anticipated by strategies of reflective figuration that preceded it. The movement of the poem may thus here be perceived as an advance beyond its moment of visionary climax through a disruptive response, which sustains and completes the symbolic action of the poem in the manner of a dialectical negation. The full import of this movement for the hermeneutical reception of the text needs to be further clarified.

What is the relation of the damsel to the pleasure-dome? How does the vision here claimed by the poetic self as something once seen relate to the development of the previous description into a poetic event? More specifically, within the temporal continuum of the poem as fictional historical narrative, how is the assertion of a particular moment of experience – "once" (38) – to be referred back to the remote setting of the opening movement? It is presumably no accident that an identical form of indeterminate generic statement with the verb *to be* occurs both at the end of the first movement and near the outset of the second: "It was . . ." (35 and 39), both times at the beginning of a line. Given the remoteness of Kubla Khan and his world to the poet and the position he occupies as speaker in time and space, the question of relationship between description and vision becomes extremely problematic. An awareness of this problem is central to the hermeneutical design of the final movement.

The subject of the damsel's song is Mount Abora, which remains unrelated, except through patterns of sound, to Xanadu and the river Alph. Yet, through a displacement of discourse into the subjunctive mood of a condition contrary to fact, a hypothetical analogy is established between the song of the Abyssinian maid and the poet's own poem. May we therefore associate the damsel's song with the simile used earlier of the "woman wailing for her demon-lover" (16), whose manner was associated with the "savage place" (14) of the river's birth? The common denominator is vision, and the medium of communication in each instance would be "symphony and song" (43), received once by the poet "in a vision" (38) and now to be revived "within me" (42) through a recreative act of the poetic imagination. The automatic and inevitable consequence of such a recreative act, we are told, would be a "music loud and long" (45). Even more, to achieve such music of vision would be to "build that dome in air, / That sunny dome! those caves of ice!" (46–47) What does this mean?

Such allusion to the earlier focus of the poem on the pleasure-dome involves a radical opposition to the project of its own discourse. Earlier the pleasure-dome and caves of ice were evoked as image and as paradigm, recalled and reconstructed within the descriptive language of the poem as fictional event. The final couplet of that movement established a reflective, hermeneutical perspective of self-reference, *as if* the assertion that "it was" had become "this is." Now all possibility of such realization is removed into a subjunctive alternative: *if only.* The poem thus seems to undo everything it earlier achieved. Equally important for a hermeneutical reading of the poem is the assertion that a reconstruction of the sunny dome and the caves of ice, the possibility of which is implicitly denied, would *not* be a reflection or shadow upon the surface of the sacred river or a mingled measure of murmuring spirit voices, but rather an aerial palace suspended impossibly in the sky like some cloud, signifying the distance and insubstantiality of poetic vision or imaginative *Schein.* How does this second dome relate to the first?

The two constructs appear initially to oppose each other, as description opposes vision, or as reality (event) opposes idea (image). Upon reflection, however, we perceive that the two are identical, both within the fictional or poetic world of the poem and within the mind of the recreative imagination, regardless of the recipient of that recreation: Kubla Khan, the Abyssinian maid (as she sings to her dulcimer), the poet (as he speaks in and through his poem), and ourselves (as we read this text). The only difference – and it is the crucial difference for hermeneutical consciousness – resides in the effect of that figurative transgression that occurred in the movement from one section of the poem to the other.

The shadow of the dome was initially affirmed as a figure of capable imagination, the product of a willing suspension of disbelief; reference to it latterly involves displacement through several levels of negation or deconstruction, so that it serves as a conscious, indeed a self-conscious, sign for the poem itself, not as it has been achieved, but as it might be in an ideal instance. The content of that sign, its transcendental referent, is thus the norm for poetic vision, performing in the manner of a transcendent signified for the discourse of the poem as a play of signifiers, against which the actual movement of that discourse may be measured as negative instance (in Hegel's sense of the negative).

How appropriate, finally, that the language of the poem shifts its focus at the end through a further ironic displacement to a hypothetical recipient for such visionary song. This recipient turns out to be, as the last playful surrogate for the identity of the text, the reader of "Kubla Khan," indeed *we ourselves,* at least within the poetic figure of a hermeneutical response. About that poet singing of his vision in a fine frenzy, whose voice until now has been tacitly accepted as the vehicle for the entire text of this poem, we ourselves are made to utter the concluding lines as a warning to dissociate ourselves from the madness of his vision:

> And all should cry, Beware! Beware!
> His flashing eyes, his floating hair!
> Weave a circle round him thrice,
> And close your eyes with holy dread,
> For he on honey-dew hath fed,
> And drunk the milk of Paradise.
> (49–54)

Everything that constituted the fiction of the pleasure-dome as event and even the damsel's song as vision has now collapsed into a hyperbole of affect. We share in it only vicariously through a distancing of perspective, a dissociation of sensibility, which we ourselves impose – or rather, which the final lines of the poem impose *for us*. The poet's state of mind as he produces his visionary song is relegated to a kind of madness, manifested by such symptoms as "his flashing eyes" and "his floating hair." The exclamation by this hypothetical audience of "all who heard" (48) even assumes the rhetorical form of a second-person address in the imperative mood. In effect, we are giving commands to each other, indeed to all readers.

The effect of such a statement, as further enhancement to the thematic reflectivity of our hermeneutical consciousness, is that the poem speaks directly to us in our own voice, so that our position and attitude are categorically differentiated from those of the poet. The discourse of the lyric, through a final transgression, thus dispels all sense of presence and breaks all sense of poetic illusion. Where does this leave us at the end but in the real world, beyond the limits of vision, outside the magic circle that we ourselves have drawn about the poet, to separate us from all possible exchange with that lunatic mind, which fed on "honey-dew" and drank "the milk of Paradise"? Our compensation must be that the language of the poem has also moved with us to this outside place, thus sharing in the breakdown of its vision, indeed causing that breakdown through an imperious usurpation of our own voice. The consequence for our hermeneutical understanding of the poem is indicated by the phrase that I have adapted from Heidegger (misrepresenting on purpose the implications of his term *Sprung*): *the fault of its vision*. The implications of all this for the concept of identity are disturbing.

It may now be instructive by way of conclusion to this essay on "Kubla Khan" to reconsider briefly the prose preface. Whether or not this preface reports accurately the biographical circumstances in which the poem was composed may be of less interest finally than the ironic thematic association of the situation there described with the hypothetical status of the poet as visionary within the poem. The opium dream in which the poem is said to have been composed may thus be identified with the frenzy of vision attributed to the poet at the end of the poem. Also important is the use of water imagery to describe the failure of the poet's vision when he endeavored to write it down after waking up. Following the interruption by his visitor from Porlock, he asserts, "all the rest [of that vision] had passed away like the images on the surface of a stream into which a stone has been cast, but, alas! without the after restoration of the latter." He then quotes a passage from his poem "The Picture: or, the Lover's Resolution," which was included in the initial publication just after "Kubla Khan," where a similar image of concentric circles upon the surface of water is used to signify the disruption of a vision, like the breaking of a spell:

> Then all the charm
> Is broken – all that phantom-world so fair
> Vanishes, and a thousand circlets spread,
> And each mis-shape[s] the other. Stay awhile,
> Poor youth! who scarcely dar'st lift up thine eyes –
> The stream will soon renew its smoothness, soon
> The visions will return! And lo, he stays,
> And soon the fragments dim of lovely forms
> Come trembling back, unite, and now once more
> The pool becomes a mirror.

The hope is there expressed that the smoothness of the surface will soon return, reestablishing the lost vision as in a mirror or a glass. May we not refer this image of the reflecting surface of the water to the central symbol of the entire poem: "The shadow of the dome of pleasure / Floated midway on the waves" (32–33)? Such continuity must be more than accidental and suggests, further, that the apparent fragmentary status of the written text may contrast with the vision it seeks to recapture in just the way the smooth surface of the water relates to the concentric rippling that results when the surface is disturbed.

A thematic analogy may also be perceived between the dissociation of the reader from the poet at the end of the poem and the interruption of the act of writing by the arrival of the visitor from Porlock. To refer both these moments of disruption to the act of reading may go beyond any apparent intention on Coleridge's part, although within the poem it seems unavoidable as an analogy *for the reader's role.* Such ironic transformations are precisely appropriate to the dialectical movement of thought. Understanding

is only achieved as the mind advances through moments of projected vision towards a position of reflective self-awareness by means of
a cognitive response to patterns of figurative transgression and the
breakdown of vision.

Not unrelated to this strategy of ironic dissociation is the initial
assertion in the preface that the author is only publishing his fragment "at the request of a poet of great and deserved celebrity" (who
scholars inform us was Lord Byron), and that, as far as the author is
concerned, the text serves "rather as a psychological curiosity, than
on the ground of any supposed *poetic* merits." May we not perceive
in this statement a bit of ironic tongue-in-cheek on the part of
Coleridge? Yet that request by a fellow-poet, perhaps in analogy to
the original decree of Kubla Khan for the construction of the pleasure dome, shifts the burden of *authority* away from the poet himself, who nonetheless remains the source of the vision represented
in the fragment. The argument for publication by the fellow-poet
thus derives also from what must be regarded as a response to *reading* the text, including presumably what I would term a hermeneutical consciousness of what the text is capable of communicating
about that vision that the poet claims to have lost.

These several levels of related paradoxical distinctions between
vision and reflection, both in the text of the poem and in the preface, serve to enhance and sustain that hermeneutical consciousness
in the reader, which I take to be the ultimate communicative purpose of this poetic text. The meaning of poetic vision thus remains
always beyond the limits of language, only accessible to our interpretive understanding – as Coleridge well knew! – from the distance of a disillusionment, like the circles upon the surface of the
water, or like the faults in a crystal, from a sense of absence or difference rather than presence, indeed as an image of a paradise
which has always just been lost at the very moment when it is
glimpsed. The measure of identity for a reader of poetry, as a reflective knowledge to be achieved, is the radical breakdown and
destruction of the principle of identity itself.

Afterthoughts

CRITIC : Will this do? I hope such a reading helps clarify some of the practical implications for literary criticism to be drawn from the theoretical issues that arose in our discussion of identity.

STUDENT : I am grateful for it. You have shown how our shared quandary about identity in a literary text could yield productive insights for the actual encounter with poems and the production of a hermeneutical consciousness through critical reading.

CRITIC : Are there any changes to be made in our earlier theoretical pronouncements?

STUDENT : Several concepts are now clearer to me. I begin to understand how Heidegger's notion of *Er-eignis* could apply to the hermeneutical reception of a text as an event in discourse. I also see how the notion borrowed from Stierle concerning the discourse of lyric as a transgression can apply to the communicative functions of figurative or metaphoric language in poetry.

CRITIC : Anything else?

STUDENT : There is one area of our discussion that did not enter at all into your reading of "Kubla Khan." I refer to the polemical point developed from Plato and Aristotle concerning the ethical value or pedagogical effect of literature, specifically with regard to the impact of poetry on the mind. Is this not implicitly an issue even for "Kubla Khan," especially if we agree that the text exhibits a communicative design intended to elicit a hermeneutical response?

CRITIC : I am puzzled. What you say about the omission of an ethical concern in my reading is true, especially recalling the apparent impasse of our challenge to traditional humanism in education. But I fail to find evidence in this text that would clarify what its function might be for education or for the general ethics of reading.

SKEPTIC : Let me once again perform my role as skeptic and offer a critique of your reading. The issue, as I see it, does not depend upon what this poem says about ethical values, but rather upon what it does *not* say. I will have to elaborate what I have in mind.

I do not believe this poem to be so politically naive as it seems. What are we to make, for instance, of Kubla Khan himself as a model for creation by decree? His historical reputation, which I assume was familiar to Coleridge, speaks for itself. He is the extreme instance of an Oriental despot or tyrant, a Mongol warrior emperor, who achieved his power and domination through vast destruction and military violence. What sort of pleasure-dome does such a monarch build? If it serves the poem as a model for paradise, should we ignore the fact that it must have been built upon human blood and sweat, violence and oppression? Nothing is said in the poem about this, unless a profound, even tragic irony is intended in the allusion to ancestral voices heard by the emperor prophesying war. What war might this have been, unless a direct outcome of the emperor's policies of violence and oppression? I think such considerations can and should affect our reading of the poem. The shadow of the pleasure-dome upon the water as a cave of ice may signify a more sinister political implication than your reading suggested. Could such dark allusions also be reconciled with your claim that the pleasure-dome serve as paradigm for art?

Consider also the historical context of the dates associated with the composition and publication of this poem. The prose preface ascribes the composition to the year 1797, and it was finally published in 1816. These dates neatly bracket the public career of Napoleon Bonaparte. Coleridge himself, as is well known, had strong political opinions concerning developments in Europe from the French Revolution to the Restoration after Napoleon's fall. Evidence could probably be assembled to support the claim that the poet regarded Napoleon as a military tyrant in the manner of a Kubla Khan. But we do not need to impose any explicit or even hypothetical political design upon the poem. My point would be that the historical context of the poem is itself sufficient to allow readers to make this connection between the two emperors. A latent ideological perspective on the political status of Romantic poetry is thus opened up on the poem, whether the author intended it or not.

If we take seriously such an analogy between internal and external historical and political contexts for despotism, what effect would there be upon our reading of "Kubla Khan"? An answer is provided only indirectly from the text, again from the evidence of what remains unspoken. The norm of visionary song evoked by this Oriental pleasure-dome is signalled by the damsel with her dulcimer. She can hardly serve as a spokesman for the political events of the Napoleonic era. But we also associated the damsel's song with the earlier simile of the woman wailing for her demon-lover. Does that simile suggest a valid model for poetic inspiration? I think not. The woman's wailing must signify either an unfulfilled sexual desire or a lament for some kind of exotic ravishment. We are either in the domain of psychopathology or the strange gothic world of the ghost-ballad.

The politics of an Oriental despotism are thus supplanted by a peculiarly inhuman model of ethical relationship, which can only have negative implications. Visionary song, however we interpret the damsel and the wailing woman, is clearly antisocial. The lyrical outburst of the damsel is also the direct cause of an emotional frenzy in the poet, when he attempts to recall the vision she conveyed. Our response as hypothetical audience to all this must be repulsion, as the final lines insist with regard to our attitude towards the poet. This yields a model of incompatibility, indeed a radical alienation, which must be regarded as the exact opposite of the Classical norm of aesthetic education. You recall our discussion of Plato's argument in *Republic* iii, where the beauty of art and music is asserted to be the mimetic outcome of a corresponding disposition in the soul, just as the proper effect of such beauty upon the mind of its recipient was argued to be a sympathetic or imitative transformation, in the manner of an aesthetic education. Nothing of all this is implied for the response to "Kubla Khan." Coleridge's text imposes a radical revision of the Classical norm regarding beauty and its effects. This constitutes a blatant challenge to the ethical values of art, just as extreme in its way as the political implications of a paradisical garden built by the decree of an Oriental despot.

To read "Kubla Khan" does not in any way improve or edify the mind, except by categorical negation and opposition. The act of reading effects an abrupt disruption even for a recollection of vision. Our function as readers, so you argued, is to break the spell of vision. My point would be that such a breaking – remember Heidegger's *Sprung*? – constitutes a catastrophe, in the original Greek sense of a reflective turning back upon itself by the mind. The consequence is a categorical destruction of all the effects of beauty. The value of art, by the example of this poem, must be understood in purely negative terms. To achieve this insight requires the substitution of an ethical criterion, however negative, for any aesthetic norm. Remember that we are left outside the magic circle of vision; we move through the poem as imagined figuration of paradise only to leave it behind. We recognize, finally, the figures of language in the poem to be the empty, lifeless, and inhuman structures, like caves of ice, for a pure reflectivity, which has no further ethical value *for us* (i.e., for the human community) than the fact that it knows itself to be thus isolated and bereft and obliges us to share that knowledge. Such knowledge is the very opposite of the traditional, humanistic edification claimed for art. It is also the basis of my fundamental skepticism concerning any claims for the identity of the literary text.

Let me conclude. The garden of vision, whether we associate it with Eden or Elysium, is beyond our access here in the fallen world. We are all subject, including the poet, to the violence and suffering of politics and time. The best that art may communicate to us is the semblance of beauty (the *Schein* of *Schönheit*), an illusion of vision, which we can and do and must see through as an elaborate fiction. The ethical, political and even ideological value of art resides precisely in the act of seeing through the fiction. We must be very careful in drawing any lessons from our experience of art, with which to make claims either for the conduct of our lives or for the education of our souls. Can we agree that such issues of ethical value need to be considered?

CRITIC : Considered by whom? I acknowledge the importance of these political and ethical issues for questions of value and ideological commitment, especially where they remain unspoken within the text. But I would also argue for suitable limits to the powers of criticism, insofar as the basis of judgment must always be the language of the text. What lies beyond or behind the text in silence may also lie beyond the certainty of our grasp. This is no longer a question of identity so much as propriety. Forgive my caution.

STUDENT : Let me plead for an appropriate balance between what is proper to criticism and what is important for political and ethical judgment. My concern as student of literature remains with the value of literary study for education. Despite your attack on traditional humanism, I still consider Plato to be our best guide for the educational effects of critical reading, above all through the example of his dialogues as a norm for such reading, indeed as an implicit norm for the development of a hermeneutical consciousness. Your comments on "Kubla Khan" may challenge the traditional assumptions concerning the value of literature for edifying the mind and guiding us to the truth and the light. There is no doubt in my mind, however, that the enlightened study of poetic texts, whatever the outcome for our understanding, will continue to be central to the procedures and the purposes of higher education.

SKEPTIC : Agreed. And in that spirit of conclusion let me quote the line from Theocritus's first Idyll, which Coleridge used in part (and slightly garbled) in the prose preface to "Kubla Khan" and which stands as motto to the essay here. The shepherd-poet addresses the Muses:

"I will sing you a sweeter song another day."[25]

ἐγὼ δ᾽ ὔμμιν καὶ ἐς ὕστερον ἅδιον ᾀσῶ.

Notes to Preface

1. Helmut Börsch-Supan, *Caspar David Friedrich,* translated from the 4th ed. by Sarah Twohig, with John William Gabriel (München, 1990), 118.

2. "The Chalk Cliffs of Rügen," in Richard Howard, *Findings* (New York, 1971), 14-17.

3. On the concept of form as *Gestalt,* see chapter 5, 201-5.

4. "Der Mönch am Meer," cat. no. 168, in Helmut Börsch-Supan and Karl Wilhelm Jähnig, *Caspar David Friedrich* (München, 1973), 302-4.

5. "Wanderer über dem Nebelmeer," cat. no. 250, ibid., 350.

6. On the hermeneutical implications of such "reciprocal recognition," see chapter 1, 45-9, where this concept from Hegel's *Phenomenology of Spirit* is discussed.

7. The emphasis here on a reversal of perspective or awareness, which includes a measure of self-reflection, anticipates arguments in what follows, especially in chapter 8, on the hermeneutics of reversal in narrative.

8. I here allude to the structure of self-consciousness as defined by Fichte in his *Wissenschaftslehre* and discussed at length in chapter 4.

9. On Emerson's famous image of the encounter with the Universal Being, when crossing the Cambridge common, where he became "a transparent eyeball," see *Nature,* in Emerson, *Essays and Lectures* (*Library of America,* New York, 1983), 10. Shortly after completing this preface it was pointed out to me that my colleague in American Studies, Bryan Wolf, in his book *Romantic Re-Vision. Culture and Consciousness in Nineteenth-Century American Painting and Literature* (Chicago, 1982), includes some brief interpretive remarks about C.D. Friedrich's "Chalk Cliffs of Rügen" (20–3). I was astonished and delighted to discover that Wolf also refers the image of landscape in Friedrich to Emerson's Nature: "like Emerson's nature, the infinitude of space, though latently threatening is present as an arena of rich visual possibility whose attainment depends solely upon the direct and unmediated encounter of foreground figures and background vista" (22).

10. For the discussion of Coleridge's "Limbo" in chapter 4, see 187-9 and 193-5 below.

11. The statement quoted here is cited at the very end of chapter 6, 287.

Notes to Foreword

1. For further discussion of this term from Gadamer, see chapter 1, 31-40.

2. "I. A. Richards (1893–1979): Grand Master of Interpretations," *University*

of Toronto Quarterly 49 (1980), 189–204.

3. Paul de Man, "The Rhetoric of Temporality," in *Interpretation: Theory and Practice*, ed. Charles S. Singleton (Baltimore, 1969), 173–209. I have also published an essay of appreciation concerning de Man's essays on Romanticism and Modernity, "Literary History beyond New Criticism," in *(Dis)continuities: Essays on Paul de Man*, ed. Luc Herman, Kris Humbeeck, and Geert Lernout (*Postmodern Studies*, vol. 2 [Amsterdam and Antwerp, 1989]), 133–48.

4. Paul Ricoeur, *La métaphore vive* (Paris, 1975); English translation by Robert Czerny, *The Rule of Metaphor* (Toronto, 1977).

5. Paul Ricoeur, *Temps et récit*, 3 vols. (Paris, 1983–85); English translation by Kathleen Blamey and David Pellauer, *Time and Narrative*, 3 vols. (Chicago, 1984–88).

6. Wolfgang Iser, *Der Akt des Lesens* (München, 1976); English trans., *The Act of Reading* (Baltimore, 1978).

7. Dieter Henrich, "Fichtes ürsprüngliche Einsicht," *Wissenschaft und Gegenwart*, Heft 34 (Frankfurt, 1967).

Notes to Chapter 1

The following essay originally appeared in *Arion: A Journal of Humanities and the Classics*, N. S. 3: 4 (1978), 385–419. Initially, the essay was intended as a review of the first English version of Gadamer's *Truth and Method* (published in 1976). As it turned out, the argument provided a programmatic introduction to my own views concerning hermeneutics and the place of interpretation in education. The essay has been substantially revised in style and formulation for the present volume.

1. In addition to the canon of criticism published by these and other writers, I have in mind as important background for this essay the influential textbooks, handbooks and histories of criticism: René Wellek and Austin Warren, *Theory of Literature* (New York, 1949); Cleanth Brooks and R. P. Warren, *Understanding Fiction* and *Understanding Poetry* (New York, 1943 and 1946); W. K. Wimsatt, Jr., and Cleanth Brooks, *Literary Criticism: A Short History* (New York, 1957).

2. I refer to work by Harold Bloom, Geoffrey Hartman, Paul de Man and J. Hillis Miller. These critics invited their readers to regard them as a kind of school by dedicating their books to each other and by frequent cross-reference. Also important as a stimulus for the theoretical views of all four was the work of Jacques Derrida.

3. I refer to Jonathan Culler, author of *Structuralist Poetics* (London and Ithaca, 1975), in his essay "Beyond Interpretation: The Prospects of Contemporary Criticism," *Comparative Literature* 28 (1976): 244–56.

4. Three works by Hans-Georg Gadamer were published in English within a single year: *Truth and Method,* ed. and trans. Garrett Barden and John Cumming [*sic*] (New York, 1975); *Philosophical Hermeneutics,* ed. and trans. David E. Linge (Berkeley, 1976); and *Hegel's Dialectic: Five Hermeneutical Studies,* trans. P. Christopher Smith (New Haven, 1976). We are fortunate now to have a much revised and improved translation of *Truth and Method* by Joel Weinsheimer and Donald G. Marshall (2d rev. ed., New York, 1991), hereafter cited as TM.

5. Gadamer, *Wahrheit und Methode: Grundzüge einer philosophischen Hermeneutik* (Tübingen, 1960). A fourth edition includes supplementary material, two essays of which, "Hermeneutics and historicism" and "To what extent does language preform thought?" are included with the English translation. (In his collected works, now in progress, Gadamer has added a volume of essays dealing with hermeneutics as a supplement to *Wahrheit und Methode.*) The 1960 edition of *Wahrheit und Methode* is hereafter cited as WM.

6. The personal background of Gadamer's philosophical concerns is outlined in the autobiographical study, *Philosophische Lehrjahre: Eine Rückschau* (Frankfurt am Main, 1977).

7. E. D. Hirsch, *Validity in Interpretation* (New Haven, 1967); Palmer, *Hermeneutics: Interpretation Theory in Schleiermacher, Dilthey, Heidegger and Gadamer* (Evanston, Ill., 1969).

8. I refer in particular to the opening section of Paul Ricoeur's *Freud and Philosophy* (entitled "On Interpretation"), translated by Denis Savage (New Haven, 1970), and to the essays in Ricoeur's *The Conflict of Interpretations: Essays in Hermeneutics,* edited by Don Ihde (Evanston, Ill., 1974).

9. Gadamer, "Hermeneutik als praktische Philosophie," *Vernunft im Zeitalter der Wissenschaft* (Frankfurt am Main, 1976), 78–109.

10. The most critical exchange in response to *Wahrheit und Methode* which has yet appeared is the volume of essays entitled *Hermeneutik und Ideologie-kritik* (Frankfurt am Main, 1971), with essays by Karl-Otto Apel, Jürgen Habermas, Claus von Bormann, Rüdiger Bubner, Hans Joachim Giegel and Gadamer himself.

11. WM, 157–61; TM, 146–50.

12. Schleiermacher, "Über den Begriff der Hermeneutik, mit Bezug auf F. A. Wolfs Andeutungen und Asts Lehrbuch" (1829), *Hermeneutik,* ed. H. Kimmerle (Heidelberg, 1959), 123–56.

13. The quotation from Ast, in my own translation, is taken from *Seminar: Philosophische Hermeneutik,* hrsg. von Hans-Georg Gadamer and Gottfried Boehm (Frankfurt am Main, 1976), 111–30, esp. 116.

14. Heidegger, *Being and Time,* trans. John Macquarrie and Edward Robinson (New York, 1962), 195.

15. A useful summary of his position on the hermeneutic circle is provided by Gadamer in a separate essay, "Vom Zirkel des Verstehens," *Kleine Schriften IV: Variationen* (Tübingen, 1977), 54–61, where the term *Vollkommenheit* figures prominently.

16. Developing the tradition of hermeneutics from Gadamer toward an independent theory of reading, Wolfgang Iser published an important study of this problem, *Der Akt des Lesens: Theorie ästhetischer Wirkung* (München, 1976); in English, *The Act of Reading* (Baltimore, 1978). A general outline of Iser's theoretical position is available in his essay "The Reading Process: A Phenomenological Approach," in *The Implied Reader: Patterns of Communication in Prose Fiction from Bunyan to Beckett* (Baltimore, 1974), 274–94. I discuss aspects of Iser's position in relation to hermeneutic theory in general in chapter 8.

17. Throughout his argument Hegel makes important use of a radical ambivalence inherent to the term *aufheben:* (1) to resolve or destroy; (2) to sustain or preserve. E. M. Wilkinson argues persuasively that Schiller was the first to apply this ambiguity to the dialectical structure of experience, in the 18th of his *Letters on Aesthetic Education.* See her notes in Schiller, *On the Aesthetic Education of Man,* ed. and trans. E. M. Wilkinson and L. M. Willoughby (Oxford, 1967), 304–5, hereafter cited as *AesthEd.*

It seems probable that Hegel was indebted to Schiller for this use of *aufheben,* as he was for so much else. In a note to his *Science of Logic,* however (*Wissenschaft der Logik,* ed. Georg Lasson, vol. 1 [Hamburg, 1934], 93ff.), Hegel refers the ambiguity of *aufheben* to a similar double sense in the Latin *tollere,* as in Cicero's pun: "tollendum esse Octavium." On the basis of this note, presumably, Hegel's term has traditionally been rendered in English as "sublate," from the past participle of the Latin verb.

18. "Der seiner selbst gewisse Geist: Die Moralität" is the title of the third section of Hegel's long chapter "Geist," which traces the historical-cultural evolution of the alienated self in Western society. The central concern of this section is the impact of Kant's moral philosophy, especially within the development of Idealism, which is perceived as a higher alternative to the politics of the French Revolution. The final stage in this development toward the Absolute Spirit is traced under the heading "Das Gewissen: Die schöne Seele, das Böse

und seine Verzeihung," Hegel, *Phänomenologie des Geistes,* ed. Johannes Hoffmeister (Hamburg, 1952), 445–72; see also the translation by A. V. Miller, *Phenomenology of Spirit* (Oxford, 1977), 383–409. Subsequent references will cite pages from both these editions, with the following abbreviations: *PhG* and *PhS*. It is primarily with the argument of this crucial and climactic section of the *Phenomenology* that I am concerned in this essay.

19. Scholars have generally acknowledged allusions in this section to Fichte and Jacobi, supported by Hegel's comments on these philosophers elsewhere in his work (see, for instance, the commentary on the *Phenomenology* by Jean Hyppolite, *Genesis and Structure: Hegel's* Phenomenology of Spirit, trans. Samuel Cherniak and John Heckman [Evanston, Ill., 1974], 491–528). Schiller's work was crucial, in my view, for Hegel's development in general, and especially for his critique of Romanticism (which is largely in sympathy with Schiller), as Hegel himself acknowledged in the introduction to his lectures on *Aesthetics* (*Ästhetik,* ed. Friedrich Bassenge [Frankfurt am Main, 1955], 1: 69ff.). My argument in this essay is based on the premise of this influence.

20. Schiller's theory of beauty as "Freiheit in der Erscheinung" was first elaborated in a series of letters to his friend Körner in January and February 1793, which were not published during his lifetime. These letters have come to be known as the "Kallias-letters" (from the title of Schiller's projected essay "Kallias, or on Beauty"; see *Schillers Briefe,* ed. Fritz Jonas, [Stuttgart, 1893], vol. 3, nos. 639, 640, 643 and 646). I discuss this theory of beauty with its several ambiguities at greater length in chapter 6.

21. *AesthEd,* 94–95. See also "The Temporality of Selfhood," 265-71.

22. *AesthEd,* 109.

23. *PhG,* 140–43; *PhS,* 110–13.

24. In order to make my paraphrase clearer, I have imposed on Hegel's language a grammatical distinction between first and third persons. The passage under discussion here, in the translation of A. V. Miller (*PhS,* 110), is as follows: "The notion of self-consciousness is only completed in these three moments: (a) the pure undifferentiated 'I' is its first immediate object. (b) But this immediacy is itself an absolute mediation, it *is* only as a supersession of the independent object, in other words, it is Desire. The satisfaction of Desire is, it is true, the reflection of self-consciousness into itself, or the certainty that has become truth. (c) But the truth of this certainty is really a double reflection, the duplication of self-consciousness. Consciousness has for its object one which, of its own self, posits its otherness or difference as a nothingness, and in so doing is independent. The differentiated, merely *living,* shape does indeed also supersede its independence in the process of Life, but it ceases with its distinctive

difference to be what it is. The object of self-consciousness, however, is equally independent in this negativity of itself; and thus it is *for itself* a genus, a universal fluid element in the peculiarity of its own separate being; it is a living self-consciousness."

25. Hegel explicitly acknowledges that language is the medium of Spirit in its self-certainty in the midst of his discussion of the beautiful soul (*PhG*, 458-60.; *PhS*, 395ff.); but a concern for the dialectical form of speech acts is implicit throughout the final pages of the chapter "Geist."

26. *PhG*, 460; *PhS*, 397.

27. Within the scope of the present essay, where a balance must be maintained among the several sections of the argument, it is impossible to do justice to the complexities of Hegel's theory concerning the ultimate transformation of the Spirit as ethical interaction into the domain of absolute knowledge. My brief comments here are developed at greater length in an essay relating these concepts from Hegel to the later poetry of Hölderlin, entitled "Dialectical Intersubjectivity: Hegel's *Phenomenology* and the Hermeneutics of Romanticism" (delivered as an address to the Academy of Literary Studies, Princeton, May 1976).

28. Goethe, "Bekenntnisse einer schönen Seele," Book 6, *Wilhelm Meisters Lehrjahre* (1795), and Schiller, "Über Anmuth und Würde" (1793). This concept was subsequently influential in the poetics of German Romanticism, as in the figure of Diotima in Hölderlin's novel *Hyperion, oder der Eremit in Griechenland* (1797–99). (Further discussion of this concept in relation to Romantic theories of Beauty is contained in my essay "'Schönheit als Erscheinung': Schiller and Hölderlin between Kant and Hegel," in *Hegel und die "Kritik der Urteilskraft,"* ed. Hans-Friedrich Fulda and Rolf-Peter Horstmann [Stuttgart, 1990], 13–44.)

29. Helpful and persuasive discussion of this question, specifically with regard to Hegel's critique of Romanticism in general, is provided by Emanuel Hirsch, "Die Beisetzung der Romantiker in Hegels Phänomenologie: Ein Kommentar zu dem Abschnitte über die Moralität," in *Materialien zu Hegels "Phänomenologie des Geistes,"* ed. Hans-Friedrich Fulda and Dieter Henrich (Frankfurt, 1973), and also by Otto Pöggeler, *Hegels Kritik der Romantik* (Bonn, 1956).

30. *PhG*, 471; *PhS*, 408.

31. Hoffmeister discusses the complex evolution of Hegel's book and its title in his introduction (*PhG*, iii–xlii).

32. Hölderlin's "Patmos" was composed, as Werner Kirchner first documented (in his introduction to the facsimile edition of the dedicatory fair copy

in the poet's hand, *Schriften der Friedrich Hölderlin Gesellschaft,* Band 1
[Tübingen, 1949]), during the final months of 1802 and was presented to the
Landgraf von Homburg on his birthday, 30 January 1803, by the poet's friend
Sinclair. All quotations from "Patmos" in the argument which follows are taken
from this version of the poem, as printed in the *Große Stuttgarter Ausgabe,* ed.
Friedrich Beißner (Stuttgart, 1952), vol. 2, pt. 1, 165–72. Quotations will be identified by line number; the accompanying prose translations are my own. I
acknowledge that a discussion of this extremely complex poem in so brief a
space, which is all the present context allows, will be inadequate to the poem
and an imposition on any reader unfamiliar with it. Since writing this essay, I
have prepared a detailed reading of "Patmos" with reference to hermeneutic
theory, to be published as an independent monograph.

Notes to Chapter 2

The following essay was written originally as a public lecture for a colloquium
on Theories of Literary History at the University of Toronto in March 1979.
The following remarks introduced the lecture at that time: "This paper is an
exercise in critical reading, which endeavors to develop through the interplay
of several selected texts a theoretical perspective on the act of reading itself.
One question that the argument intends to address is the uncertain status of
tradition within the broader enquiry of literary history (with which this colloquium is concerned) and the extent to which the act of reading itself demonstrates, at least in specific instances, the manner in which interpretation is necessarily a reappropriation of tradition, whereby even the theoretical perspectives achieved through such endeavor remain cognitive of their own essential
historicity."

    1. Dante, *The Divine Comedy, Purgatory,* canto 2. In the Latin Vulgate Bible
the psalm is numbered 113. I follow the numbering of modern Bibles.

    2. Dante's letter to Can Grande, originally in Latin, is available in the
English translation by Paget Toynbee, *Letters of Dante* (2d ed., Oxford, 1967).
There is an extensive literature on the letter to Can Grande, with some arguments that Dante is not the author. Such questions do not pertain to my concern here.

    3. *Letters of Dante,* 199.

    4. "di quel salmo è poscia scripto" (*Purgatory* 2.48).

    5. For convenience I cite the English text of the psalm from the King James
Bible.

6. I have consulted a number of commentaries on this psalm, but given the informal nature of a public lecture, it seemed inappropriate to address specific scholarly opinion, especially since my own competence in this highly specialized field is very limited. I try to offer in my own comments the consensus of scholarship insofar as I am able to perceive it.

7. Cross references to related biblical passages are commonplace in most Bibles and reflect a long tradition of exegesis. My own references are dependent throughout on such traditions.

8. The question of origin for so complex a cultural tradition as the feast of Passover is beyond my own competence to address. So far as I can judge there is consensus among biblical historians and archaeologists about the seasonal ritual contained in the sacrifice of lambs in springtime.

9. It is apparent from the commentaries that the Hebrew text of the psalm is uncertain at this point. I am not competent to address the philological questions involved.

10. In all likelihood the psalm here alludes to the events described in Exod. 17:1–2, Num. 20:1ff., and Deut. 8:15ff.

11. Charles Singleton, "In Exitu Israel de Aegypto," *Annual Report of the Dante Society* (Boston, 1960), 1–24.

12. This term from 19th-century German biblical scholarship would normally apply primarily to the cultural origins of a biblical text. I here apply it more loosely to the tradition of worship in general.

13. A convenient description of the Hallel may be found in *The Anchor Bible Dictionary,* ed. D. N. Freedman (New York, 1992), 3:30.

14. I here follow standard commentaries on the account of the Passover in Egypt in relation to the subsequent traditions of celebrating and commemorating the event, as implied in the account in Exodus.

15. Commentaries on both Psalm 114 and on the description in Joshua of the entry into the Promised Land are in general agreement on this point.

16. I have no persuasive authority for this connection between the Last Supper and Psalm 114, though the traditional use of the psalm in the liturgy of Easter would indicate that the connection has some validity.

17. Apart from the fact that the psalm is still recited as part of the service on Easter Sunday and commentaries are universally agreed on its usage in liturgy, I have no reliable information on the origins of this practice. I assume that it extends back to the early church.

18. So far as I am aware, the *tonus peregrinus* has been used exclusively for Psalm 114 since the Middle Ages.

19. "più di cento spirti" (2.45); "cantavan tutti insieme ad una voce" (2.47).

20. I have consulted such commentaries on *The Divine Comedy* in English as those by Grandgent, Plumptre and Sinclair.

21. Singleton, "In Exitu Israel de Aegypto" (n. 11 above).

22. Erich Auerbach, *Dante als Dichter der irdischen Welt* (Berlin and Leipzig, 1929); in English, *Dante: Poet of the Secular World,* trans. Ralph Manheim (Chicago, 1961). Auerbach's famous study concerns itself primarily with the *Inferno.*

23. Wolfgang Iser, *The Act of Reading,* 225–31 (see chap. 1, n. 16); also see my discussion of Iser in chapter 8.

24. See p. 328 below.

25. See Hegel, *Wissenschaft der Logik,* part 2 (Zweites Buch: Das Wesen; Erster Abschnitt: Das Wesen der Reflexion in ihm selbst; Erstes Kapitel: Der Schein), ed. Georg Lasson, *Die philosophische Bibliothek,* 57 (repr. Hamburg, 1966), 7–23.

26. See p. 204 below.

27. Gadamer, "Horizontverschmelzung," *WM,* 286–90; *TM,* 302–7 (see chap. 1, nn. 4–5).

28. Paul de Man, "Literary History and Literary Modernity," *Blindness and Insight: Essays in the Rhetoric of Contemporary Criticism,* 2d rev. ed. (Minneapolis, 1983): 142–65, esp. 151.

29. I have kept the original spelling and orthography as printed in the critical edition by Herbert J. C. Grierson, *The Poems of John Donne,* vol. 1 (Oxford, 1912), 368–69.

30. See Rom. 5:12ff. and 1 Cor. 15:22.

31. I have published a more comprehensive reading of Hölderlin's "Andenken" since writing this essay: "Die Poetik des Gedächtnisses," *Hölderlin-Jahrbuch* (1984–85), 119–38.

32. Hölderlin, "Andenken," in *Große Stuttgarter Ausgabe,* Friedrich Beißner, ed., vol. 2, pt. 1, 188–89.

33. The exact date of composition is uncertain. Hölderlin's stay in Bordeaux did include the month of March 1802, and it seems reasonable, following the surmise of Friedrich Beißner, editor of the *Große Stuttgarter Ausgabe,* that the poem was composed a year later, very near the end of Hölderlin's productive career. The editor of the competing critical edition, Dietrich Sattler, has proposed a date as late as 1806, which seems quite preposterous to me. The poem was published by a friend of Hölderlin, Leo von Seckendorf, in his *Musenalmanach für das Jahr 1808.* No manuscript for the poem survives, apart from a variant of the concluding lines.

34. On the symbolism of the fig tree, see Anselm Haverkamp, "Verschwie-

gener Lorbeer," *Laub voll Trauer: Hölderlins späte Allegorie* (München, 1991), 71–92; in English, *Leaves of Mourning: Hölderlin's Late Work, with an Essay on Keats and Melancholy,* trans. Vernon Chadwick (Albany, 1996), 56-77.

35. *Hyperion, oder der Eremit in Griechenland,* 2 vols., 1797–99; trans. Willard Trask, rev. David Schwarz, in *"Hyperion" and Selected Poems,* ed. Eric Santner (New York, 1990). The entire novel consists of the correspondence of Hyperion to his friend in Germany. The name has been interpreted symbolically to signify the "beautiful German" (*Bell[e]-Arminius*). The novel is discussed in detail in chapter 4.

36. Hölderlin's theory of poetic composition is discussed more fully in chapters 6 and 8.

Notes to Chapter 3

First drafted for a special session on "Literary Hermeneutics: Historicity, Historiography and Theology," chaired by Jeffrey Peck, at the meeting of the Modern Language Association, San Francisco, December 1979. Expanded version read as a lecture in Comparative Literature, University of Iowa, February 1980, and the University of California Irvine, May 1980. Subsequently revised and expanded, the essay was published in *New Literary History* 13 (1981–82), 205–30.

1. Gadamer, "Was ist Praxis? Die Bedingungen gesellschaftlicher Vernunft," and "Hermeneutik als praktische Philosophie," in *Vernunft im Zeitalter der Wissenschaft* (Frankfurt am Main, 1976), 54–77, 78–109.

2. *WM,* 286–90; *TM,* 302–7 (see chap. 1, nn. 4–5).

3. See chapter 4.

4. Hegel, *Phänomenologie des Geistes,* ed. Hans-Friedrich Wessels and Heinrich Clairmont (Hamburg, 1988), 120–56, esp. 127ff. I discuss this concept and its significance for a hermeneutical theory of reading in chapter 1, 46-9.

5. See chapter 7.

6. Citations from *Tristram Shandy* are given by volume and chapter for convenience of reference. I have used the text in the Norton Critical Edition, ed. Howard Anderson (New York, 1977).

7. See *The Complete Works and Life of Laurence Sterne,* ed. Wilbur L. Cross, vol. 5, pt. 2 (New York and London, 1905), 99–117.

8. Of interest is the fact that Hegel later located conscience (*Gewissen*) in the *Phenomenology of Spirit* under the heading of *self-certainty* in the Spirit ("der seiner selbst gewisse Geist").

9. Laurence Sterne, *A Sentimental Journey through France and Italy,* ed. Wilbur L. Cross (New York, 1926), 156-60.

10. I cite the Latin text of Augustine's *Confessions* from the Loeb Classical Library, ed. W. H. D. Rouse, in 2 vols. (London and Cambridge, Mass., 1977). Citations in English are from the translation by John K. Ryan (New York, 1960).

11. Since this was written, a hermeneutical reading of the concept of time in Book xi of St. Augustine's *Confessions* has been published by Paul Ricoeur in *Temps et récit* (Paris, 1983), 1: 19–53; in English, *Time and Narrative,* trans. Kathleen McLaughlin and David Pellaur (Chicago and London, 1984), 1: 5–30. I have learned much from Ricoeur's work and am grateful to find my own reading of St. Augustine confirmed by his argument.

12. "statim quippe cum fine huiusce sententiae, quasi luce securitatis infusa cordi meo, omnes dubitationis tenebrae diffugerunt."

13. "tu autem, domine, inter verba eius retorquebas me ad me ipsum, auferens me a dorso meo, ubi me posueram, dum nollem me adtendere; et constituebas me ante faciem meam, ut viderem, quam turpis essem, quam distortus et sordidus, maculosus et ulcerosus."

14. "et adhuc ascendebamus, interius cogitando et loquendo et mirando opera tua, et venimus in mentes nostras."

15. "et loquatur ipse solus non per ea, sed per se ipsum, ut audiamus verbum eius, non per linguam carnis neque per vocem angeli nec per sonitum nubis nec per aenigma similitudinis, sed ipsum, quem in his amamus, ipsum sine his audiamus."

16. Dieter Henrich, *Fichtes ursprüngliche Einsicht, Wissenschaft und Gegenwart,* Heft 34 (Frankfurt, 1967).

17. Geoffrey Hartman, "Romanticism and 'Anti-Self-Consciousness,'" in *Romanticism and Consciousness: Essays in Criticism,* ed. Harold Bloom (New York, 1970), 46–56.

18. See chapter 4.

19. See chapters 6 and 7.

20. Geoffrey Hartman, "From the Sublime to the Hermeneutic," in *The Fate of Reading and Other Essays* (Chicago, 1975), 114–23.

21. See chapter 1.

22. Gadamer's work on Plato is now conveniently available in vol. 7 of his collected works, *Plato im Dialog* (Tübingen, 1991).

23. Iser, *The Act of Reading* (see chap. 1, n. 16). See also chapters 2 and 5.

24. See chapter 8.

Notes to Chapter 4

In its earliest version this essay, the first to be written of those contained in this volume, was presented at a meeting of the Canadian Comparative Literature Association in St. John's, Newfoundland, in June 1971. Subsequently in an expanded version – though several sections had to be omitted because of its length – it was published in *Genre* VI (1973), 142-77, in a special issue on autobiography edited by Christie MacDonald. The discussion of Wordsworth's *Prelude* benefited in many important ways from a graduate seminar on the poem taught by my mentor and friend at the University of Toronto, Kenneth MacLean. The discussion of Coleridge's late poetry was developed in response to the essay by I. A. Richards (cited in the text), which he sent to me while I was still a graduate student in Comparative Literature at Yale. The concept of self-consciousness as central to the poetics of European Romanticism first became clear to me from the treatise on Fichte's "original insight" by Dieter Henrich, which he presented to me when I first visited him in Heidelberg in 1968. For the present collection the essay has been greatly revised, the discussion of Hölderlin's *Hyperion* significantly expanded and the implicit hermeneutical concern of the original made more explicit.

1. Pope, "An Essay on Man," Epistle II, 1–2.

2. Quoted from Pierre Charron, preface to his *Treatise on Wisdom,* cited in the Twickenham Edition of Pope, ed. Maynard Mack, vol. 3, bk. 1 (New Haven, 1950), 54.

3. Quoted from Mark Pattison in the Twickenham Edition of Pope, vol. 3, bk. 1, 53.

4. A convenient survey of the Classical references on the Delphic inscription and related material is found in the commentary of John E. B. Mayor on Juvenal, *Thirteen Satires* (London, 1888), 2: 186–87.

5. I. A. Richards, "Coleridge's Other Poems" (originally published in 1960 with the title "Coleridge's Minor Poems"), in *Poetries: Their Media and Ends* (The Hague, 1974), 112–27.

6. Juvenal, 11: 27.

7. *The Complete Poetical Works of Samuel Taylor Coleridge,* ed. E. H. Coleridge (Oxford, 1912), 1: 487.

8. Wolfgang Schadewaldt, "Der Gott von Delphi und die Humanitätsidee," *Opuscula* 23 (Pfullingen, 1965), 17.

9. Juvenal, 11: 35–36.

10. Bloom, *Romanticism and Consciousness* (New York, 1970), 1.

11. Hartman, "Romanticism and 'Anti-Self-Consciousness,'" *Romanticism and Consciousness,* 49.

12. Dieter Henrich, *Fichtes ursprüngliche Einsicht* (see chap. 3, n. 16).

13. "...das Resultat des tätigen Setzens ist ein Wissen" (Ibid., 20–21).

14. Walter Silz, "Hölderlin and Wordsworth: Bicentenary Reflections," *Germanic Review* 45 (1970): 259–72.

15. Paul de Man, "Wordsworth und Hölderlin," *Schweizer Monatshefte* 45 (1965–66): 1141–55.

16. On *Hyperion,* see Lawrence Ryan, *Hölderlins "Hyperion": Exzentrische Bahn und Dichterberuf* (Stuttgart, 1965), and Friedbert Aspetsberger, *Welteinheit und epische Gestaltung: Studien zur Ichform von Hölderlins Roman "Hyperion"* (München, 1971); on *The Prelude,* see Herbert Lindenberger, *On Wordsworth's Prelude* (Princeton, 1963), and Geoffrey Hartman, *Wordsworth's Poetry, 1787–1814* (New Haven, 1964).

17. Persuasive evidence has been published that Coleridge was influenced by Fichte's *Wissenschaftslehre* around 1801 and that he, in turn, communicated Fichte's ideas to Wordsworth. See Daniel Stempel, "Revelation on Mount Snowdon: Wordsworth, Coleridge and the Fichtean Imagination," *Journal of Aesthetics and Art Criticism* 29 (1971): 371–84.

18. Henrich, 33. A useful survey of the concept of intellectual intuition is offered by John Neubauer, "Intellektuelle, intellektuale and ästhetische Anschauung: Zur Entstehung der romantischen Kunstauffassung," *Deutsche Vierteljahrsschrift für Literaturwissenschaft und Geistesgeschichte* 46 (1972): 294–319.

19. "Mein ganzes Wesen verstummt und lauscht, wenn die zarte Welle der Luft mir um die Brust spielt. Verloren in's weite Blau, blik' ich oft hinauf an den Aether und hinein in's heilige Meer, und mir ist, als öffnet' ein verwandter Geist mir die Arme, als löste der Schmerz der Einsamkeit sich auf in's Leben der Gottheit.

. . . Auf dieser Höhe steh' ich oft, mein Bellarmin! Aber ein Moment des Besinnens wirft mich herab. Ich denke nach und finde mich, wie ich zuvor war, allein, mit allen Schmerzen der Sterblichkeit, und meines Herzens Asyl, die ewigeine Welt, ist hin; die Natur verschließt die Arme, und ich stehe, wie ein Fremdling, vor ihr, und verstehe sie nicht."

Friedrich Hölderlin, *Hyperion,* vol. 1, p. 10, lines 6–10, and p. 11, lines 8–13 (orig. pagination with line nos., hereafter cited as *Hyp*); Hölderlin, *Sämtliche Werke* (*Große Stuttgarter Ausgabe,* hereafter cited as *GStA*), vol. 3, pp. 8–9. English translation by Willard R. Trask, *Hyperion and Selected Poems,* ed. Eric L. Santner (New York, 1990), pp. 3–4.

20. "Wie Jupiters Adler dem Gesange der Musen, lausch' ich dem wunder-

baren unendlichen Wohllaut in mir. Unangefochten an Sinn' und Seele, stark und fröhlich, mit lächelndem Ernste, spiel' ich im Geiste mit dem Schicksaal und den drei Schwestern, den heiligen Parzen. Voll göttlicher Jugend frohlokt mein ganzes Wesen über sich selbst, über Alles. Wie der Sternenhimmel, bin ich still und bewegt." (*Hyp*, 1: 85.2–7; *GStA*, 3: 48).

21. "Warum erzähl' ich dir und wiederhole mein Leiden und rege die ruhelose Jugend wieder auf in mir? Ists nicht genug, Einmal das Sterbliche durchwandert zu haben? warum bleib' ich im Frieden meines Geistes nicht stille?

Darum, mein Bellarmin! weil jeder Athemzug des Lebens unserm Herzen werth bleibt, weil alle Verwandlungen der reinen Natur auch mit zu ihrer Schöne gehören....Lieber Bellarmin! ich habe eine Weile geruht; wie ein Kind, hab' ich unter den stillen Hügeln von Salamis gelebt, vergessen des Schiksaals und des Strebens der Menschen. Seitdem ist manches anders in meinem Auge geworden, und ich habe nun so viel Frieden in mir, um ruhig zu bleiben, bei jedem Blik ins menschliche Leben....ich meine, du solltest sogar meinen Briefen es ansehn, wie meine Seele täglich stiller wird und stiller" (*Hyp*, 2: 20.6–21; *GStA*, 3: 102–3).

22. "So schrieb Notara; und du fragst, mein Bellarmin! wie jezt mir ist, indem ich diß erzähle?

Bester! ich bin ruhig, denn ich will nichts bessers haben, als die Götter. Muß nicht alles leiden? Und je treflicher es ist, je tiefer! Leidet nicht die heilige Natur? O meine Gottheit! daß du trauern könntest, wie du seelig bist, das konnt' ich lange nicht fassen. Aber die Wonne, die nicht leidet, ist Schlaf, und ohne Tod ist kein Leben" (*Hyp*, 2: 106.11–17; *GStA*, 3: 150).

23. See Lawrence O. Frye, "Seasonal and Psychic Time in the Structuring of Hölderlin's *Hyperion*," in *Friedrich Hölderlin: An Early Modern*, ed. Emery E. George (Ann Arbor, 1972), 148–79.

24. "Wie der Zwist der Liebenden, sind die Dissonanzen der Welt. Versöhnung ist mitten im Streit und alles Getrennte findet sich wieder.

Es scheiden und kehren im Herzen die Adern und einiges, ewiges, glühendes Leben ist alles" (*Hyp*, 2: 124.6–11; *GStA*, 3: 160).

25. We have no manuscript for the final text of the novel and must assume that Cotta's original edition preserved the punctuation of the author.

26. Passages cited in this paragraph are from *Hyp*, 2: 121.19–124.11; *GStA*, 3: 158ff.

27. The identification of Diotima with Hyperion's poetic Muse is discussed by both Ryan and Aspetsberger (in the works cited in n. 16 above and referred to in notes below as *Hyperion*).

28. "Diotima, rief ich, wo bist du, o wo bist du? Und mir war, als hört' ich

Diotimas Stimme, die Stimme, die mich einst erheitert in den Tagen der
Freude –
Bei den Meinen, rief sie, bin ich, bei den Deinen, die der irre Menschengeist
misskennt!"

29. Ryan, *Hyperion*, 229–36.

30. Ibid., 220 ff.

31. Aspetsberger, *Hyperion*, 93–103 and 132–39.

32. "Das Product dieser schöpferischen Reflexion ist die Sprache," *GStA*, 4, 1,
263, 23–24 (discussed by Aspetsberger, 137–38).

33. See, for instance, Aspetsberger, *Hyperion*, 137.

34. Ibid., 102 ff.

35. Ryan, *Hyperion*, 228–29.

36. "Hyperion! mich deucht, du bist zu höhern Dingen geboren. Verkenne
dich nicht!…Du mußt, wie der Lichtstral, herab, wie der allerfrischende Regen,
mußt du nieder in's Land der Sterblichkeit, du mußt erleuchten, wie Apoll,
erschüttern, beleben, wie Jupiter, sonst bist du deines Himmels nicht werth" (3:
87–88).

37. "Sie [the people] müssen heraus, sie müssen hervorgehn, wie die jungen
Berge aus der Meersfluth, wenn ihr unterirrdisches Feuer sie treibt….Es werde
von Grund aus anders! Aus der Wurzel der Menschheit sprosse die neue Welt!
Eine neue Gottheit walte über ihnen, eine neue Zukunft kläre vor ihnen sich
auf" (3: 88–89).

38. "Du frägst nach Menschen, Natur? Du klagst, wie ein Saitenspiel, worauf
des Zufalls Bruder, der Wind, nur spielt, weil der Künstler, der es ordnete,
gestorben ist? Sie werden kommen, deine Menschen, Natur! Ein verjüngtes
Volk wird dich auch wieder verjüngen, und du wirst werden, wie seine Braut
und der alte Bund der Geister wird sich erneuern mit dir.
Es wird nur Eine Schönheit seyn; und Menschheit und Natur wird sich
vereinen in Eine allumfassende Gottheit" (3: 90).

39. See p. 143-4.

40. Hölderlin, *Hyperion oder der Eremit in Griechenland*; in *Sämtliche Werke
und Briefe*, ed. Jochen Schmidt (*Bibliothek Deutscher Klassiker*, Frankfurt am
Main, 1994), 174 f.

41. *Hyperion and Selected Poems*, 133.

42. Wolfgang Binder, "Hölderlins Dichtung im Zeitalter des Idealismus,"
Hölderlin-Aufsätze (Frankfurt am Main, 1970), 9–26.

43. Wordsworth and Coleridge, Preface of 1800, *Lyrical Ballads*; see edition
by R. L. Brett and A. R. Jones (London, 1965), 266.

44. See Herbert Lindenberger, *On Wordsworth's Prelude* (Princeton, 1963),

and Geoffrey Hartman, *Wordsworth's Poetry, 1787–1814* (New Haven, 1964).

45. Passages from *The Prelude* are cited (except where noted as 1805) from the 1850 version (from the edition by E. de Selincourt, rev. by Helen Darbishire [Oxford, 1959]), with line numbers (and book if necessary) given in parentheses following the quotation.

46. Concerning the relation of this image to Wordsworth's concept of poetic visitation, see M. H. Abrams, "The Correspondent Breeze: A Romantic Metaphor," *Kenyon Review* 19 (1957): 113–30.

47. Hartman, "Romanticism and 'Anti-Self-Consciousness,'" 48–49.

48. Hartman, *Wordsworth's Poetry*, esp. section 4 of the chapter "Via Naturaliter Negativa," 45–48. The point about the autonomy of the imagination is made in various contexts by Hartman (consider such a statement as "his imagination is not only not naturalized but perhaps utterly transcendent," 251).

49. De Man, "Intentional Structure of the Romantic Image," *Romanticism and Consciousness,* 75–76.

50. Hartman, *Wordsworth's Poetry,* 45–48; also 238 and 271.

51. Abrams, *Natural Supernaturalism: Tradition and Revolution in Romantic Literature* (New York, 1971), 71, 94, 117.

52. Abrams, "Structure and Style in the Greater Romantic Lyric," in *From Sensibility to Romanticism: Essays Presented to F. A. Pottle,* ed. F. W. Hilles and H. Bloom (Oxford, 1965); also included in *Romanticism and Consciousness,* 201–29.

53. For the dates of composition of *Hyperion,* see Beißner's *Entstehungsgeschichte, GStA,* 3: 296–335, esp. 310–11.

54. "An die Parzen" (1798), *GStA,* 1, 1: 241.

55. Ryan, *Hyperion,* 228 (also 236).

56. Ryan, *Hölderlins Lehre vom Wechsel der Töne* (Stuttgart, 1960).

57. *GStA,* 4, 1: 241–65. For an exhaustive analysis of this essay, see Michael Konrad, *Hölderlins Philosophie im Grundriß* (Bonn, 1967).

58. See "Brod und Wein," st. 7; also "Der Rhein," st. 14 (*GStA,* 2, 1: 93–94 and 148).

59. See "Patmos," sts. 13 and 15 (last 7 lines); *GStA,* 2, 1: 170ff.

60. Richards, *Coleridge on Imagination,* 2d ed. (London, 1950), 141–63, esp. 145.

61. Ibid., esp. 148–56.

62. Abrams, "The Correspondent Breeze."

63. Richards, *Coleridge on Imagination,* 163.

64. See Hölderlin's notes to Sophocles' *Oedipus* and *Antigone, GStA* 5: 196, 265.

65. "... die Feier des Lebens mythisch feiern," "Über Religion," *GStA*, 4, 1: 281, 21–22.

66. *Complete Poetical Works*, 1: 429 ff.

67. Richards, "Coleridge's Minor Poems," 25, also thinks ahead (by a few years chronologically) to Shelley's *Prometheus Unbound*.

68. *Complete Poetical Works*, 1: 455–46.

69. A helpful discussion of the Brocken-spectre and the pertinent documents for Coleridge's experience of it is found in Stephen Prickett, *Coleridge and Wordsworth: The Poetry of Growth* (Cambridge, 1970), chap. 1: "An Image with a Glory round Its Head," 22–45.

70. Ibid., 37–43.

71. Richards, "Coleridge's Minor Poems," 23, and Prickett, 24.

72. *GStA*, 2, 1: 268, and 2, 2: 900.

Notes to Chapter 5

This essay was written by invitation for a special issue of *boundary 2: A Journal of Postmodern Literature* concerned with new approaches to literary texts (*boundary 2*, 7, no. 3 [1979]: 1–30). The reading of Coleridge's "Dejection: An Ode" was first presented as a lecture at Victoria College, University of Toronto. The supplementary discussion of the odes by Keats and Shelley was developed through teaching a course in English Romantic poetry at the University of Toronto.

1. The phrase "Gleichgültigkeit des Stoffes" is attributed to Goethe and Schiller by Elizabeth M. Wilkinson, in her important essay "'Form' and 'Content' in the Aesthetics of German Classicism," in *Stil- und Formprobleme in der Literatur*, ed. Paul Böckmann, (Heidelberg, 1959), 18–27, esp. 26. Hegel makes essentially the same claim for the content of Romantic art in the following statement: "derselbe Inhalt [wird] zur bloßen Zufälligkeit herabgesetzt, die keine selbständige Gültigkeit in Anspruch nehmen darf ..." *Ästhetik*, ed. Friedrich Bassenge (Frankfurt am Main, 1955), 1: 500. Subsequent references to this work will cite volume and page from this edition (hereafter *Äst*), as well as volume and page of the English translation by T. M. Knox: *Hegel's Aesthetics: Lectures on Fine Art* (Oxford, 1975), hereafter *Aes*. The text by Hegel that I address centrally in this essay is his general introduction to the Romantic form of art (*Äst* 1: 498–508; *Aes* 1: 517–28).

2. Hegel, *Phänomenologie des Geistes*, ed. Johannes Hoffmeister, 460; *Phenomenology of Spirit*, 397 (see chap. 1, n. 18). Subsequent references will be abbreviated *PhG* and *PhS*.

The implications of this passage for hermeneutic theory in general are considered in more detail in chapter 1, 45-9. My comments on form in what follows make no claim to address the philosophical implications of the concept as elaborated by Hegel in the extremely complex argument of his *Logic* (see *Wissenschaft der Logik*, ed. Georg Lasson, vol. 2 [Hamburg, 1939; repr. 1966], 66–76). My concern here is to apply concepts derived from Hegel to the interpretation of literary texts, even at the risk of abandoning the philosophical context in which those concepts are established.

3. "Dies in sich Unendliche und an und für sich Allgemeine, ist die absolute Negativität von allem Besonderen, die einfache Einheit mit sich, die...alle Beschränktheit des geistigen Daseins verzehrt und alle besonderen Götter zu der reinen unendlichen Identität mit such aufgelöst hat" (*Äst*, 1: 500; *Aes*, 1: 519).

4. "Das wirkliche Subjekt [ist] die Erscheinung Gottes...die neue Aufgabe der Kunst [kann] nur darin bestehen...die Zurücknahme des Inneren in sich, das geistige Bewußtsein Gottes im Subjekt zur Anschauung zu bringen" (*Äst*, 1: 501; *Aes*, 1: 520).

5." Denn wie Gott zunächst die endliche Wirklichkeit von sich ausscheidet, so erhält auch der endliche Mensch, der von sich ausserhalb des göttlichen Reiches anfängt, die Aufgabe, sich zu Gott zu erheben, das Endliche von sich loszulösen, die Nichtigkeit abzutun und durch dieses Ertöten seiner unmittelbaren Wirklichkeit das zu werden, was Gott in seiner Erscheinung als Mensch als die wahrhafte Wirklichkeit objektiv gemacht hat" (*Äst*, 1: 503; *Aes*, 1: 522).

6. "Dieser Inhalt jedoch führt zugleich die Bestimmung mit sich, daß er als bloß äußerlicher Stoff gleichgültig und niedrig ist und nur erst seinen eigentlichen Wert erhält, wenn das Gemüt sich in ihn hineingelegt hat und er nicht das Innerliche nur, sondern die *Innigkeit* aussprechen soll, die, statt sich mit dem Äußeren zu verschmelzen, nur in sich mit sich selber versöhnt erscheint. Das Innere in diesem Verhältnis, so auf die Spitze hinausgetrieben, ist die äußerlichkeitslose Äußerung, unsichtbar gleichsam nur sich selber vernehmend, ein Tönen als solches ohne Gegenständlichkeit und Gestalt, ein Schweben über den Wassern, ein Klingen über einer Welt, welche in ihren und an ihren heterogenen Erscheinungen nur einen Gegenschein dieses Insichseins der Seele aufnehmen und widerspiegeln kann" (*Äst*, 1: 508).

7. "Das Lyrische ist für die romantische Kunst gleichsam der elementare Grundzug, ein Ton, den auch Epopöe und Drama anschlagen und der selbst die Werke der bildenden Kunst als ein allgemeiner Duft des Gemüts umhaucht, da hier Geist und Gemüt durch jedes ihrer Gebilde zum Geist und Gemüt sprechen wollen" (*Äst*, 1: 508; *Aes*, 1: 528).

8. I allude here to the complex history in linguistic theory of the distinction between the sign and what it signifies (between *signifiant* and *signifié*, to use the terms established by de Saussure). For a helpful survey of this history see Jonathan Culler, *Structuralist Poetics* (Ithaca, 1975).

9. The influence of Romantic poetic theory on Hegel, primarily in the years preceding the writing of the *Phenomenology* (1807), remains a complex subject for research, despite such works as Otto Pöggeler, *Hegels Kritik der Romantik* (Bonn, 1956), and Ernst Behler, "Friedrich Schlegel und Hegel," *Hegel-Studien* 2 (1963): 203–50. Aspects of poetic theory from Schelling and Schlegel pertinent to my argument here are further discussed, respectively, in chapters 6 and 7.

10. See chapters 1 and 8.

11. Hegel does not, of course, apply his concept of *Er-Innerung* to the act of reading or even to the act of communication. In addition to the passage from the *Phenomenology* discussed in the next paragraph with regard to its implications for hermeneutics, see *PhG*, 39 and 564; *PhS*, 28 and 492.

12. *Wahrheit und Methode*, 160–61; *Truth and Method*, 167–69 (see chap. 1, nn. 4–5). Future references to this work will be abbreviated *WM* and *TM*.

13. Hegel's use of the phrase *für uns* as a central strategy of argument in the *Phenomenology*, crucial for its implied hermeneutics, is discussed by Kenley R. Dove, "Hegel's Phenomenological Method," *New Studies in Hegel's Philosophy*, ed. Warren E. Steinkraus (New York, 1971), 34–56.

14. "Aber wie das Mädchen, das die gepflückten Früchte darreicht, mehr ist, als die in ihre Bedingungen und Elemente, den Baum, Luft, Licht u.s.f. ausgebreitete Natur derselben, welche sie unmittelbar darbot, indem es auf eine höhere Weise dies alles in den Strahl des selbstbewußten Auges und der darreichenden Gebärde zusammenfaßt, so ist der Geist des Schicksals, der uns jene Kunstwerke darbietet, mehr als das sittliche Leben und Wirklichkeit jenes Volkes, denn er ist die *Er-Innerung* des in ihnen noch *veräußerten* Geistes, – er ist der Geist des tragischen Schicksals, das alle jene individuelle Götter und Attribute der Substanz in das Eine Pantheon versammelt, in den seiner als Geist selbstbewußten Geist" (*PhG*, 523–24).

Hegel here shares a basic elegiac stance toward the Classical art of antiquity, which survives only in fragments and ruins, with his friend Hölderlin, who celebrated the glories of ancient Greece in various poems as something lost *for us*. See, for example, the elegy "Brod und Wein" (lines 99–104, discussed below, p. 206-7). As Gadamer argues with reference to Hegel (see n. 13 above), this is the fundamental condition of all art, which must be recollected and remembered, reconstituted through the hermeneutical process of interpretation, *not* as a living presence, but as a meaning that is thus mediated and understood.

15. For an authoritative survey of the complex history in Western metaphysics regarding the concept of *form*, see the article by Johannes Hoffmeister in *Wörterbuch der philosophischen Begriffe*, 2d ed. (Hamburg, 1955), p. 235.

16. See Kant, "The Ground of the Distinction of all Objects in General into Phenomena and Noumena," *Critique of Pure Reason*, trans. Norman Kemp Smith (New York, 1965), 257–75.

17. I refer specifically to Socrates' *palinode* in the *Phaedrus*, where inspiration is discussed under the heading of recollection (248e–250d). (See also my discussion of the *Phaedrus* in chapter 7.)

18. Gadamer develops his concept with reference to Husserl's phenomenological theory as central to historical consciousness (*WM*, 232–33, 286ff.; *TM*, 245–46, 302ff.).

19. Anthony Burgess, *ABBA ABBA* (London, 1977), 81–82 (my emphasis).

20. J. Hillis Miller, "The Still Heart: Poetic Form in Wordsworth," *New Literary History* 2 (Winter 1971): 297–310. Also of interest is the sequel article to this piece, "The Stone and the Shell: The Problem of Poetic Form in Wordsworth's Dream of the Arab," in *Mouvements premiers: Études critiques offertes à Georges Poulet* (Paris, 1972), 125–47.

21. Miller indicates his developing interest in post-structuralist sign theory with a reference to Derrida's essay "La structure, le signe et le jeu dans le discours des sciences humaines," in *L'écriture et la différence* (Paris, 1967) ("Still Heart," 298 n.). The influence of Heidegger's views on language is most apparent in the use of etymological arguments in a more recent essay by Miller, "Ariadne's Thread: Repetition and the Narrative Line," *Critical Inquiry* 3 (Autumn 1976): 57–77.

22. Pertinent texts on the concept of *concretisation* by Ingarden and Vodička are conveniently collected in a volume of essays entitled *Rezeptionsästhetik: Theorie und Praxis*, ed. Rainer Warning (München, 1975).

23. Iser, *Der Akt des Lesens* (see chap 1, n. 16), esp. "Die passiven Synthesen des Lesevorgangs," 219–56.

24. St. Augustine, *Confessiones*, Book xi, chap. 28: "atque distenditur vita huius actionis meae in memoriam propter quod dixi et in expectationem propter quod dicturus sum." This passage and its hermeneutical implications are discussed at greater length in chapter 3.

25. Translated by Knox as "the pure appearance of the Idea to sense." *Äst*, 1: 117; *Aes*, 1: 111.

26. The most comprehensive and authoritative defense of the unitary tradition in Romantic thought is provided by the work of M. H. Abrams, notably in *The Mirror and the Lamp: Romantic Theory and the Critical Tradition* (New

York, 1953), and *Natural Supernaturalism: Tradition and Revolution in Romantic Literature* (New York, 1971). Opposing arguments addressing Abram's view of Romanticism are made by Paul de Man, "The Rhetoric of Temporality," in *Interpretation: Theory and Practice,* ed. Charles S. Singleton (Baltimore, 1969), 173–209, and by J. Hillis Miller, "Tradition and Difference," *Diacritics* 2 (Winter 1972): 6–13. Of particular interest with regard to the ambiguity of *Schein* in art as either *videtur* or *lucet* is the exchange of letters between Emil Staiger and Martin Heidegger with regard to the final line of Eduard Mörike's poem "Auf eine Lampe": "Was aber schön ist, selig *scheint* es in ihm selbst" ("Ein Briefwechsel mit Martin Heidegger," in Staiger, *Die Kunst der Interpretation,* 2d ed. [Zürich, 1957], 34–49; my emphasis).

27. It is not possible to attempt an adequate discussion here of Hegel's concept of negativity, nor would I feel competent to deal with its metaphysical implications. Helpful guidelines for the discussion of Hegel within the parameters of critical theory are provided by essays contained in *Positionen der Negativität,* ed. Harald Weinrich, *Poetik und Hermeneutik,* 6 (München, 1975), esp. essays by Wolfgang Hübener, "Hegels Idee der Negativität und die metaphysische Tradition," 476–81, and by Dieter Henrich, "Substantivierte und doppelte Negation," 481–85. For Hegel's application of the concept to his theory of Romantic art, discussed in this essay, see *Äst,* 1: 504; *Aes,* 1: 523–24.

28. Further discussion of the hermeneutical implications of Hegel's concept of negativity is contained in chapter 2.

29. The concepts of irony and metaphor in poetic and narrative discourse are developed further in my essays, respectively, in chapters 6 and 7. The point of departure for my argument in these essays is the position of Paul de Man with regard to allegory and irony in "The Rhetoric of Temporality."

30. On Hegel's concept of *Aufhebung,* see his note in the *Wissenschaft der Logik,* 1, 93ff. This term is also discussed on p. 396, n. 17.

31. *WM,* 329–44; *TM,* 346–62.

32. Kurt Schlüter, *Die englische Ode* (Bonn, 1964), discussed by Hartman in "Poem and Ideology: A Study of Keats's 'To Autumn,'" in *The Fate of Reading and Other Essays* (Chicago, 1975), 124–46, esp. 126–27 and 138–39.

33. Hartman, "From the Sublime to the Hermeneutic," in *The Fate of Reading,* 114–23. Hartman uses Hegel as his central focus for a general argument concerning a shift in attitude toward poetry during the Romantic period, which is sympathetic to my argument here.

34. See also Hartman, "Toward Literary History," in *Beyond Formalism: Literary Essays 1958–1970* (New Haven, 1970), 356–86, and "History Writing as Answerable Style," in *The Fate of Reading,* 101–13.

35. An important connection between German Romantic theory and the tradition of the *querelle* is made by Hans Robert Jauss in his essay "Schlegels und Schillers Replik auf die 'Querelle des Anciens et Modernes,'" in *Literaturgeschichte als Provokation* (Frankfurt am Main, 1970), 67–106.

36. "Brod und Wein," 109–14; my translation.

37. "Patmos," *GStA*, 2, 2: 191–96 (see chap. 1, n. 32); my translation.

38. "Stutgard," 105ff.; my translation.

39. In the argument that follows I use the final text of "Dejection," as printed in *Complete Poetical Works*, 1: 362–68 (see chap. 4, n. 7), with variant readings from the earlier versions (excluding the original verse letter to Sara Hutchinson) in the apparatus. Passages quoted from the ode will be identified in parentheses by stanzas (in Roman numerals) and line numbers.

40. This point deserves emphasis since critics of Wordsworth do not seem generally aware either that the poem was first published with such a simple generic title or that the Latin motto was borrowed from this Virgilian source.

41. Wordsworth's thematic grouping of his poems is maintained, for instance, in the critical edition by Ernest de Selincourt and Helen Darbishire, *Poetical Works*, 2d ed., 5 vols. (Oxford, 1952–1972), where the ode is still located separately and in isolation at the end of vol. 4, 279–85.

42. Shelley's "Hymn to Intellectual Beauty" (generally argued to be influenced by Wordsworth's ode) and "Mont Blanc" were composed in 1816. "Ode to the West Wind" was composed in the autumn of 1819 and published with *Prometheus Unbound* in 1820. Keats's odes (with the exception of "To Autumn") were composed in the spring of 1819 and published in *Lamia, Isabella, etc.* in 1820.

43. The text of the verse letter published by de Selincourt in 1937 is reprinted in his collected essays, *Wordsworthian and Other Studies* (Oxford, 1947), 57–76. House includes the text as an appendix to his published lectures, *Coleridge* (London, 1953), 157–65. In his discussion of the ode (133–41) he expresses – presumably as the first to do so in print – a decided preference for the verse letter. An authoritative critical edition of the text is provided, with a facsimile of the opening page of the manuscript, in an appendix to George Whalley, *Coleridge and Sara Hutchinson and the Asra Poems* (Toronto, 1955), 155–64.

44. The most conspicuous celebration of the verse letter at the expense of the ode occurs in an essay by David Pirie, "A Letter to [Asra]," in *Bicentenary Wordsworth Studies,* ed. Jonathan Wordsworth (Ithaca, 1970), 294–339. Symptomatic of such judgment is the selection of *Coleridge's Verse* edited by Pirie with William Empson (London, 1972), in which *Dejection* is omitted in favor of the verse letter!

45. Richards, "Coleridge's Other Poems" (see chap. 4, n. 5).

46. Of interest are the transformations of addressee which occurred in the evolution of the ode. In the original verse letter Sara herself is addressed by name. In early draft versions of the ode, during the initial period of preparing the poem for publication in the summer of 1802, Coleridge shifts his addressee to Wordsworth, making the ode a communication to his fellow poet. This shift may be documented from several letters, namely those to W. Sotheby on 19 July, to Southey on 29 July, to Allsop on 30 September, and to Josiah Wedgewood on 20 October, each quoting lines from the poem. In the first published version in the *Morning Post* a neutral substitute for his friend is introduced under the pseudonym Edmund. Only in the final text, included in *Sibylline Leaves*, does the more general title of *Lady* reintroduce a female recipient for the ode, though without any hint of personal reference.

47. I discuss Hölderlin's theory of tonal variation in the context of Romantic poetics in chapters 4, 6 and 8.

48. Thomas Percy, *Reliques of Ancient English Poetry* (London, 1765), 1: 62–64.

49. No satisfactory explanation is known to me for Coleridge's substitution (in line 120) of Otway as attributed author of the "tender lay." The verse letter reads "thou thyself" (meaning Sara Hutchinson) and the text of the *Morning Post* reads "Edmund's self," presumably replacing an allusion to Wordsworth in the draft versions of the ode, supporting the notion that Coleridge here intends an allusion to the poem "Lucy Gray" from *Lyrical Ballads*. My assumption is that the popularity of *The Orphan* on the eighteenth-century London stage, *not* necessarily the content of the play, justifies associating Otway with the tradition of authentic, "natural" discourse, to which the popular ballad of Sir Patrick Spence belongs and to which the *Lyrical Ballads* aspired.

50. The general assumption, which I do not wish to pursue further here, is that the passage in stanza vi (i.e., 76–86; 231–42 in the verse letter), which contrasts the poet's childhood state of mind, characterized by his natural powers of Fancy and his "shaping spirit of Imagination," with his present condition of diminished spirit and dejection, responds intentionally to a similar pattern of contrast through recollection in the first four stanzas of the "Immortality-ode," which Coleridge had presumably seen in manuscript just before writing the verse letter.

51. I allude specifically to Gadamer's theory of experience (*WM*, 329–44; *TM*, 346–62) and to Ricoeur's concept of reflectivity in "On Interpretation," the opening section of *Freud and Philosophy*, trans. Denis Savage (New Haven,

1970), and in several essays collected in Ricoeur, *The Conflict of Interpretations: Essays in Hermeneutics,* ed. Don Ihde (Evanston, Ill., 1974).

52. The passage in the verse letter is as follows:

It was as calm as this, that happy night
When Mary, thou, & I together were,
The low decaying Fire our only Light,
And listen'd to the Stillness of the Air!
O that affectionate & blameless Maid,
Dear Mary! on her Lap my head she lay'd –
Her hand was on my Brow,
Even as my own is now;
And on my Cheek I felt thy eye-lash play.
(99–107)

53. Richards, "Coleridge's Other Poems," 118.

54. Reeve Parker, *Coleridge's Meditative Art* (Ithaca, 1975), 185ff. Further references will be abbreviated as *CMA*.

55. The implications of this image in English Romantic poetry are outlined with authority by M. H. Abrams in his essay "The Correspondent Breeze: A Romantic Metaphor" (see chap. 4, n. 46): 113–30.

56. *Paradise Lost,* II, 990ff.; VIII, 174ff.; see *CMA*, 197–98.

57. Milton, "On the Morning of Christ's Nativity," lines 1–3; *CMA*, 205–6.

58. See *CMA*, 202.

59. *Collected Letters of Samuel Taylor Coleridge,* ed. E. L. Griggs, vol. 2: 1801–1806 (Oxford, 1956), 377.

60. A useful survey of critical opinions concerning the end of "Dejection" with regard to the poet's state of mind (e.g., is he still dejected? or is he now joyous? etc.) is provided by Thomas M. Raysor and Max F. Schulz in their bibliography of the poet, *The English Romantic Poets: A Review of Research and Criticism,* ed. Frank Jordan, 3d rev. ed. (New York, 1972), 202.

61. *Äst,* 1: 508; *Aes,* 1: 528.

62. "In der romantischen Kunst ist der Tod nur ein Ersterben der natürlichen Seele und endlichen Subjektivität, ein Ersterben, das sich nur gegen das in sich selbst Negative negativ verhält, das Nichtige aufhebt und dadurch die Befreiung des Geistes von seiner Endlichkeit und Entzweiung sowie die geistige Versöhnung des Subjekts mit dem Absoluten vermittelt" (*Äst,* 1: 504).

63. "In der romantischen Weltanschauung aber hat der Tod die Bedeutung der Negativität, d.h. der Negation des Negativen, und schlägt deshalb ebensosehr zum Affirmativen, als Auferstehung des Geistes aus seiner blossen

Natürlichkeit und unangemessenen Endlichkeit, um. Der Schmerz und der Tod der sich ersterbenden Subjektivität verkehrt sich zur Rückkehr zu sich, zur Befriedigung, Seligkeit und zu jenem versöhnten affirmativen Dasein, das der Geist nur durch die Ertötung seiner negativen Existenz, in welcher er von seiner eigentlichen Wahrheit und Lebendigkeit abgesperrt ist, zu erringen vermag. Diese Grundbestimmung betrifft deshalb nicht nur das Faktum des von der Naturseite her an den Menschen herantretenden Todes, sondern ist ein Prozess, welchen der Geist auch unabhängig von dieser äusserlichen Negation, um wahrhaft zu leben, in sich selber durchführen muß" (*Äst*, 1: 504).

64. The discussion of Keats and Shelley which follows was originally written as part of the essay on the Romantic ode, prepared for publication in *boundary 2* in 1978. Due to limitations of space it was omitted from that publication. For the present collection I have added the text in considerably revised form. No attempt has been made, however, to include references to the vast critical literature on such poems as "Ode to a Nightingale" and "Ode to the West Wind." Mention should be made, however, of the single most important book to have appeared on the subject of the Romantic ode, Paul H. Fry, *The Poet's Calling in the English Ode* (New Haven, 1980). I only became familiar with this book after my essay was published (and after the section on Keats and Shelley had been written in draft form), as I also first met Paul Fry after I returned to Yale in 1983. I have learned much from this important book on all aspects of the English ode, but I do not find any significant concern in Fry's work for what I have called in this essay "the hermeneutics of form." The focus of Fry's argument, as indicated by the title, is exclusively on the ode as poetic event with reference to the role of the poet and the kind of experience represented in the poems for the poet as author and origin of the poem. My concern focuses on the reader of the ode and the question of what kind of experience is conveyed to us through a reading of the poem. This is a crucial distinction for hermeneutics.

65. The single most important study of Keats's odes is the book by Helen Vendler, *The Odes of John Keats* (Cambridge, Mass., 1983). This book appeared several years after this chapter was written, including my draft for Keats's "Ode to a Nightingale." Despite the authority of the readings offered by Vendler, however, there is no concern whatsoever at any point in her book for what I am calling the hermeneutics of form. As even a quick perusal of her argument will reveal, she addresses exclusively the implied perspective of the poet Keats. This will be apparent from the number of sentences page by page in which the name Keats occurs as grammatical subject. Following a critical tradition of implied identification between author and reader which was central to New

Criticism, Vendler consistently claims the privilege of speaking on behalf of the author. Were there an opportunity to consider the difference in the perspective of a hermeneutical reading of the ode from the author-oriented approach of Vendler's book on Keats, it would demonstrate precisely what is distinctive about my appeal for a hermeneutics of form in the critical study of the Romantic ode.

66. The paradigm of modern criticism on Shelley, celebrating him as a poet of vision, is found in two works which influenced an entire generation of students: Harold Bloom, *Shelley's Mythmaking* (New Haven, 1959), and Earl Wasserman, *Shelley: A Critical Study* (Baltimore, 1972).

67. See chapter 4.

68. See chapter 1.

Notes to Chapter 6

The following essay was originally written in response to a series of lectures on the topic of metaphor, given at the University of Toronto during the fall semester 1971 in conjunction with a special faculty seminar on that topic by Paul Ricoeur. The essay originally appeared, along with essays by Ricoeur, Francis Sparshott and Robert Weimann, in *New Literary History* (vol. 6, 1974–75), 169–93. Ricoeur's work from the seminar subsequently appeared as a book, *La Metaphore vive* (1975), translated into English by Robert Czerny, *The Rule of Metaphor: Multi-Disciplinary Studies of the Creation of Meaning* (Toronto, 1978). Ricoeur's essay from the lecture series, entitled "Metaphor and the Central Problem of Hermeneutics," is also contained in *Hermeneutics & the Human Sciences,* ed. and trans. by John B. Thompson (Cambridge, 1981), 165–81. I gratefully acknowledge my debt to Prof. Ricoeur throughout the argument which follows.

1. Essays by René Wellek under the general headings of "terms" and "concepts" are collected in *Concepts of Criticism,* ed. S. G. Nichols Jr. (New Haven, 1963) and in *Discriminations: Further Concepts of Criticism* (New Haven, 1970). Wellek's essential concern, with which I fully concur, is formulated in the final paragraph of his essay "The Term and Concept of Classicism in Literary History," *Discriminations,* 55–89, esp. 87–88. What Wellek there describes as "word history," the history of "key-words of our civilization," unites lexicography with the history of ideas, based to a large extent on the pioneering work of Leo Spitzer. Wellek's essays also should be compared to corresponding arguments by I. A. Richards with regard to what Richards terms "The Resource-

fulness of Words" (in a lecture of 1940 included in *Speculative Instruments* [Chicago, 1955], 72ff.). Richards's approach to the history of words and concepts is further developed in his book *How to Read a Page: A Course in Effective Reading with an Introduction to a Hundred Great Words* (London, 1943). Where Richards is concerned primarily with semantic fields of interaction, Wellek addresses the historical development of central critical concepts.

2. As a convenient instance of such concern, see Bloom, *Romanticism and Consciousness* (New York, 1970), especially W. K. Wimsatt, Jr., "The Structure of Romantic Nature Imagery," and Paul de Man, "Intentional Structure of the Romantic Image."

3. On such alternative terms for metaphor, see chapter 9.

4. Richards, *The Philosophy of Rhetoric* (New York, 1936), esp. lectures 5 and 6, "Metaphor" and "The Command of Metaphor." It is not clear to me how Richards came to use the terms *tenor* and *vehicle* for his theory of metaphor.

5. The crucial landmark for this influence is Richards's study of Coleridge's poetic theory, *Coleridge on Imagination* (London, 1934), which marked a revolution in critical attitudes toward Romantic poetry in English studies.

6. "The poet, described in *ideal* perfection, brings the whole soul of man into activity, with the subordination of its faculties to each other, according to their relative worth and dignity. He diffuses a tone and spirit of unity, that blends and (as it were) *fuses,* each into each, by that synthetic and magical power, to which we have exclusively appropriated the name of imagination. This power...reveals itself in the balance or reconciliation of opposite or discordant qualities: of sameness, with difference; of the general, with the concrete; the idea, with the image; the individual, with the representative; the sense of novelty and freshness, with old and familiar objects; a more than usual state of emotion, with more than usual order; judgement ever awake and steady self-possession, with enthusiasm and feeling profound or vehement; and while it blends and harmonizes the natural and the artificial, still subordinates art to nature; the manner to the matter; and our admiration of the poet to our sympathy with the poetry." Coleridge, *Biographia Literaria,* ed. J. Shawcross (London, 1907), 2: 12. This passage is cited by Richards as early as *Principles of Literary Criticism* (1925; rpt. New York, n.d.), chap. 32, "The Imagination," 239–53, esp. 242.

Coleridge explains *esemplastic,* his neologism from the Greek εἰς ἓν πλάττειν, at the beginning of chapter 10 of *Biographia* (1: 107). The footnote by Shawcross (249) acknowledges, but seeks to deny, the probable source for the term in Schelling's use of *Einbildungskraft.*

7. In addition to the footnote by Shawcross mentioned above, Coleridge's

editor discusses the question of indebtedness to Schelling in his general introduction to the work (*Biographia* 1, lxii–lxiii). Shawcross offers a translation
from Schelling's *System des transzendentalen Idealismus, Sämmtliche Werke*
(*Werke*, 1858), 3: 626, a passage discussed below in my essay, and refers to two
later works by Schelling (*Darlegung des wahren Verhältnisses der Naturphilosophie zu der verbesserten Fichteschen Lehre, Werke*, 7: 60, and *Vorlesungen
über die Methode des akademischen Studiums, Werke*, 5: 348). Wellek, *A History
of Modern Criticism: 1750–1950*, vol. 2, *The Romantic Age* (New Haven, 1955),
also discusses Coleridge's relation to Schelling with reference to the false etymology of *Einbildungskraft* (see esp. 163 and 392 n. 62). What neither
Shawcross nor Wellek seems to acknowledge is the apparent responsibility of
Schelling, not Coleridge, for this etymological interpretation of the German
term.

8. "Das treffliche deutsche Wort Einbildungskraft bedeutet eigentlich die
Kraft der *Ineinsbildung*, auf welcher in der That alle Schöpfung beruht."
Schelling, *Philosophie der Kunst* (ca. 1804), §22, *Werke*, 5: 386. This passage
seems to be the most important source for Schelling's etymological definition
of the poetic imagination. It has not been noted before in discussions of
Schelling's aesthetics, so far as I know. It should be acknowledged that this
work was not published until 1859, after his death; Schelling's son edited these
lecture notes for the complete works, and dated them from about 1804, when
Schelling was in Würzburg (*Werke*, 5: vii). It has been demonstrated, however,
that Schelling lectured on the philosophy of art as early as the winter semester
of 1799–1800 in Jena; see F. W. J. Schelling, *Briefe und Dokumente*, vol. 1,
1775–1809, ed. Horst Fuhrmans (Bonn, 1962), 163, 174 n. 24. It is thus possible
that the arguments in the lecture notes derive from the same period as
Schelling's *System of Transcendental Idealism.*

9. In the final meeting of his seminar on metaphor at the University of
Toronto in 1971, Ricoeur surveyed the place of the term in German Idealist philosophy. Regrettably, he did not include his discussion of German Romantic
theories of the imagination in *The Rule of Metaphor.*

10. Aristotle defines *mythos* in chapter 6 of the *Poetics* as one of the six
essential elements of tragedy, *lexis* being another of these six. The relation of
mythos to structural and mimetic functions of the poetic work is clarified
within the context of Aristotle's argument in general. For this point I defer to
the comments made by Ricoeur on this question in his essay, "Metaphor and
the Main Problem of Hermeneutics," *New Literary History* 6.

11. Here again I defer to the authority of Ricoeur's arguments, especially as
presented in chapter 7 of *The Rule of Metaphor.*

12. My judgment here is based on a preliminary assessment of a most complex and relatively neglected field. Thorough exploration is needed of the interaction between theoretical views of language at that time and the development of a general poetics or aesthetics. Philosophical idealism provides one area of concern (with Hegel very much at the center); the aesthetic theory of Humboldt in relation to his later work on language provides another.

13. "Preface to *Lyrical Ballads, with Other Poems*" (1800), *Literary Criticism of William Wordsworth,* ed. Paul M. Zall (Lincoln, Neb., 1966), 15–32, esp. 22.

14. *Biographia Literaria,* chaps. 14 and 17–20, esp. vol. 2, pp. 28 ff.

15. "Preface to *Lyrical Ballads,*" 19, 27–28.

16. Schiller's letters to Körner on beauty are dated as follows: 25 January, 8 February, 18 February, 23 February and 28 February 1793 (nos. 639, 640, 643, 644 and 646 in *Schillers Briefe,* ed. Fritz Jonas [Stuttgart, 1893], vol. 3). I quote from the study edition of Schiller's works, *Sämmtliche Werke,* ed. Fricke and Göpfert (München, 1959), vol. 5, where the letters are printed as a separate essay ("Kallias oder über die Schönheit"), 394–433.

17. Reference will be made to the bilingual edition of Schiller's *Letters,* translated with introduction and commentary by Elizabeth M. Wilkinson and L. A. Willoughby (Oxford, 1967).

18. "Kallias," 400.

19. I allude here to the argument between Martin Heidegger and Emil Staiger concerning the aesthetic concept of *Scheinen* with reference to Mörike's poem "Auf eine Lampe," in Staiger, *Die Kunst der Interpretation,* 9–49 (see chap. 5, n. 26).

20. "Kallias," 400.

21. This process of transformation in Romantic aesthetics, especially as it occurred in England, is the subject of the well-known study by M. H. Abrams, *The Mirror and the Lamp* (Oxford, 1953).

22. *Erster Teil:* "Die Idee des Kunstschönen oder das Ideal"; *Erstes Kapitel:* "Begriff des Schönen überhaupt"; §3, "Die Idee des Schönen," in *Äst,* 1: 117. In the Knox translation, the definition is rendered ". . . the beautiful is characterized as the pure appearance of the Idea to sense" (*Aes,* 1: 111).

23. Kant, *Kritik der Urteilskraft,* ed. Karl Vorländer, *Philosophische Bibliothek,* 39a (Hamburg, 1924), 211–15. Of particular importance for the influence of this paragraph in Kant's *Third Critique* on Romantic theory is the discussion in Gadamer's *Wahrheit und Methode,* "Die Grenze der Erlebniskunst: Rehabilitierung der Allegorie," 66–77 (*TM,* 70–81). (See chap. 1, nn. 4–5.)

24. The passage occurs in the final paragraph of letter 15 (*Letters,* 108–9). This passage is discussed at greater length in chapter 1.

25. My comments on the sublime proceed from the general context of eighteenth-century theory, as represented especially in Burke and Kant and as discussed in the well-known study by Samuel H. Monk, *The Sublime: A Study of Critical Theories in Eighteenth Century England* (New York, 1935). Much attention has recently been given to various aspects of the sublime in the Kantian tradition throughout the Romantic era, as for instance in the important work by Thomas Weiskel, *The Romantic Sublime: Studies in the Structure and Psychology of Transcendence* (Baltimore, 1976).

26. I do not here consider (though this could be done) the validity for my argument of Schiller's several shorter essays on the sublime, in particular "Vom Erhabenen" and "Über das Pathetische" (both 1793) and "Über das Erhabene" (1801).

27. Schiller's theoretical discussion of the developmental process of the individual mind in letters 11 to 15 was directly influenced by Fichte's *Grundlage der gesamten Wissenschaftslehre* (1794), as acknowledged in a long note to letter 13 (*Letters*, 84ff.). Schiller's new concept of human freedom is introduced in letter 14 (par. 5, 96–97) and subsequently discussed again at the end of letter 19 (186–87). Wilkinson provides a valuable commentary on the concept in the glossary.

28. The opposing urges are introduced in letter 12; their reciprocal balance is described in letter 13 (*Letters*, 78–89).

29. The term *Spieltrieb* is introduced in letter 14 (par. 3, *Letters*, 96–97); the phrase *lebende Gestalt* occurs in the letter 15 (par. 2, 100–101.).

30. Whether Schiller was himself aware that his notion of *Spieltrieb* corresponded to theories of the imagination is difficult to ascertain. He himself used the term *Einbildungskraft* in a corresponding manner in his important review of the poems of Matthisson ("Über Matthissons Gedichte," *Sämmtliche Werke*, 5: 992–1011, esp. 994ff.).

31. "Gäbe es aber Fälle,...wo [der Mensch] sich zugleich seiner Freiheit bewußt würde und sein Dasein empfände, wo er sich zugleich als Materie fühlte und als Geist kennen lernte, so hätte er in diesen Fällen, und schlechterdings nur in diesen, eine vollständige Anschauung seiner Menschheit, und der Gegenstand, der diese Anschauung ihm verschaffte, würde ihm zu einem Symbol seiner *ausgeführten Bestimmung*, folglich (weil diese nur in der Allheit der Zeit zu erreichen ist) zu einer Darstellung des Unendlichen dienen" (95).

32. The translation of the philosophical term *Anschauung* as "intuition" is based on the evidence that Kant used the term in his critical philosophy as an equivalent for the concept of *intuitio* in medieval scholasticism. Schiller's phrase *vollständige Anschauung seiner Menschheit* assumes implications,

whether intended or not, that are essentially identical with Kant's notion of *intellektuelle Anschauung*. On this concept, see chapter 4.

33. In my comments here I assume that the term *Gegenstand* may legitimately be applied from Schiller's argument to the work of art. As the statement is formulated, it is apparent that Schiller intended to leave the question of referent open, in order not to delimit the validity of his argument. Justification for my interpretation is derived from the kind of application that was subsequently made, whether or not explicitly with reference to this passage, by Romantic theories of the work of art as Symbol.

34. Needless to say, I do not accept the conventional distinction in German literary history between *Klassik* and *Romantik* – whereby Schiller is grouped with Goethe in opposition to the Romantics – as valid in any way for a discussion of European Romanticism.

35. I allude once again to para. 59 of the *Kritik der Urteilskraft*, "Schönheit als Symbol der Sittlichkeit" (see n. 23) and to Gadamer's discussion of its influence.

36. Once again, it should be emphasized that I use the term Romanticism in the context of European literary and intellectual history with reference to the period around the turn of the eighteenth to the nineteenth century. Justification for such a broad application is provided by evidence assembled in exemplary fashion by René Wellek in his crucial study of 1949, "The Concept of Romanticism in Literary History," *Comparative Literature* 1 (1949): 1–23 and 147–72 (reprinted in *Concepts of Criticism*, 128–98). Within such a European framework, of course, such writers as Goethe and Schiller must be seen as central for Romanticism, not to mention others, such as Jean Paul, Hölderlin and Kleist, who are often excluded from consideration in German literary histories of *Romantik*. What precisely the concept of Romanticism implies for such usage remains an open question, to the discussion of which this essay on metaphor in Romantic theory intends to contribute.

37. The terms *Selbstbewußtsein* and *Tathandlung* are central to Fichte's *Wissenschaftslehre* and would have been familiar as such to Schiller, as to any reader of the *Grundlage* of 1794 (see n. 27). These terms are discussed also at the beginning of chapter 4.

38. The problematic history of this term in literary criticism has been traced by Gadamer (*wm*, 60–66; *tm*, 64–70), and by René Wellek, "Genre Theory, the Lyric and *Erlebnis*," *Discriminations* (1970), 225–52.

39. I refer to Hegel's definition of Romantic art ("Vom Romantischen überhaupt," the general introduction to *Die Romantische Kunstform* in part 2 of the *Äesthetik*, vol. 1, 498–508). The term *Romantic* for Hegel, of course, did not

refer to his own era, but rather to the Christian middle ages, as it did for all theorists of Romantic art from the Schlegels on. For further discussion of this concept as used in Hegel's *Aesthetics,* see chapter 5.

40. A discussion of *irony* in the theory and practice of Schlegel's *Dialogue on Poetry* is contained in chapter 7. The key to a theory of *dialectical* form in poetry, based on Hegel's philosophical practice, is the concept of *negativity,* which is discussed chapters 2, 5 and 8.

41. *WM,* 39–77, esp. 66ff.; *TM,* 42–81.

42. De Man, "The Rhetoric of Temporality," *Interpretation: Theory and Practice,* ed. Charles S. Singleton (Baltimore, 1969), 173–209. The essay was subsequently included in the expanded second edition of de Man's *Blindness and Insight* (Minneapolis, 1983), 187–228.

It has become apparent to me since first writing this essay that the crucial and difficult use of the term *allegory* by Walter Benjamin in his book *Ursprung des deutschen Trauerspiels* also influenced de Man's use of this concept in his essay. My views on the contribution of de Man to the critical study of Romanticism have been summarized in a commemorative essay, "Literary Criticism beyond New Criticism: de Man's Essays on Romanticism and Modernity," *(Dis)continuities: Essays on Paul de Man,* ed. L. Herman, K. Humbeeck and G. Lernout, *Postmodern Studies* 2 (Amsterdam and Antwerp, 1989): 133–48.

43. "Rhetoric of Temporality," 174; *Blindness and Insight,* 189.

44. "Rhetoric of Temporality," 179ff.; *Blindness and Insight,* 194ff. De Man refers specifically to Abrams, "Structure and Style in the Greater Romantic Lyric," in *From Sensibility to Romanticism: Essays Presented to F. A. Pottle,* ed. F. W. Hilles and H. Bloom (New York, 1965); and to Earl Wasserman, "The English Romantics: The Grounds of Knowledge," *Essays in Romanticism* 4 (1964).

45. "Rhetoric of Temporality," 180; *Blindness and Insight,* 196.

46. De Man, "Genesis and Genealogy in Nietzsche's *Birth of Tragedy,*" lecture delivered at the University of Toronto, fall 1971 (subsequently published in *Diacritics*); "Theory of Metaphor in Rousseau's *Second Discourse,*" in *Romanticism: Vistas, Instances, Continuities,* ed. David Thorburn and Geoffrey Hartman (Ithaca, 1973), 83–114. The later stages in de Man's thinking about figuration in literature may be traced through the essays contained in his book *Allegories of Reading: Figural Language in Rousseau, Nietzsche, Rilke and Proust* (New Haven, 1979), including both the essays cited above (as chaps. 4 and 7).

47. The clearest formulation of this threefold structure of history occurs in the opening section (letters 1–9) of Schiller's *Letters on Aesthetic Education.* It

may also be perceived to underlie (with some differences) later Idealist philosophies of history, e.g., Schelling's incomplete *Weltalter* and Hegel's Berlin lectures on *Philosophie der Geschichte.*

48. Abrams, "English Romanticism: The Spirit of the Age," in *Romanticism Reconsidered,* ed. Northrop Frye (New York, 1963), 37.

49. "Ich bin gewiss, daß Du indessen zuweilen meiner gedachtest, seit wir mit der Loosung – Reich Gottes! von einander schieden." Hölderlin to Hegel, 10 July 1794, in *Briefe,* ed. Adolph Beck, *Große Stuttgarter Ausgabe* (hereafter cited as *GStA*), 4, 1, 126.

50. *Äst,* 1: 71; *Aes,* 1: 63.

51. Schelling, *System des transzendentalen Idealismus,* ed. Ruth-Eva Schulz (*Philosophische Bibliothek,* 254 [Hamburg, 1957]), 5 (subsequent references by page in parentheses within the text).

52. "*Identität des Bewußten* und *Bewußtlosen* im *Ich* und *Bewußtsein dieser Identität*" (281). Schelling's definition, in the translation of Albert Hofstadter, is as follows: "The postulated intuition [of art] should comprehend what exists separated in the appearance of freedom and in the intuition of the product of nature, namely *identity of conscious and unconscious in the ego and consciousness of this identity*." *Philosophies of Art and Beauty: Selected Readings in Aesthetics from Plato to Heidegger,* ed. Hofstadter and Richard Kuhns (New York, 1964), 362.

53. "Darstellung des Absoluten mit absoluter Indifferenz des Allgemeinen und Besonderen im Besonderen ist nur symbolisch möglich," *Philosophie der Kunst,* 39; *Gesammelte Werke* (1859), 5: 406.

54. I recognize that Schelling subsequently transformed the abstract, almost schematic structure of his argument in the *System* to achieve a view of myth as a comprehensive and dynamic principle of human culture and thought in general. The outline of mythology in art, which he provides in the *Philosophie der Kunst* (414–51), was later elaborated into almost unlimited scope in the lectures on the *Philosophy of Mythology and Revelation* (4 vols., published posthumously). My remarks in this essay pertain to the *System* of 1800 only and are not intended to address Schelling's later development in any way.

55. "...so ist kein wahrer, objektiver Gegensatz zwischen Schönheit und Erhabenheit; das wahrhaft und absolut Schöne ist immer auch erhaben, das Erhabene (wenn dies wahrhaft) ist auch schön" (290).

56. "...dieses Reflektiertwerden des absolut Unbewußten und Nichtobjektiven [ist] nur durch einen ästhetischen Akt der Einbildungskraft möglich" (18).

57. F. Schlegel, *Gespräch über die Poesie; Kritische Ausgabe,* vol. 2: *Charakter-*

istiken und Kritiken I (1796–1802), ed. Hans Eichner (Paderborn, 1967), 284ff. A detailed discussion of irony in Schlegel's *Dialogue* is contained in chapter 7.

58. "Jenen ewigen Widerstreit zwischen unserem Selbst und der Welt zu endigen, den Frieden alles Friedens, der höher ist, denn alle Vernunft, den wiederzubringen, uns mit der Natur zu vereinigen zu Einem unendlichen Ganzen, das ist das Ziel all' unseres Strebens, wir mögen uns darüber verstehen oder nicht" (*GStA,* 3: 236).

59. *GStA,* 4, 1: 289. "What I lack is less of power than of levity, less of ideas than of nuances, less of a basic tone than of manifold ordered tones, less of light than of shadow, and all this for One reason: I shy away too much from the common and the usual in actual life."

60. Evidence for such an interpretation of the meaning of the tones does not derive from the names assigned to them as such, but rather from the general context of Hölderlin's argument, where the central qualities and attributes associated with the tones frequently occur also in Hölderlin's poetic work (especially in his novel *Hyperion*). The influence of Schiller on Hölderlin's theoretical writings, as on his poetic practice, is everywhere apparent. There is no space to pursue this claim here.

61. See "Über den Unterschied der Dichtarten," *GStA,* 4, 1: 266–72. Hölderlin interchanges the phrases *geistige Behandlung* and *idealische Behandung.* Questions of consistency in terminology further complicate the challenge of deciphering his argument.

62. "...wenn die idealische Behandlung [= geistige Behandlung] in ihrer Metapher, ihrem übergang, ihren Episoden, mehr vereinigend ist, hingegen der Ausdruk, die Darstellung in ihren Karakteren, ihrer Leidenschaft, ihren Individualitäten, mehr trennend, so stehet die Bedeutung zwischen beiden, sie zeichnet sich aus dadurch, dass sie sich selber überall entgegengesezt ist..." (*GStA,* 4, 1: 245).

63. "...in der rhythmischen Aufeinanderfolge der Vorstellungen, worinn der *Transport* sich darstellt" (*GStA,* 5: 196, lines 9–10). The phrase cited in the text here occurs in Hölderlin's notes to his translations from Sophocles. Hölderlin also speaks in his "Notes to Sophocles" of a "categorical reversal" [kategorischer Umkehr] with reference to the moment of climax and catastrophe in the drama.

64. This Fichtean term is used repeatedly in the longer essay ("Über die Verfahrungsweise"), where Hölderlin is describing the climax of the poem (*GStA,* 4, 1: 249–50).

65. The Aristotelian implications of Hölderlin's theory of the tragic turn, or reversal, are especially apparent in the essay "Grund zum Empedokles" (*GStA,*

4, 1: 249–62, esp. 149, 152ff.) and in the "Notes to Sophocles" (*GStA*, 5: 195–202, 265–72, esp. 201–2, 269ff.).

66. Concerning the validity of this phrase for Hölderlin, as for the other theorists of German Romantic idealism, see John Neubauer, "Intellektuelle, intellektuale und ästhetische Anschauung: Zur Entstehung der romantischen Kunstauffassung," *Deutsche Vierteljahrsschrift für Literatur- und Geistesgeschichte* 46 (1972): 294–319. Also very helpful for Hölderlin's use of the phrase is a long footnote in the monograph by Jochen Schmidt, *Hölderlins letzte Hymnen: "Andenken" und "Mnemosyne"* (Tübingen, 1970), 38–39.

67. This phrase (or related epithets) appears in various poems, such as "Der Zeitgeist," "Mein Eigentum," line 46; "An Eduard," lines 35–36; "Brod und Wein," line 54; "Heimkunft," lines 89ff.; etc. (*GStA*, 1, 1: 300, 307; 2, 1: 42, 91, 99). To pursue so complex and central a theme in Hölderlin in this context would be inappropriate.

68. See the ode with this title, *GStA*, 2, 1: 64–65, subsequently changed to "Blödigkeit."

69. "Das tragische, dem Schein nach heroische Gedicht ist in seiner Bedeutung idealisch. Es ist die Metapher einer intellectuellen Anschauung" (*GStA*, 4, 1: 266, lines 6ff).

Notes to Chapter 7

This essay was written for a special issue of the *Canadian Review of Comparative Literature* on the subject of Dialogue, edited by Christie MacDonald, vol. 2 (1976): 66–77. It was presented as a public lecture at Boston University in the preceding year.

1. "Der platonische Dialog war gleichsam der Kahn, auf dem sich die schiffbrüchige ältere Poesie samt allen ihren Kindern rettete: auf einem engen Raum zusammengedrängt und dem einen Steuermann Sokrates ängstlich untertänig, fuhren sie jetzt in eine neue Welt hinein, die an dem phantastischen Bilde dieses Aufzugs sich nie sehen konnte. Wirklich hat für die ganze Nachwelt Plato das Vorbild einer neuen Kunstform gegeben, das Vorbild des *Romans*." Friedrich Nietzsche, *Die Geburt der Tragödie,* para. 14. Translation by Walter Kaufmann, *The Birth of Tragedy,* 90–91.

2. Ernst Behler, *Klassische Ironie, Romantische Ironie, Tragische Ironie: Zum Ursprung dieser Begriffe* (Darmstadt, 1972), esp. 15ff. Thomas Mann, "Freiheit," chap. 5, *Der Zauberberg* (Frankfurt a.M., 1960), 3: 309.

3. There is an extensive literature on this subject, including Walter Rehm,

Griechentum und Goethezeit; Henry Hatfield, *Aesthetic Paganism in German Literature*; and even E. S. Butler, *The Tyranny of Greece over Germany*. Still worth consulting on Goethe is the study by Humphrey Trevelyan, *Goethe and the Greeks*.

4. For a more detailed discussion of Schiller's *Letters,* see chapters 1 and 6.

5. *Briefe über die ästhetische Erziehung des Menschen,* letter 15, in: *Schiller Nationalausgabe,* vol. 20, no. 1: *Philosophische Schriften,* ed. B. v. Wiese (Weimar, 1962), 359ff.

6. *Über Naive und Sentimentalische Dichtung, Schiller Nationalausgabe,* 20, 1: 424ff.

7. Ibid., 433ff.

8. "Unser Herz macht beim Lesen einen Stillstand und entfernt sich von dem Objekte gern, um in sich selbst zu schauen." Ibid.

9. Wilhelm von Humboldt, *Aesthetische Versuche, Erster Theil: Ueber Göthes Herrmann und Dorothea,* chaps. xxi–xxx, in W. v. Humboldt, *Werke in fünf Bänden,* ed. A. Flitner and K. Giel (Darmstadt, 1961), 2: 178–94.

10. ". . . *ein einziges, unteilbares, vollendetes Gedicht." Gespräch über die Poesie,* ed. Hans Eichner (Stuttgart, 1968), 313.

11. Schelling, *Philosophie der Kunst,* par. 42 (Darmstadt, 1966), 58–95 (photographic reproduction of the original edition of 1859). An English translation has now been published: Schelling, *The Philosophy of Art,* trans. Douglas W. Scott (Minneapolis, 1989).

12. "Alle Gedichte des Altertums schließen sich eines an das andre, bis sich aus immer größern Massen und Gliedern das Ganze bildet; alles greift in einander, und überall ist ein und derselbe Geist nur anders ausgedrückt." *Gespräch über die Poesie,* 313.

13. Nietzsche, *Die Geburt der Tragödie,* par. 12, in: *Werke in drei Bänden,* ed. K. Schlechta (München, 1954), vol. 1, 71–75.

14. For Hegel's attack on F. Schlegel with reference to the concept of irony, see *Philosophy of Right,* par. 140 (esp. section f and note), and the introduction to *Aesthetics,* under "Irony" (3.B.3).

15. A useful survey of German theories of Romantic irony is Helmut Prang, *Die romantische Ironie (Erträge der Forschung* 12 [Darmstadt, 1972]), with a bibliography. Important also are the books by Beda Allemann, *Ironie und Dichtung* (Pfullingen, 1956), and Ingrid Strohschneider-Kohrs, *Die romantische Ironie in Theorie und Gestaltung* (Tübingen, 1960), and the essays by Raymond Immerwahr, "The Subjectivity or Objectivity of F. Schlegel's Poetic Irony," *Germanic Review* 26 (1951): 173–90, and Peter Szondi, "Friedrich Schlegel und die romantische Ironie," *Euphorion* 48 (1954): 397–411.

16. The two most authoritative discussions of Schlegel's *Dialogue* are both primarily concerned with aspects of theory and doctrine: Franz Norbert Mennemeier, *Friedrich Schlegels Poesiebegriff dargestellt anhand der literaturkritischen Schriften: Die romantische Konzeption einer objektiven Poesie* (München, 1971), esp. 313–66; and Karl Konrad Polheim, *Die Arabeske: Ansichten und Ideen aus Friedrich Schlegels Poetik* (Paderborn, 1966), esp. 55–197.

17. Concerning Schlegel's relations with Schleiermacher regarding plans for a translation of Plato, see Wilhelm Dilthey, *Leben Schleiermachers, Erster Band: Abhandlungen aus dem Nachlaß W. Diltheys zur Fortsetzung seiner Schleiermacher-Biographie (3. und 4. Buch: 1803–1807)*, chap. 4: "Schleiermachers Übersetzung des Platon," and *Zweiter Band: Schleiermachers System als Philosophie und Theologie: Aus dem Nachlaß...*, ed. Martin Redeker (Berlin, 1966), vol. 1, bk. 2, pp. 37–75, and vol. 2, bk. 2, pp. 678–83.

18. See Dilthey, "Der Platon Friedrich Schlegels," in *Leben Schleiermachers*, vol. 1, bk. 2, 46ff.

19. Derrida, "La Pharmacie de Platon," *Tel Quel* 32 (1968): 3–48; and 33 (1968): 18–59; repr. in *La Dissémination* (Paris, 1972).

20. "Wie der Kern der Erde sich von selbst mit Gebilden und Gewächsen bekleidete, wie das Leben von selbst aus der Tiefe hervorsprang, und alles voll ward von Wesen die sich fröhlich vermehrten; so blüht auch Poesie von selbst aus der unsichtbaren Urkraft der Menschheit hervor, wenn der erwärmende Strahl der göttlichen Sonne sie trifft und befruchtet" (339; 285).

All references to Schlegel's *Dialogue* in the argument that follows will be included in parentheses immediately following the quotations. The first number in these parentheses refers to the pages of the edition by Jacob Minor, *Friedrich Schlegel, 1794–1802: Seine prosaischen Jugendschriften*, 2 (Vienna, 1882): 338–85; the second to the pages of the edition by Ernst Behler and Hans Eichner, *Friedrich Schlegel, Kritische Ausgabe seiner Werke in 35 Bänden*, vol. 2: *Charakteristiken und Kritiken I (1796–1802)* (Paderborn, 1967), 284–362. English translations – unless otherwise noted – are taken from *Dialogue in Poetry and Literary Aphorisms*, trans. Ernst Behler and Roman Struc (University Park, Pa., 1968).

21. Hans Eichner discusses such biographical identification briefly in his "Nachwort" to his separate edition of the *Gespräch* in the *Sammlung Metzler* (*Realienbücher für Germanisten*, Abt. G: *Dokumentationen*, Reihe a: *Aus der Geschichte der Literaturwissenschaft und Literaturkritik*, M 70) (Stuttgart, 1968), 13*.

22. "[Dieses Gespräch] soll ganz verschiedene Ansichten gegeneinander stellen, deren jede aus ihrem Standpunkte den unendlichen Geist der Poesie in

einem neuen Lichte zeigen kann, und die alle mehr oder minder bald von dieser bald von jener Seite in den eigentlichen Kern zu dringen streben" (340; 286).

23. The conclusion of the original version of the *Gespräch* in 1800 is laconic and abrupt. The much expanded version of 1823 (prepared by Schlegel for the collected edition of his work), which has only been readily available since the appearance of the critical text edited by Behler and Eichner (see n. 20; 2: 352–62), is far more sophisticated and rhetorically persuasive, even though the views there expressed reflect a considerable change in Schlegel's own outlook more than twenty years after the dialogue was first composed.

24. "So lassen Sie uns lieber den schönen Garten unsrer neuen Poesie sorgfältig verschließen, damit wir nichts vernehmen von dem widrigen Lärm da draußen auf den Gassen und von dem literarischen Jahrmarkte herüber. Da wollen wir dann ungestört und einsam wandeln unter den hohen Zedern-bäumen, uns an dem Duft der blühenden Pomeranzenhaine erquicken, in den lieblichen Rosengängen verweilen, oder das Auge an der prachtvollen Hyazinthenflur weiden" (362).

25. "Jeder, oder zunächst nur wer eben am meisten Lust habe, solle einmal seine Gedanken über Poesie, oder über einen Teil, eine Seite derselben von Grund des Herzens aussprechen, oder lieber ausschreiben, damit mans schwarz auf weiß besitze, wies jeder meine" (341; 287).

26. "Jenes unsichtbare, welches uns die verborgne Wurzel und Quelle aller Dichtung und Sage in der wunderbaren Kraft der Fantasie enthüllt, deren ewiges Wirken und Schaffen in der symbolischen Welt der Mythologie, oder in der Natursage wie in der Naturanschauung daheim ist" (1967 ed., 356).

27. "Dasselbe Element hat unser humoristischer Freund nur von einer andern Seite ergriffen, und es in seinem ewigen Kampfe mit der prosaischen Wirklichkeit dargestellt; denn aller wahrhaft poetische Witz und dichterische Humor ist doch nur eine angewandte Fantasie; oder eine indirekte Äußer-ungsart derselen" (1967 ed., 356).

28. "Mich däucht wer das Zeitalter, das heißt jenen großen Prozeß allge-meiner Verjüngung, jene Prinzipien der ewigen Revolution verstünde, dem müßte es gelingen können, die Pole der Menschheit zu ergreifen und das Tun der ersten Menschen, wie den Charakter der goldnen Zeit die noch kommen wird, zu erkennen und zu wissen. Dann würde das Geschwätz aufhören, und der Mensch inne werden, was er ist, und würde die Erde verstehn und die Sonne" (363; 322).

29. "Ich muß, was ich gestern zu Ihrer Verteidigung zu sagen schien, zurücknehmen, liebe Freundin! und Ihnen so gut als völlig unrecht geben. Sie

selbst geben es sich am Ende des Streites darin, daß Sie sich so tief eingelassen, weil es gegen die weibliche Würde sei, aus dem angebornen Element von heiterm Scherz und ewiger Poesie zu dem gründlichen oder schwerfälligen Ernst der Männer sich, wie Sie es richtig nannten, herabzustimmen. Ich stimme Ihnen gegen Sie selbst bei, daß Sie unrecht haben. Ja ich behaupte noch außerdem, daß es nicht genug sei, Unrecht anzuerkennen; man muß es auch büßen, und die wie mirs scheint, ganz zweckmäßige Buße dafür, daß Sie sich mit der Kritik gemein gemacht haben, soll nun sein, daß Sie sich die Geduld abnötigen, diese kritische Epistel über den Gegenstand des gestrigen Gesprächs zu lesen" (367; 329).

30. "Romantisch ist, was uns einen sentimentalen Stoff in einer fantastischen Form darstellt" (370; 333). For an authoritative discussion of these terms as Schlegel uses them, see Hans Eichner, "F. Schlegel's Theory of Romantic Poetry," *PMLA* 71 (1956): 1018–41.

Notes to Chapter 8

This essay in a much shorter version was first written for a conference on literary narrative sponsored by the Graduate Program in Comparative Literature at the University of Toronto in the spring of 1976, subsequently published in *The Interpretation of Narrative,* ed. M. J. Valdés and O. J. Miller (Toronto, 1978), 61–77. For the present collection it has been revised and expanded, with the addition of the section on Shakespeare.

1. I. A. Richards, "Reversals in Poetry," *Poetries: Their Media and Ends* (The Hague, 1974), 59–70.

2. Richards, *The Philosophy of Rhetoric* (New York, 1936), 85.

3. Richards, *How to Read a Page: A Course in Efficient Reading with an Introduction to a Hundred Great Words* (New York, 1942).

4. Richards, "The Future of Poetry," lecture delivered at Victoria College, Toronto, in 1958, repr. in his collection *So Much Nearer* (New York, 1968), 150–82.

5. See esp. Richards, *Speculative Instruments* (Chicago, 1955).

6. Iser, *Der Akt des Lesens,* 348–55; *The Act of Reading,* 225–31 (see chap. 1, n. 16). This work is also discussed in chapters 2 and 5.

7. *Positionen der Negativität,* ed. Harald Weinrich, *Poetik und Hermeneutik,* 6 (München, 1975).

8. Iser, "Die Appellstruktur der Texte: Unbestimmtheit als Wirkungsbedingung literarischer Prosa," *Konstanzer Universitätsreden,* no. 28 (Konstanz, 1970).

9. Iser, "The Patterns of Negativity in Beckett's Prose," *Georgia Review* 29 (Fall 1975): 706–19.

10. "[E]ine Spur des Nicht-Gegebenen," *Der Akt des Lesens*, 348–49.

11. See W. K. Wimsatt, Jr., "Aristotle's Answer: Poetry as Structure," *Literary Criticism: A Short History* (New York, 1957), 21–34; also "Aristotle and Oedipus or Else," his essay directed against the extensive commentary on the *Poetics* by Gerald Else, in *Hateful Contraries: Studies in Literature and Criticism* (Lexington, Ky., 1965), 72–89.

12. Hans Robert Jauss, "Negativität und Identifikation: Versuch zur Theorie der ästhetischen Erfahrung," in *Positionen der Negativität*, 263–339, esp. 300ff.

13. A more detailed interpretation of this sonnet is included in my introductory essay on Rilke for the collection of translations by Walter Arndt, *The Best of Rilke* (Hanover, N.H., 1989), xiii–xxvi.

14. *GStA*, 5: 195–202, 265–72.

15. See chap. 1, n. 18.

16. "Darum der immer widerstreitende Dialog, darum der Chor als Gegensaz gegen diesen. Darum das allzukeusche, allzumechanische und factisch endigende Ineinandergreifen zwischen den verschiedenen Theilen, im Dialog, und zwischen dem Chor und Dialog und den großen Parthien oder Dramaten, welche aus Chor und Dialog bestehen" (201).

17. "Dadurch wird die Aufeinanderfolge des Kalkuls, und der Rhythmus getheilt, und bezieht sich, in seinen zweien Hälften so aufeinander, daß sie, als gleichwiegend, erscheinen" (196).

18. "In solchem Momente vergißt der Mensch sich und den Gott, und kehret, freilich heiliger Weise, wie ein Verräther sich um. - In der äußersten Gränze des Leidens bestehet nemlich nichts mehr, als die Bedingungen der Zeit oder des Raums.

In dieser vergißt sich der Mensch, weil er ganz im Moment ist; der Gott, weil er nichts als Zeit ist; und beides ist untreu, die Zeit, weil sie in solchem Momente sich kategorisch wendet, und Anfang und Ende sich in ihr schlechterdings nicht reimen läßt; der Mensch, weil er in diesem Momente der kategorischen Umkehr folgen muß, hiermit im Folgenden schlechterdings nicht dem Anfänglichen gleichen kann" (202).

19. "[D]er Gott der Mythe" (*GStA*, 4, 1: 281); "in diesem Puncte [ist] der Geist in seiner Unendlichkeit fühlbar" (*GStA*, 4, 1: 249–50).

20. "[A]ls eigene Welt der Form nach, als Welt in der Welt, und so als Stimme des Ewigen dargestelltwird" (*GStA*, 4, 1: 250).

21. "[Der Begriff], indem [es] das eigene Selbst des Gegenstandes ist, das sich als *sein Werden* darstellt, ist...der sich bewegende und seine

Bestimmungen in sich zurücknehmende Begriff. In dieser Bewegung *geht* jenes ruhende Subjekt selbst *zugrunde*; es geht in die Unterschiede und den Inhalt ein und macht vielmehr die Bestimmtheit, d. h. den unterschiednen Inhalt wie die Bewegung desselben aus, statt ihr gegenüberstehen zu bleiben" (*PhG*, 45; my emphasis).

22. For example, the essay by Jere Paul Surber, "Hegel's Speculative Sentence," *Hegel-Studien* 10 (1975): 211–30.

23. "Der feste Boden, den das Räsonnieren an dem ruhenden Subjekte hat, schwankt also, und nur diese Bewegung selbst wird Gegenstand. Das Subjekt, das seinen Inhalt erfüllt, hört auf, über diesen hinaus zu gehen, und kann nicht noch andre Prädikate oder Akzidenzen haben. Die Zerstreutheit des Inhalts ist umgekehrt dadurch unter das Selbst gebunden; er ist nicht das Allgemeine, das frei vom Subjekte mehrern zukäme. Der Inhalt ist somit in der Tat nicht mehr Prädikat des Subjekts, sondern ist die Substanz , ist das Wesen und der Begriff dessen, wovon die Rede ist. Das vorstellende Denken, da seine Natur ist, an den Akzidenzen oder Prädikaten fortzulaufen und mit Recht, weil sie nicht mehr als Prädikate und Akzidenzen sind, über sie hinauszugehen, wird, indem das, was im Satze die Form eines Prädikates hat, die Substanz selbst ist, in seinem Fortlaufen *gehemmt*. Es erleidet, es so vorzustellen, einen *Gegenstoß*. Vom Subjekte anfangend, als ob dieses zum Grunde liegen bliebe, findet es, indem das Prädikat vielmehr die Substanz ist, das Subjekt zum Prädikat übergegangen und hiemit *aufgehoben*; und indem so das, was Prädikat zu sein scheint, zur ganzen und selbständigen Masse geworden, kann das Denken nicht frei herumirren, sondern ist durch diese Schwere aufgehalten" (*PhG*, 45; my emphasis).

24. "Dieser Konflikt der Form eines Satzes überhaupt und der sie zerstörenden Einheit des Begriffs ist dem ähnlich, der im Rhythmus zwischen dem Metrum und dem Akzente stattfindet" (*PhG*, 46).

25. "Der Rhythmus resultiert aus der schwebenden Mitte und Vereinigung beider [i.e., meter and accent]. So soll auch im philosophischen Satze die Identität des Subjekts und Prädikats den Unterschied derselben, den die Form des Satzes ausdrückt, nicht vernichten, sondern ihre Einheit [soll] als eine Harmonie hervorgehen. Die Form des Satzes ist die Erscheinung des bestimmten Sinnes oder der Akzent, der seine Erfüllung unterscheidet; daß aber das Prädikat die Substanz ausdrückt und das Subjekt selbst ins Allgemeine fällt, ist die *Einheit*, worin jener Akzent verklingt" (*PhG*, 46).

26. "Daß die Form des Satzes aufgehoben wird, muß nicht nur auf *unmittelbare* Weise geschehen, nicht durch den bloßen Inhalt des Satzes. Sondern diese entgegengesetzte Bewegung muß ausgesprochen werden" (*PhG*, 48).

27. Richards, "*Troilus and Cressida* and Plato," *Speculative Instruments* (see chap. 6, n. 1), 198–213.

28. Richards, "What Is Saying?" repr. in *Poetries: Their Media and Ends,* 222.

Notes to Chapter 9

This dialogue was originally composed as a contribution to a yearlong series of lectures on the Identity of the Literary Text, sponsored by the Center for Comparative Literature at the University of Toronto in 1981–82. The essay on Coleridge's "Kubla Khan" was written as a supplement to the dialogue at that time but was based on my teaching of English Romantic poetry in the English Department of that university during the preceding decade. The "Afterthoughts" were added somewhat later, based above all on a detailed critique of the dialogue and essay by my friend Geoff Waite at Cornell University. The entire text, minus about ten pages of the essay on "Kubla Khan," was published in the collection of essays from the lecture series edited by M. J. Valdés and O. J. Miller, *Identity of the Literary Text* (Toronto, 1985), 119–45. The text has been slightly revised for the present collection.

The following (imagined) dialogue attempts to explore the question of identity in the literary text in a manner that reflects what I take to be a genuine quandary for criticism.

1. Stanley Fish, *Is There a Text in This Class? The Authority of Interpretive Communities* (Cambridge, Mass., 1980), vii.

2. E. D. Hirsch, *Validity in Interpretation* (New Haven, 1967), 46.

3. This statement by Gadamer derives from the seminar on Hermeneutics that he taught at the University of Toronto in the fall of 1970.

4. Dieter Henrich, "'Identität' – Begriffe, Probleme, Grenzen," in *Identität,* ed. Odo Marquard and Karlheinz Stierle, *Poetik und Hermeneutik,* 8 (München, 1979): 133–86. The examples cited in the paragraphs that follow are borrowed from Henrich's authoritative argument.

5. Heidegger, "Der Satz der Identität," in *Identität und Differenz* (Pfullingen, 1957): 13–34. The discussion of *Er-eignis* occurs on pp. 28–29; the phrase "der in sich schwingende Bereich," on p. 30; and the concept of *Sprung* on p. 32. The following statement is summarized here: "Im Er-eignis schwingt das Wesen dessen, was als Sprache spricht, die einmal das Haus des Seins genannt wurde. Satz der Identität sagt jetzt: Ein Sprung, den das Wesen der Identität verlangt, weil es ihn braucht, wenn anders das Zusammen*gehören* von Mensch und Sein in das Wesenslicht des Ereignisses gelangen soll" (32).

6. Heidegger, "Der Ursprung des Kunstwerks," in *Holzwege,* 3d ed. (Frankfurt, 1957), 7–68. The essay appeared separately as a Reclam paperback (Stuttgart, 1960), with an important introduction by Hans-Georg Gadamer. The concept of *Riß* is developed in the final section of the essay, "Die Wahrheit und die Kunst," esp. 51ff.

7. The position outlined here derives in large part from the important essay by Roman Jakobson, "Linguistics and Poetics," in *Style and Language* (Cambridge, Mass., 1960), 350–77. Also important for my thinking on such theoretical issues are the views of I. A. Richards, notably in his essays "Toward a Theory of Comprehending," in *Speculative Instruments* (Chicago, 1955), 17–38, and "The Future of Poetry," in *So Much Nearer* (New York, 1968), 150–82; also "Factors and Functions in Linguistics," Richards's discussion of Jakobson's essay, in *Poetries: Their Media and Ends,* 1–16. I have outlined my view of Richards's theory in a commemorative essay, "I. A. Richards (1893–1979): Grand Master of Interpretations," *University of Toronto Quarterly* 49, no. 3 (spring 1980): 189–204.

8. The text of Aristotle is cited from the bilingual (Greek and English) edition in the Loeb Classical Library: Aristotle, *The Organon,* trans. Harold P. Cooke (Cambridge, Mass., 1938), 114–15.

9. Plato, *The Republic,* 2-volume bilingual (Greek and English) edition in the Loeb Classical Library: *Plato,* vols. 5 and 6, trans. Paul Shorey (repr. Cambridge, Mass., 1970). I have also consulted the translation of *The Republic* by Allan Bloom (New York, 1968).

10. Karlheinz Stierle, "Die Identität des Gedichts – Hölderlin als Paradigma," in *Identität,* 505–52. The discussion of transgression occurs in section 1.3 of the essay (513–23). Particularly important for my argument is the following statement by Stierle: "Das 'Poetische' der Lyrik geht hervor aus der unaufhebbaren Einheit von formaler Artikulation auf der Ebene des Textes und reflexiver Funktion des Diskurses im Hinblick auf ein Subjekt, das in seiner emotiven Gestalt nicht mehr aufgeht, sondern zum Fluchtpunkt wird für eine Pluralität simultaner Kontexte" (521).

11. Michel Foucault, *L'Ordre du discours* (Paris, 1971), and Pierre Macherey, *Pour une théorie de la production littéraire* (Paris, 1966). Stierle discusses these works in relation to his own theory on pp. 510–13 of his essay.

12. My translation. "Die Metapher ist in der Lyrik nicht eine Figur der Identität, die den Schein der Divergenz an sich hat, sondern umgekehrt eine Möglichkeit, das scheinbar Identische in seinen Differenzen sichtbar zu machen und so den primären Kontext zu multiplizieren." Stierle, "Die Identität des Gedichts," 521.

13. Hegel, *Wissenschaft der Logik,* part 2 (Zweites Buch: Das Wesen; Erster Abschnitt: Das Wesen der Reflexion in ihm selbst; Erstes Kapitel: Der Schein), ed. Georg Lasson, *Die philosophische Bibliothek,* 57 (repr. Hamburg, 1966), 7–23. Invaluable for the study of this text is the detailed commentary by Dieter Henrich, "Hegels Logik der Reflexion: Neue Fassung," in *Die Wissenschaft der Logik und die Logik der Reflexion,* ed. Dieter Henrich, *Hegel-Studien, Beihefte,* 18 (Bonn, 1978), 204–324. Valuable material on the concept of negativity is also contained in *Positionen der Negativität* (see chap. 8, n. 7). I do not claim any competence to address Hegel's text directly. The value of the concept of negativity for literary theory is briefly discussed in chapter 5.

14. Later collections published during the poet's lifetime – in 1828, 1829 and 1834, respectively – did include the three poems of 1816.

15. Richard Hoffpauir, "'Kubla Khan' and the Critics: Romantic Madness as Poetic Theme and Critical Response," *English Studies in Canada* 2 (1976), 402-22.

16. John Livingston Lowe, *The Road to Xanadu: A Study in the Ways of the Imagination* (Boston and New York, 1927).

17. The so-called "Crewes" manuscript of "Kubla Khan" in Coleridge's hand was acquired by the British Museum in 1962. An essay by T. C. Skeat, "Kubla Khan" (*The British Museum Quarterly* 26 [1963], 77-83), with facsimiles of the manuscript (Plates xxx-xxxi), outlines the history of this document so far as was then known, and describes its variants from the published text of 1815.

18. Elisabeth Schneider, *Coleridge, Opium and "Kubla Khan"* (New York, 1953).

19. Kenneth Burke, "'Kubla Khan,' Proto-Surrealist Poem," in *Language as Symbolic Action: Essays on Life, Literature, and Method* (Berkeley, 1968), 201–22; esp. 209–10.

20. Kathleen Raine, "Traditional Symbolism in *Kubla Khan,*" *Sewanee Review* 72 (1964), 626-42.

21. Norman Fruman, *Coleridge, The Damaged Archangel* (New York, 1971).

22. Elinor Shaffer, *"Kubla Khan" and "The Fall of Jerusalem": The Mythological School in Biblical Criticism and Secular Literature, 1770–1880* (Cambridge, 1975).

23. Title of a well-known philosophical poem by Goethe, "Dauer im Wechsel," *Werke,* ed. Erich Trunz (*Hamburger Ausgabe,* Hamburg, 1949), 1: 247-48.

24. The basic ambivalence of the term *Schein* for aesthetic theory was first perceived by Schiller in his letters to Körner in 1793, which have come to be known as the *Kallias-Briefe,* since he there outlines plans for an essay on the

theory of beauty to be entitled "Kallias." The letters are printed together in the volume of *Theoretische Schriften,* in the edition of Schiller's works, ed. Fricke and Göpfert (München, 1959), 5: 394–433. For Hegel on *Schein,* see n. 13 above. I discuss this ambivalence in chapter 6.

25. Theocritus, *Idylls,* I, 145.

Index of Names

This book is set in Minion, a type face
based on 15th and 16th century models
adapted for electronic typesetting. The
Minion family of typefaces is designed
for Adobe Systems by Robert Slimbach.

The printer is Reprographics and Imaging
Services, a division of Information
Technology Services at Yale University.
The text is composed by Vincent Oneppo
on a Macintosh computer using
QuarkXPress, and printed on a Xerox
Docutech. The image of the painting by
Caspar David Friedrich is made on an Agfa
Scanner by Richard Benson and printed on
a Canon Color Laser Printer 1000.

The binder of the clothbound books is
Acme Bookbinding of Charlestown,
Massachusetts, using double-fanned cold
vinyl adhesive; the cloth is Brillianta.
The binder of the paperbound books is Yale
University's Reprographic and Imaging
Services.

The paper is Mohawk Superfine Recycled,
which is acid-free and made from alpha
cellulose fibers.

The book is designed by Alvin Eisenman.